Let's Draw MANGA 漫画

ALL ABOUT FIGHTING

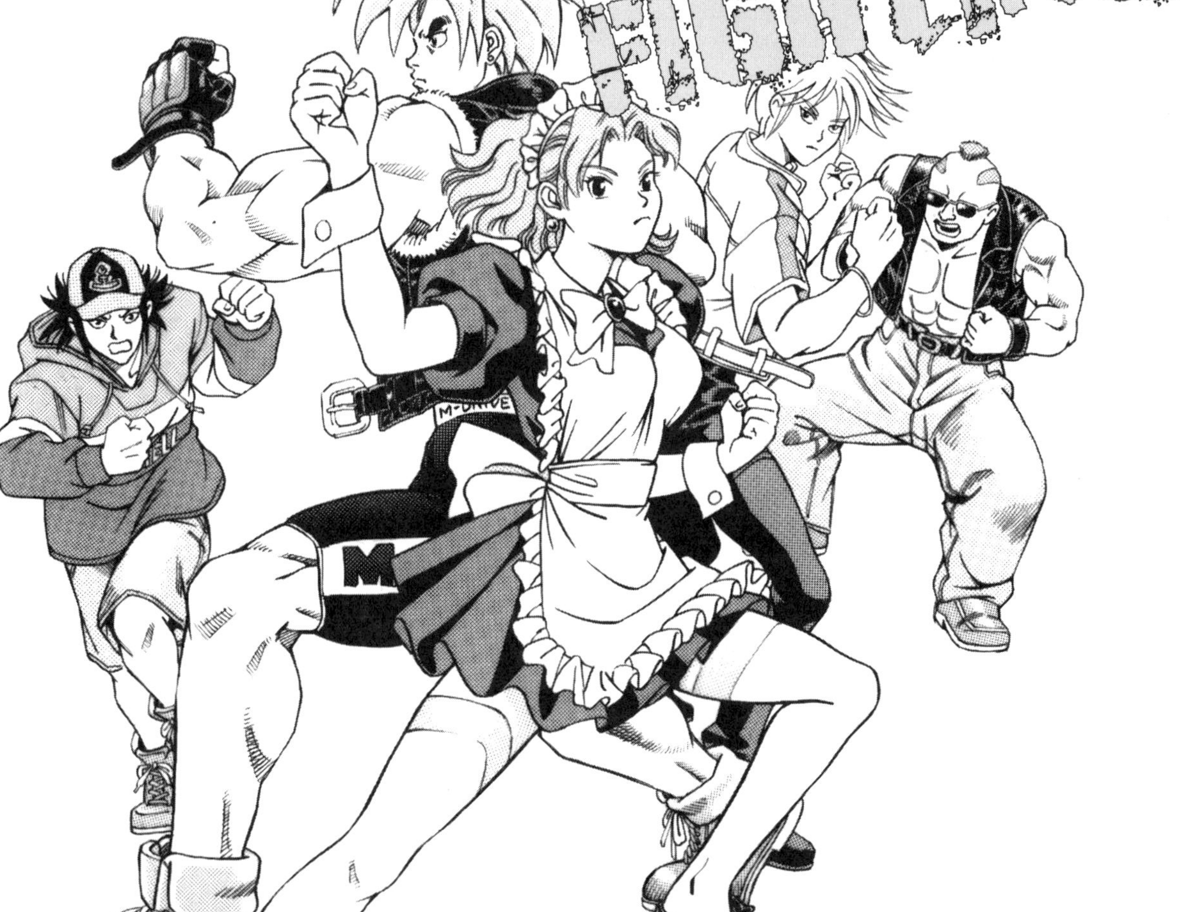

Presented by Big Mouth Factory

MAKOTO NAKAJIMA

大口工場

DIGITAL MANGA PUBLISHING

Los Angeles

Composition:	KEN SASAHARA
	MAKOTO NAKAJIMA
Storyboarding:	MAKOTO NAKAJIMA
	ASTER NORIKO
Artists:	MAKOTO NAKAJIMA
	TETSUYA YAMAMOTO
	BUNTA 625
	ASTER NORIKO
Assistant Artists:	KENICHIROH HAYASHI
	NORIKO NAKAJIMA
Original Cover Art:	MAKOTO NAKAJIMA
	TETSUYA YAMAMOTO
	BUNTA 625
	ASTER NORIKO
Cover Art (Coloring):	MIE HAYASHI (MILKY WORLD)
Art Director:	MAKOTO NAKAJIMA
Assistance:	MILKY WORLD
	www.mangazoo.jp/studio/milk/
Publisher:	HIKARU SASAHARA
Japan Relations:	JOHN WHALEN
Print Production Manager	FRED LUI

LET'S DRAW MANGA
All About Fighting

English Edition Published by
DIGITAL MANGA PUBLISHING
1123 Dominguez Street, Unit K
Carson, CA 90746
www.emanga.com
tel: (310) 604-9701
fax: (310) 604-1134

Distributed Exclusively in North America by
WATSON-GUPTILL PUBLICATIONS
a division of VNU Business Media
770 Broadway, New York, NY 10003
www.watsonguptill.com

ISBN: 1-56970-987-4
Library of Congress Control Number: 2003098728
First Edition September 2004
10 9 8 7 6 5 4 3 2 1

Printed in China

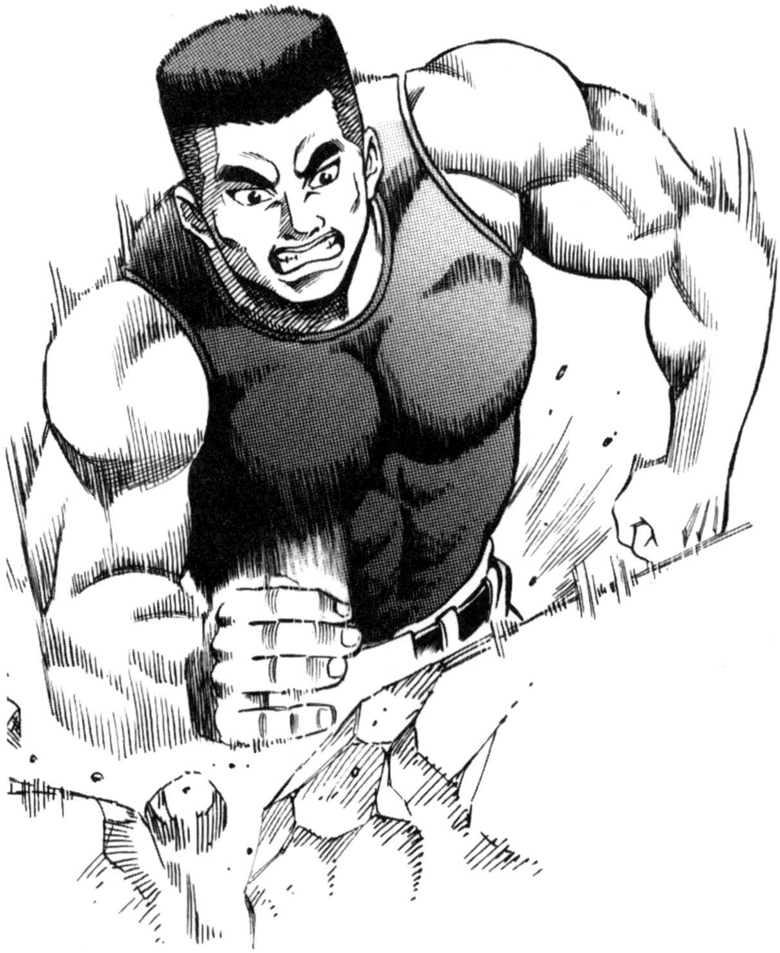

Contents

PURPOSE OF THIS BOOK

We created this book because we wanted to give American manga fans an overview of how to draw fighting scenes in the Japanese manga style. From the manga neophyte to the blossoming pen-master, we are confident that everyone will find its pages packed with useful and entertaining tips.

First off, we should emphasize that this book is not simply another collection of character poses; there are more than enough of those around already, and many of them are–to put it bluntly–totally worthless. In fact, we can't think of a single professional manga artist in Japan who keeps this kind of book at hand. A real artist doesn't need to rely on such crutches to create original drawings.

Aren't there a lot of you in the States who are fed up with insipid "manga pose resources"? We think so. That's why with this book, we aimed to break the mold and adopt, from the get-go, methods that show you the mechanics behind drawing imaginative manga characters that literally "kick ass". These same methods allow even new comers to get a foothold in the manga world by reading this book. A good idea? Yeah, we're pretty proud of ourselves.

Furthermore, we introduced a variety of specific character archetypes in each section that are designed to stimulate your imagination. Before you know it, you'll be creating your own unique storylines! In a nutshell, we wanted to make this book fun to look at, fun to read, and above all, fun for your imagination.

As you are probably aware, manga has grown to become a major part of Japanese culture. There are people here who claim, "All I really needed to know I learned through manga!" (Kindergarten ranks a distant second.) Your humble writer remembers first learning about American literature through manga. The heroine of this particular manga was a middle school girl who was feeling anxious about getting accepted into a top-ranked high school. One of her classmates gets a crush on her, but he turns out to be her complete opposite. Despite earning excellent grades, he has no aspirations to enter a good high school. "Why slave away at a big league high school? I'd rather have the freedom to try lots of new things, like join different clubs or read *Flowers for Algernon* in English... Doesn't it get you excited?" Sadly, your manga-geek author did poorly in school, never mastered English, and read only the Japanese translation of the great Daniel Keyes novel.

Anyway, all of us at the Big Mouth Factory sincerely hope that American readers will, throughly studying this book, start to understand and appreciate Japanese manga–and by derivation, Japanese culture itself. We are sure that you will find the art to be as fun and exciting as we do.

Makoto Nakajima
Big Mouth Factory

CHAPTER 1

「素手で戦う」

WEAPONLESS FIGHTING

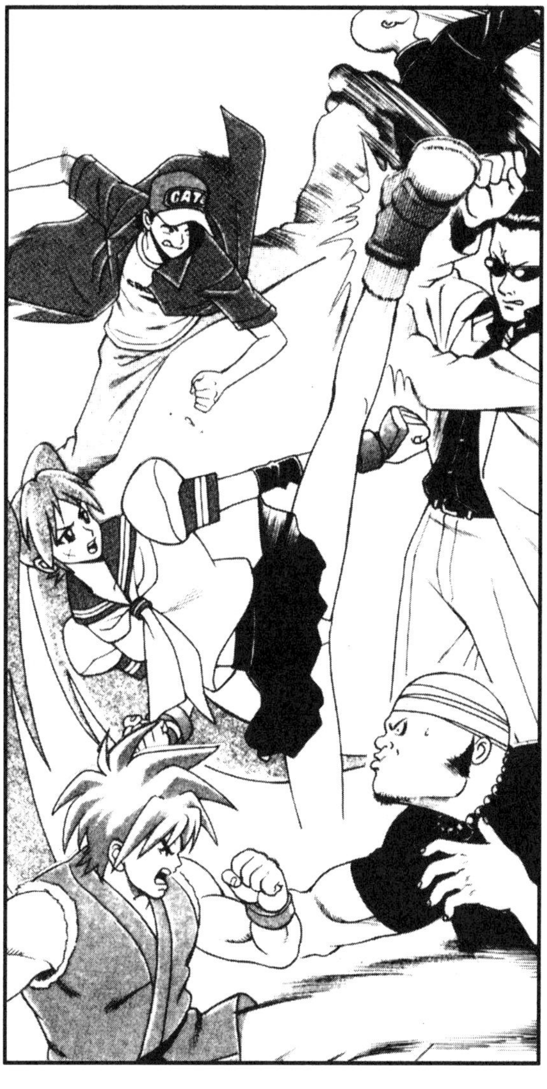

殴る!

How to Draw a Fistfight!

Tokyo: the capital of Japan. Within its throbbing heart, hot-blooded youth gather nightly in bustling districts like Shibuya and Ikebukuro. We'll use these mean streets as our backdrop and show you some useful techniques for drawing street fight scenes in the manga style.

Our main character is "Reiji", a seventeen-year-old Shibuya street hero who possesses a strong sense of loyalty and justice.

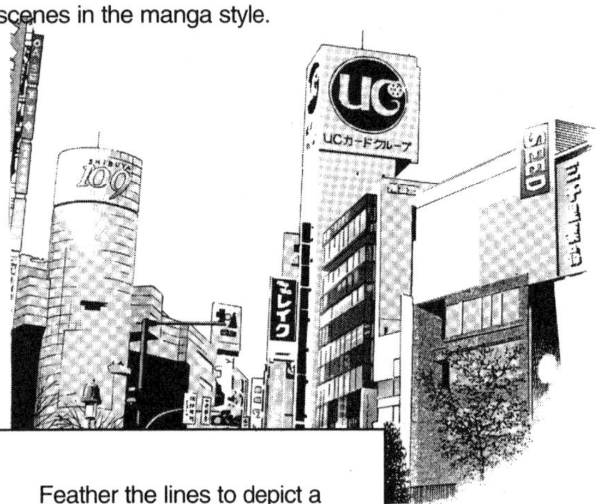

Feather the lines to depict a rapid movement. This technique is a characteristic of Japanese manga.

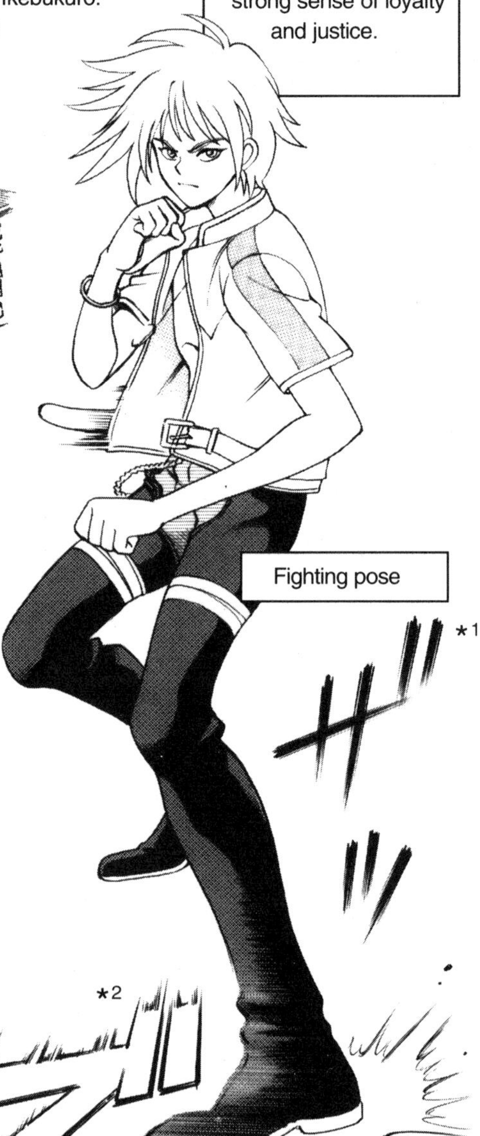

Fighting pose

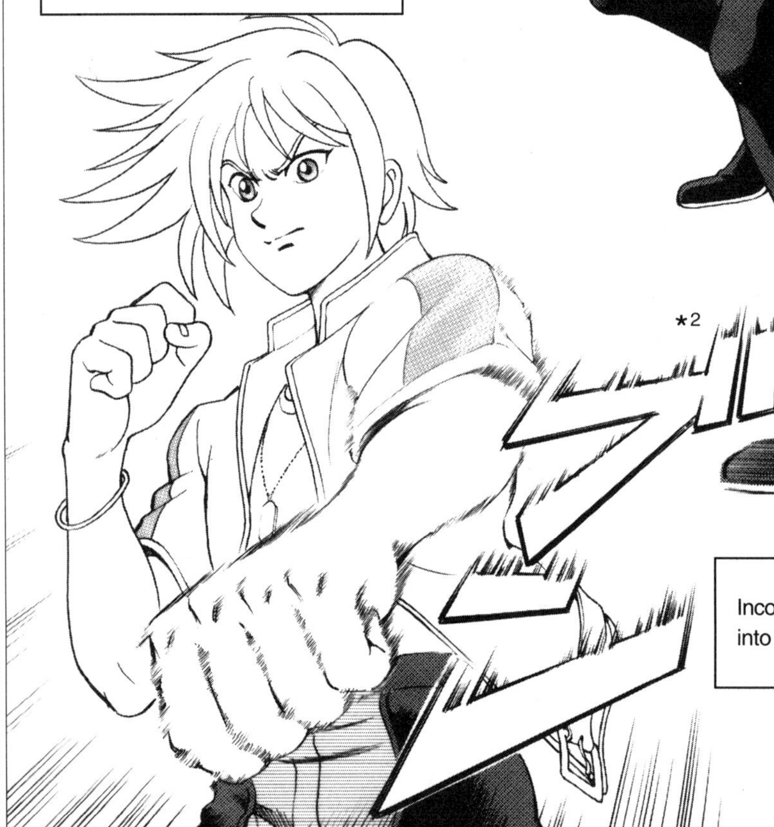

Incorporate sound effects into your illustration.

★1:Krkkch! ★2:woosh!

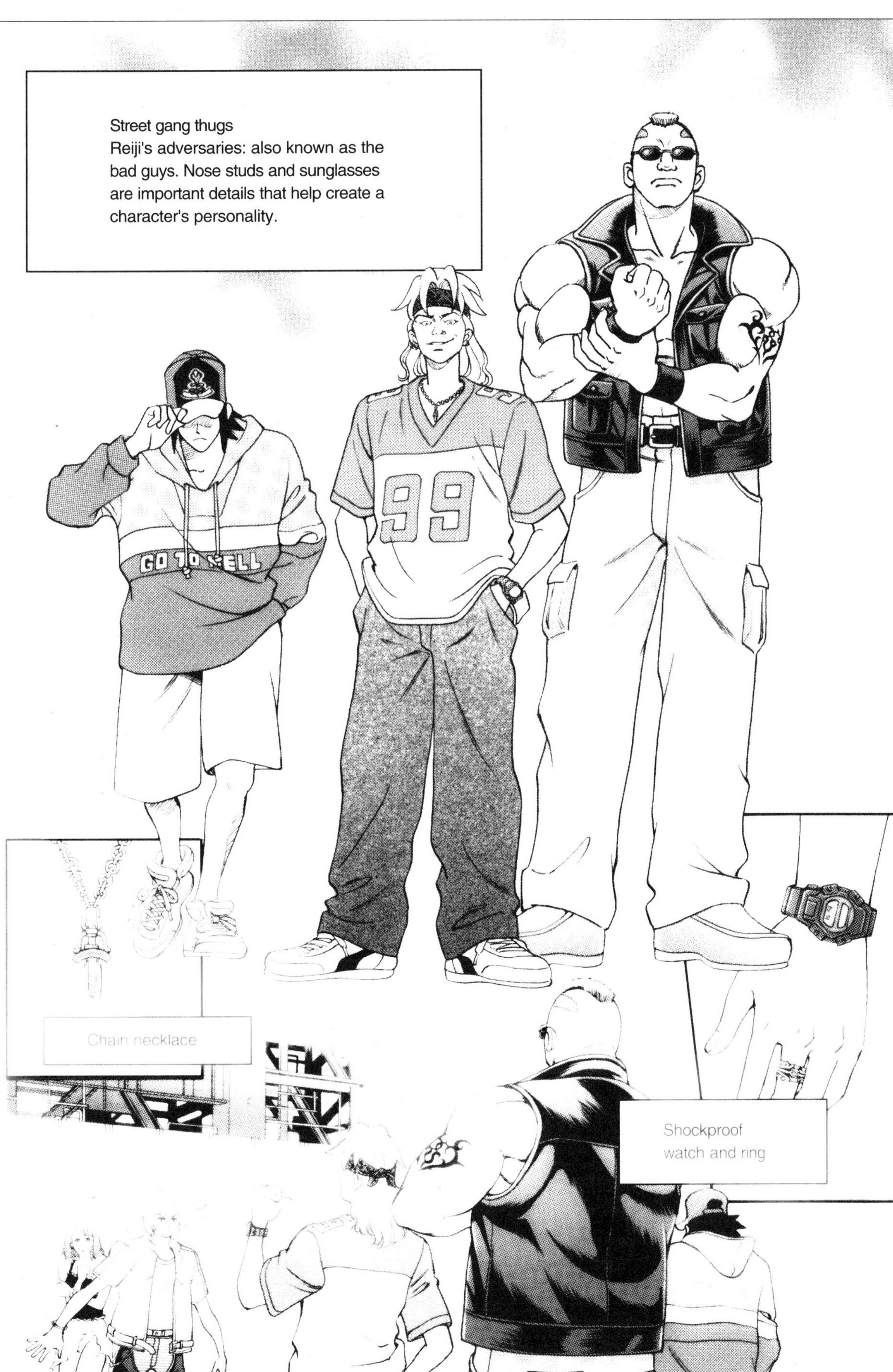
Street gang thugs
Reiji's adversaries: also known as the bad guys. Nose studs and sunglasses are important details that help create a character's personality.
99
GO TO HELL
Chain necklace
Shockproof
watch and ring

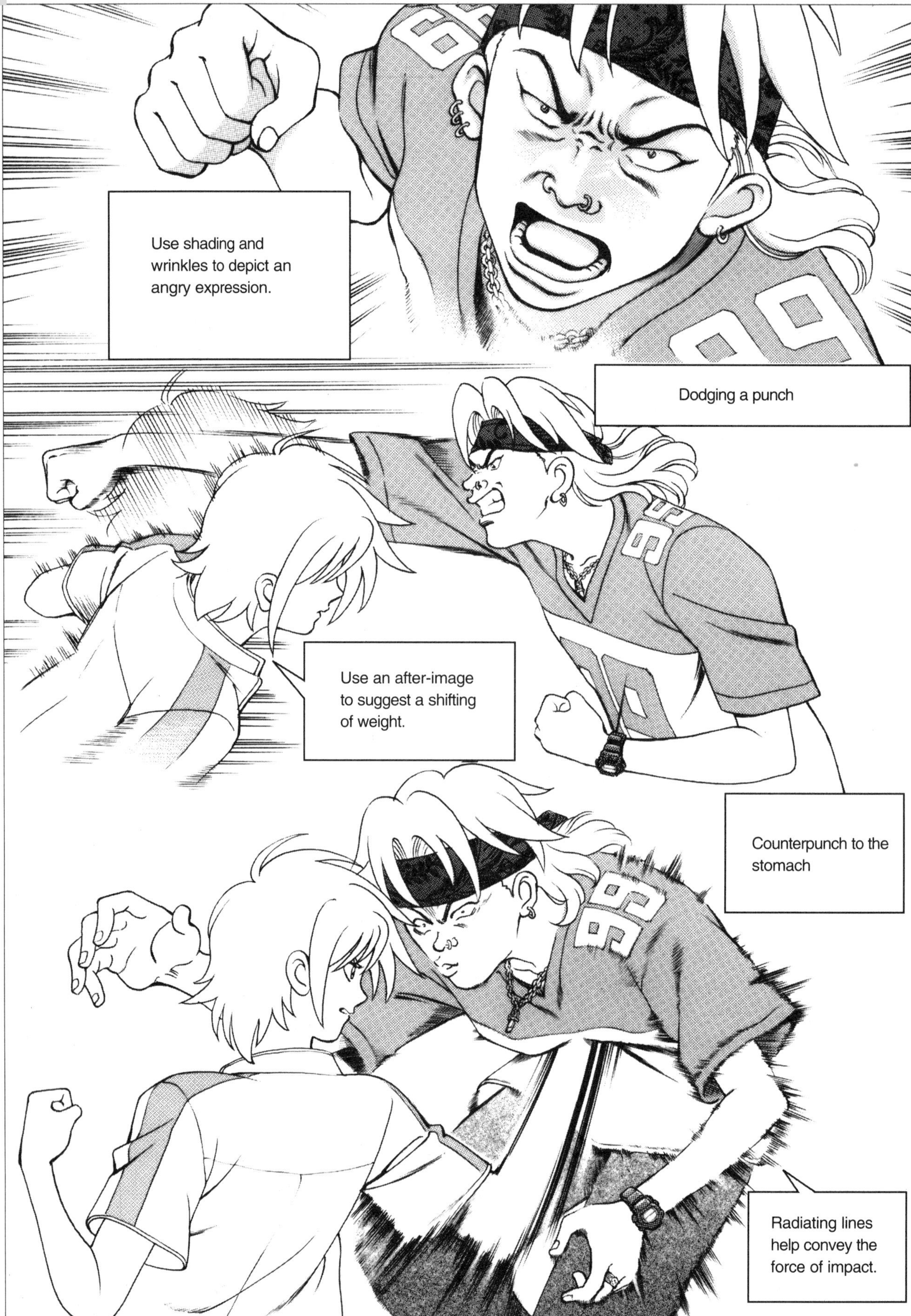
Use shading and wrinkles to depict an angry expression.
Dodging a punch
Use an after-image to suggest a shifting of weight.
Counterpunch to the stomach
Radiating lines help convey the force of impact.

A body punch seen from a different angle

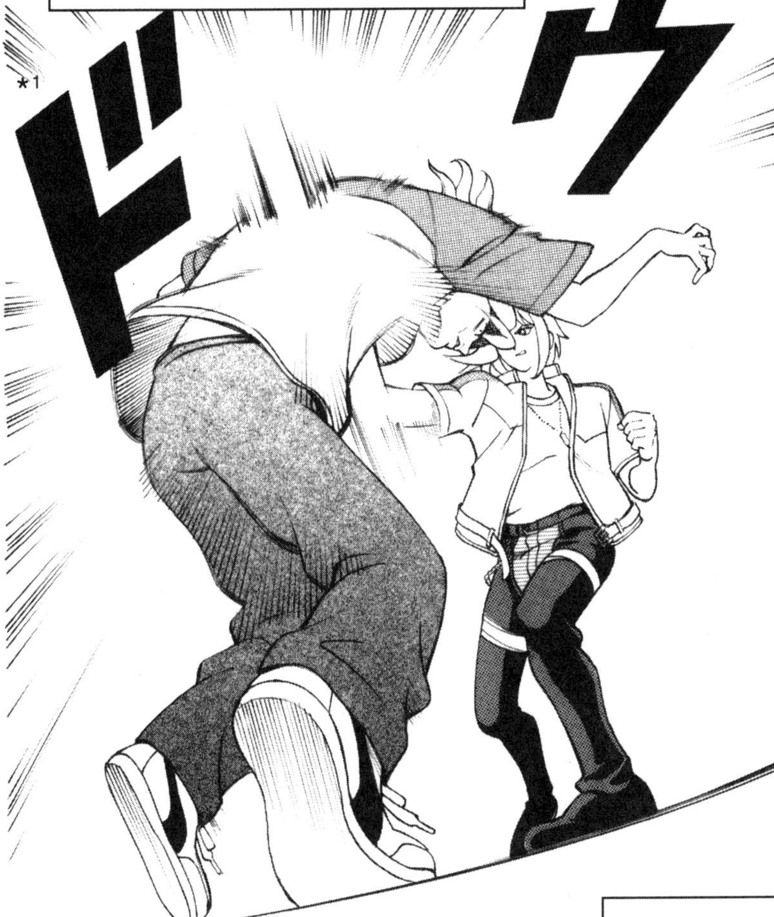

Japanese manga techniques use parallel kinetic lines to depict a rapid movement.

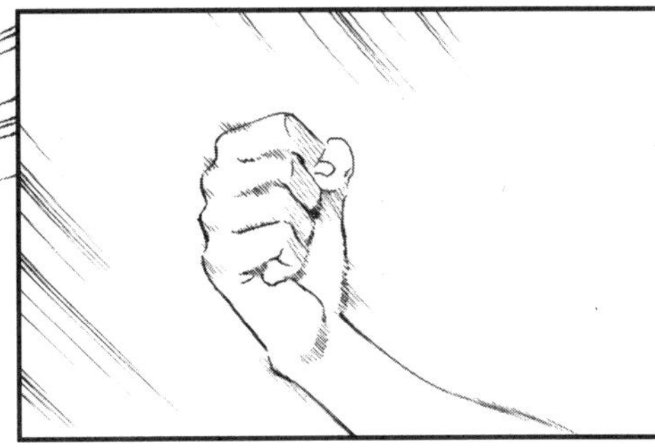

The faster the motion, the longer and more ragged the lines.

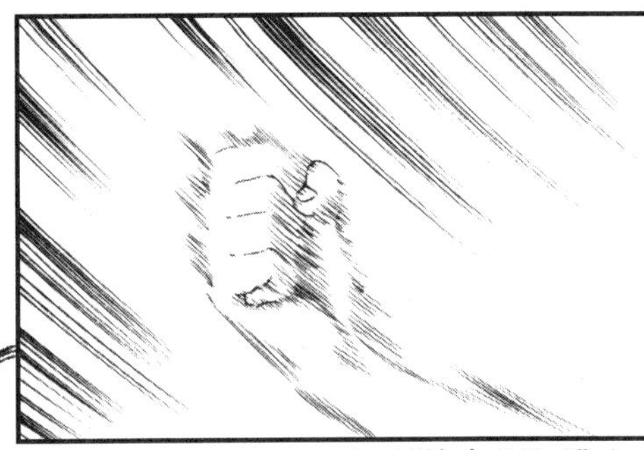

Gasping for breath after a painful blow to the stomach

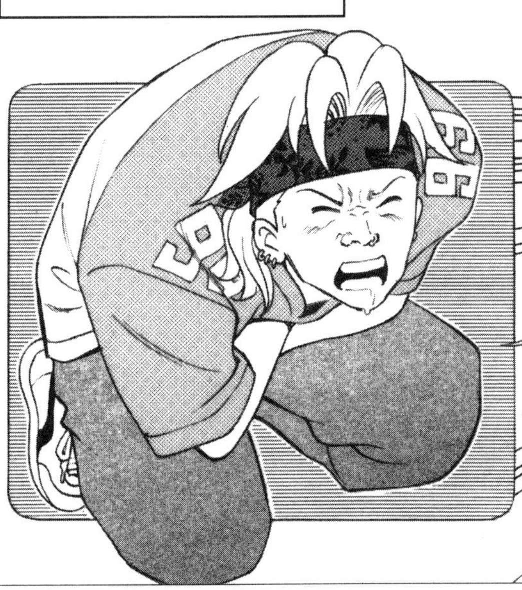

Centrifugal subjective motion lines are used to show a person rapidly approaching from afar.

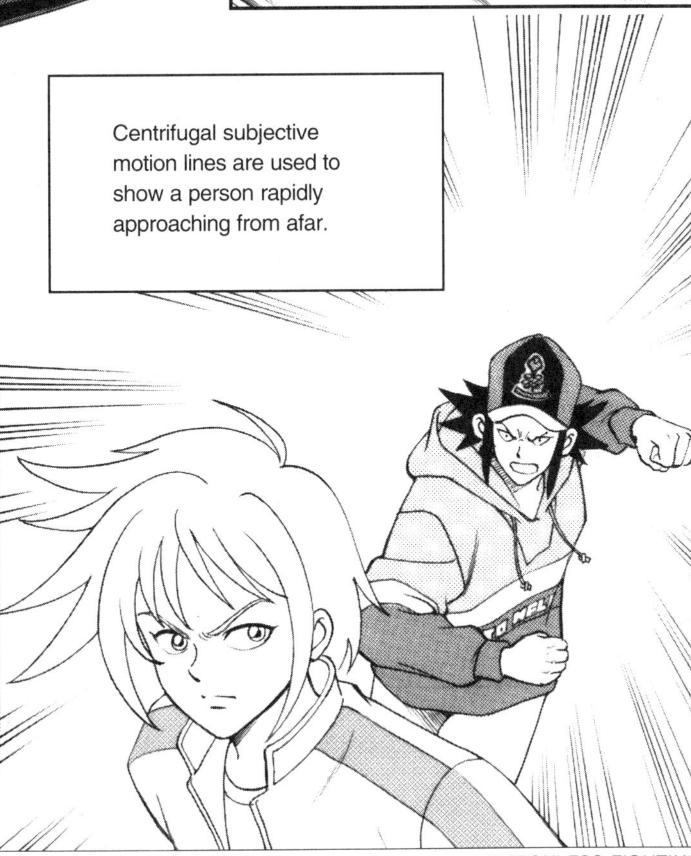

*1: Doof!

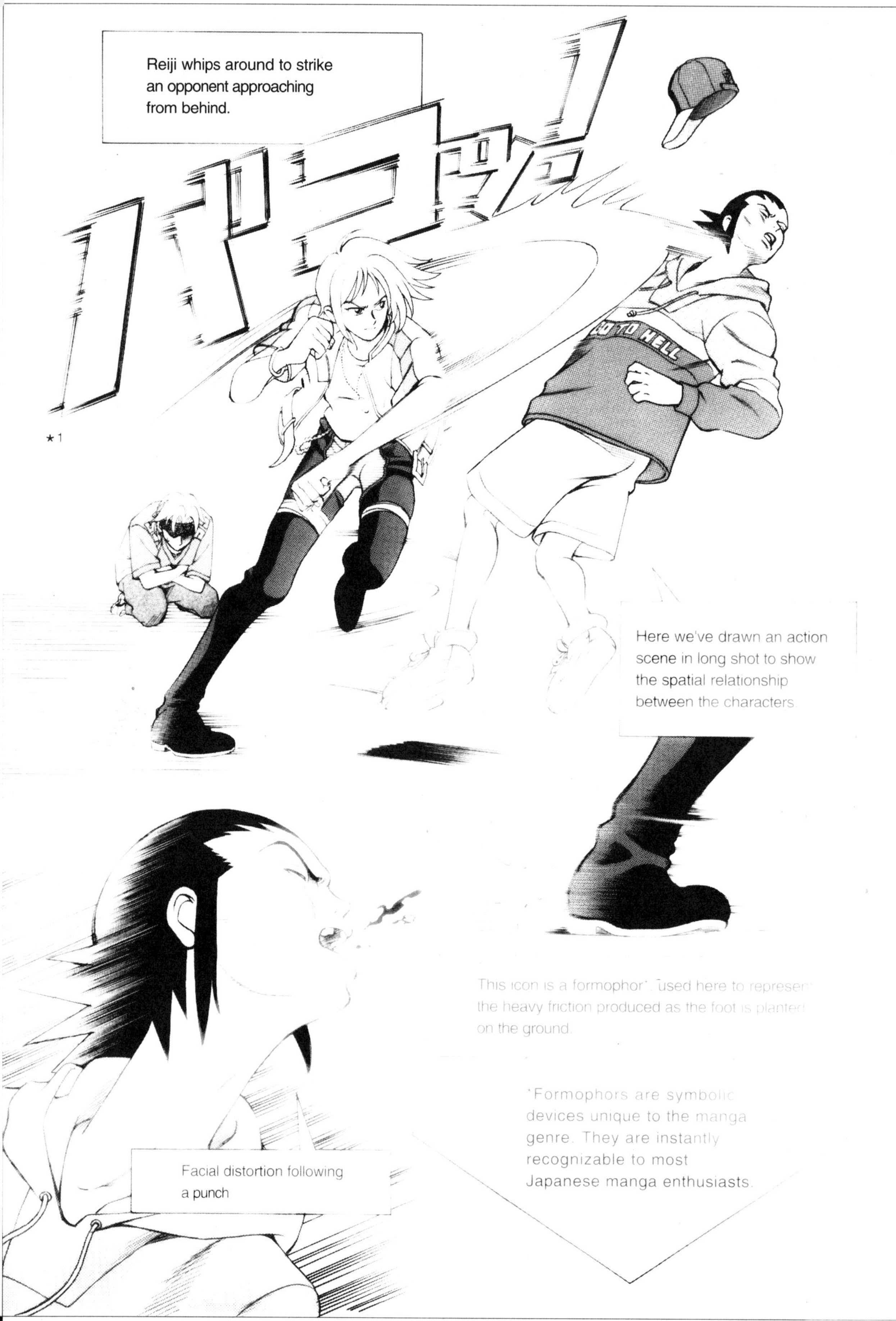

Reiji whips around to strike an opponent approaching from behind.

★1

Here we've drawn an action scene in long shot to show the spatial relationship between the characters.

This icon is a formophor*, used here to represent the heavy friction produced as the foot is planted on the ground.

*Formophors are symbolic devices unique to the manga genre. They are instantly recognizable to most Japanese manga enthusiasts.

Facial distortion following a punch

★1: Whack!

Reiji sends a gang member flying.

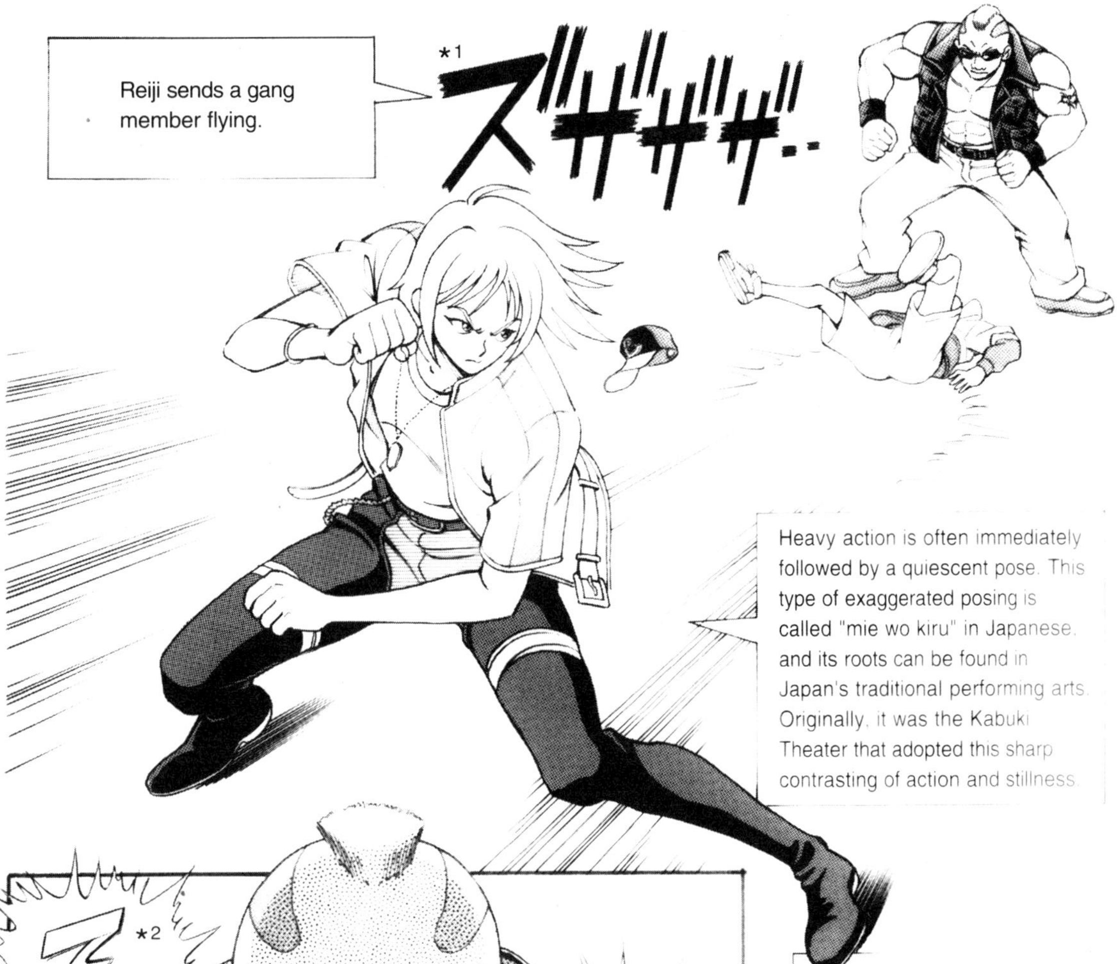

Heavy action is often immediately followed by a quiescent pose. This type of exaggerated posing is called "mie wo kiru" in Japanese, and its roots can be found in Japan's traditional performing arts. Originally, it was the Kabuki Theater that adopted this sharp contrasting of action and stillness.

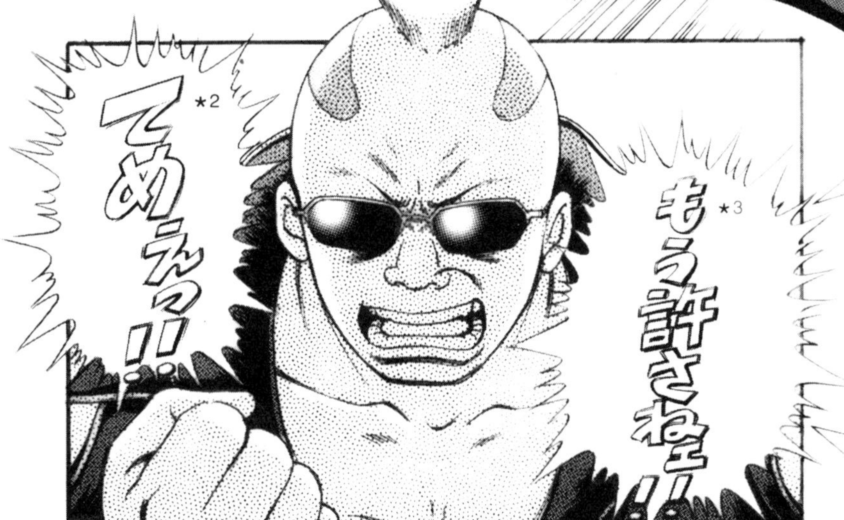

This icon, the text bubble, is used to represent speech.

The text bubble and the dialogue itself are incorporated into the illustration. In this instance, jagged, explosion-style bubbles and handwritten dialogue help convey the character's rage.

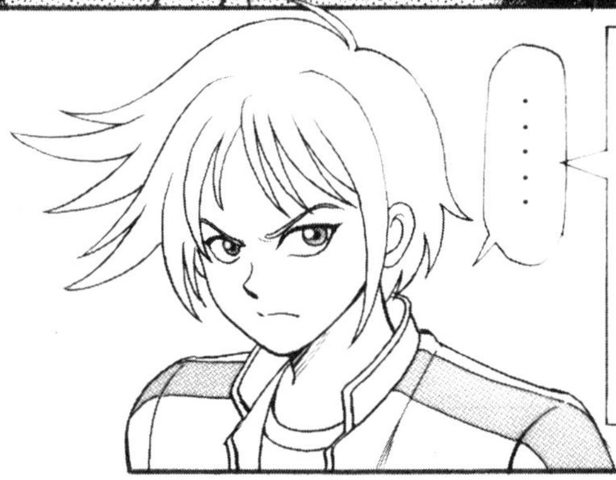

Reiji keeps his cool and remains stoically silent. Just one text bubble can give clues to a character's personality. For example, if Reiji were a wimp...

...we might draw his bubble like this.

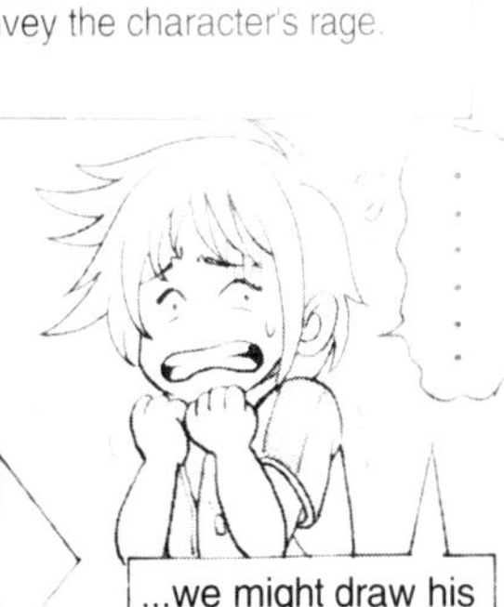

★1:Szkrshhhhhn! ★2:Why you little... ★3:You're dead meat!

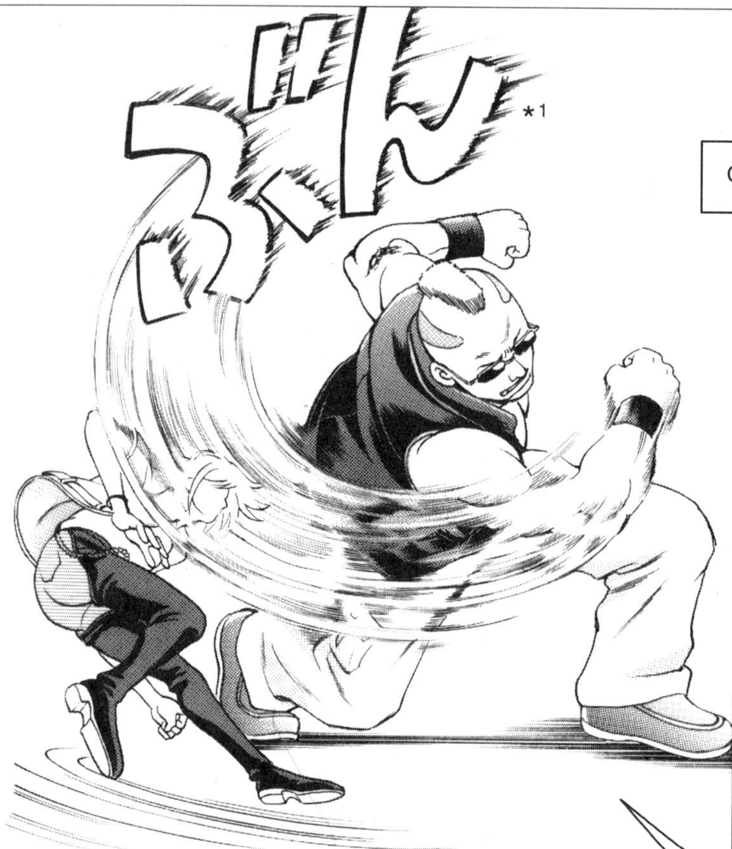

Curved subjective motion lines

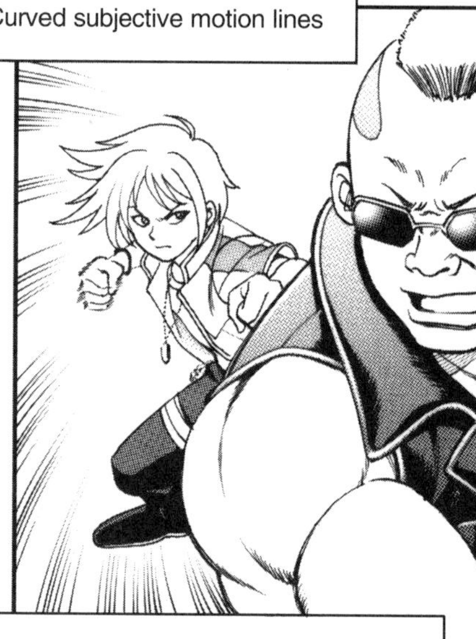

There are three types of letters in the Japanese language: "Hiragana," "Katakana," and "Kanji." Use each kind to suit the situation. This echoic word is the same sound as that of page 6, while the letter style is different. Notice how the size of the sound effect lettering supports the overall feel of the illustration.

Leave out the motion lines and sound effects, and the illustration takes on a freeze-frame quality. This stylistic change immediately lets the reader know that the fight is over.

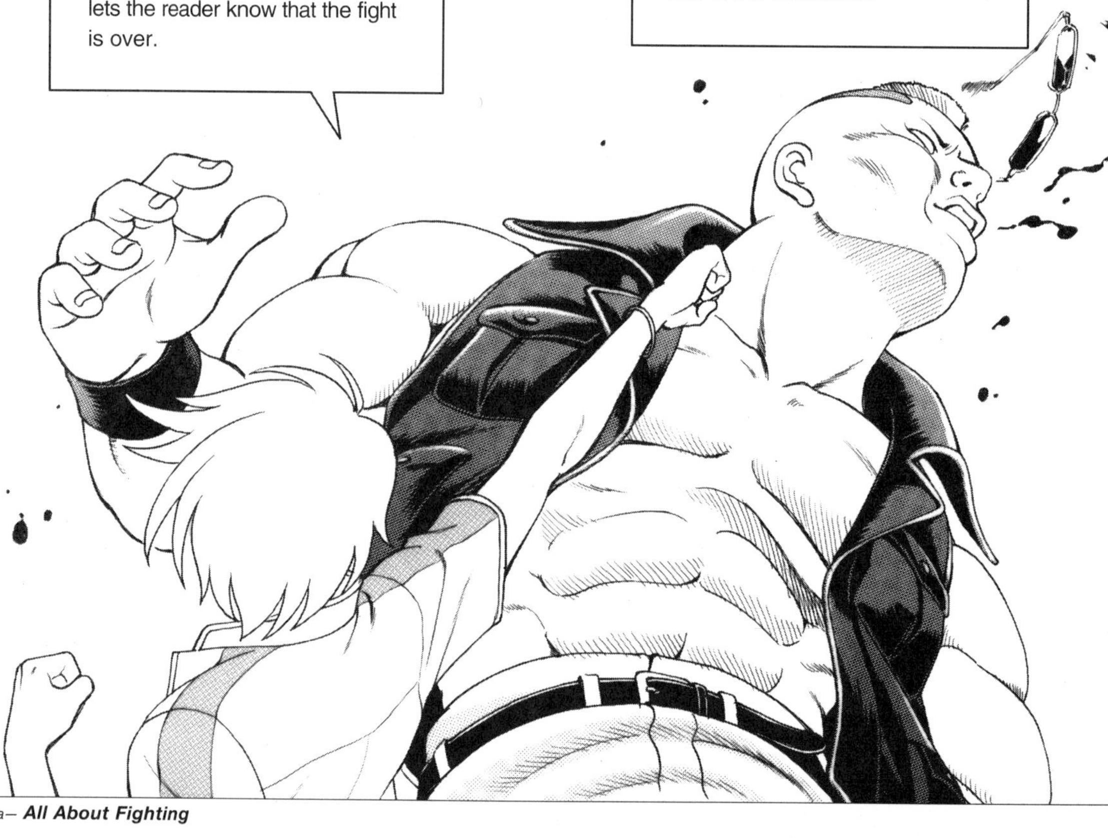

*1:Fsssssh!

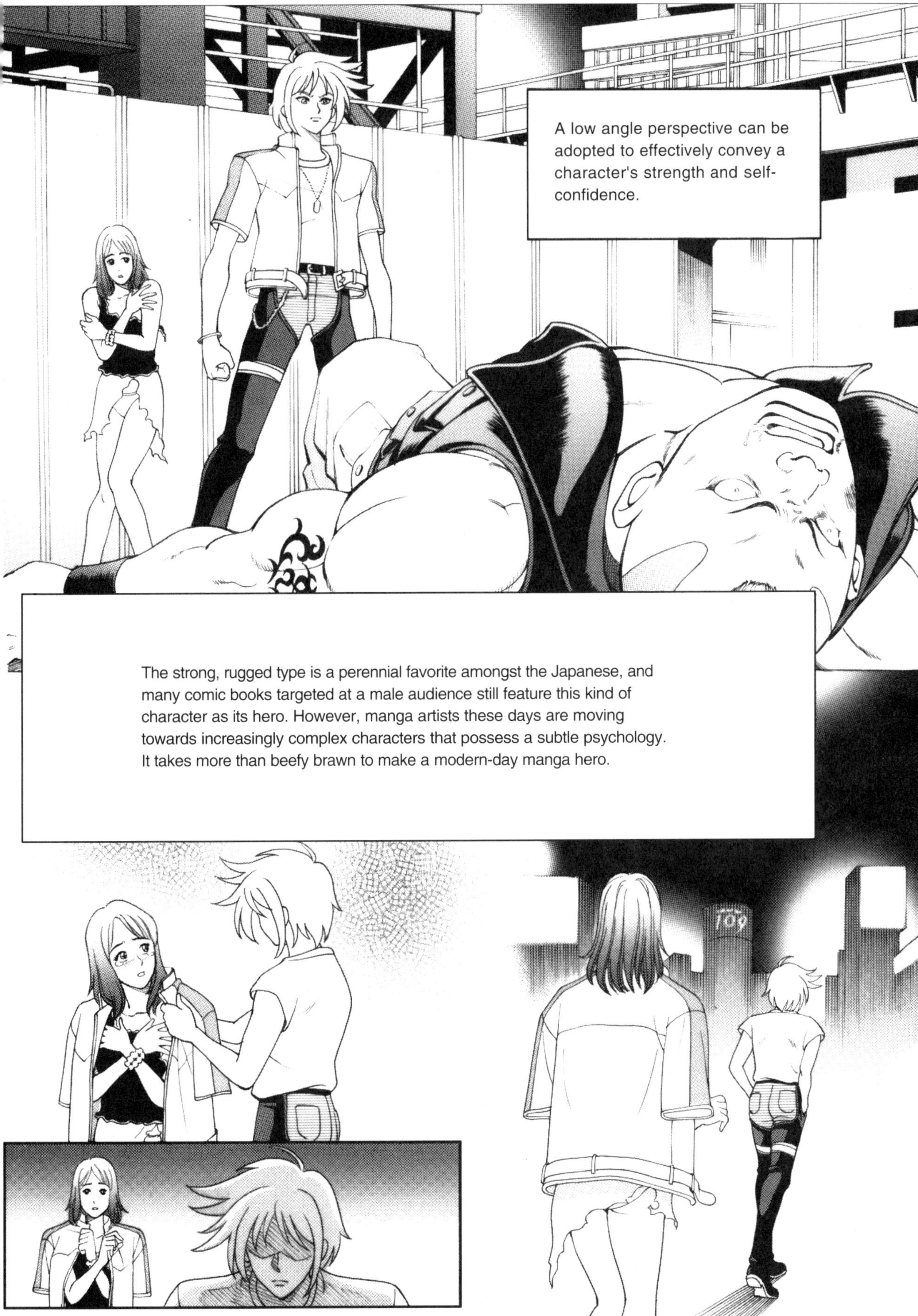

A low angle perspective can be adopted to effectively convey a character's strength and self-confidence.

The strong, rugged type is a perennial favorite amongst the Japanese, and many comic books targeted at a male audience still feature this kind of character as its hero. However, manga artists these days are moving towards increasingly complex characters that possess a subtle psychology. It takes more than beefy brawn to make a modern-day manga hero.

How the characters in this book were drawn-Part 1

Let's take a closer look at how the figures in this book were created.

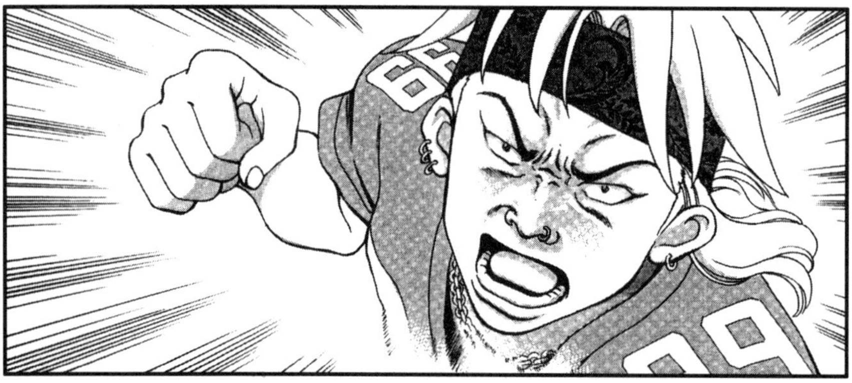

Here's a street punk coming in fast to strike a blow. In a situation like this, it's important to draw a facial expression that effectively conveys the character's rage.

First, we must thoroughly understand the figure's motion.

Although professional manga artists hardly ever start with this kind of figure sketch, they are included here because they serve as a useful learning tool for the novice manga artist.

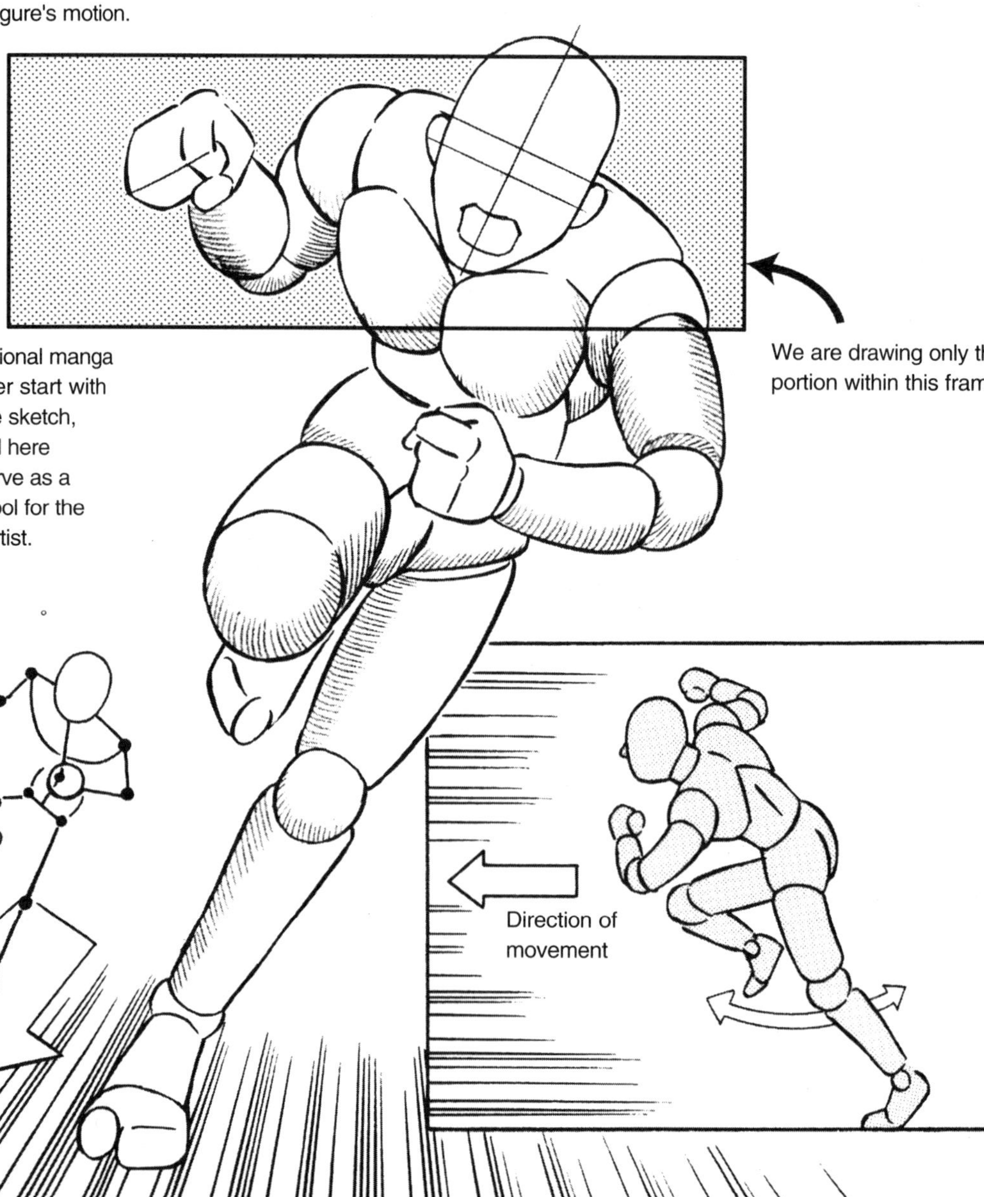

We are drawing only the portion within this frame.

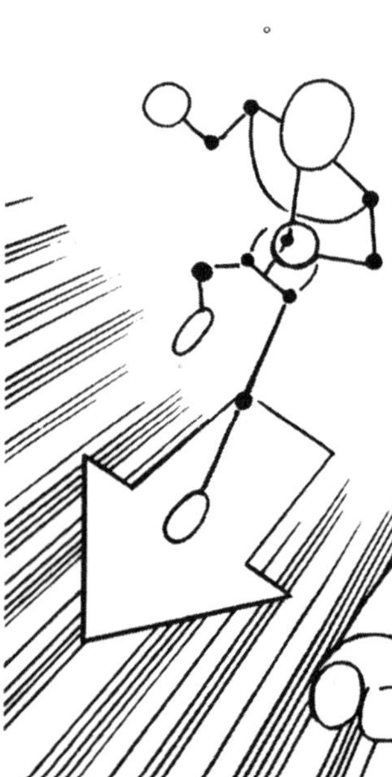

Important Manga Fact: The face makes the character!!

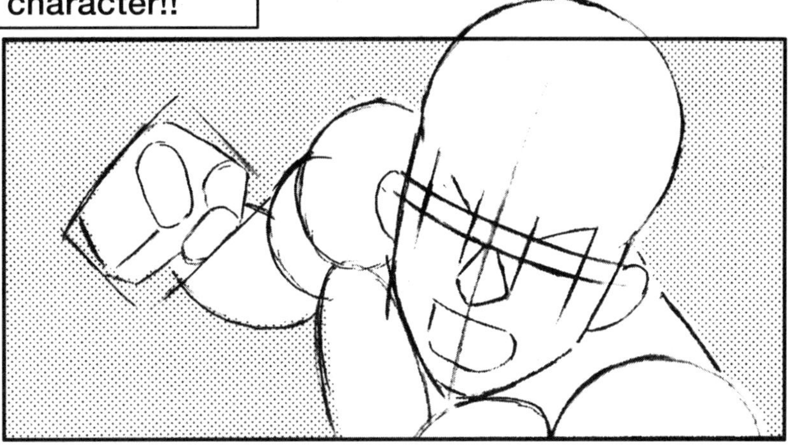

When drawing manga, facial expressions are of prime importance. Try studying your own face in a mirror to get a grasp of how expressions reflect the psychological subtleties of a character.

Typical facial expressions (the arrows indicate the direction of muscle contraction)

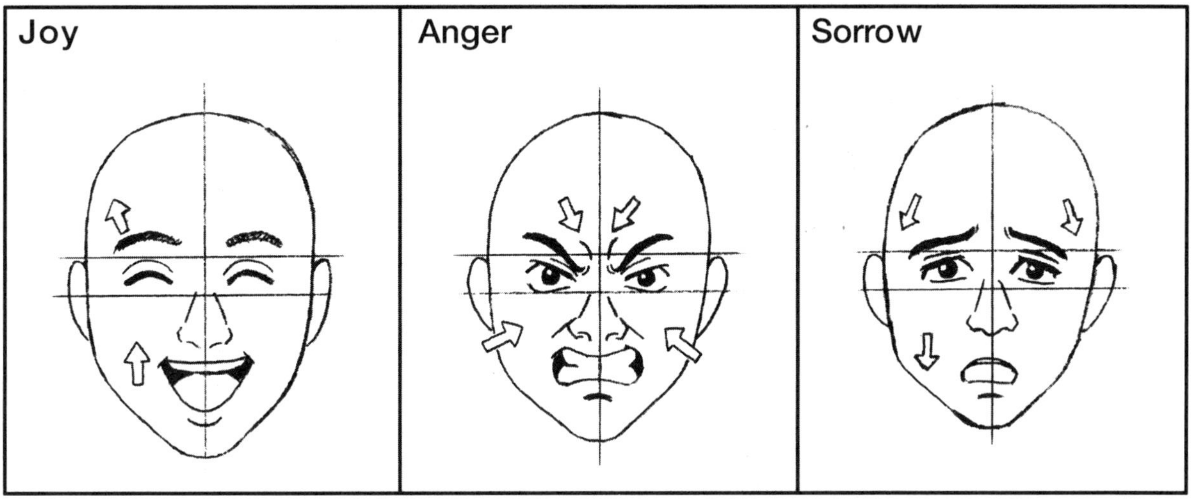

Sketch in the details after the eyes, nose, and mouth have been positioned.

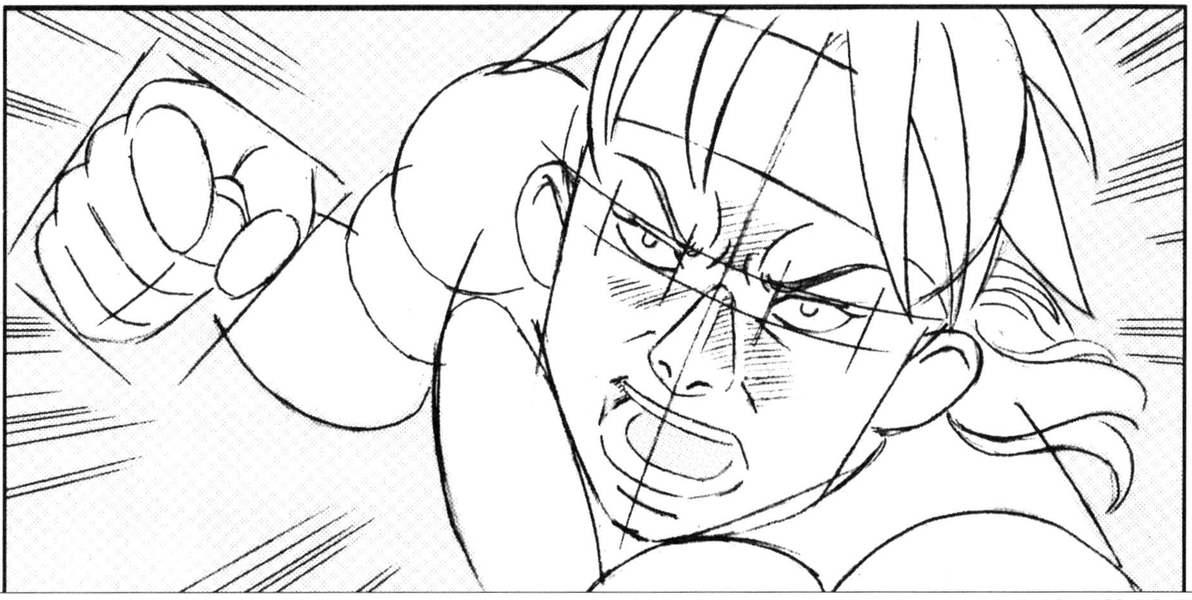

Let's try drawing faces from different angles.

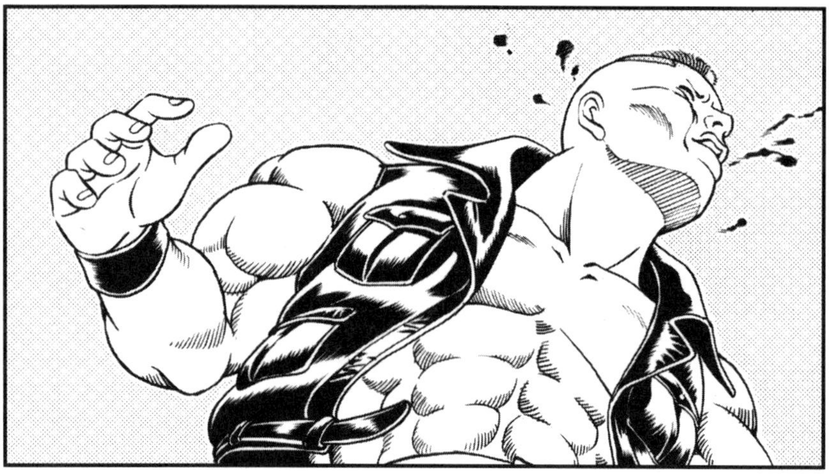

We'll examine a couple of characters getting punched (panels from this book) to see how to draw faces from various angles. The arrows indicate the direction of the punch.

A preliminary figure sketch comprised of circles and ovals is helpful when drawing "muscleman" characters.

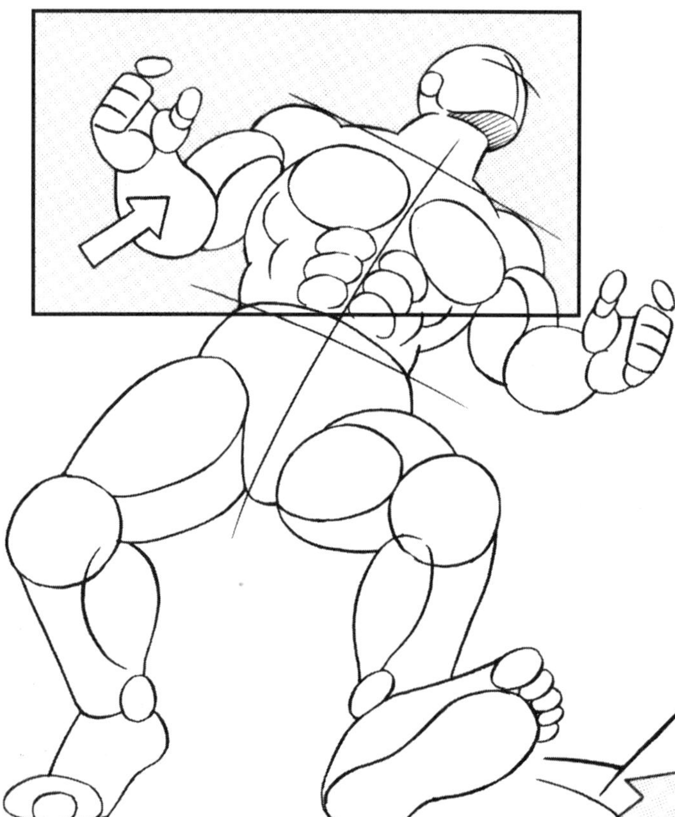

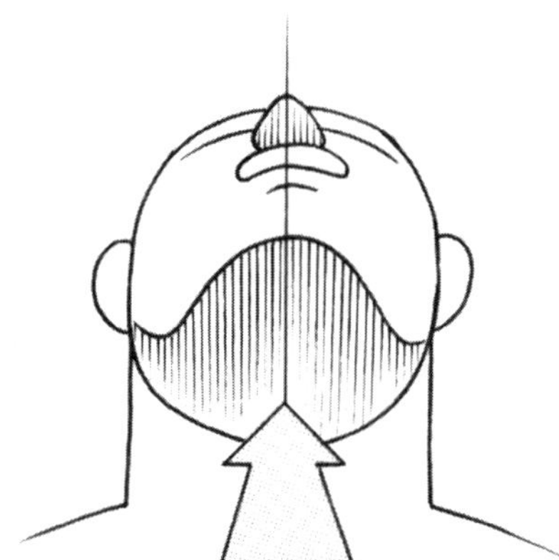

Low angle view from underneath the chin

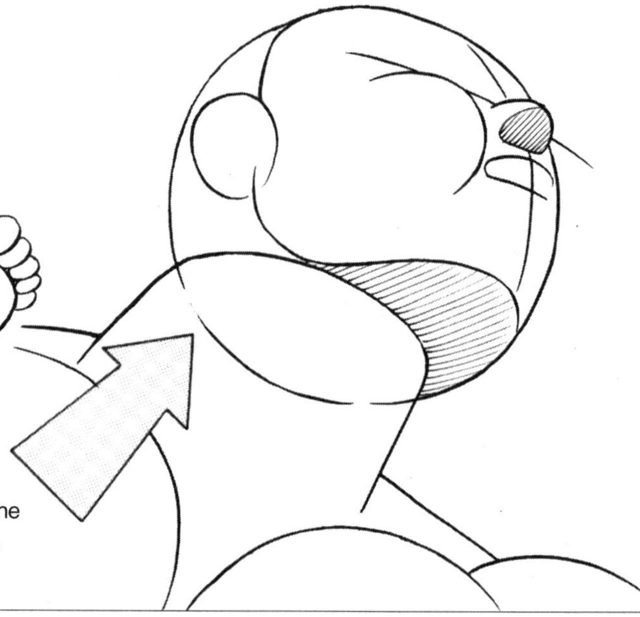

The buckling of the cheek accentuates the impact of the punch.

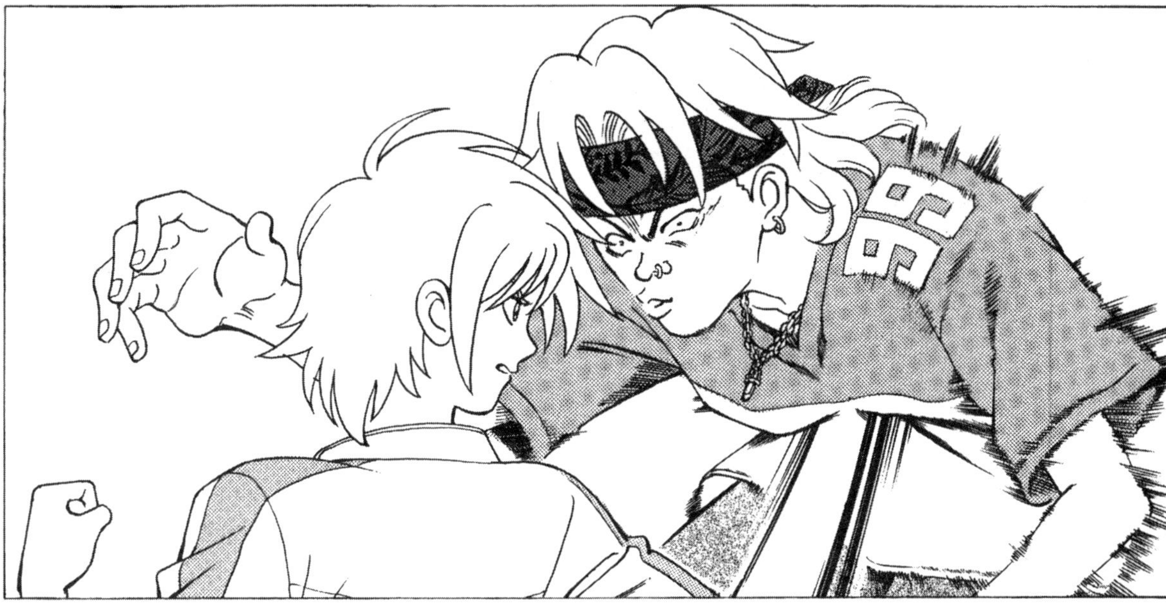

The character's face contorts as he gets slugged in the gut. His eyes are wide open and his face is scrunched in toward its center.

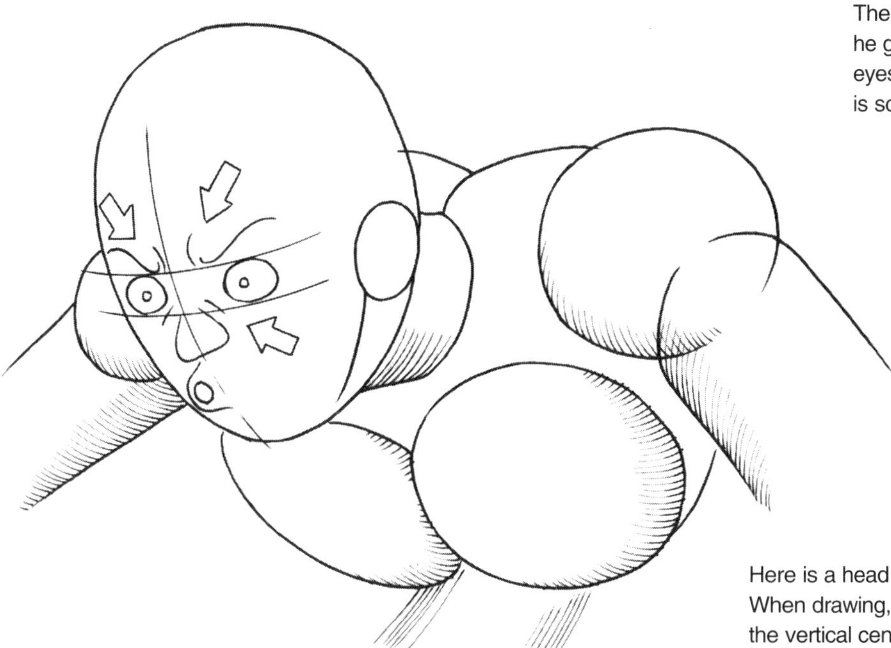

Here is a head seen from different angles. When drawing, you should pay attention to the vertical center line of the face.

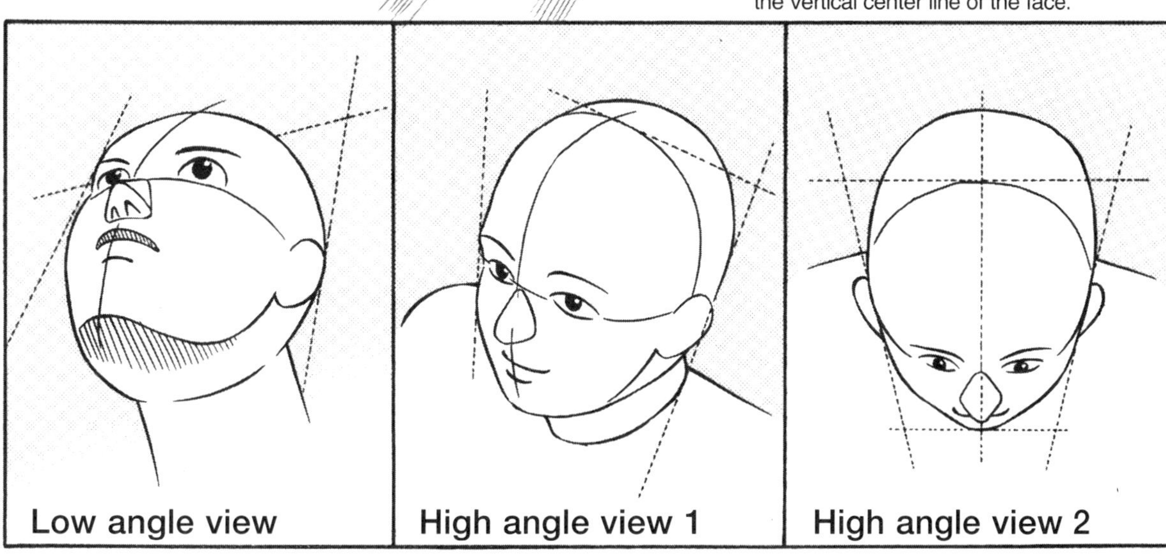

描いてみよう

Putting Pen to Paper

Drawing punches

What you need:
Paper (bond or Kent)
Pencil
Eraser

With your pencil, try sketching a scene you have visualized in your mind.

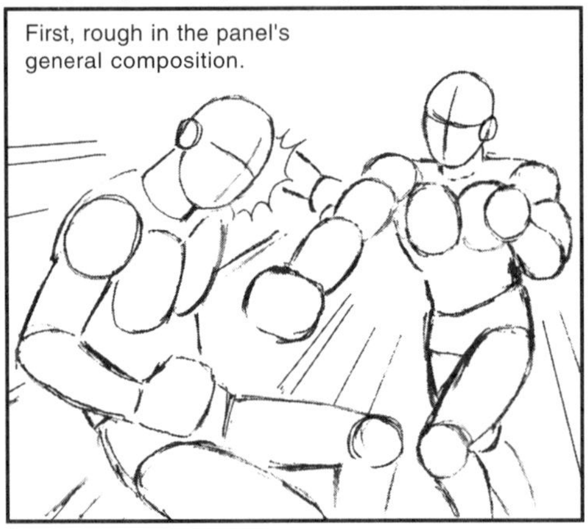

First, rough in the panel's general composition.

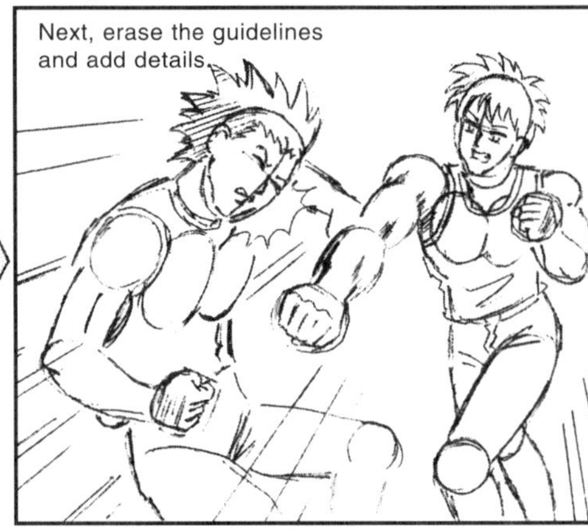

Next, erase the guidelines and add details.

The finished pencil sketch

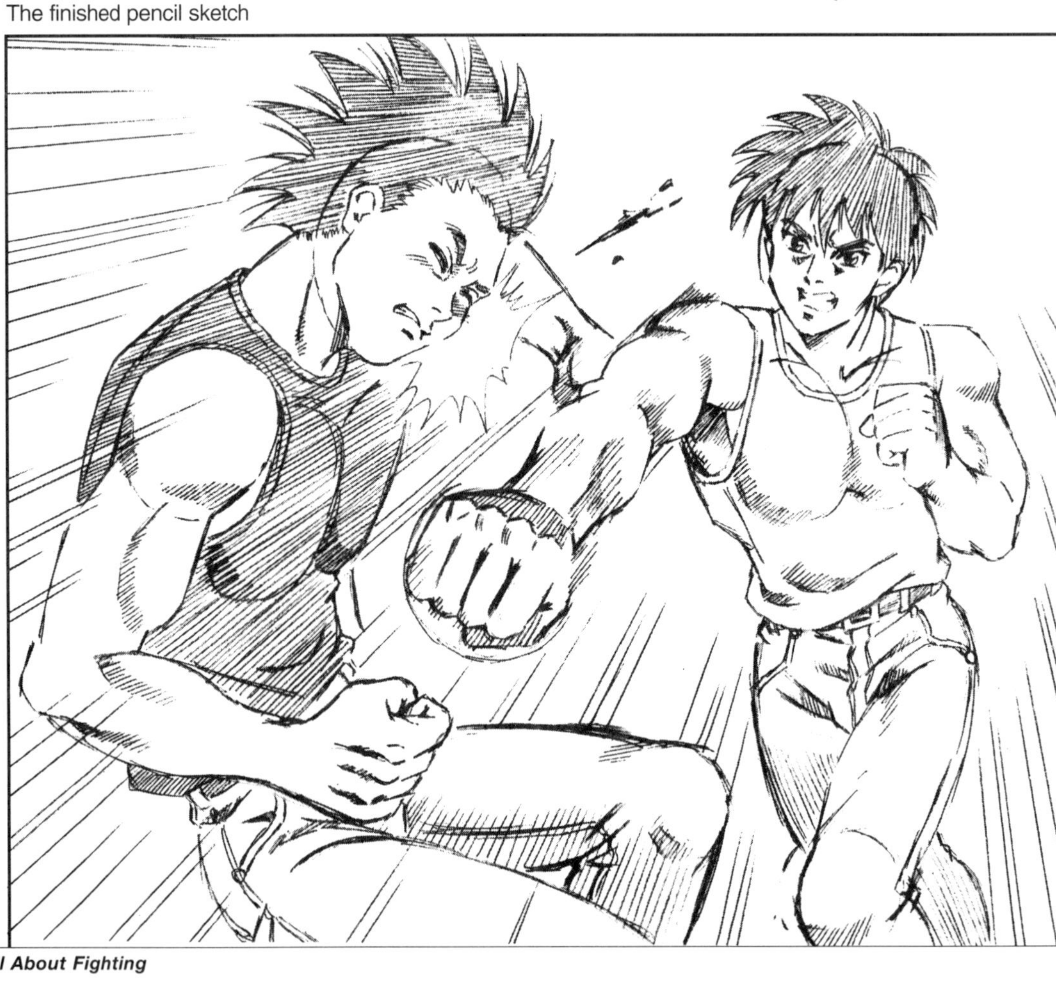

Drawing various punches

Hook
A slightly low angle perspective

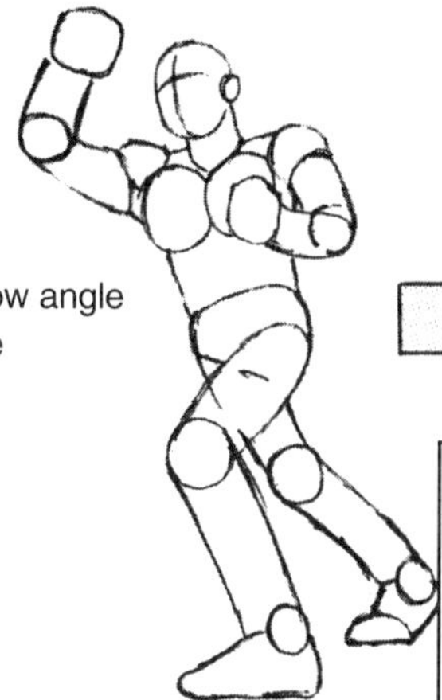

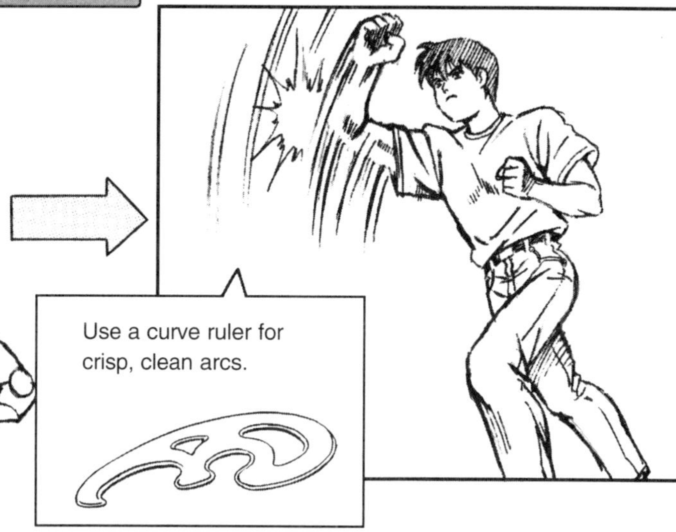

Straight right punch
A slightly high angle perspective

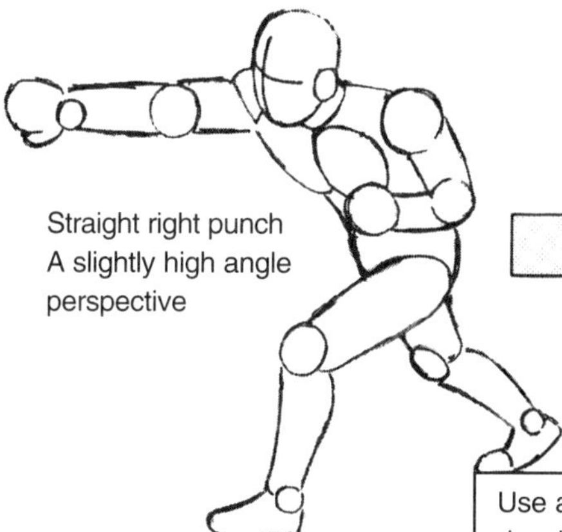

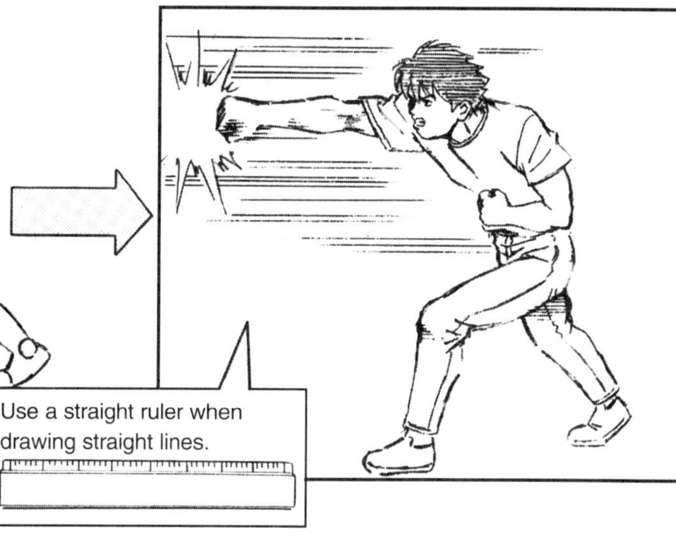

Straight right punch
Head-on perspective

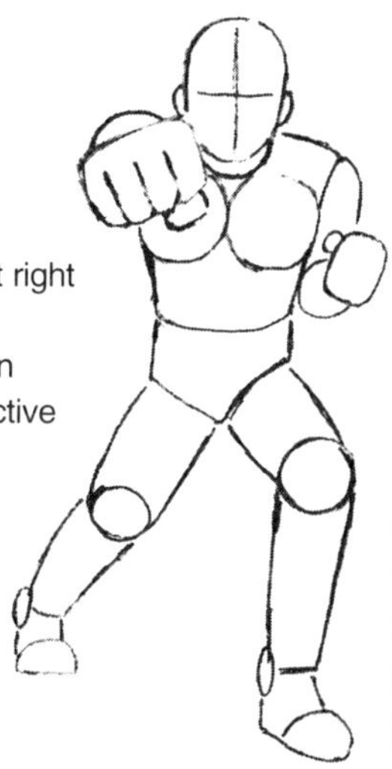

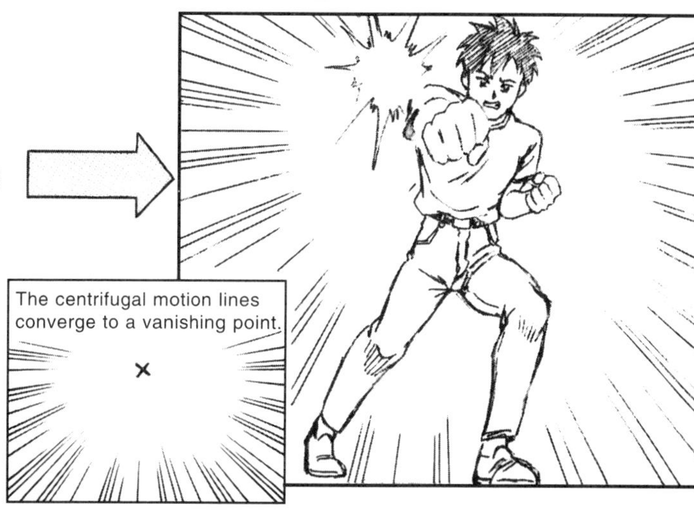

Inking with black ink

In contrast to American comics, which tend to be in full-color, most Japanese manga are drawn in black-and-white. Ink your pencil sketch with black India ink.

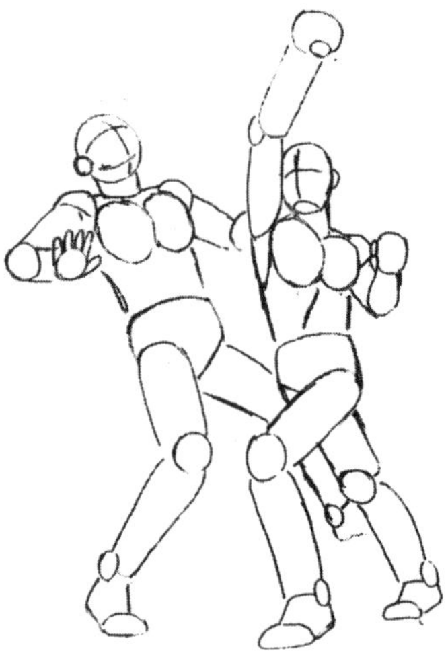

Here we have a preliminary pencil sketch of a figure throwing an uppercut.

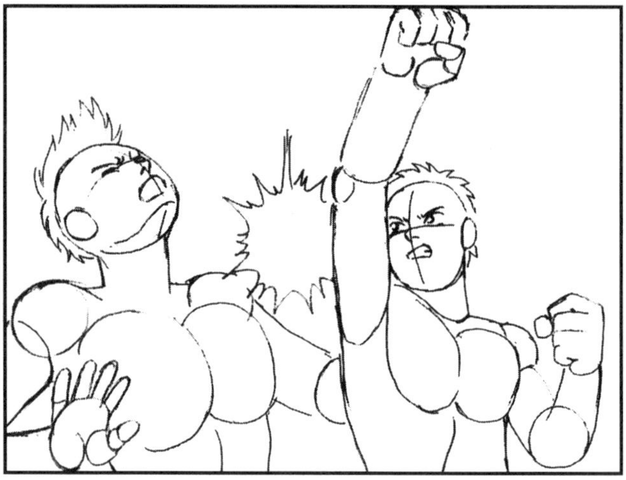

We'll make it a close-up of the upper body to bring out the force of impact. The next step is to add details to the rough sketch.

Once you are finished with penciling, you are ready to start inking. Use India (black) drawing ink in this step. (If adding color, make sure to use waterproof ink.)

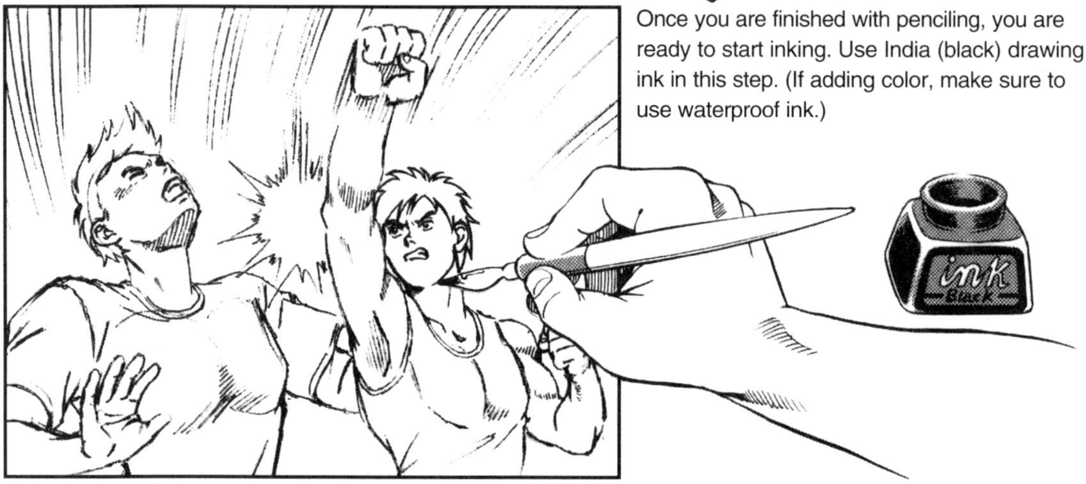

Pen nibs and line thicknesses (try several to find which one suits your style)

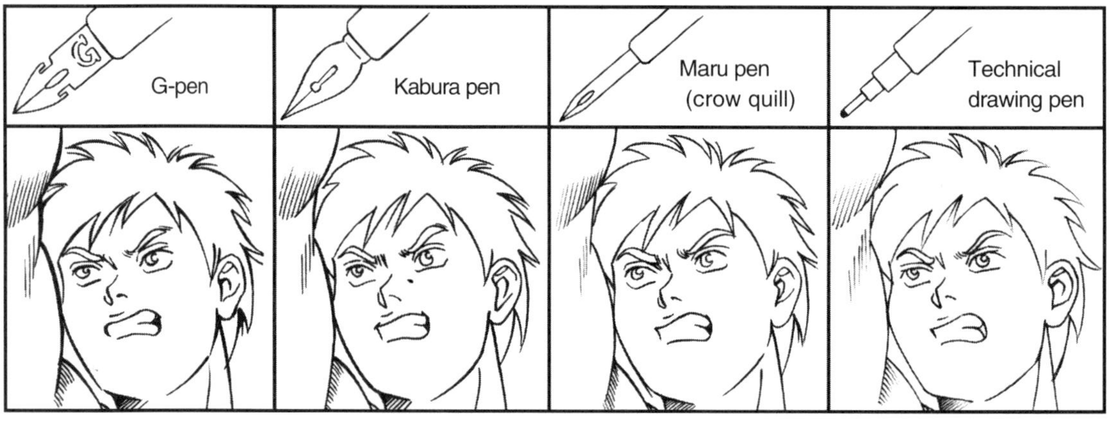

Use a straight ruler or curve ruler when drawing motion lines. Angle the nib against the ruler's edge so as to prevent the ink from bleeding.

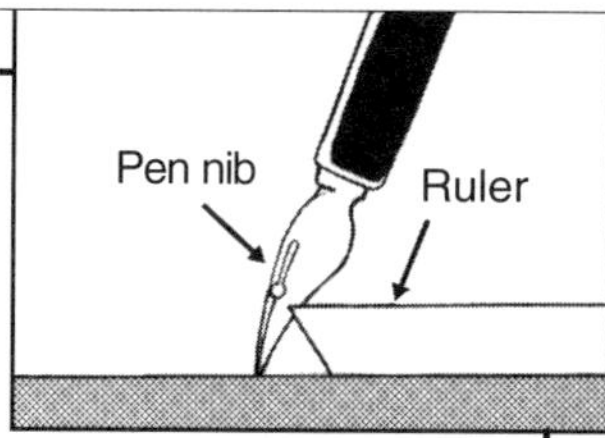

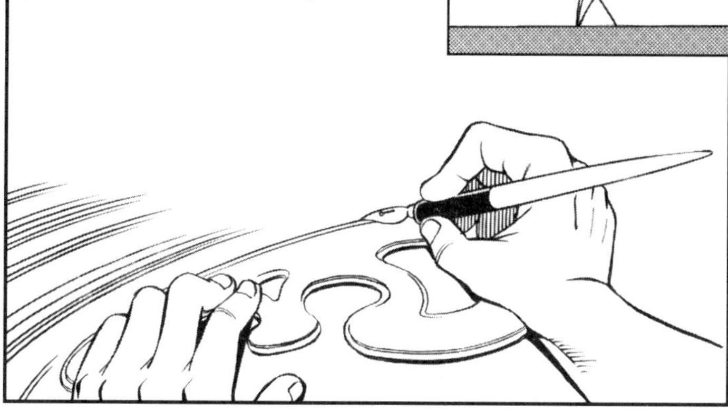

Use an ink brush or brush pen to fill in areas with a solid color. After the ink has dried, rub out the pencil lines with an eraser.

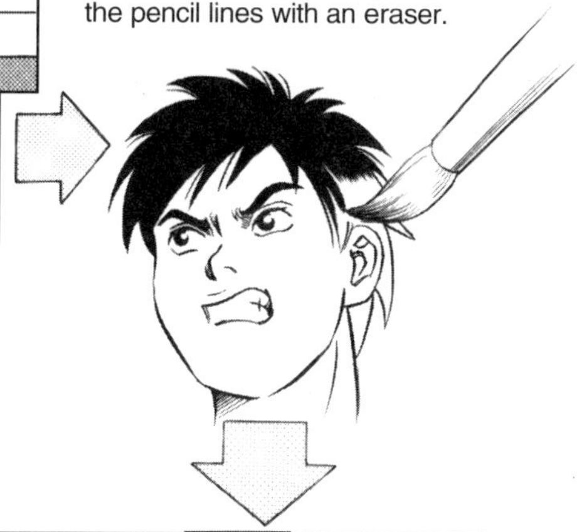

Use a commercially available screentone if your illustration requires one. After the tone has been applied, sections can be trimmed away with an exacto knife.

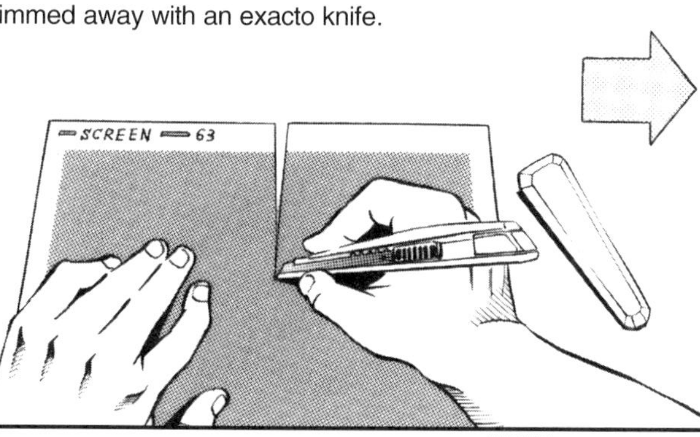

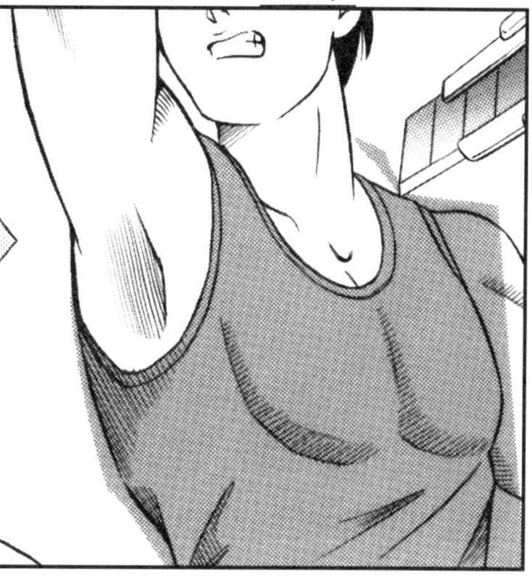

Screentone designs

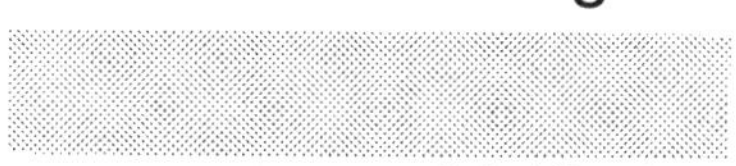

Dots / Gray tone

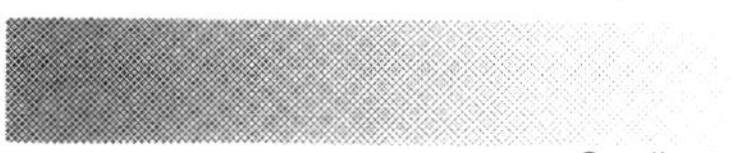

Gradient

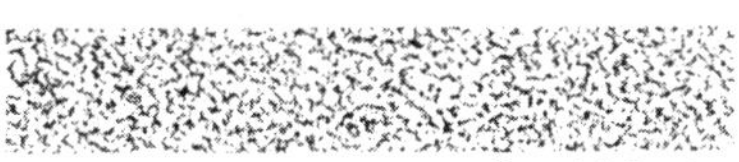

Sand / Static

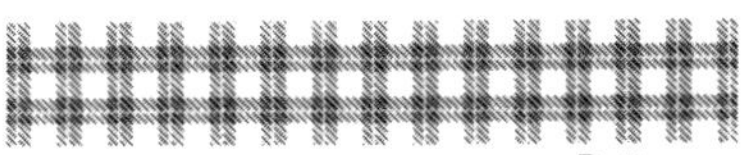

Patterns

Many additional designs can be found at any Japanese art supply store.

White out any protruding lines to complete your illustration.

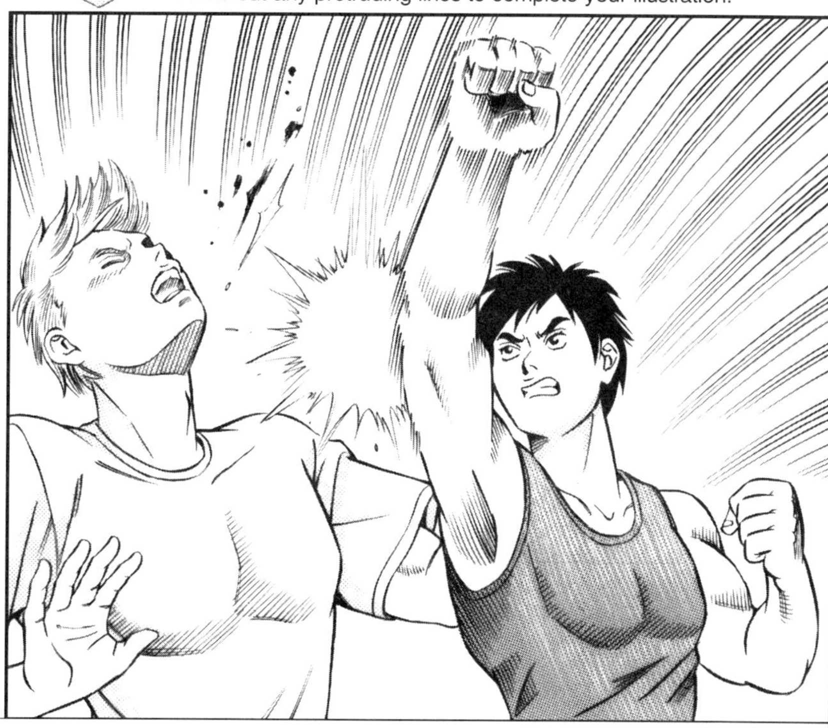

蹴る!

How to Draw Karate Kicks!

We'll cast Reiji as a high school sophomore.

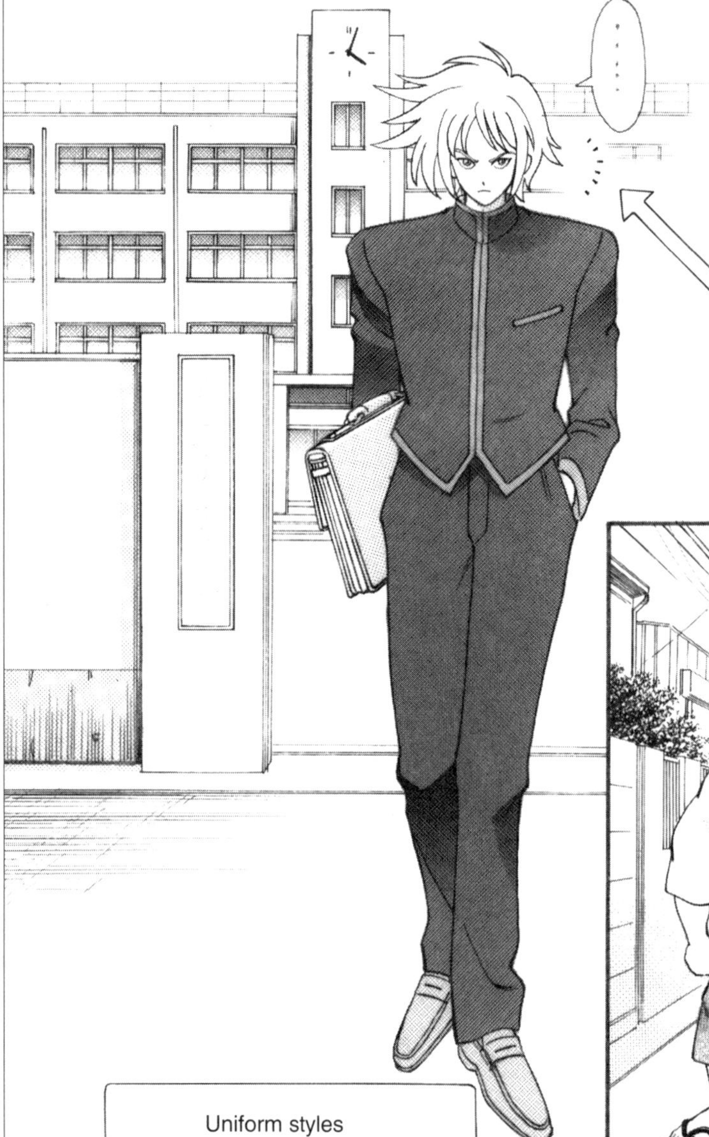

Most Japanese high schoolers are required to wear uniforms to school. Every school has its own distinct uniform style, and nowadays, this alone can heavily influence a school's popularity.

Here is another formophore. It usually indicates either a sudden discovery or mild astonishment.

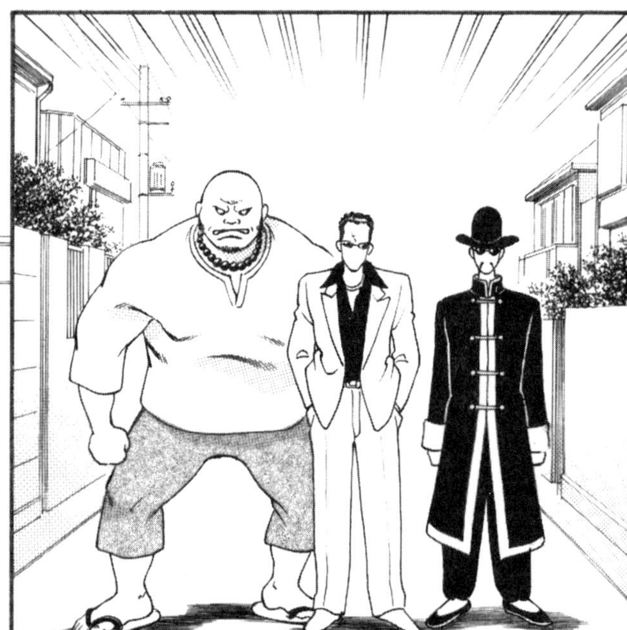

Uniform styles

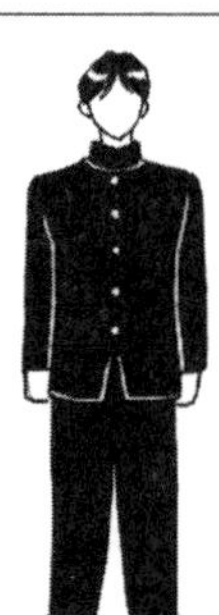

Standard

The stereotypical "juvenile delinquent" style. A flamboyant design is normally embroidered onto the jacket's back lining.

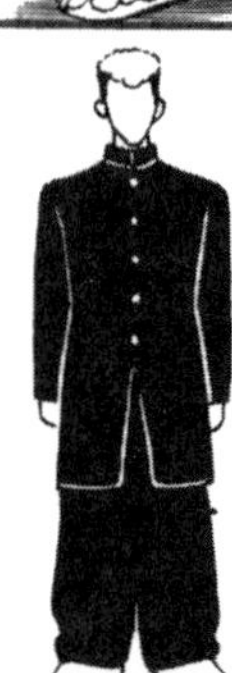

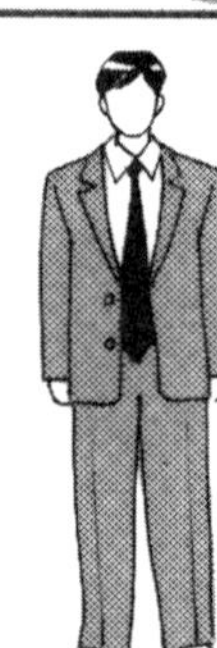

Many schools have adopted this type of "Ivy style" blazer combo.

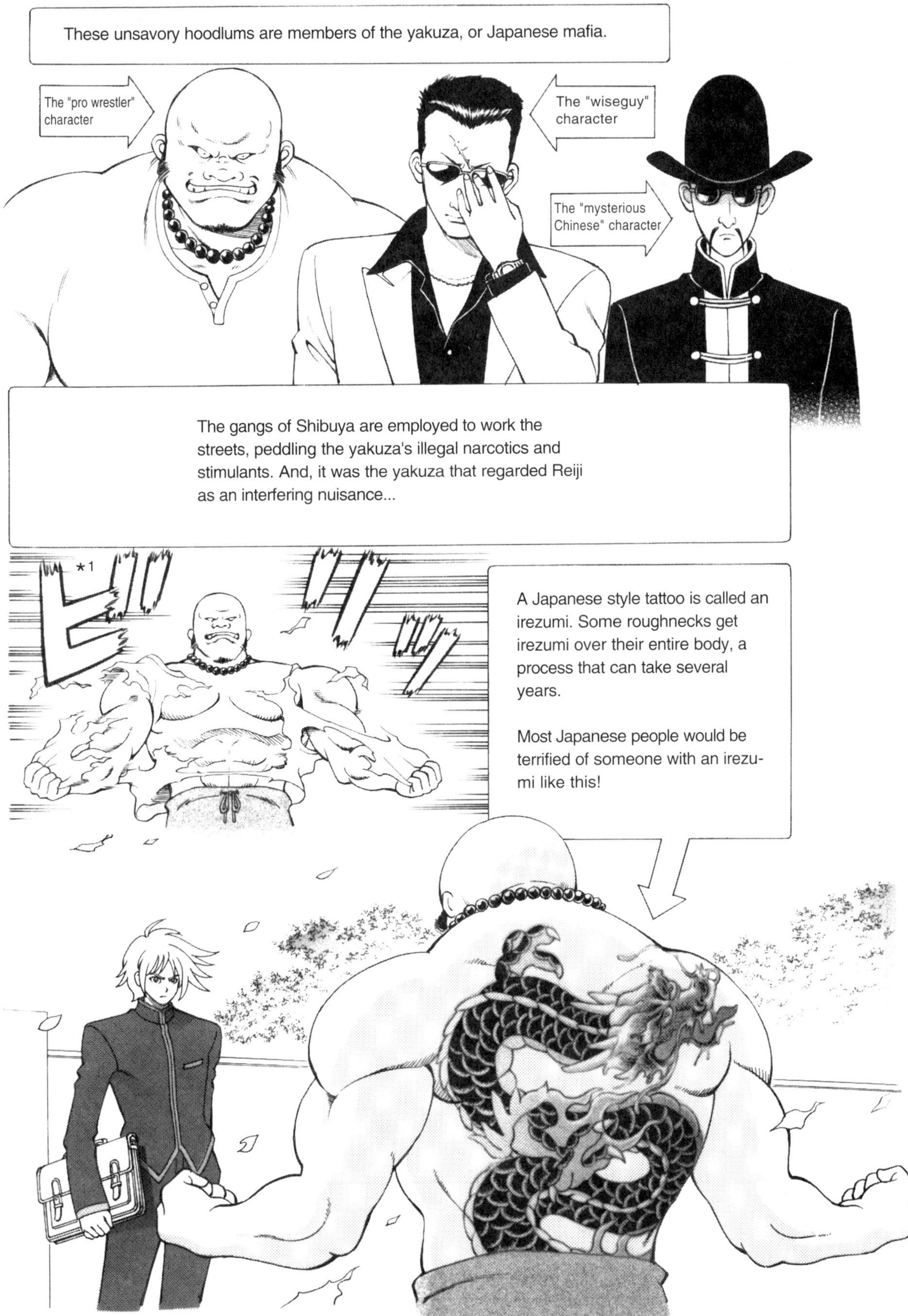
These unsavory hoodlums are members of the yakuza, or Japanese mafia.
The "pro wrestler" character
The "wiseguy" character
The "mysterious Chinese" character
The gangs of Shibuya are employed to work the streets, peddling the yakuza's illegal narcotics and stimulants. And, it was the yakuza that regarded Reiji as an interfering nuisance...
★1
A Japanese style tattoo is called an irezumi. Some roughnecks get irezumi over their entire body, a process that can take several years.
Most Japanese people would be terrified of someone with an irezumi like this!

★1:Rrrripp!

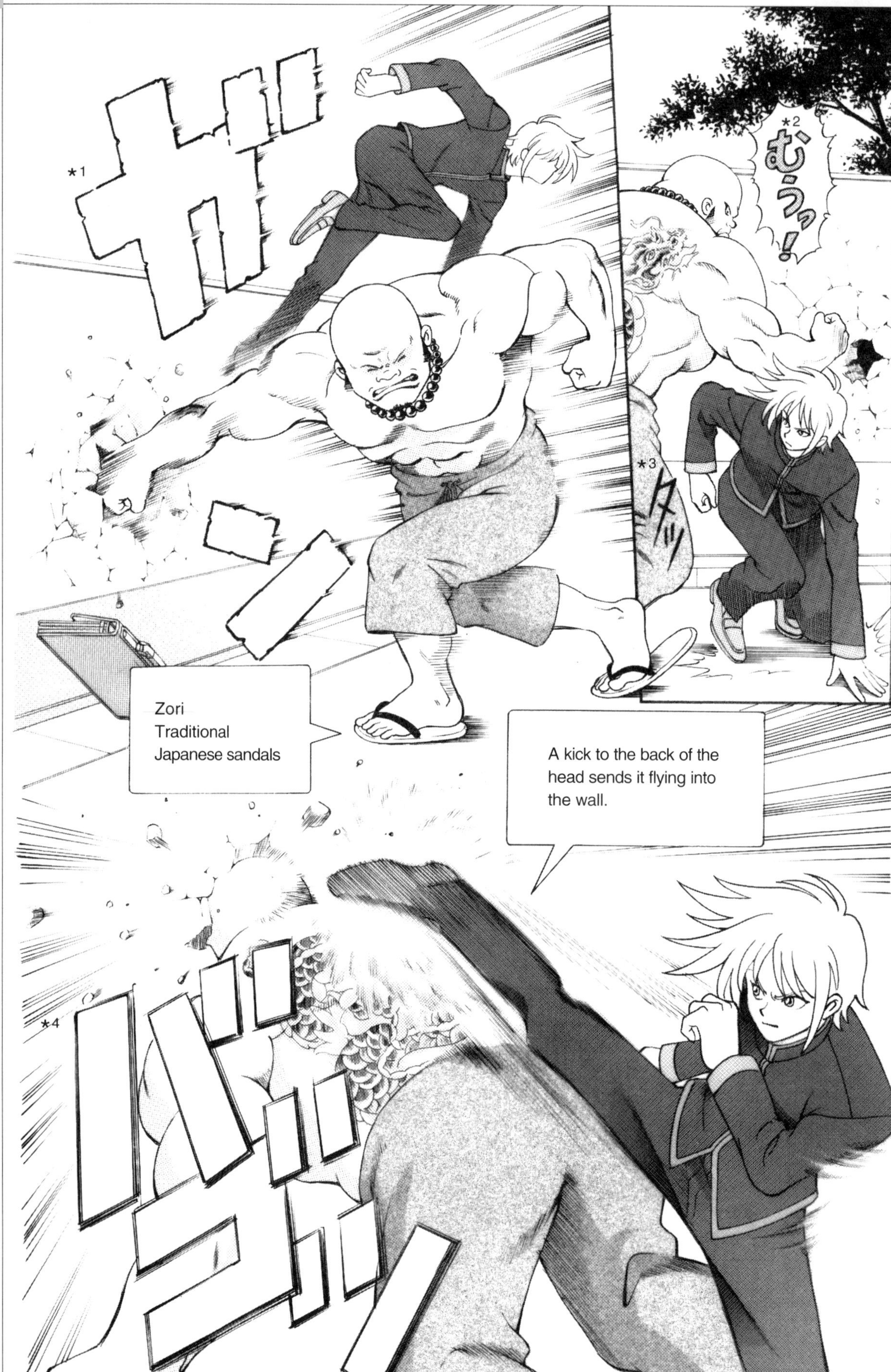

★1:Bash! ★2:Huh?! ★3:Ffft ★4:Thrak!

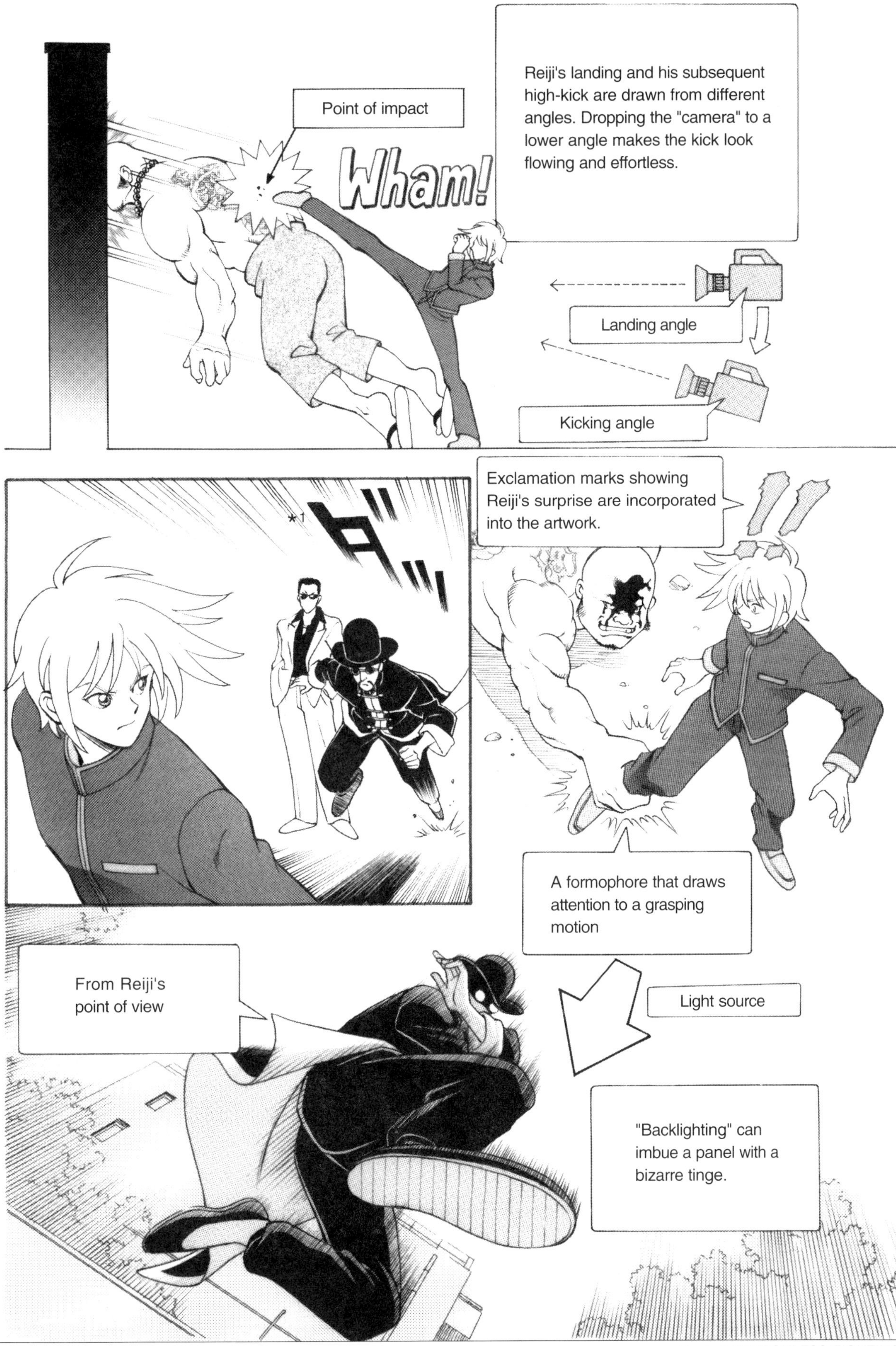
Reiji's landing and his subsequent high-kick are drawn from different angles. Dropping the "camera" to a lower angle makes the kick look flowing and effortless.
Point of impact
Wham!
Landing angle
Kicking angle
Exclamation marks showing Reiji's surprise are incorporated into the artwork.
★1
A formophore that draws attention to a grasping motion
From Reiji's point of view
Light source
"Backlighting" can imbue a panel with a bizarre tinge.

★1:Sfft

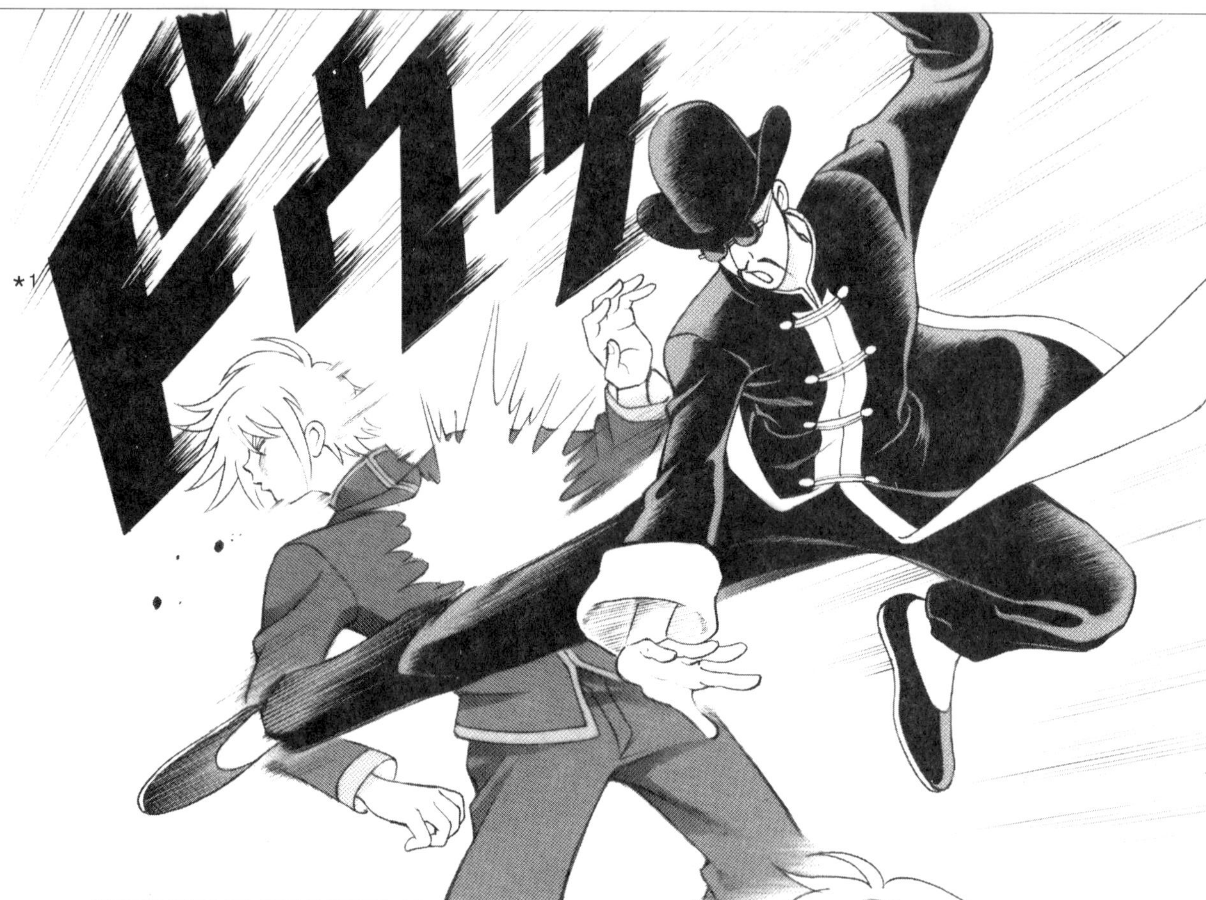

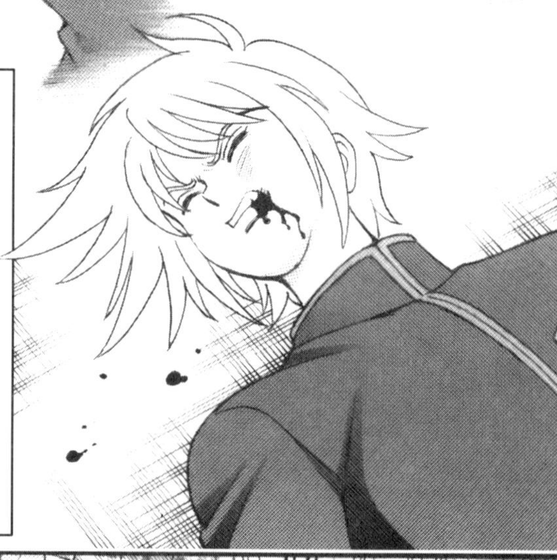

Japanese manga has frequently faced criticism for its excessive violence. Certainly, manga that feature meaningless violence can be a problem. To its credit, most manga don't glorify violence for its own sake, and the intelligent reader should have no problem avoiding those that do.

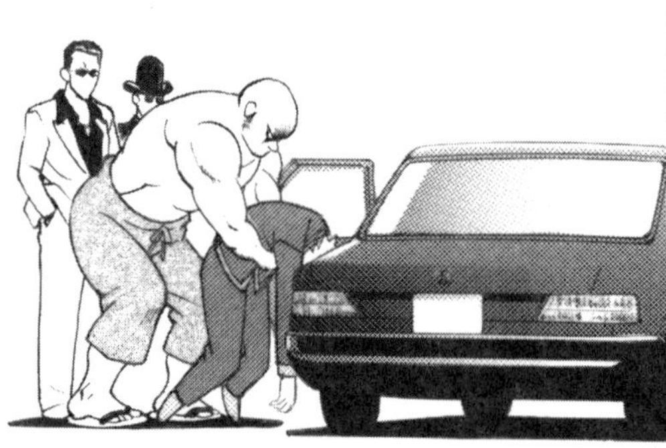

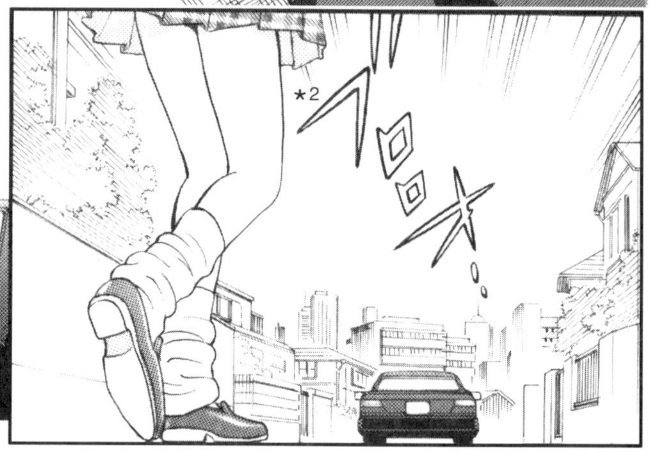

★1:Crrack! ★2:Vrooom

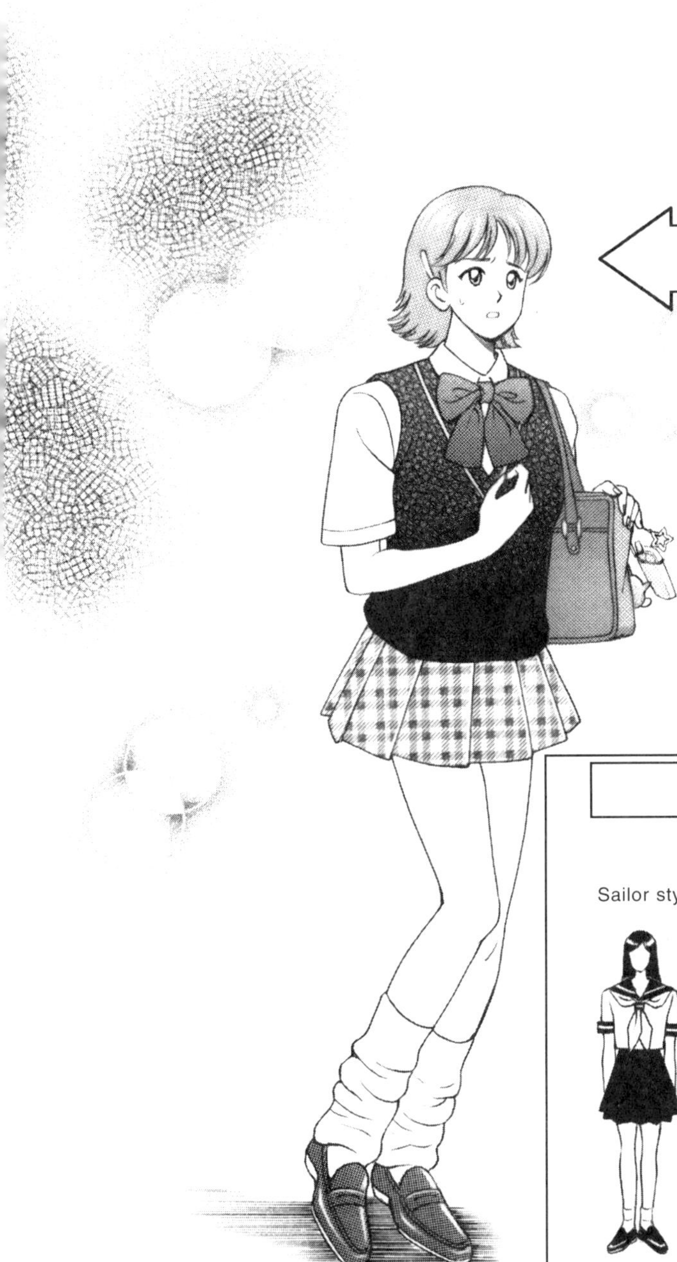

Reiji's 17-year old classmate, Kaori

We previously mentioned that most Japanese high schools require uniforms. Girls, too, must abide by this rule, but their uniforms are marked by even greater school-specific design differences that contribute markedly to a school's popularity or lack thereof. While the word "uniform" may bring to mind a buttoned-down, formal image, many schoolgirls enjoy accessorizing and turning their uniform into a fashion statement.

High-school girls' uniforms

Sailor style — Jacket style — Vest style — Necktie style (popularized by the Russian vocal duo t.A.T.u.)

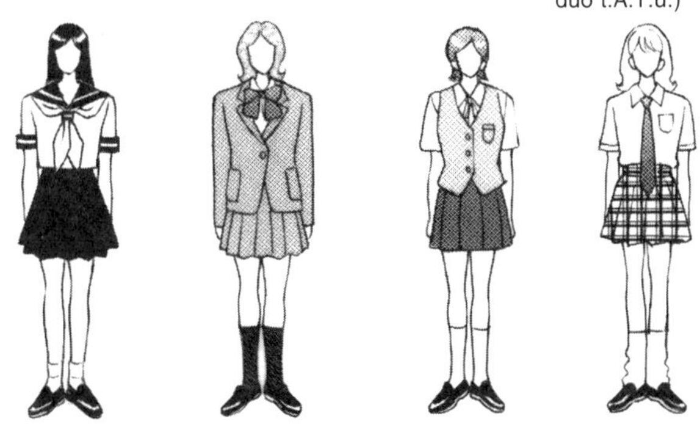

The most popular skirt style among schoolgirls is the "micro-mini", so called for its ultra-high hemline. Uniforms of both boys and girls show certain differences between the summer and winter styles.

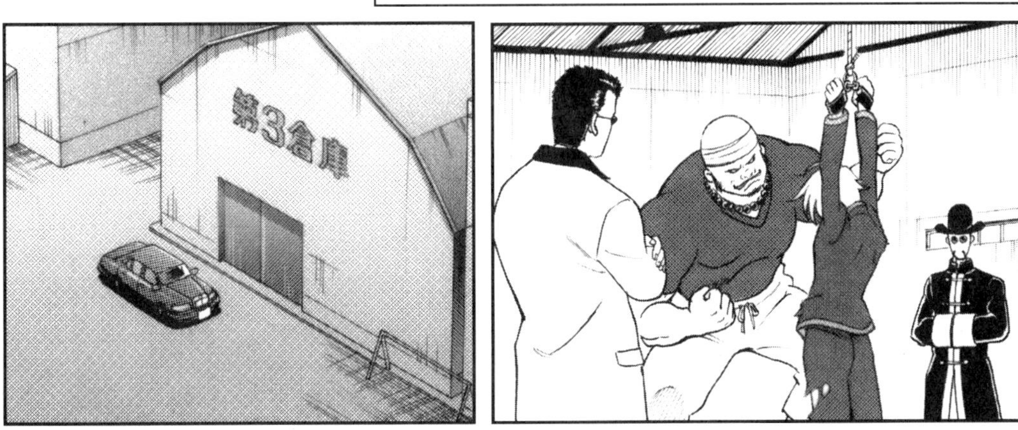

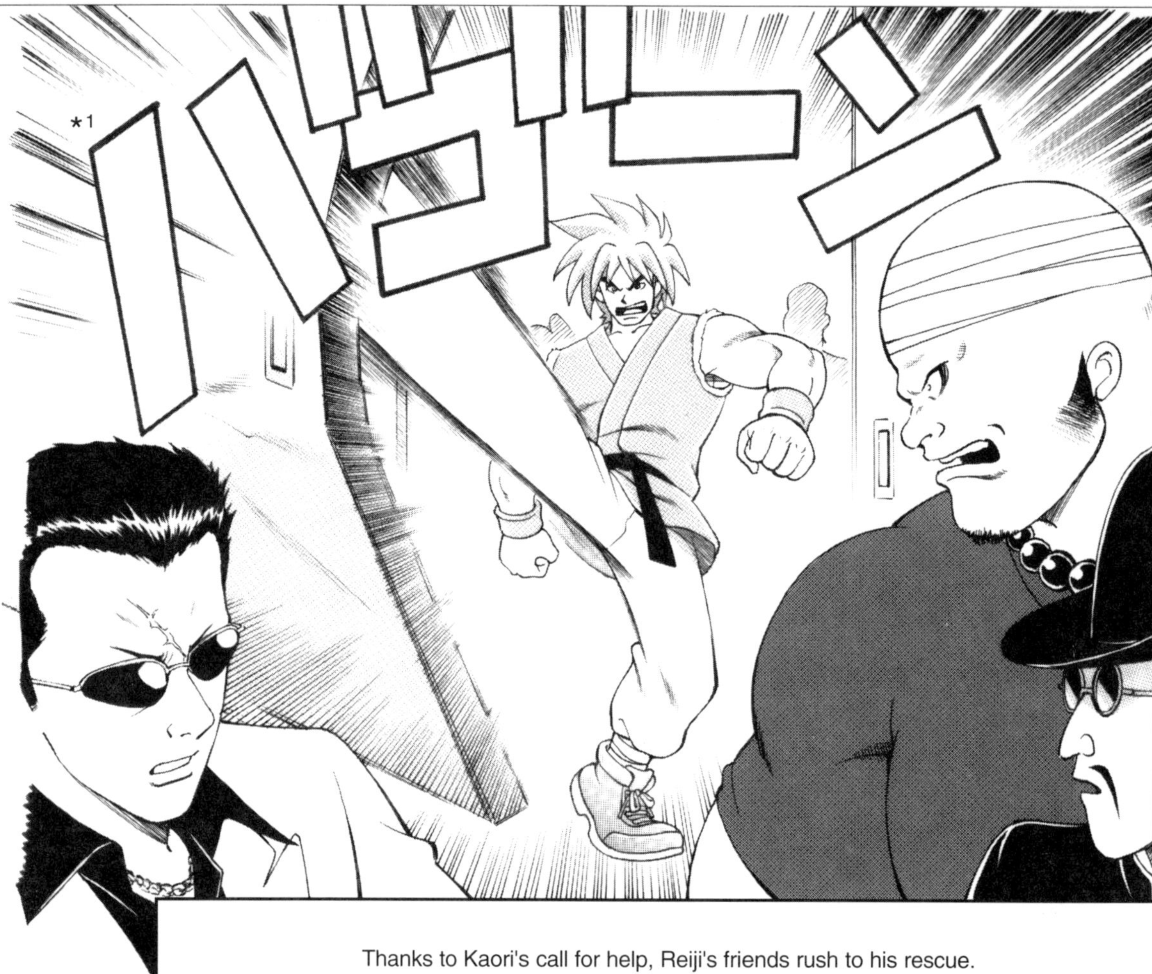

Thanks to Kaori's call for help, Reiji's friends rush to his rescue. At one time, these young fighters were Reiji's adversaries, but they have since become trusted allies.

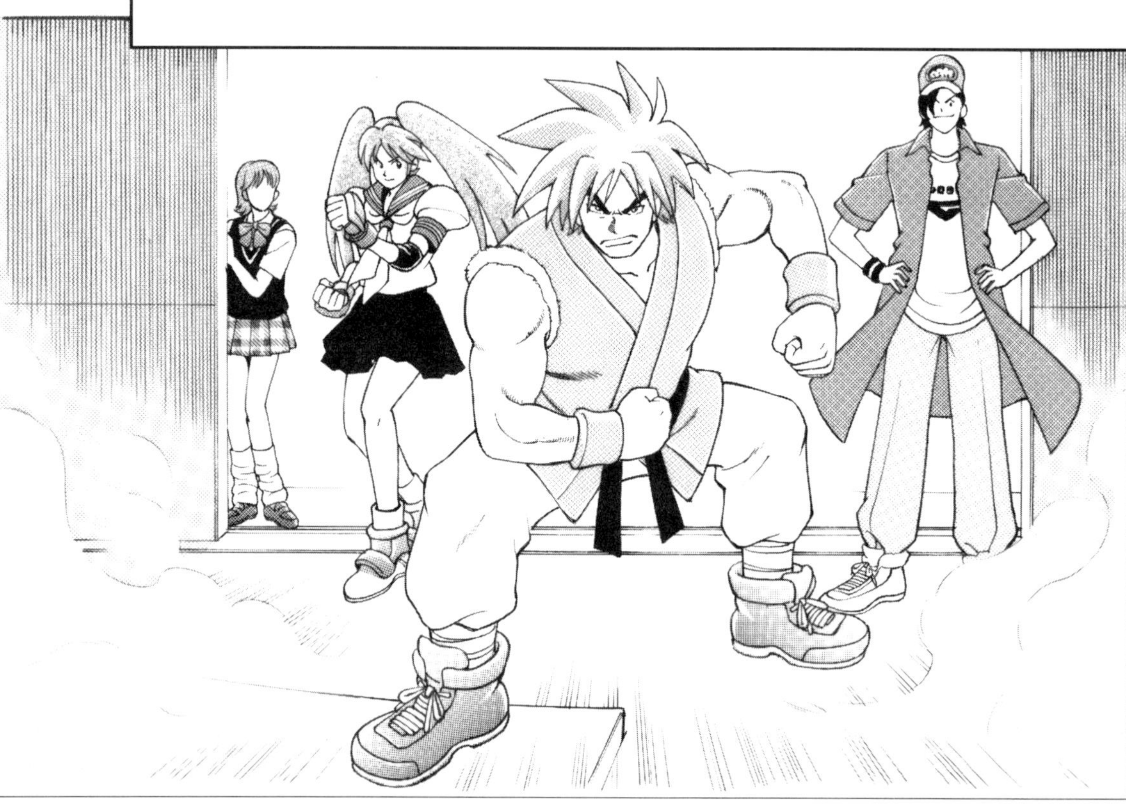

⋆1:Smash!

A narrative pattern typical of Japanese fighting manga

Hero "A"

VS.

Rival "B"

→ Hero "A" wins the battle, but in the process, "A" and "B" come to see eye to eye and wind up becoming friends.

→ Enter the even stronger enemy "C", who is defeated through the combined forces of "A" and "B".

It is said that the Japanese have held dear their "spirit of harmony" since time immemorial. The concept of wa, which includes elements of both cooperation and harmony, is fundamentally about showing good will to your fellow man. It's interesting to note that the majority of Japanese manga fans tend to prefer storylines in which rival characters grow to understand each other and ultimately reconcile their differences. Less popular are those that feature characters battling it out until one is destroyed.

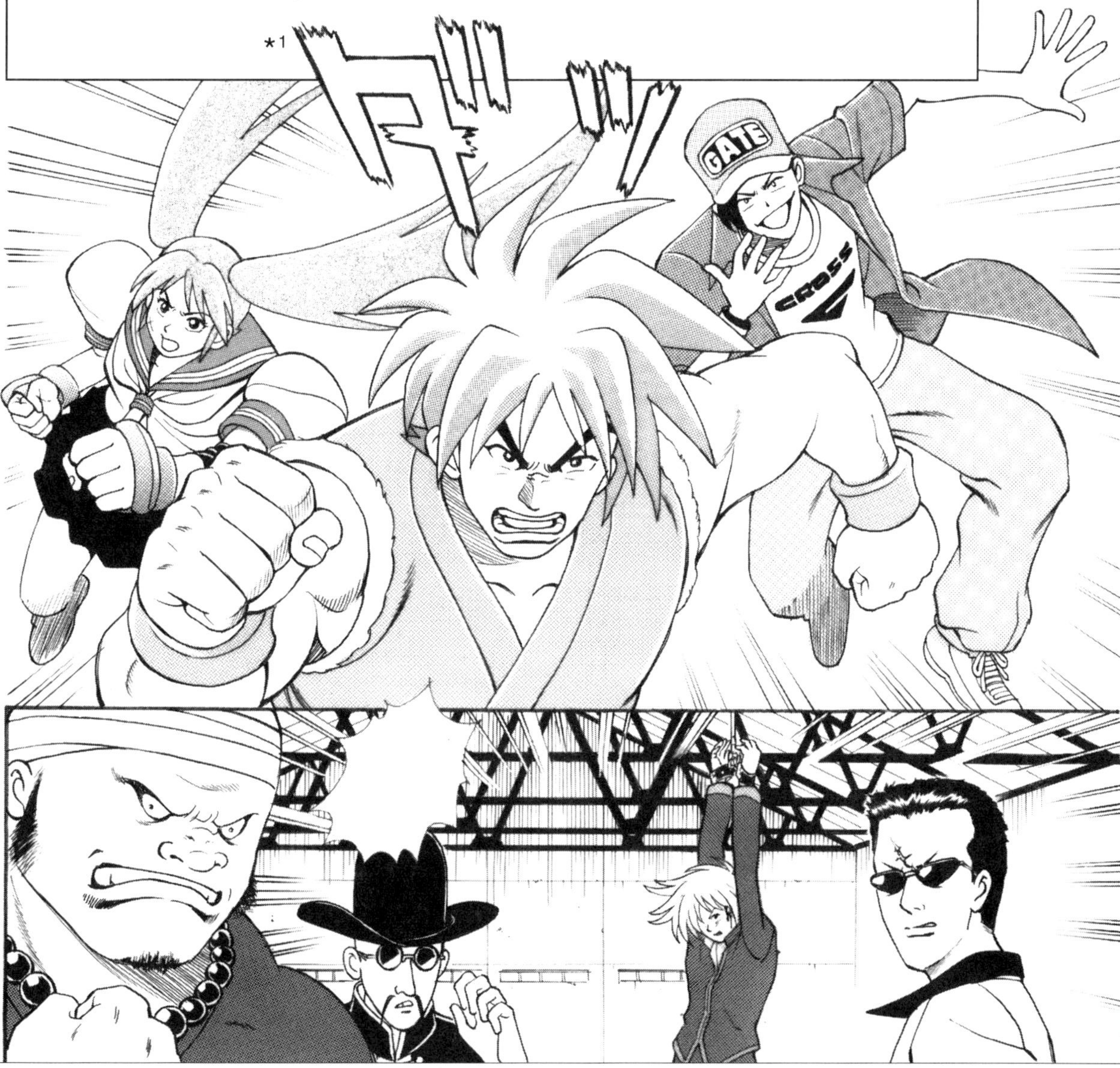

*1: Yaaaaa!!

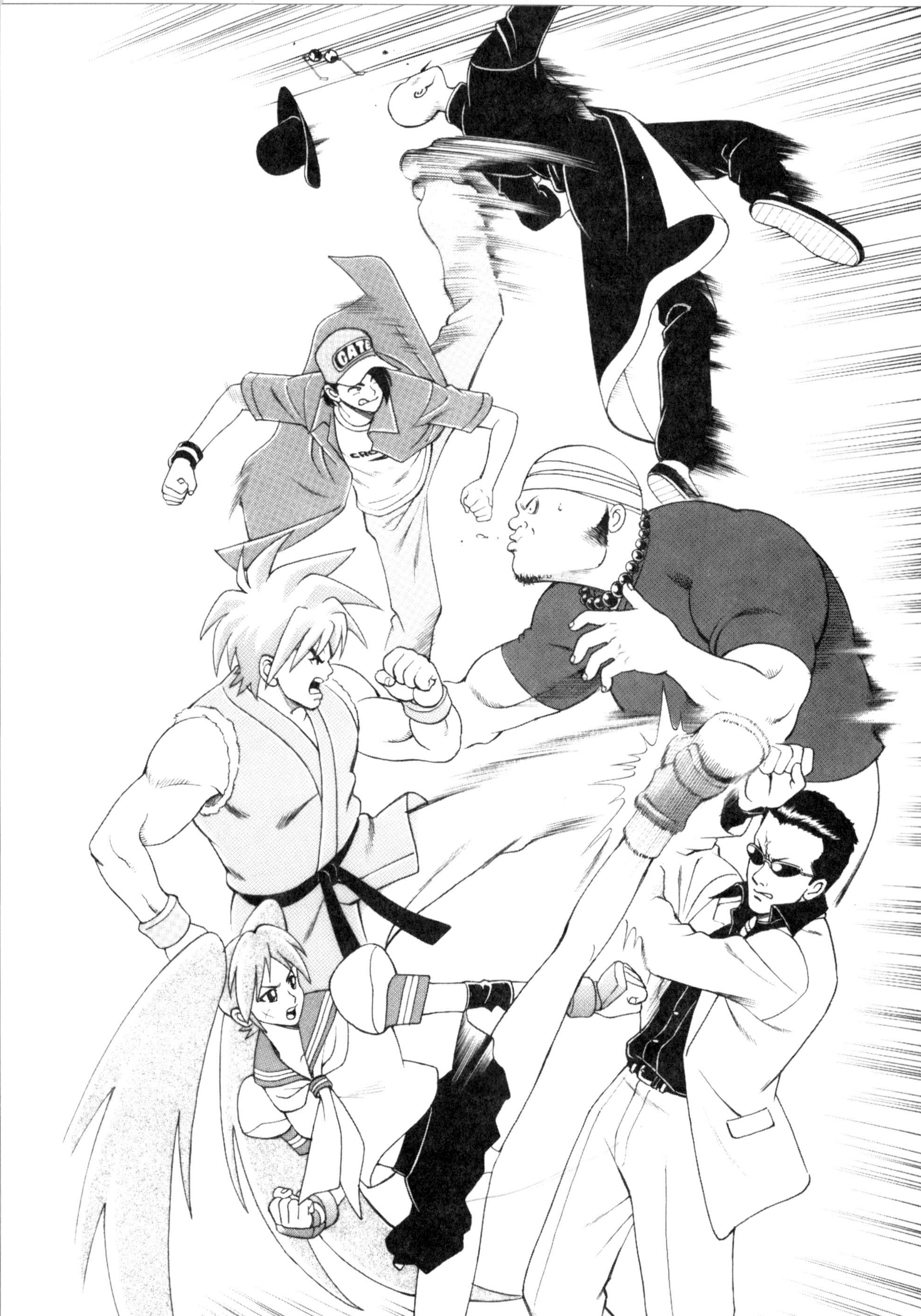
GATE

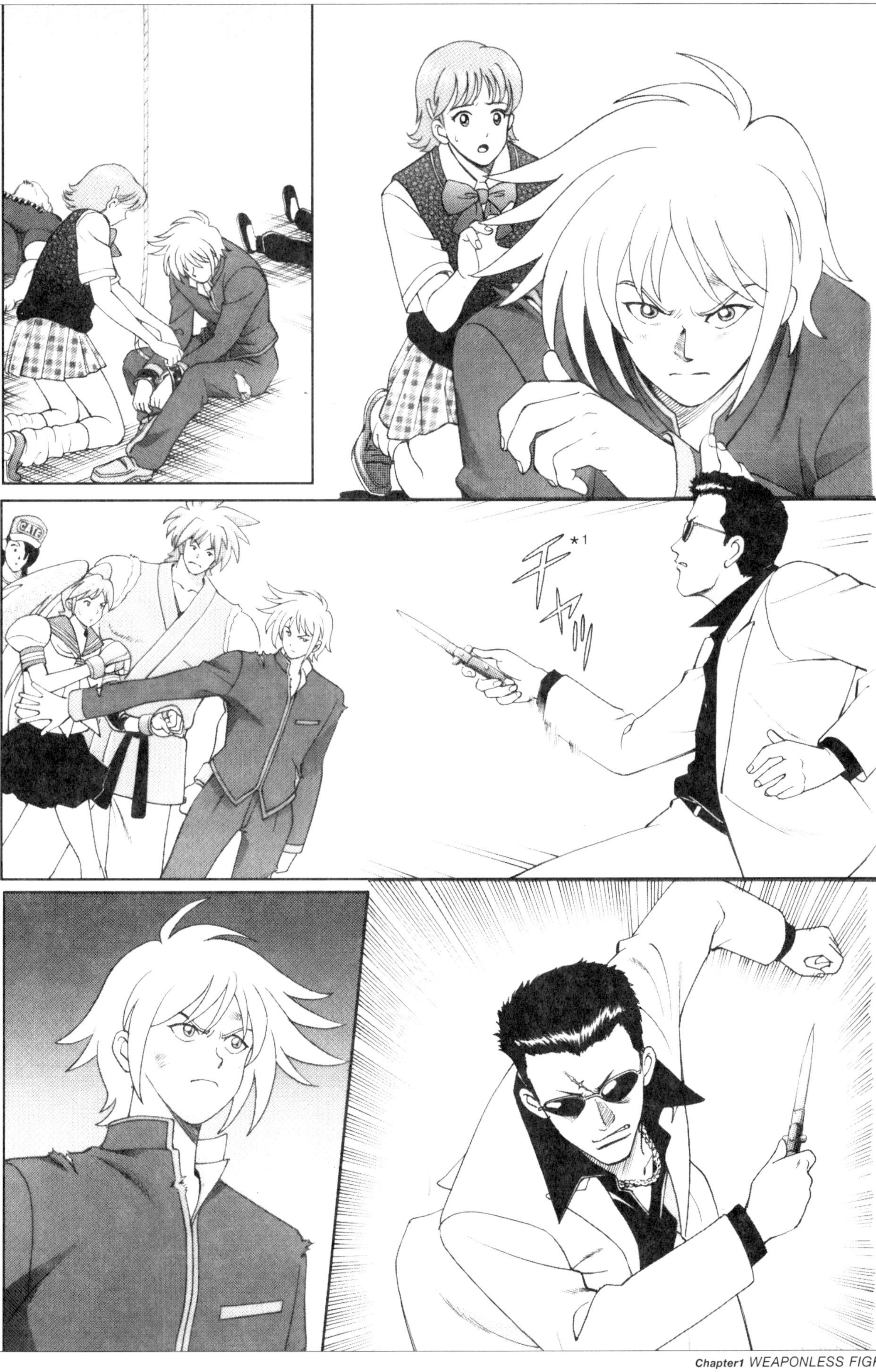

★1:Chikt

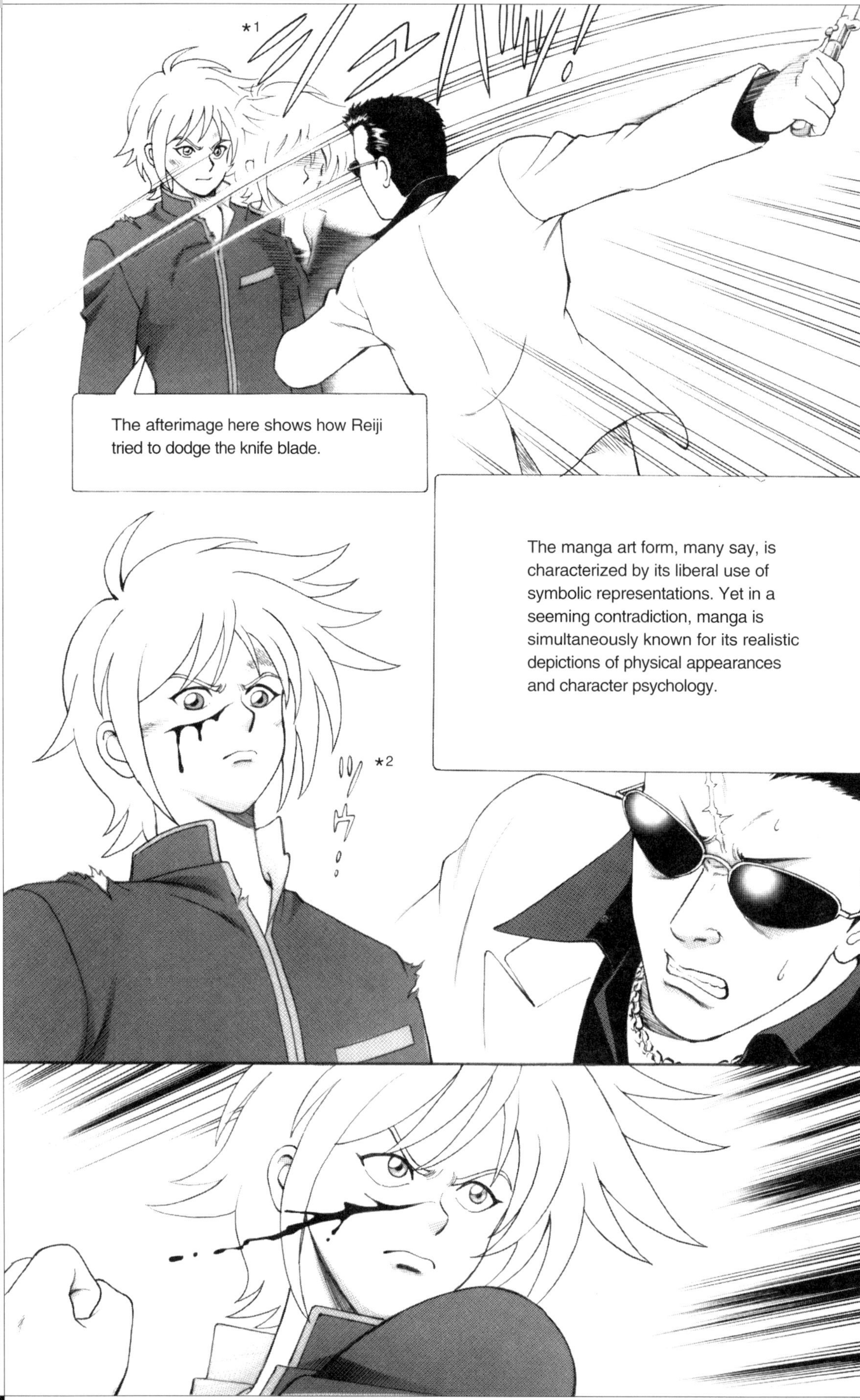

The afterimage here shows how Reiji tried to dodge the knife blade.

The manga art form, many say, is characterized by its liberal use of symbolic representations. Yet in a seeming contradiction, manga is simultaneously known for its realistic depictions of physical appearances and character psychology.

★1:Slisssh ★2:Hmm...

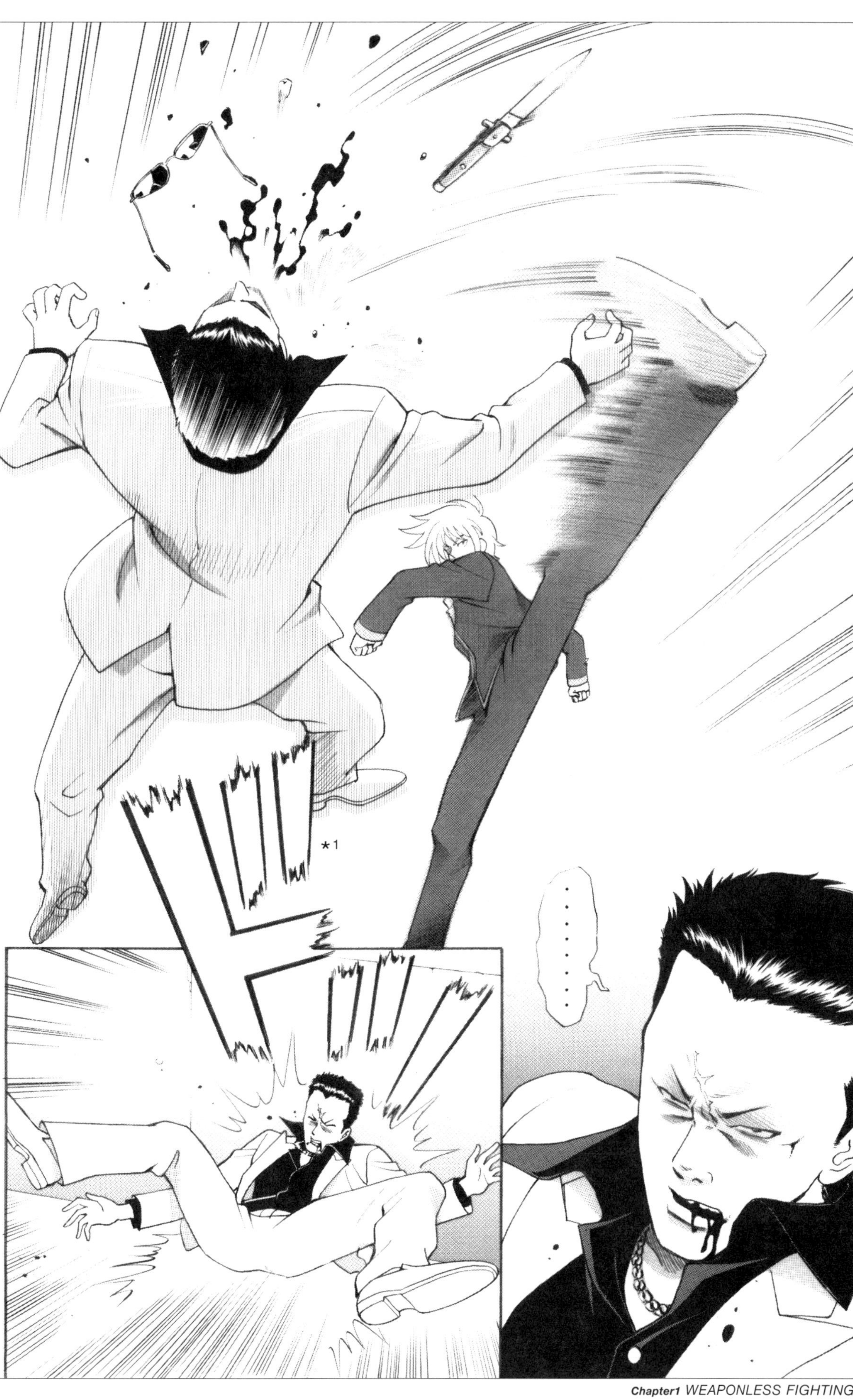

★1:Kathud!

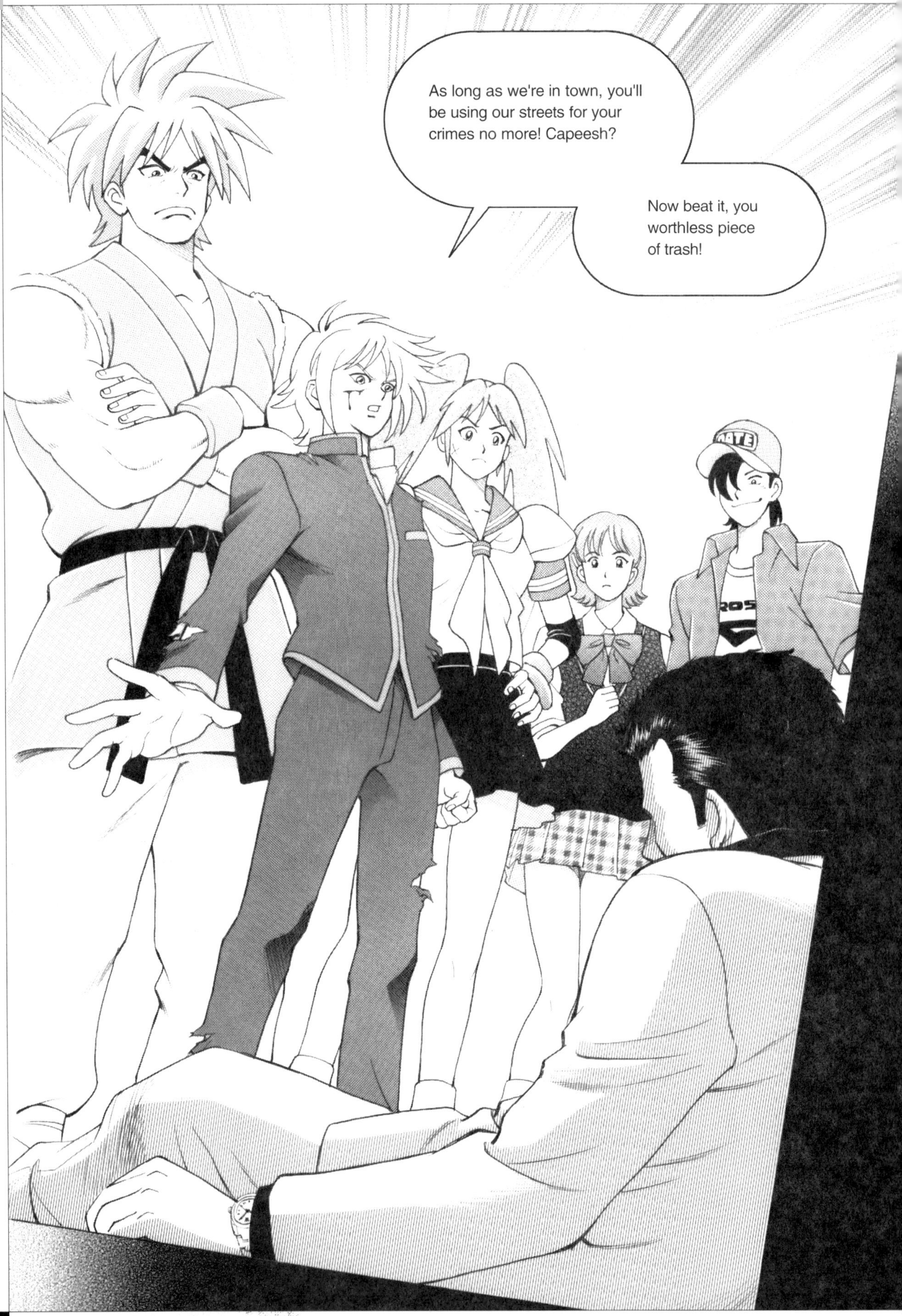
As long as we're in town, you'll be using our streets for your crimes no more! Capeesh?
Now beat it, you worthless piece of trash!
ROTE
ROS

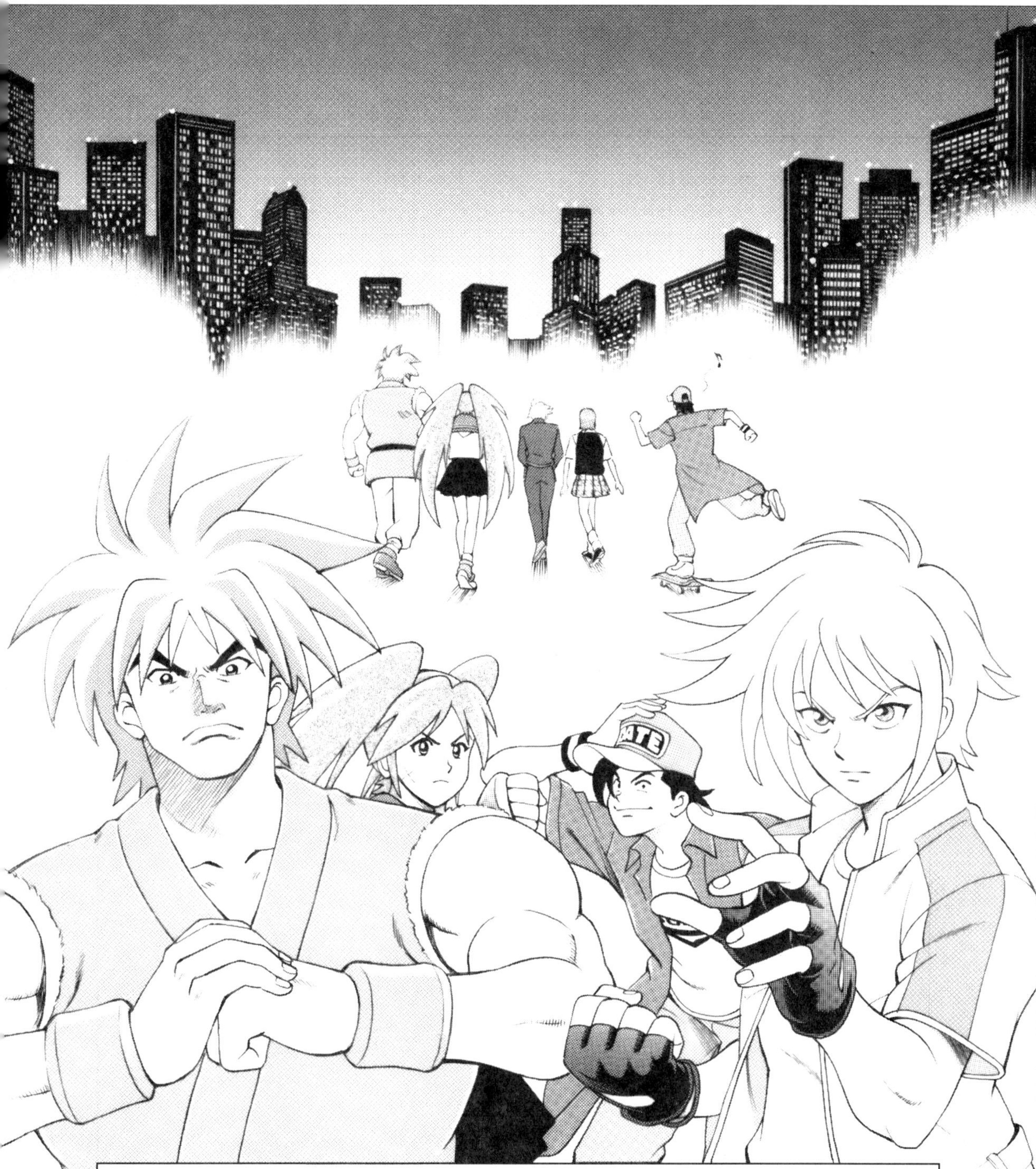

So far in this book, we've covered techniques for drawing fistfights and karate kicks. In the next chapter, we'll take a closer look at how these types of moves apply to fighting scenes that feature a variety of characters.

How the characters in this book were drawn-Part 2

Distorted features help the reader easily tell the characters apart. Check out the two panels below.

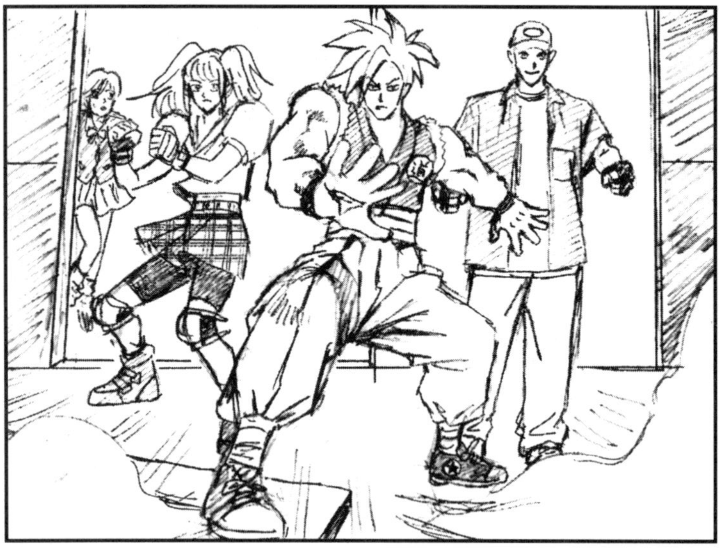

The manga appearing in this book were drawn by four artists, based on storyboards sketched by Makoto and Aster Noriko. The upper panel, from Makoto's storyboard, formed the basis for the lower panel, Tetsuya's final version.

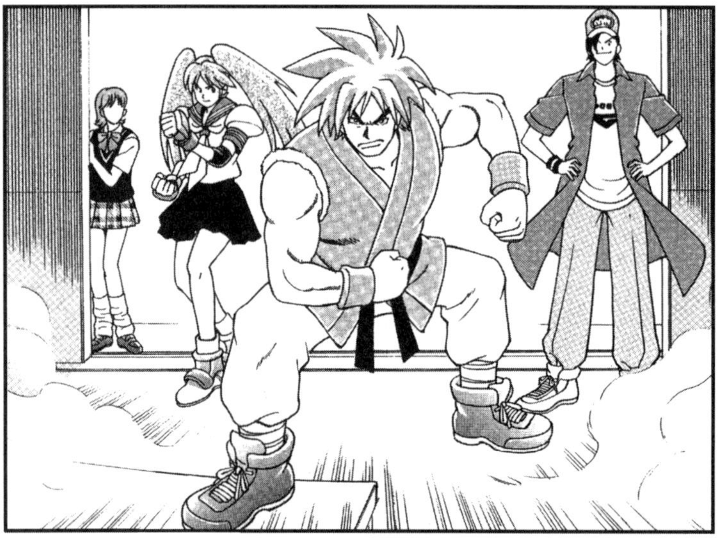

In contrast to Makoto's drawing, Tetsuya's style is marked by a touch of playful humor. Notice how much more distorted the features are in Tetsuya's panel.

The power of distortion
Extra-big hair adds to a character's overall visual impact.

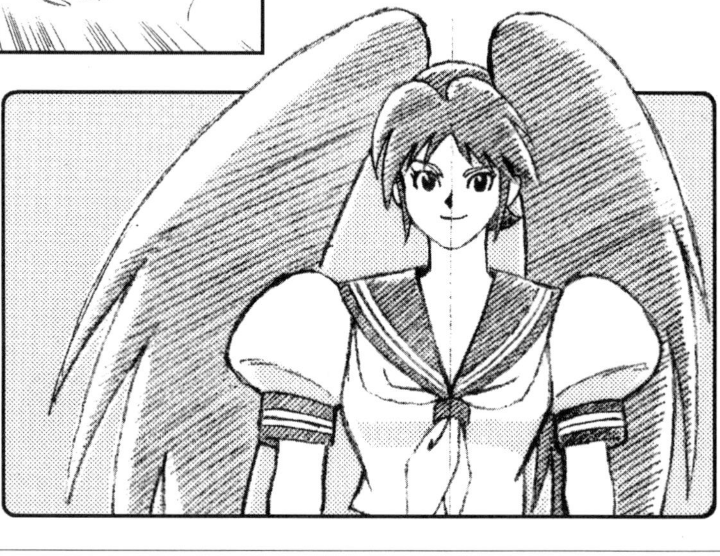

Distortion of facial features

The face on the left is a realistically drawn, strong-minded woman's face. The face on the right exhibits the exaggerated features typical of anime.

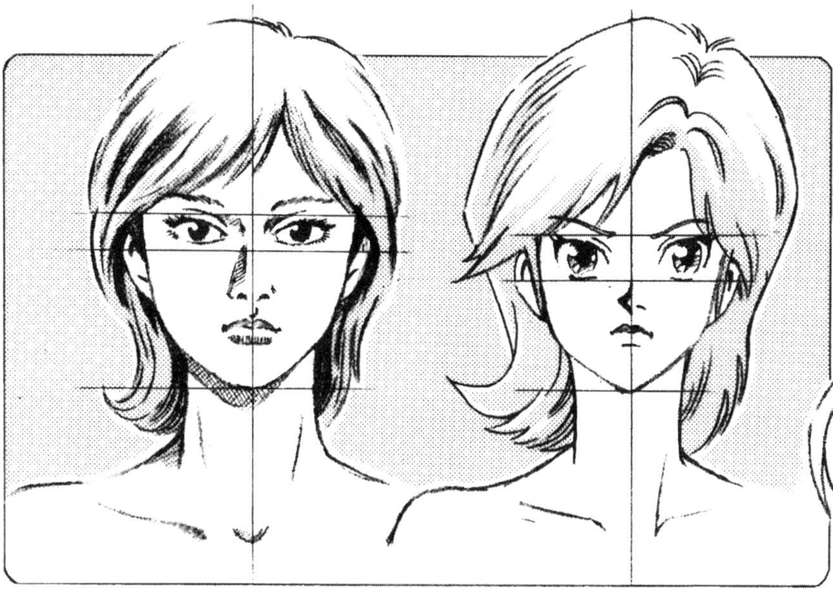

The figure on the right has oversized eyes and a proportionately larger head.

In profile

The smallish nose is given an upward slant. Nostrils are often not drawn.

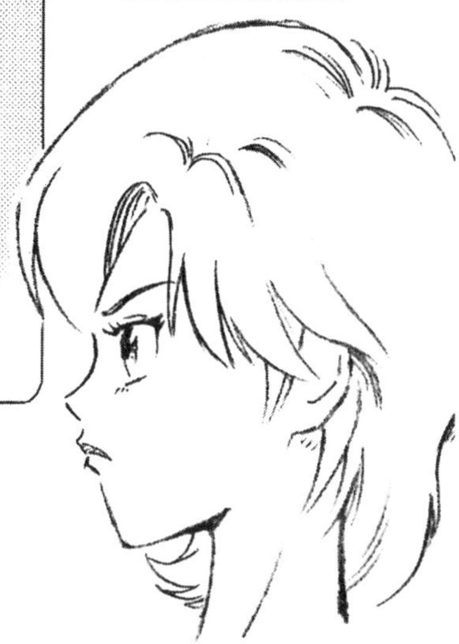

Distorted motion

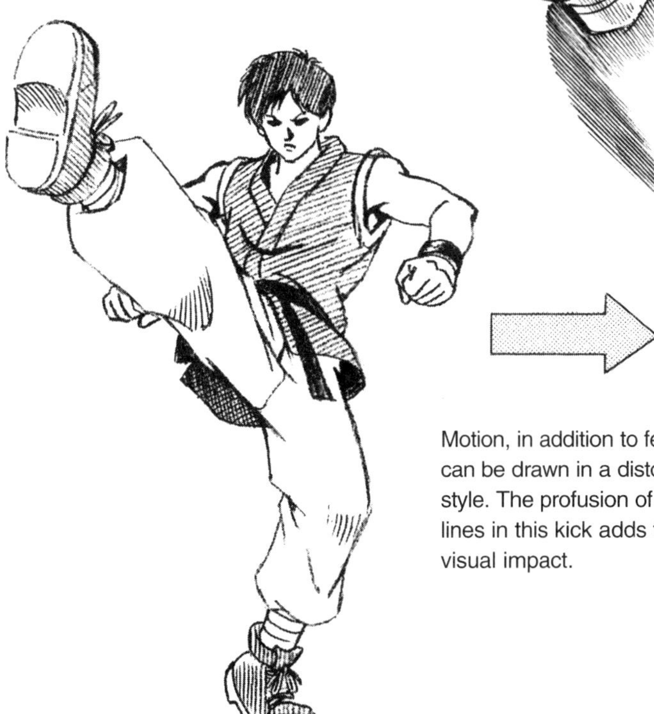

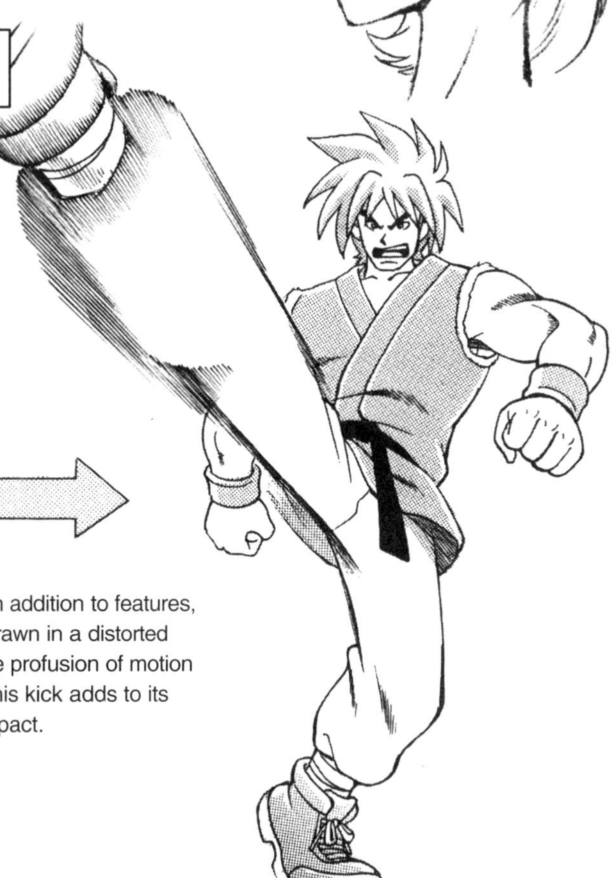

Motion, in addition to features, can be drawn in a distorted style. The profusion of motion lines in this kick adds to its visual impact.

キャラクター別ファイティングアクション

Drawing Various Characters in Fight Scenes

The Muscle-bound Hero

Comic book heroes with muscular physiques are popular amongst male readers in Japan. More often than not, such characters are dynamic, cheerful and easy-going. The beefcake presented here is twenty-two years old.

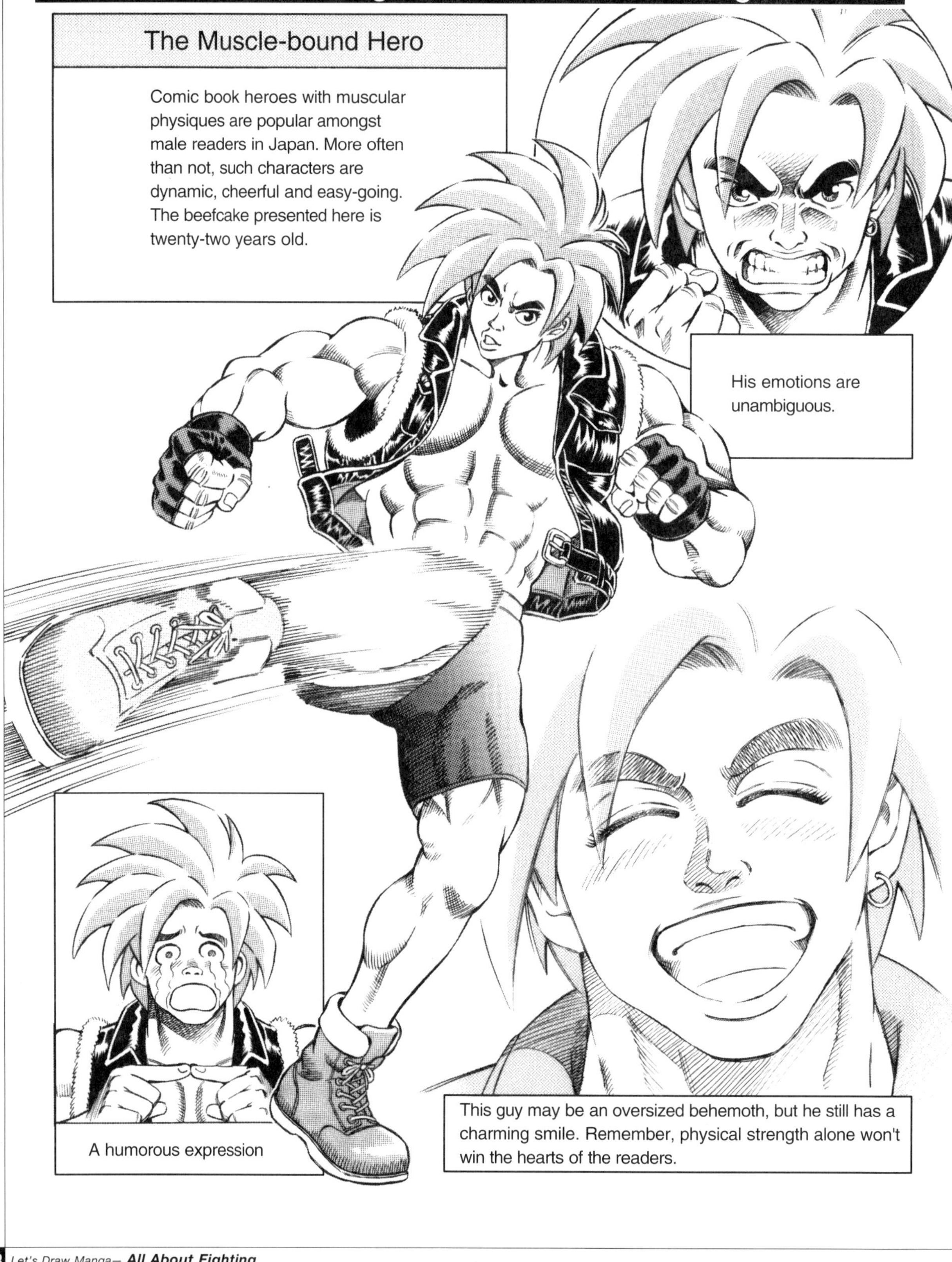

His emotions are unambiguous.

A humorous expression

This guy may be an oversized behemoth, but he still has a charming smile. Remember, physical strength alone won't win the hearts of the readers.

Above all, this character is dynamic in his motions. Think of his behavior and actions as reflections of his personality.

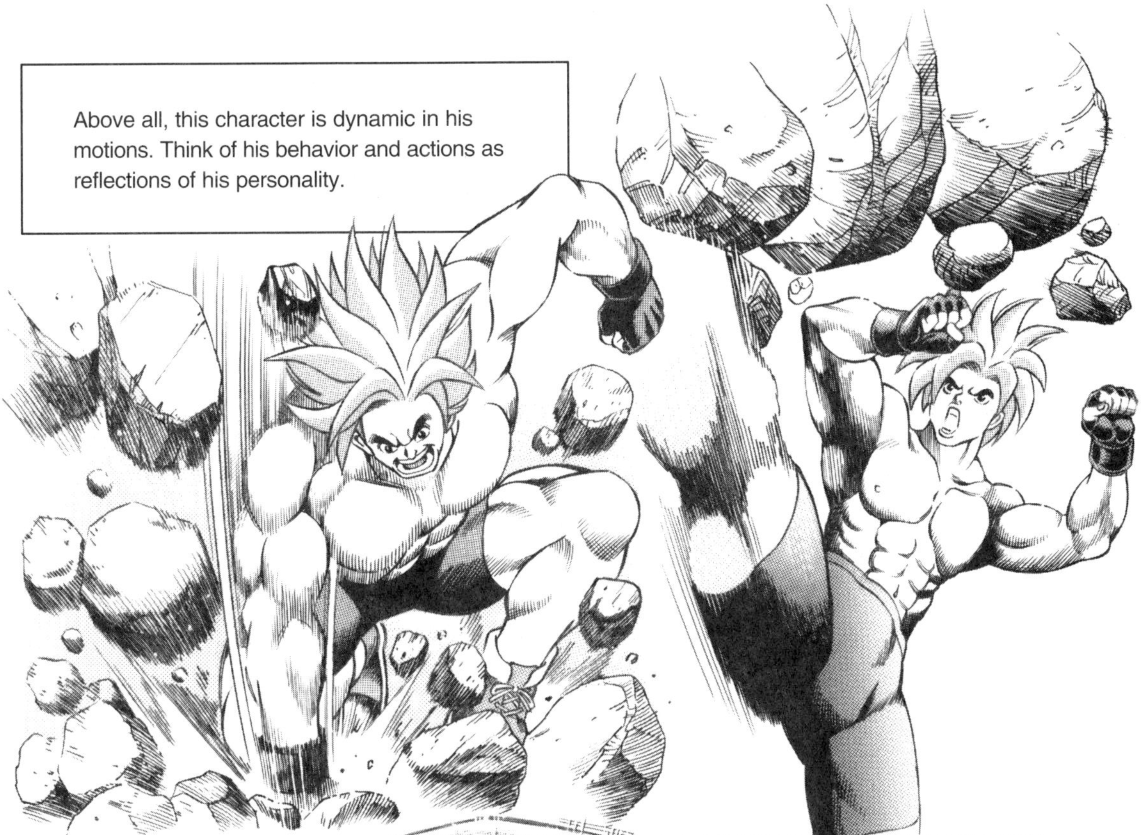

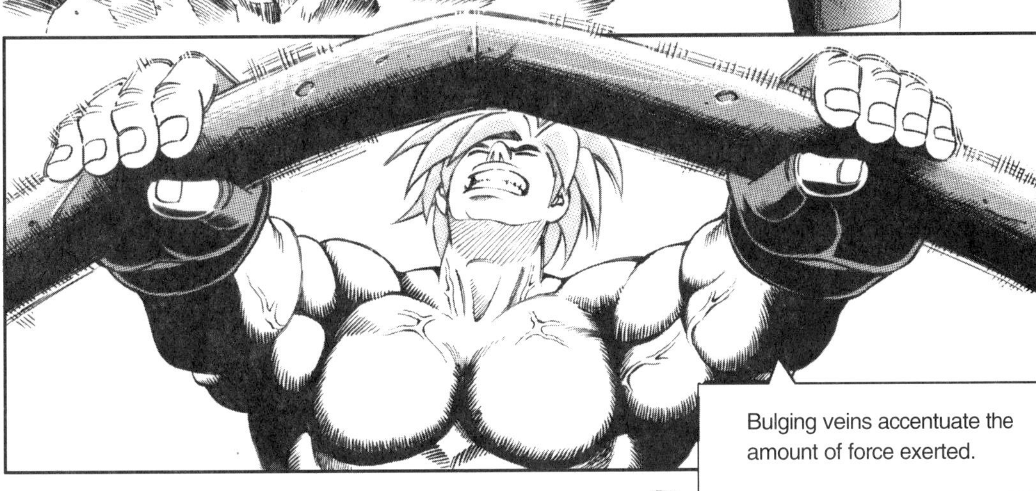

Bulging veins accentuate the amount of force exerted.

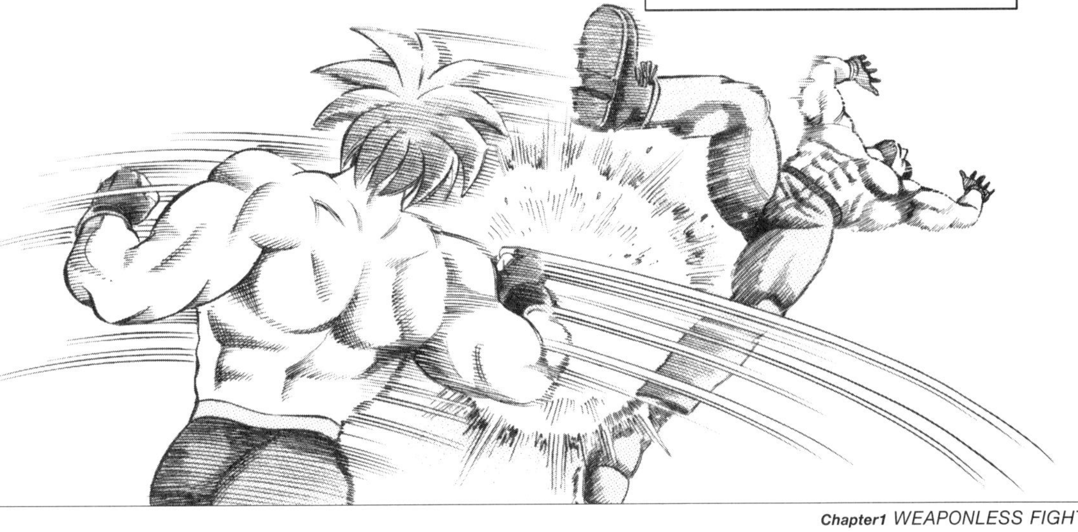

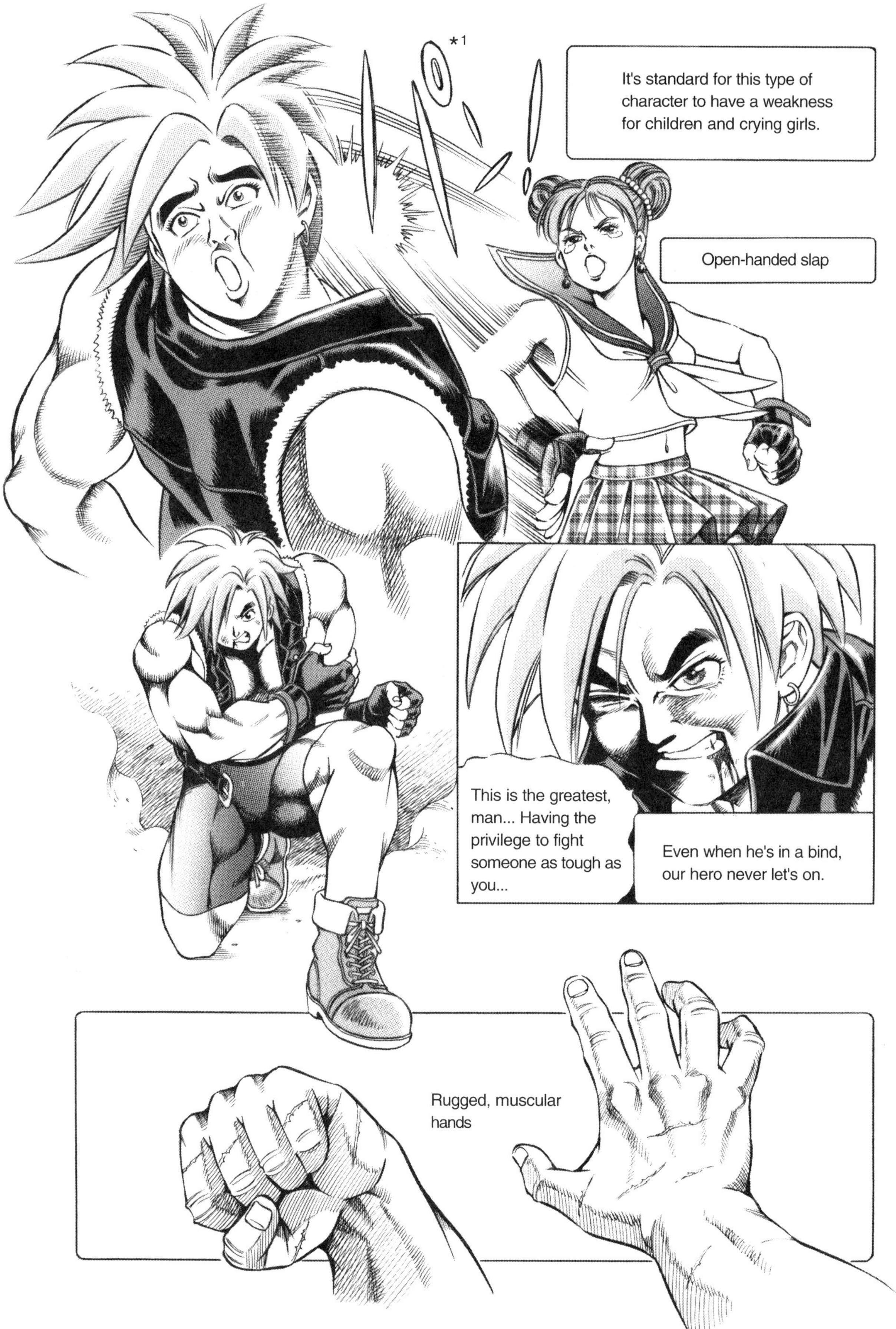

★1
It's standard for this type of character to have a weakness for children and crying girls.
Open-handed slap
This is the greatest, man... Having the privilege to fight someone as tough as you...
Even when he's in a bind, our hero never let's on.
Rugged, muscular hands

★1: Wham!

Drawing muscles (examples)

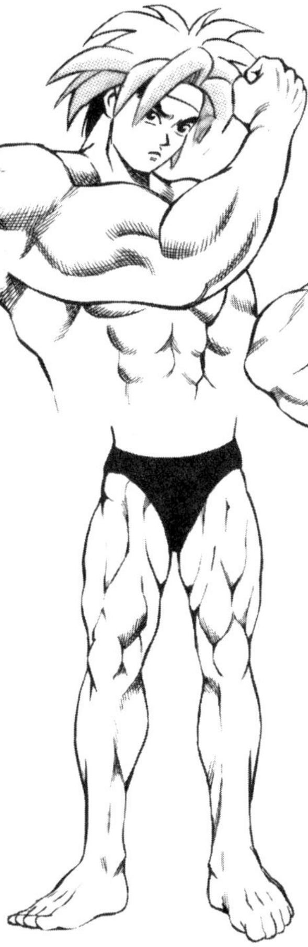

Illustrators have their own personal style when it comes to drawing muscles. The figures here are drawn in a rather stylized, "comic-book" style.

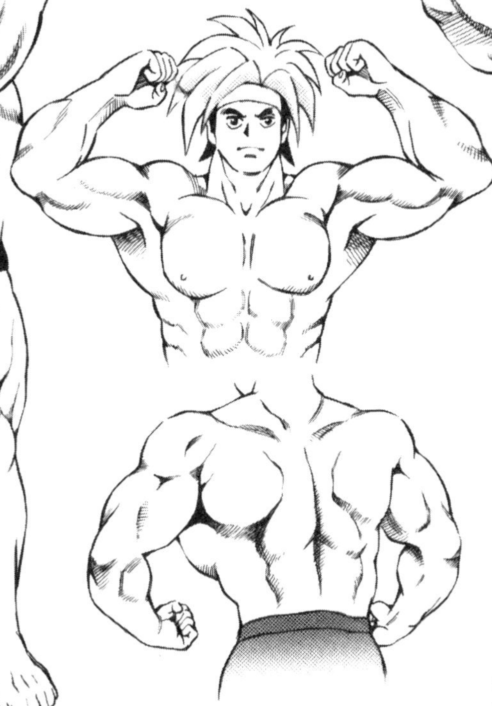

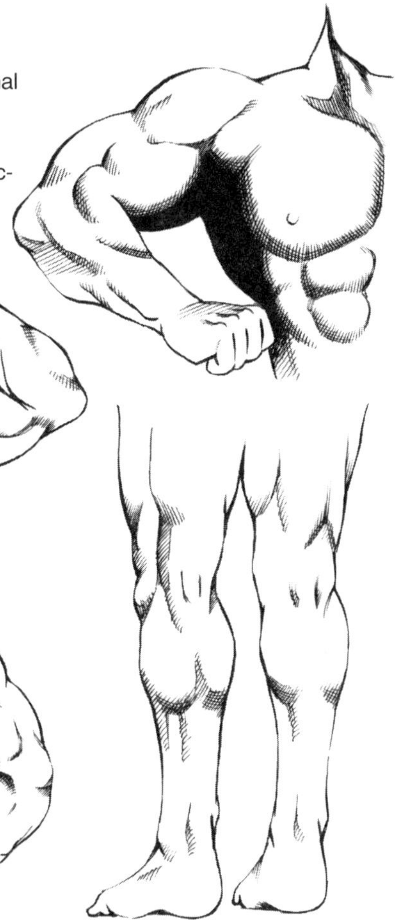

Variations on the muscle-bound hero

The silent, serious ex-military type. This character never makes a good protagonist, but he's often cast in an important supporting role. The fellow here is about thirty years old.

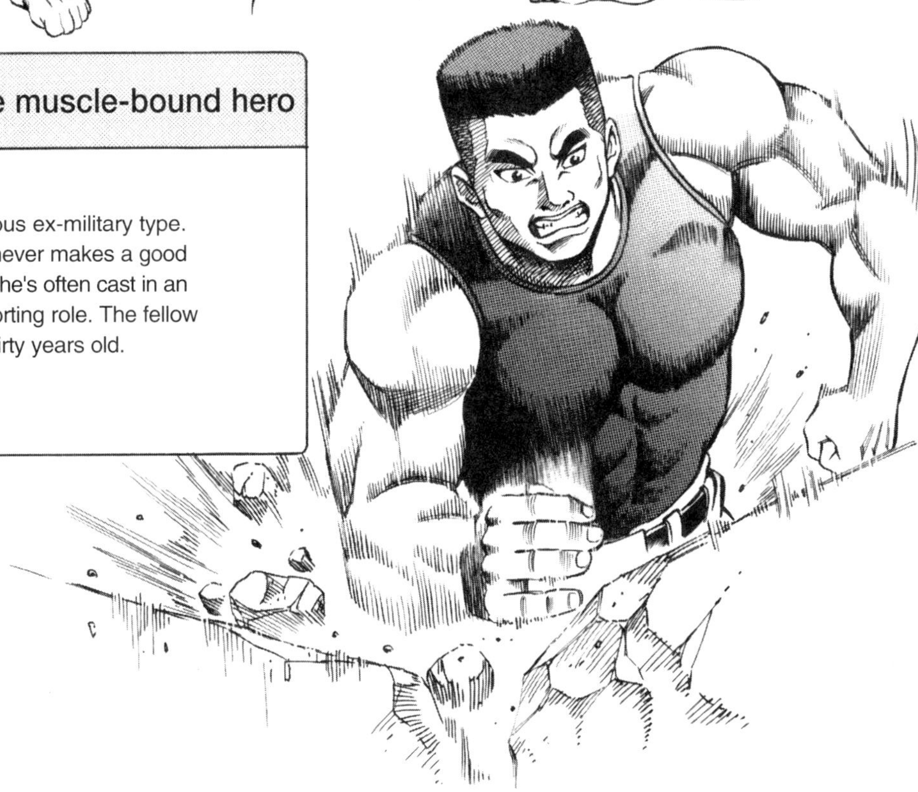

The Adonis Hero

Often depicted as somewhat of a nihilistic pretty boy, the Adonis character might be the kind of guy you love to hate. But first impressions can be deceiving; reveal a personal history plagued by misfortune and you've won the sympathy of your readers. In Japan, this character is especially popular amongst female manga fans. The lad illustrated here is about seventeen years old.

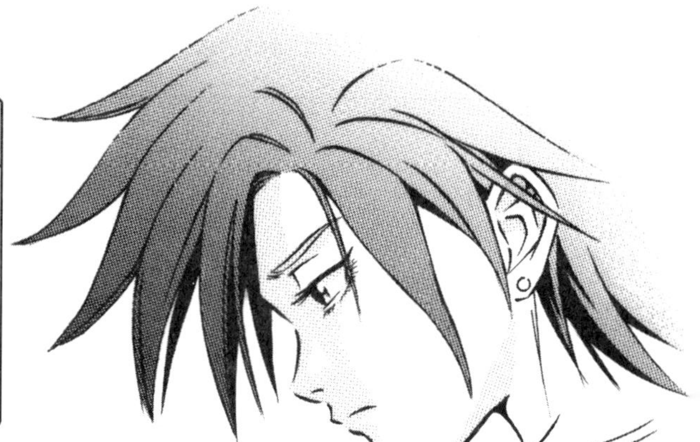

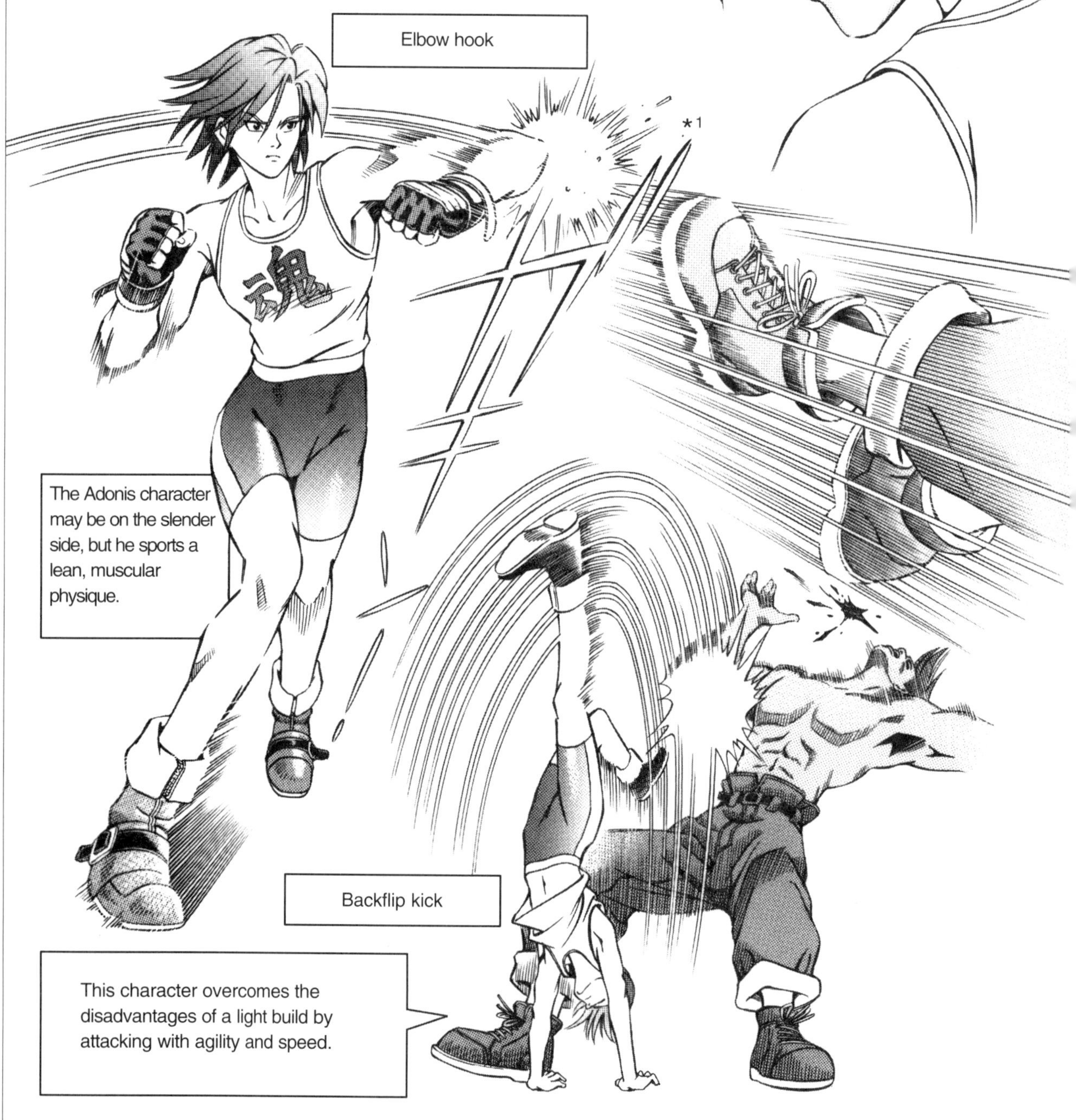

The Adonis character may be on the slender side, but he sports a lean, muscular physique.

This character overcomes the disadvantages of a light build by attacking with agility and speed.

★1: Wham!

Fight scenes should take full advantage of the Adonis character's light frame.

Moving from a forward handspring into a kick. Take special care to make this character look good when he's fighting in mid-air.

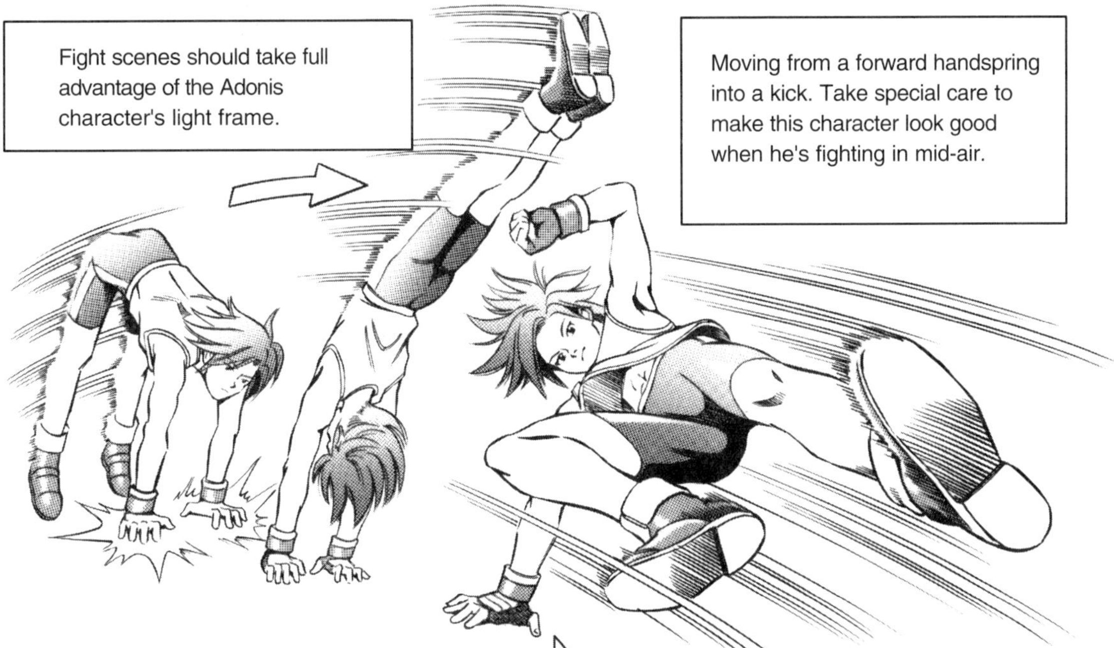

Why fight such a colossal foe?

A Japanese proverb states that, "a mud wall deadens a cannon ball". In other words, even a little guy can defeat a big guy if he is clever enough. The martial art of judo is based on this philosophy. So how does the little guy prevail against such overwhelming odds? This is a key question not only for judo, but for the entertainment world as well.

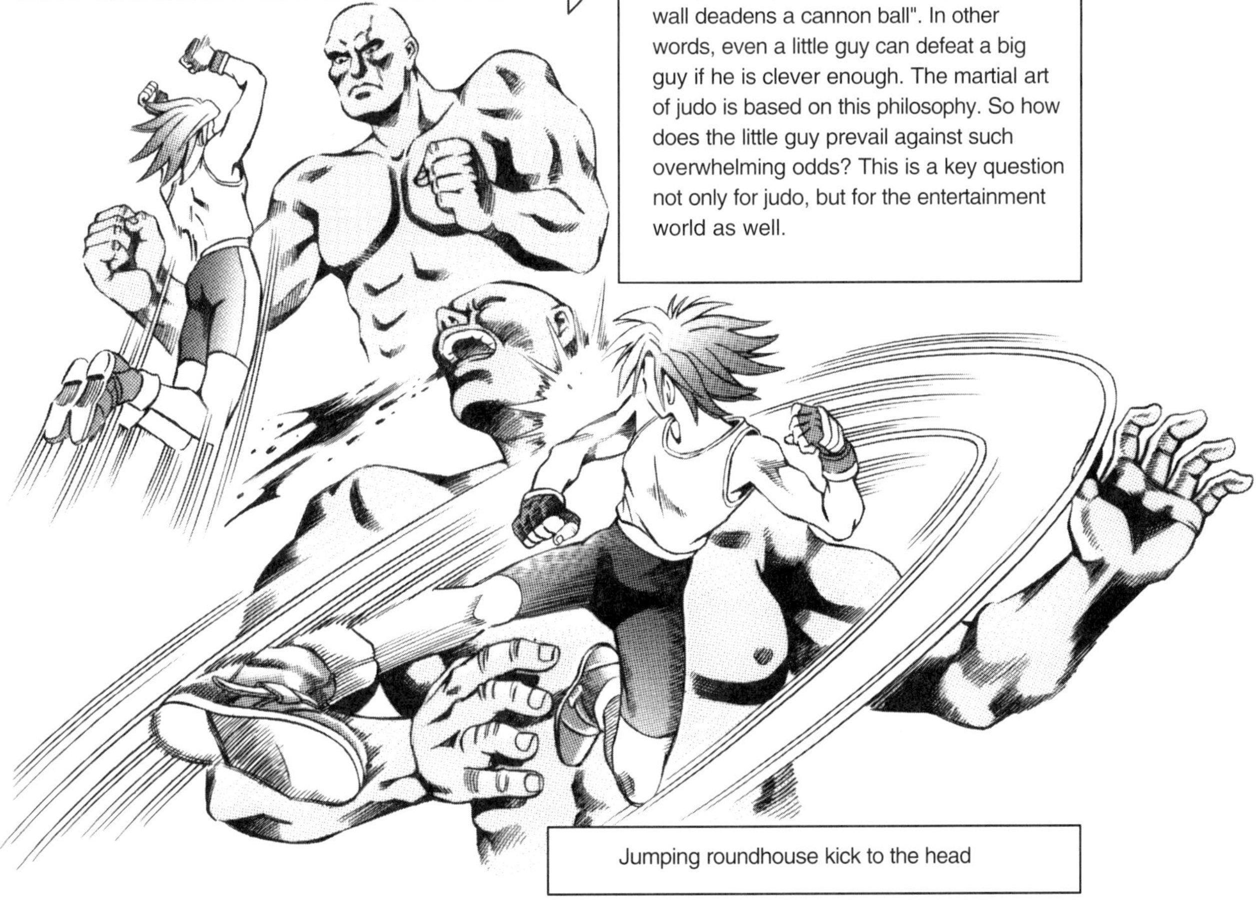

Jumping roundhouse kick to the head

The Adonis Hero (second type)

This seventeen year-old Adonis is skilled in the art of kung fu. When illustrating kung fu, pay special attention to the distinctive positioning of the waist, wrists and ankles.

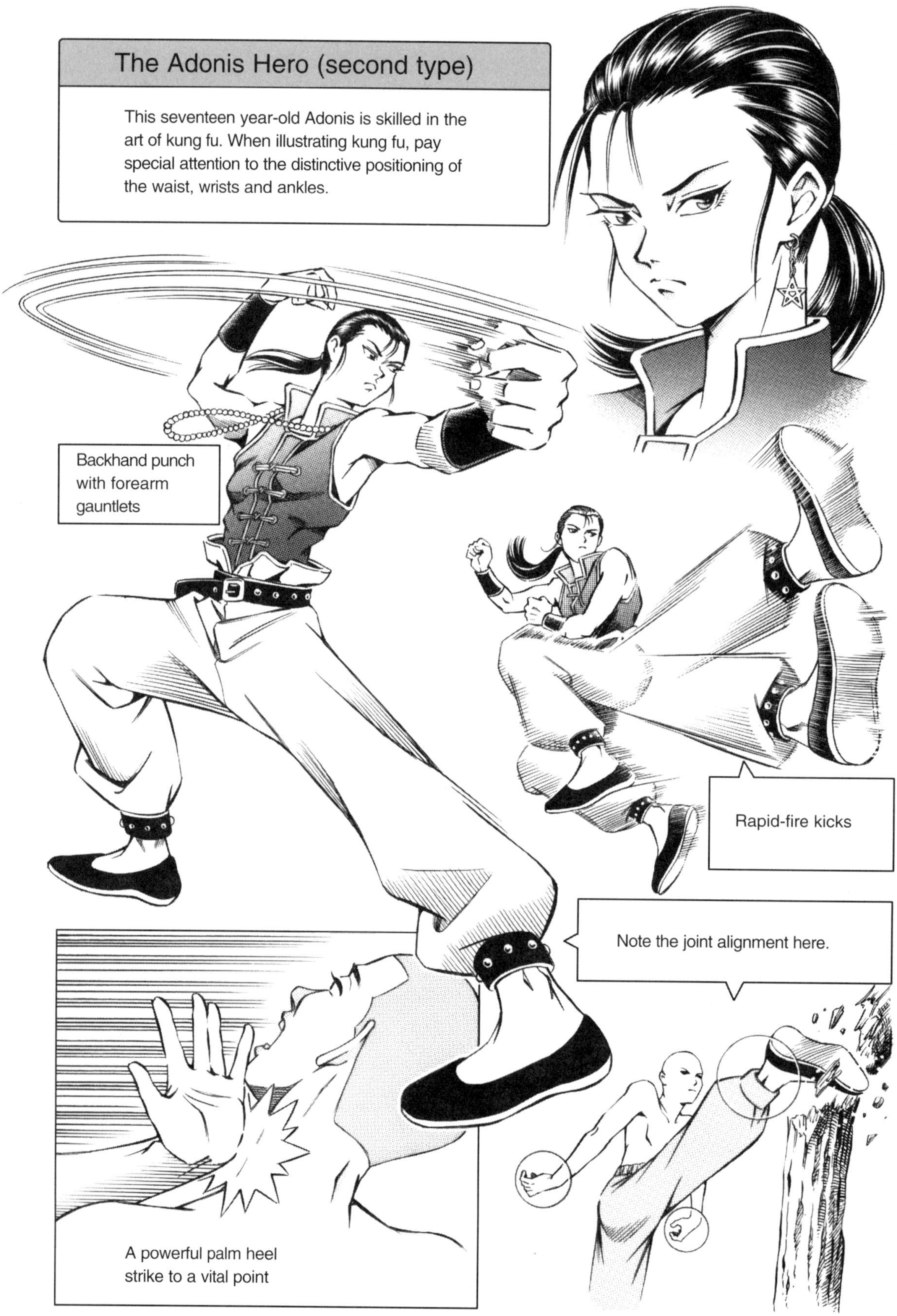

The Boy Hero

When it comes to characters featured in youth-oriented manga, the boy hero takes the crown. He is a cheerful, energetic and optimistic character that personifies the ethic of "effort, triumph, and friendship" embraced by such manga publications. This youngster is around twelve years old.

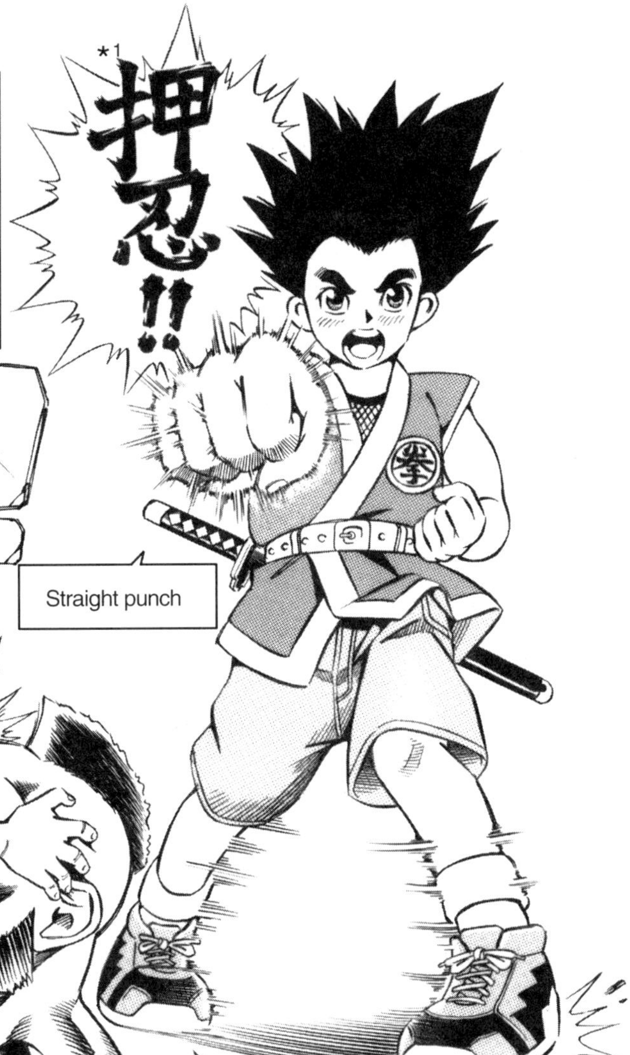

Straight punch

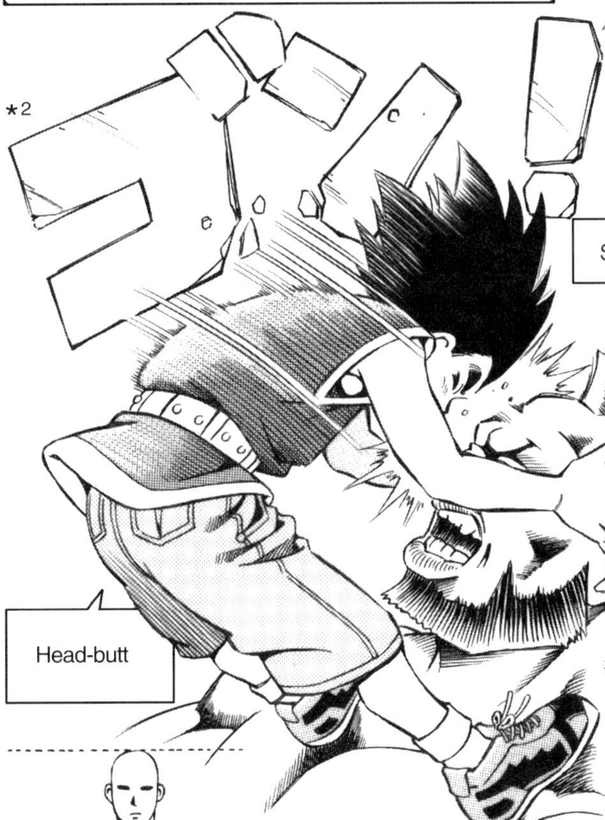

Head-butt

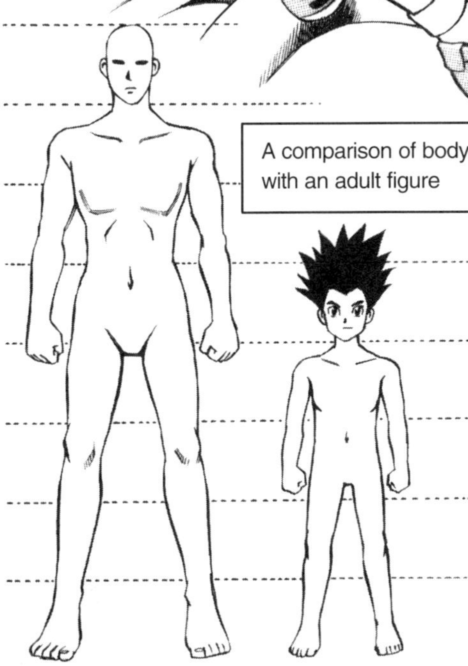

A comparison of body proportions with an adult figure

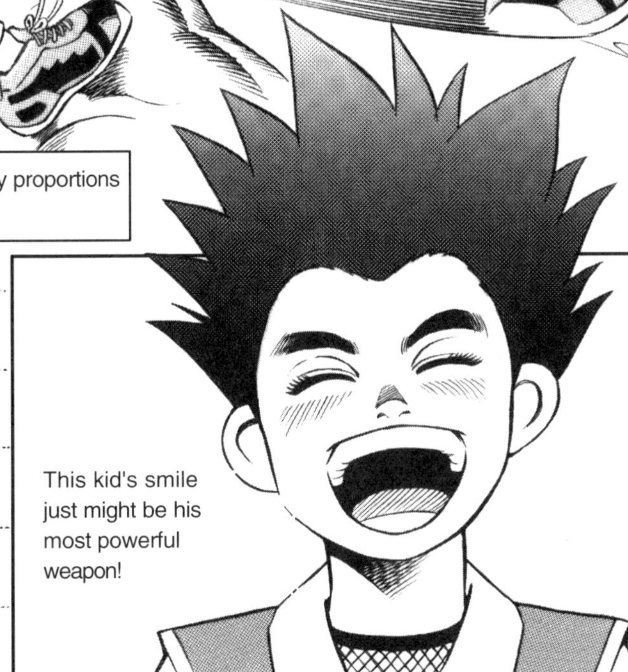

This kid's smile just might be his most powerful weapon!

★1:Hi-Ya!! ★2:Crack!

Special Moves by Character

Professional Wrestling (ex. 1)

Body slam: The opponent is lifted up onto the shoulders and thrown down to the ground.

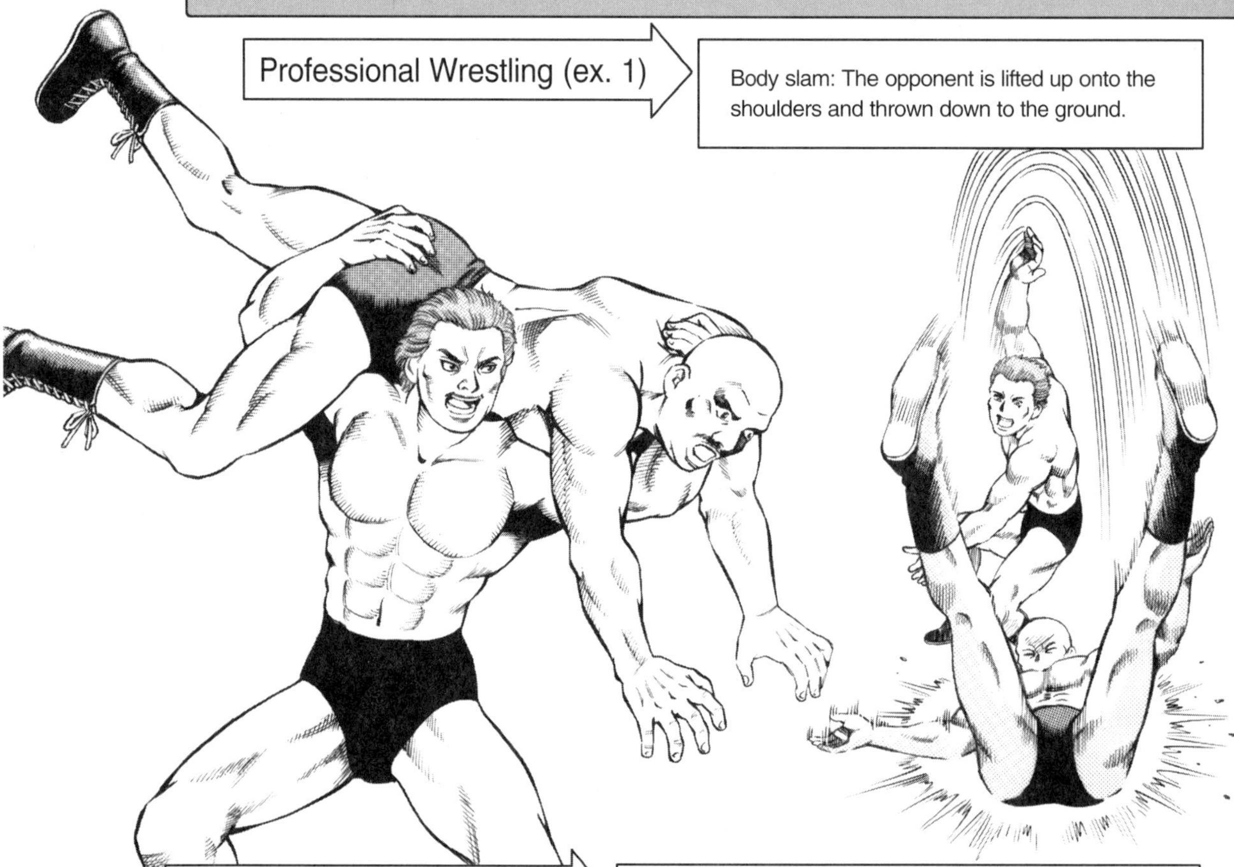

Professional Wrestling (ex. 2)

Western lariat: The crook of the elbow is flung under the opponent's chin and into the neck.

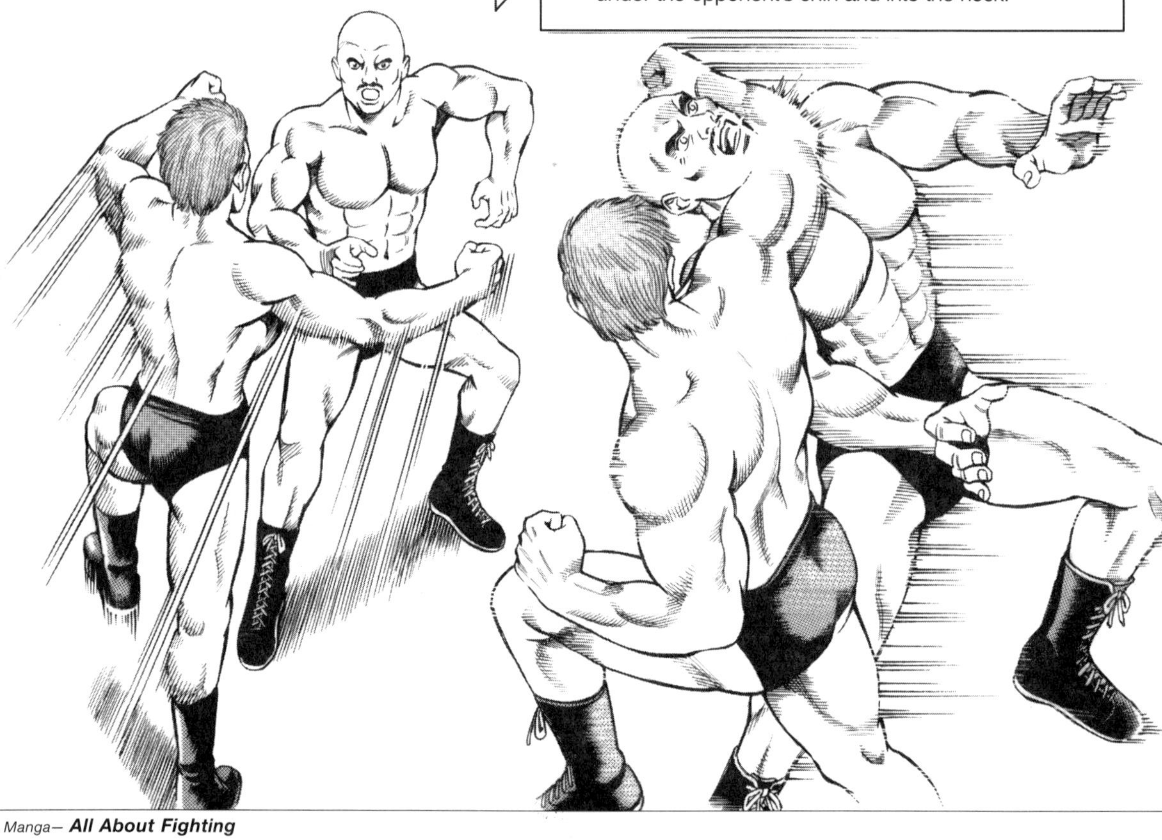

Professional Wrestling / Greco-Roman Wrestling / Jujitsu

Choke sleeper: At first glance, chokeholds may not look like anything special, but they are actually a dangerous class of moves that can easily kill a person.

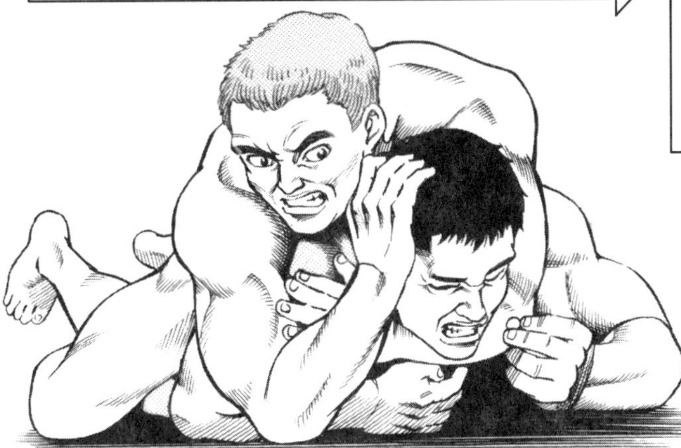

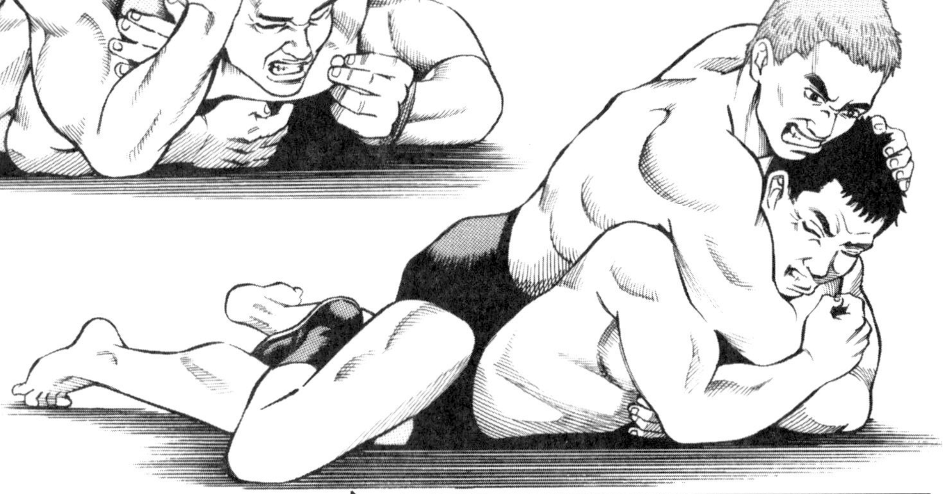

Karate

Axe kick. After the leg is swung upwards, the heel is brought down onto the opponent's head.

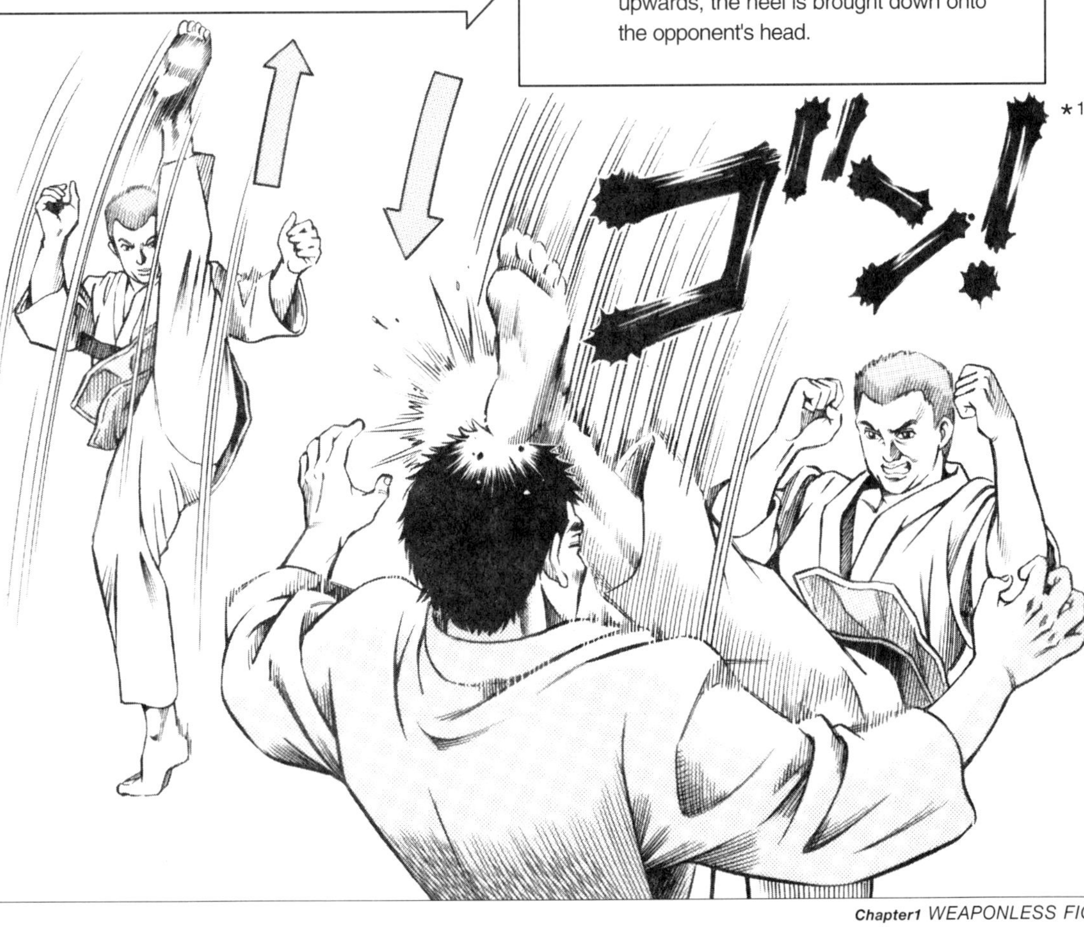

★1:Thump!

Sumo Wrestling

Despite being Japan's national sport, few manga publications today feature sumo fighting. This is truly a shame, as the genre gave rise to numerous manga masterpieces in years past.

Sumo wrestlers fight inside a circular ring called a dohyo. The first to fall down or step outside the dohyo is the loser. Tournaments are held over a period of fifteen days, six times a year. Each wrestler fights in one match a day, and the winner of the most matches is the tournament's grand champion.

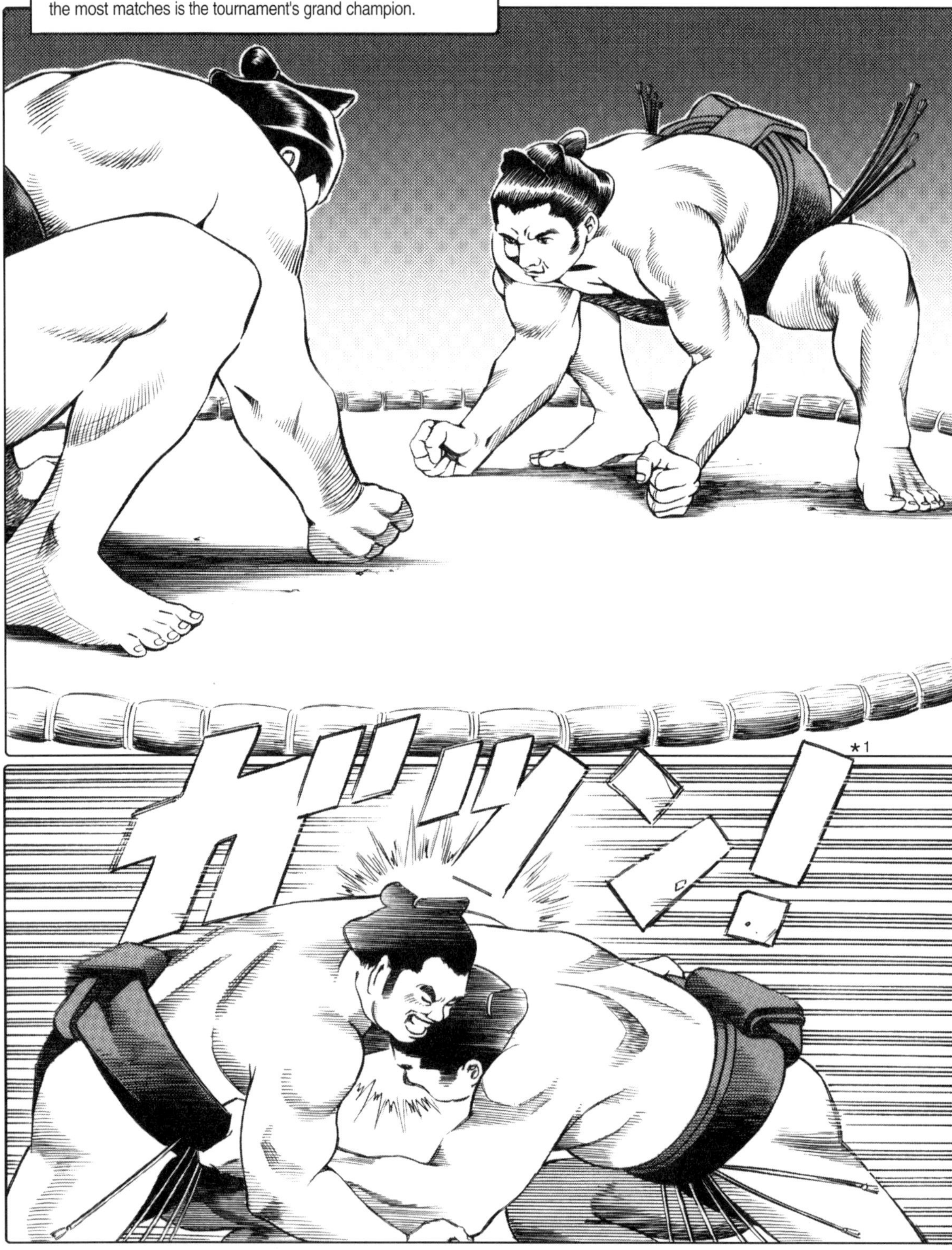

*1:Slam!

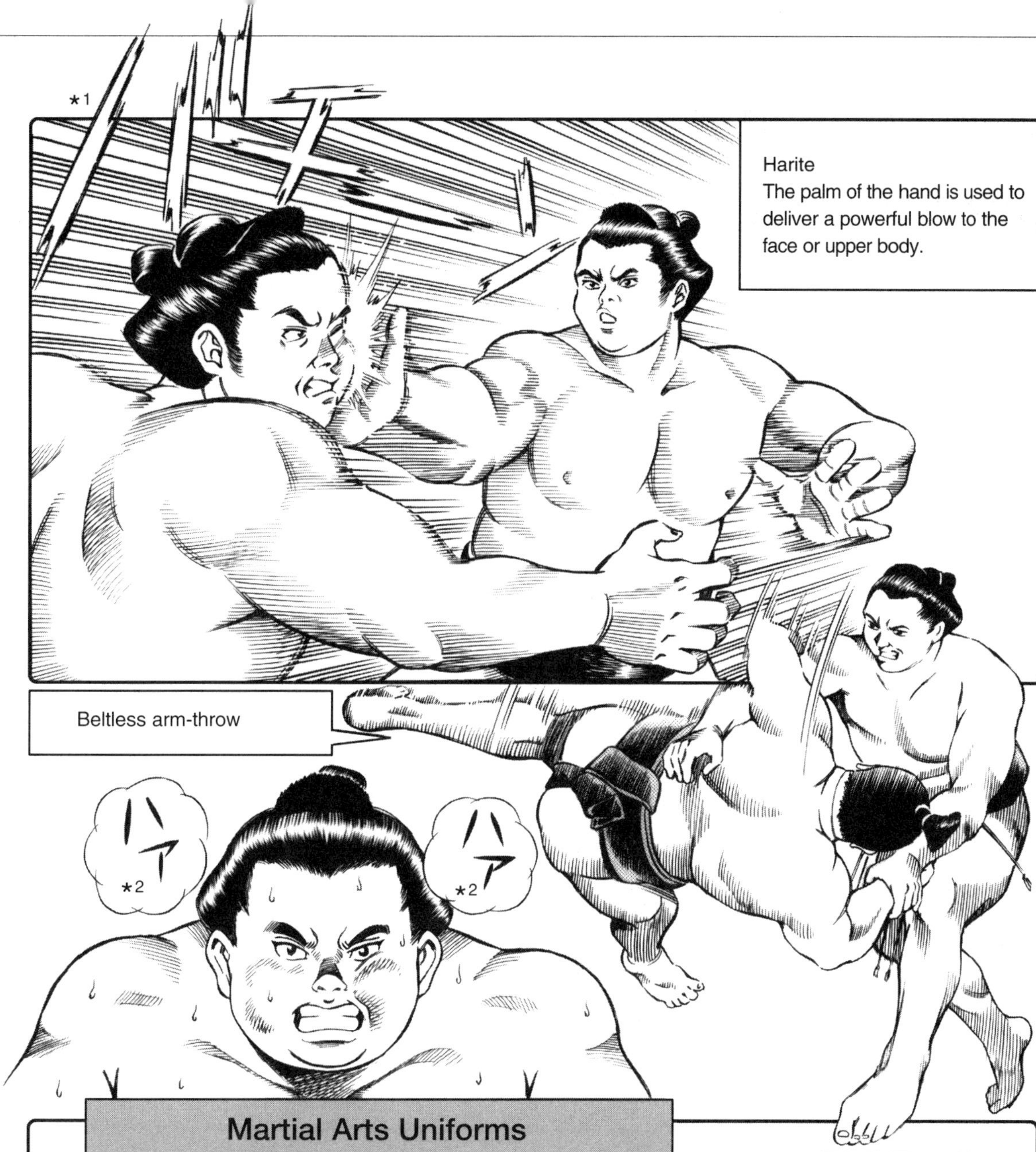

Martial Arts Uniforms

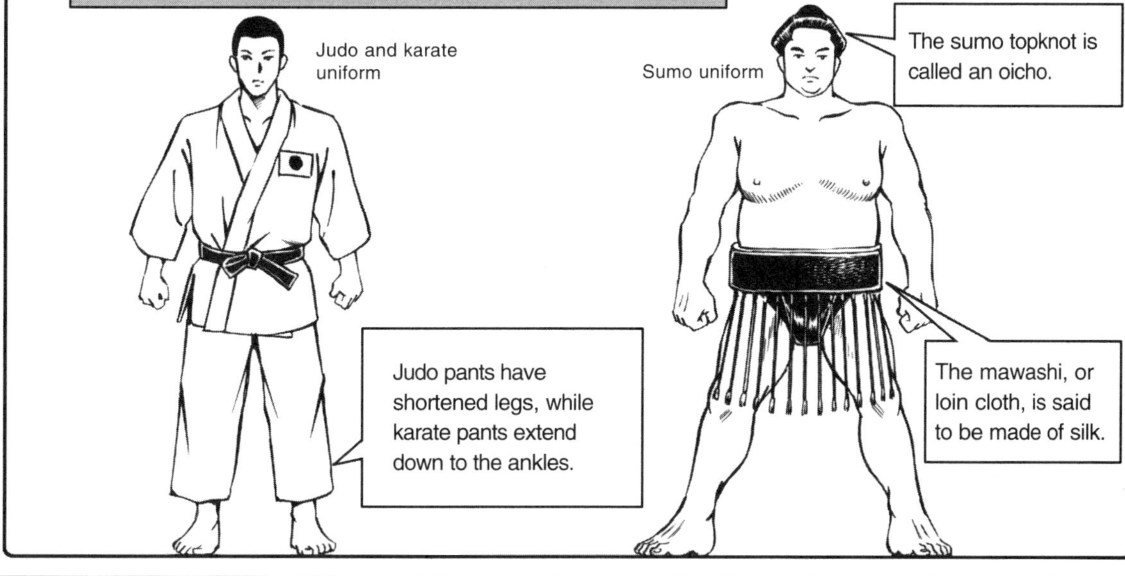

★1:Smack! ★2:Pant

女性闘士

How to Draw Female Fighters!

In the past, manga characters had clearly defined gender roles; the men were fighters and the women were lovers. Oh, how times have changed! Female characters these days can be seen kicking ass on practically every other page. It's anyone's guess as to how female roles will evolve in the future.

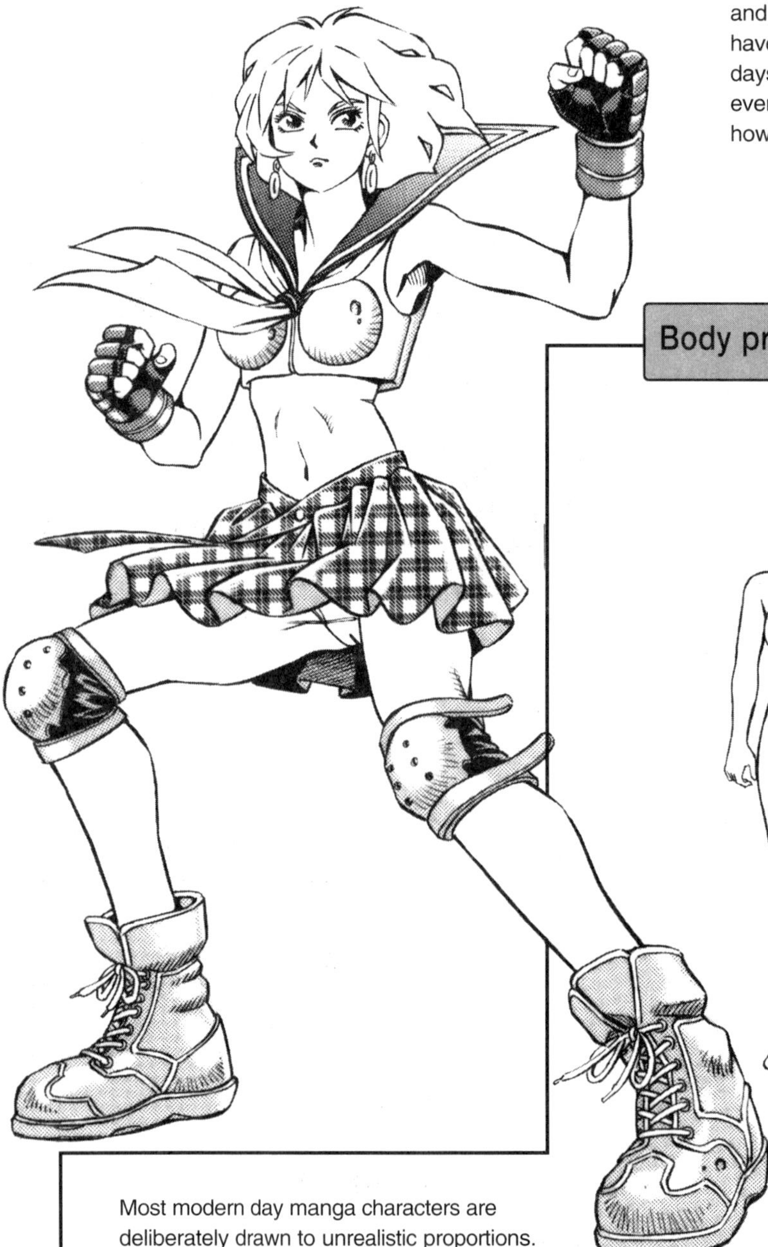

Body proportions:realistic vs. anime

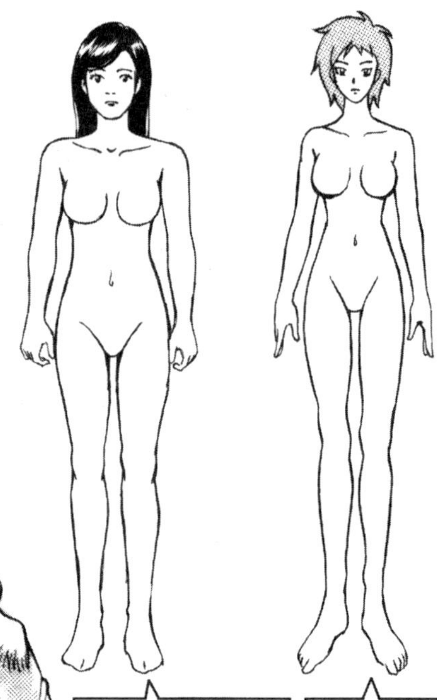

Realistic style

Anime style

Most modern day manga characters are deliberately drawn to unrealistic proportions. This so-called "anime style" shows the heavy influence of Japanese animation and its associated stylistic conventions. Anime is characterized by its symbolic representation of elements– a convention that developed out of the necessity for several animators to draw the same character. Raised on a steady diet of animated TV programs, the current generation of manga artists and fanboys has grown to prefer the anime style over any other.

Female office worker

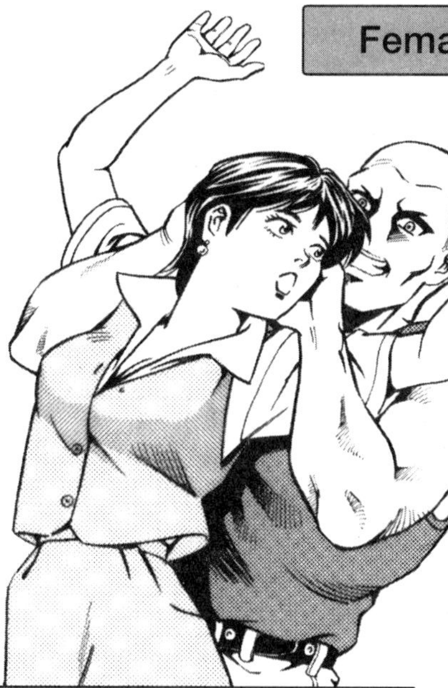

Trapped in a full nelson

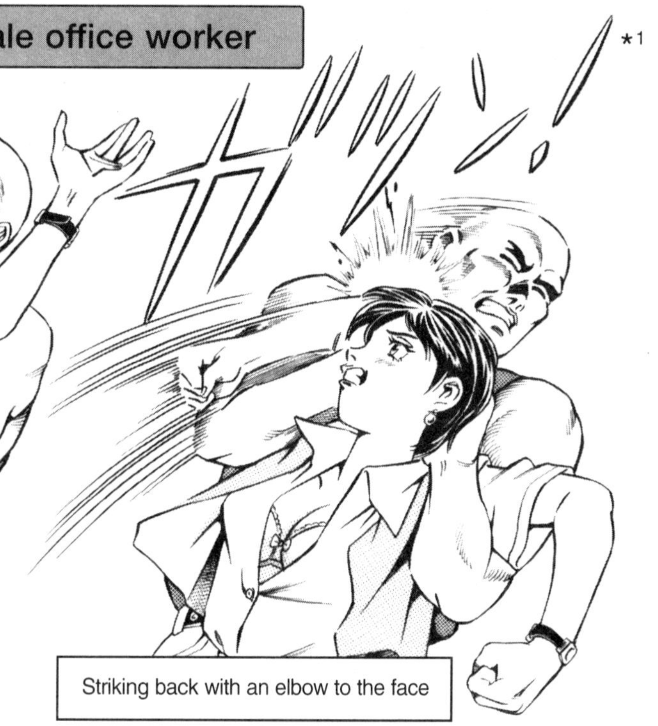

Striking back with an elbow to the face

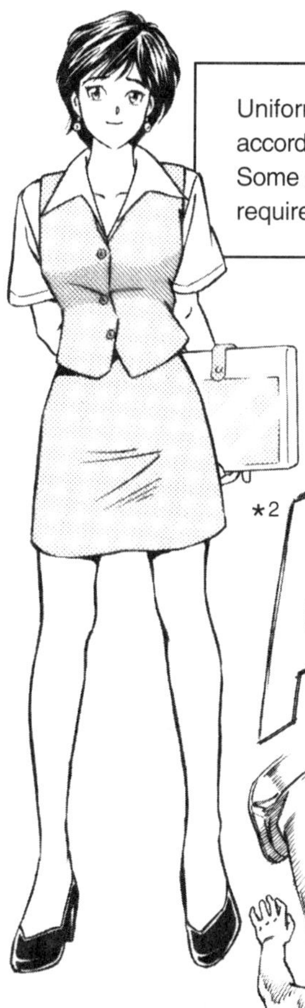

Uniform styles differ according to the company. Some companies don't require uniforms at all.

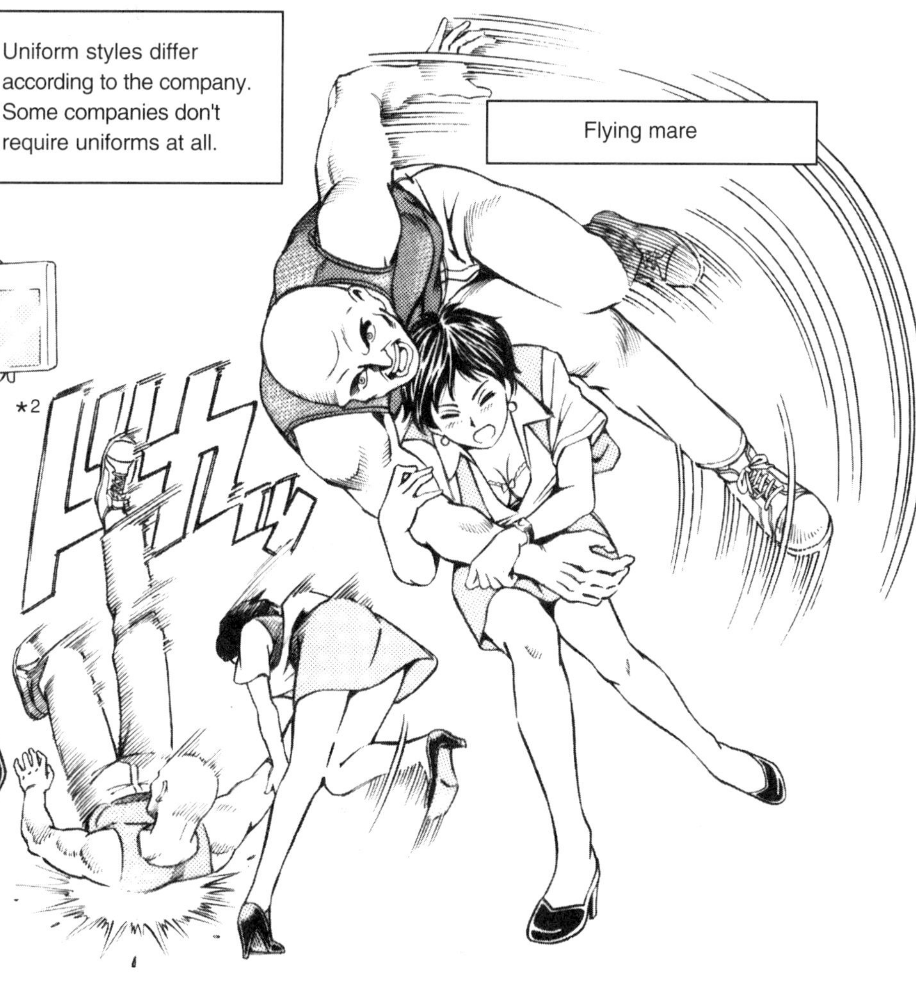

Flying mare

★1:Crack! ★2:Thud!

Policewoman

More often than not, female police officers featured in manga are dressed in sexy outfits. This is, of course, nothing more than artistic embellishment; uniforms worn by real-life policewomen are considerably more modest.

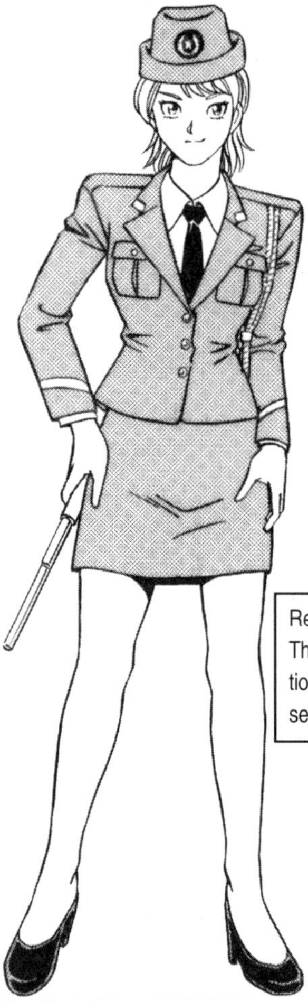

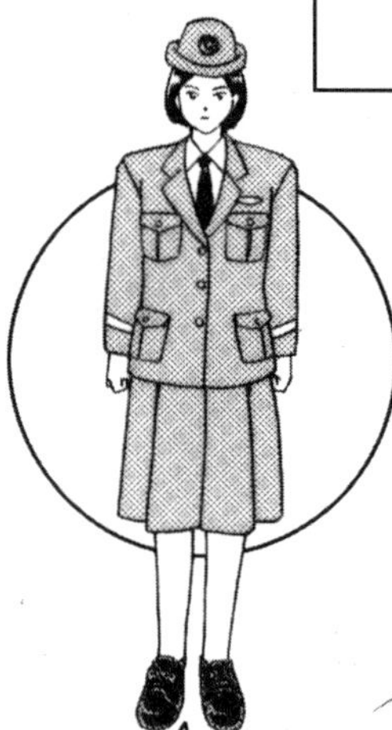

Real-life uniform (winter)
There are a number of additional uniform styles that serve specific functions.

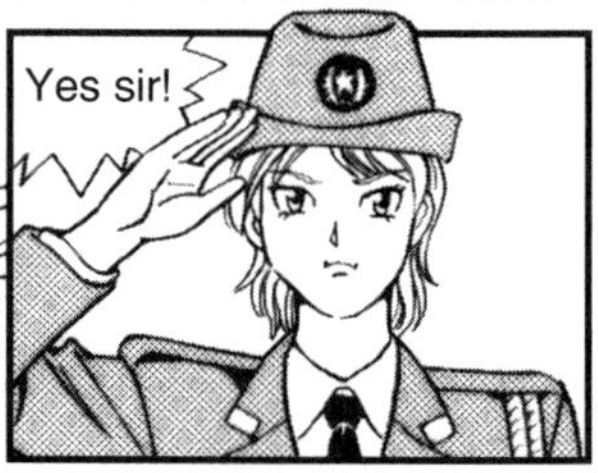

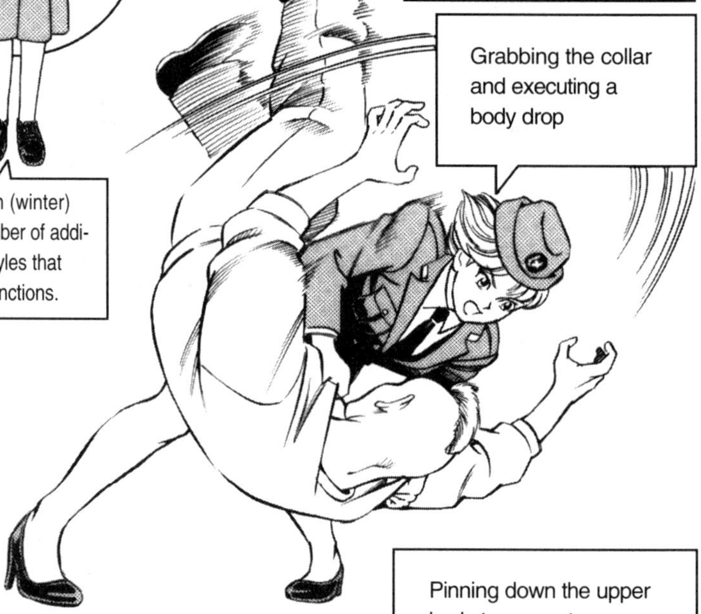

Grabbing the collar and executing a body drop

Real-life uniform (summer)

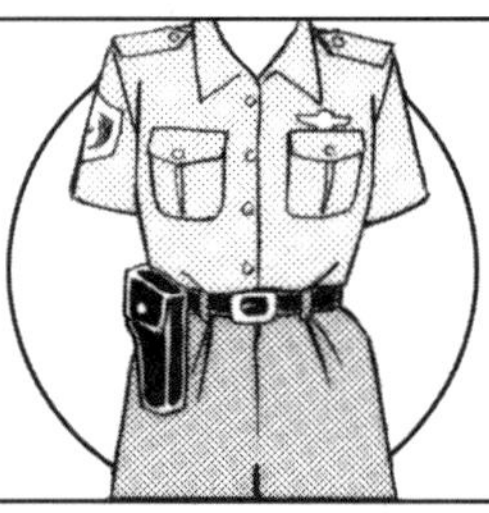

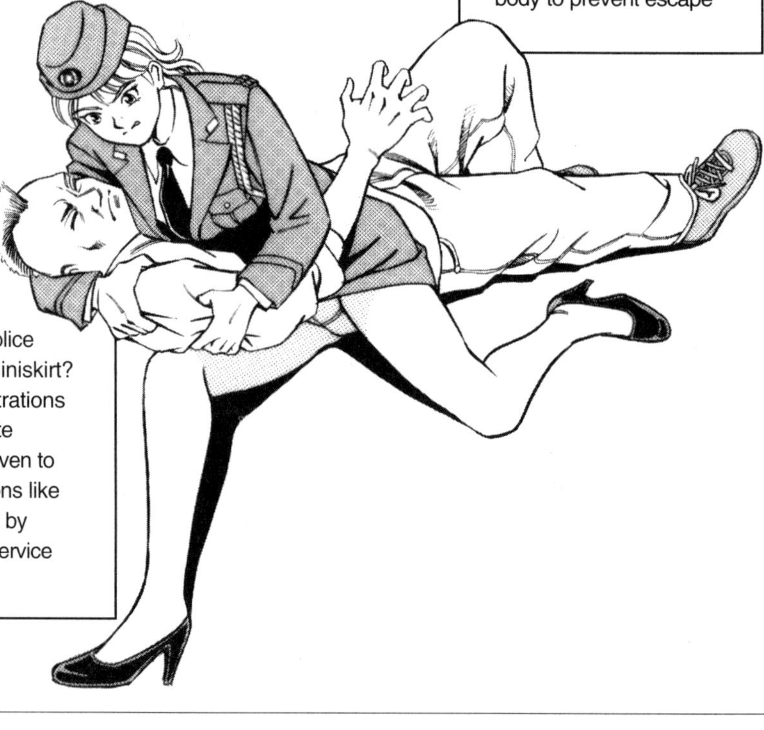

Pinning down the upper body to prevent escape

In Japan, these thigh-revealing cops of the manga world are popularly known as mini-suka police (miniskirt police). But why the miniskirt? The answer is simple: sexy illustrations attract readers. In fact, a moderate amount of sexiness has been proven to boost magazine sales. For reasons like this, the manga artist is regarded by some to be an employee of the service sector.

Cabin attendant (stewardess)

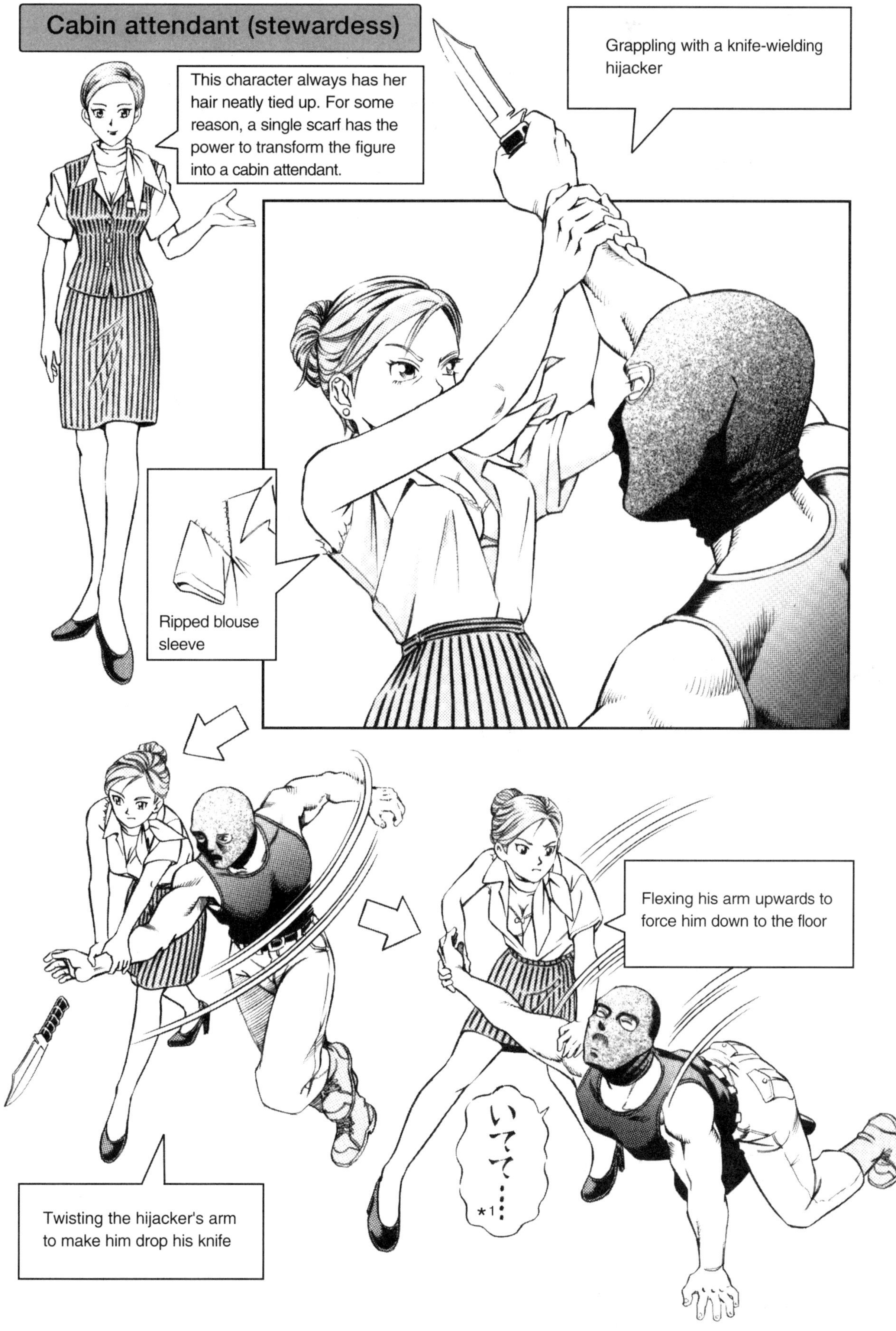

★1:Ow ow ow!

Chinese women

A Chinese-dress clad woman has become a fixture of numerous manga publications that feature fight scenes. Notice the single-edged eyelid and slanted eyes; these features have come to represent Chinese characters in the manga world.

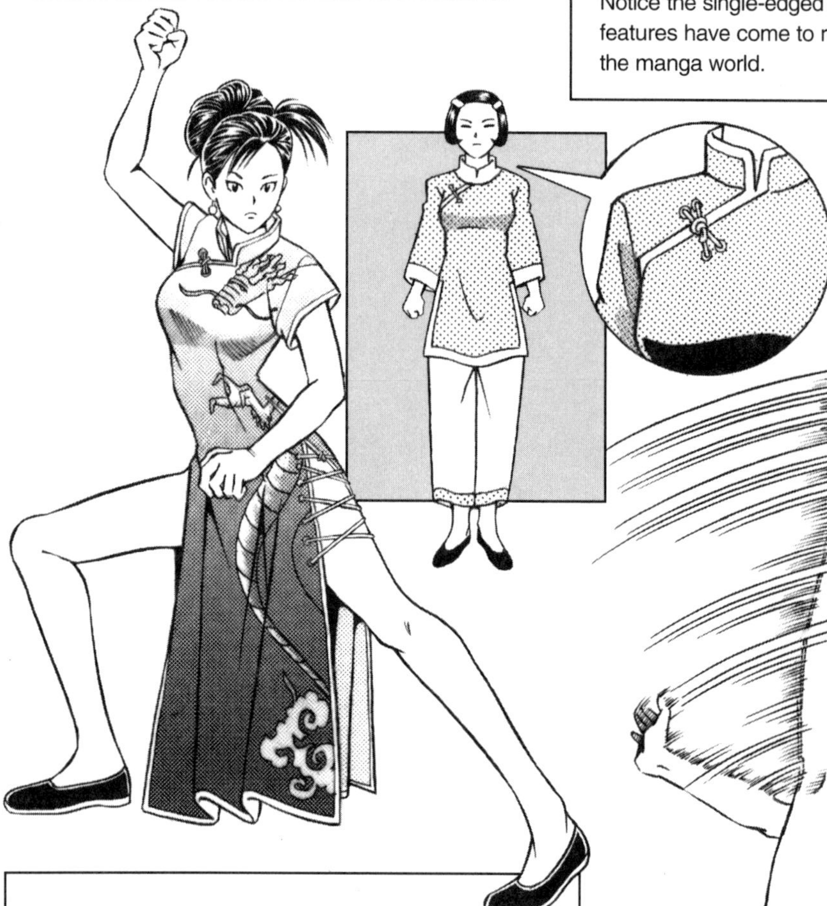

A real Chinese dress is fairly subdued in design. The long side slit and ultra-sexiness of the manga version is simply another "special service for the reader".

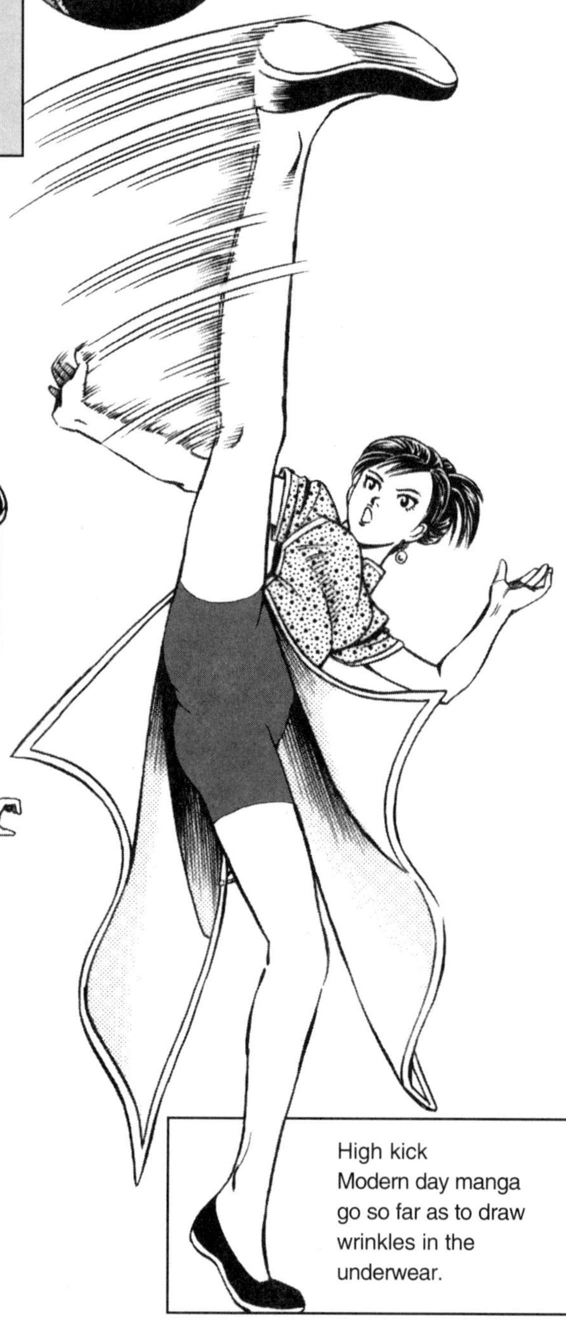

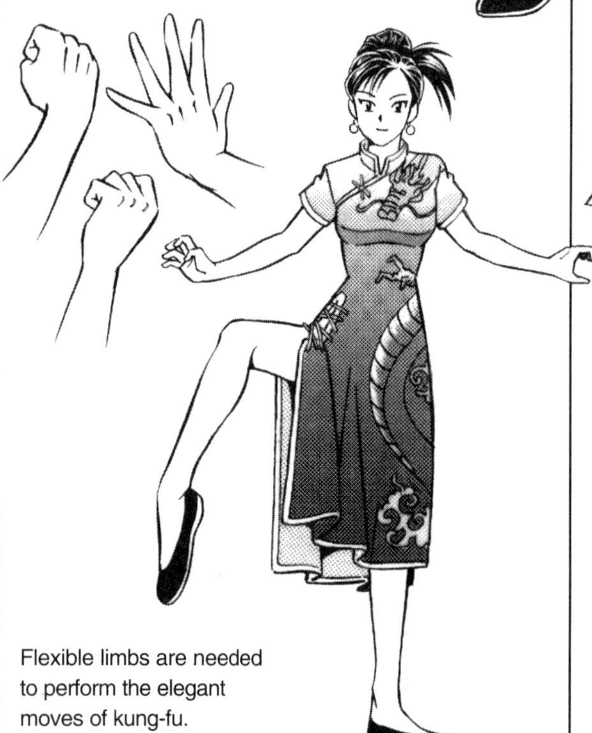

Flexible limbs are needed to perform the elegant moves of kung-fu.

High kick
Modern day manga go so far as to draw wrinkles in the underwear.

Traditional Japanese attire for women

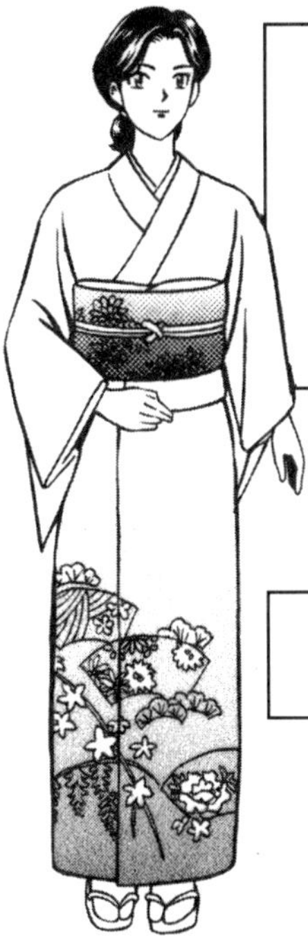

Kimono

The kimono dress, still frequently worn at ceremonial functions, remains the most popular of the traditional garments.

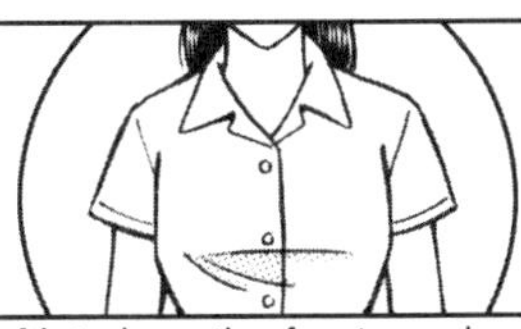

Note how the front overlaps opposite that of a Western garment.

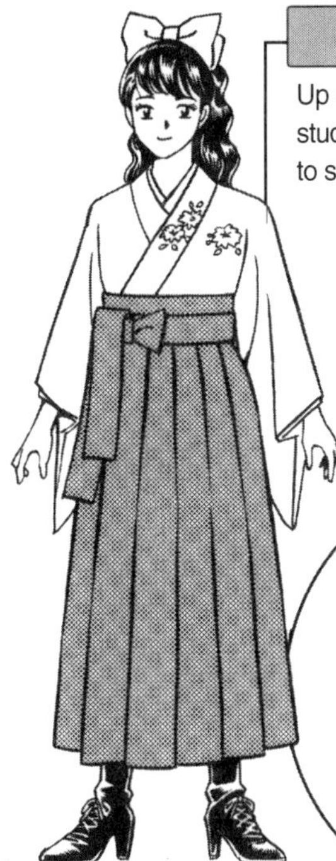

Hakama

Up until fifty years ago, all female students in Japan wore a hakama to school. Although students these days have but one occasion to don the garment (their college graduation ceremony), hakama are frequently featured in manga and video games.

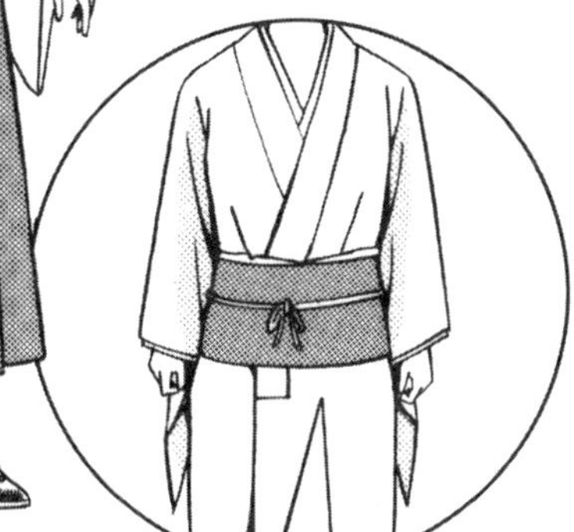

The placement of the obi, or sash, is incorrect in this illustration. This wrapping of the obi around the waist can often be seen in second-rate Hollywood flicks (whose directors ought to spend some time learning about other cultures).

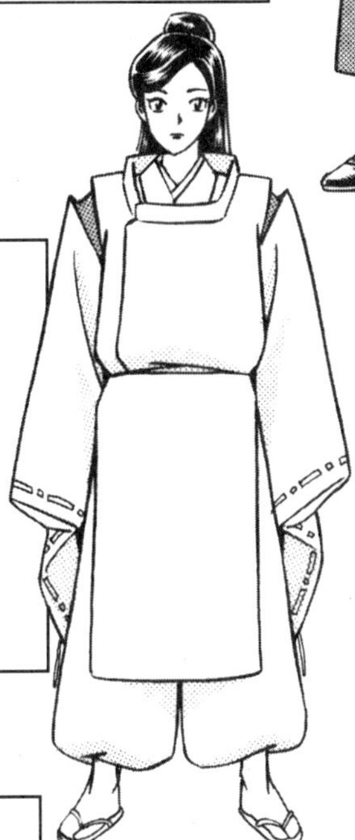

Ikansokutai

This is a costume traditionally worn by male Shinto priests. However, recent manga in the "occult" genre have featured women wearing ikansokutai.

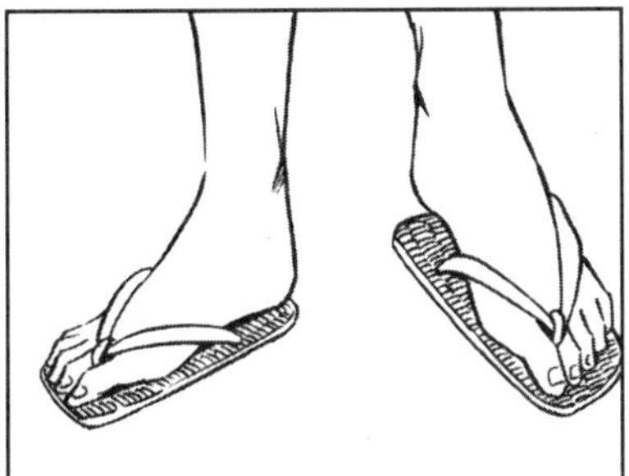

Zori are traditional sandals woven out of straw.

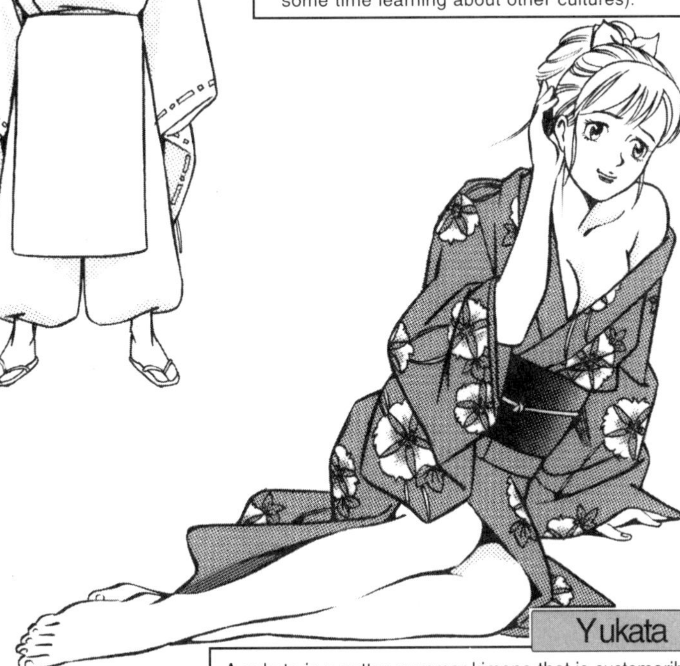

Yukata

A yukata is a cotton summer kimono that is customarily put on after taking a bath. It can be found in most hotel rooms across Japan. Worn directly over the skin, this light garment is typically worn by Japanese women when attending summertime festivals and enjoying fireworks.

Erotic action scenes

Japan's manga market is a diverse panoply of genres that cater to the interests of all age groups. Generally classified according to their target audience, there are magazines for children; young men (shonen-shi); young women (shojo-shi); and magazines for older readers, like seinen-shi for men, and jyosei-shi for women. Publications targeted at an adult audience usually contain at least some sexual content.

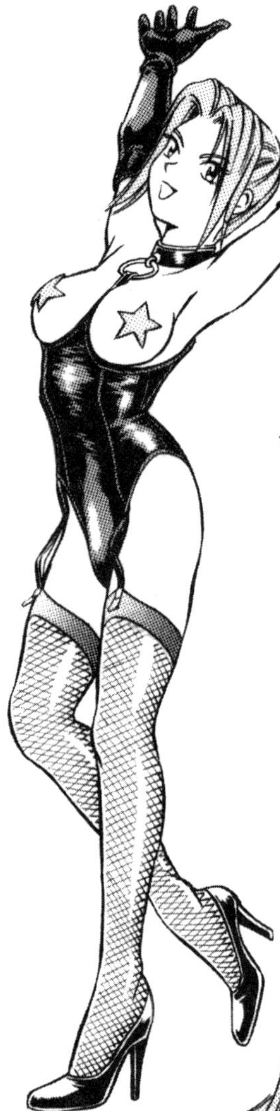

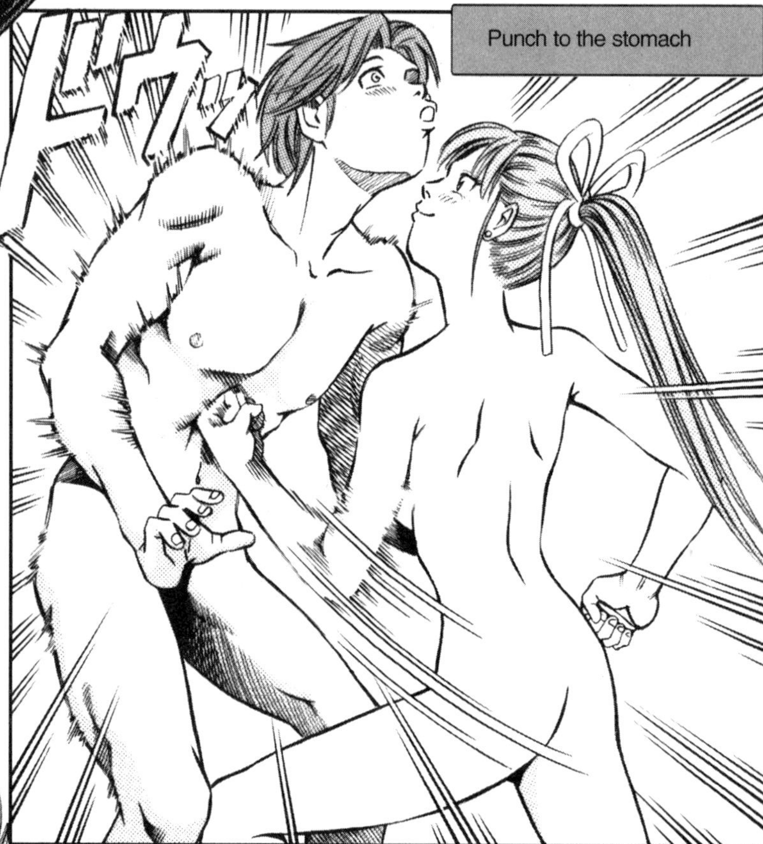

Punch to the stomach

★1

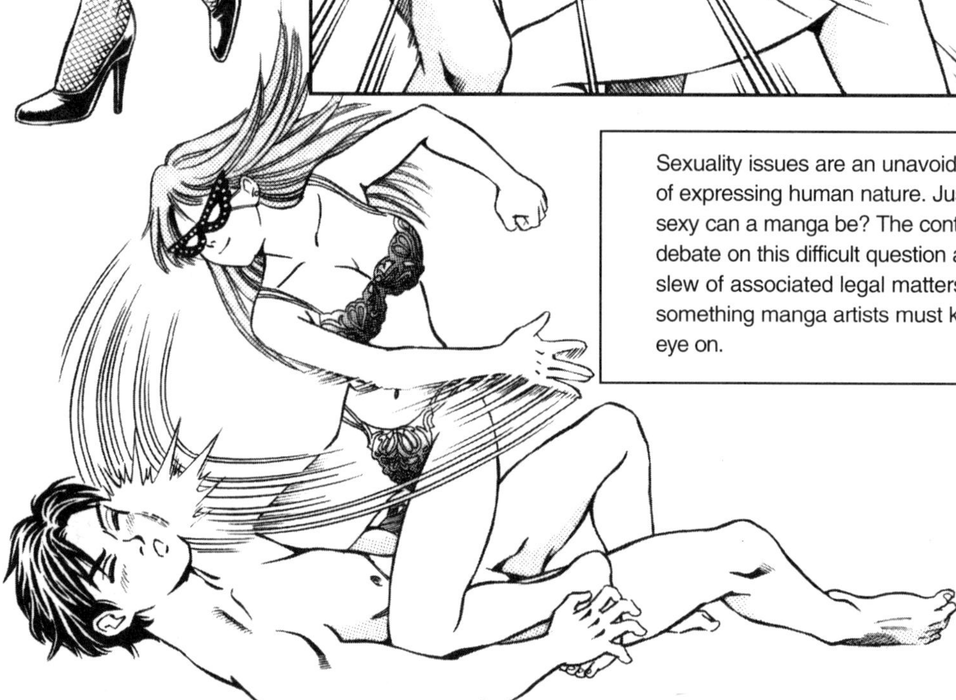

Sexuality issues are an unavoidable part of expressing human nature. Just how sexy can a manga be? The continuing debate on this difficult question and its slew of associated legal matters is something manga artists must keep an eye on.

★1:Ooof!

Erotic action scenes

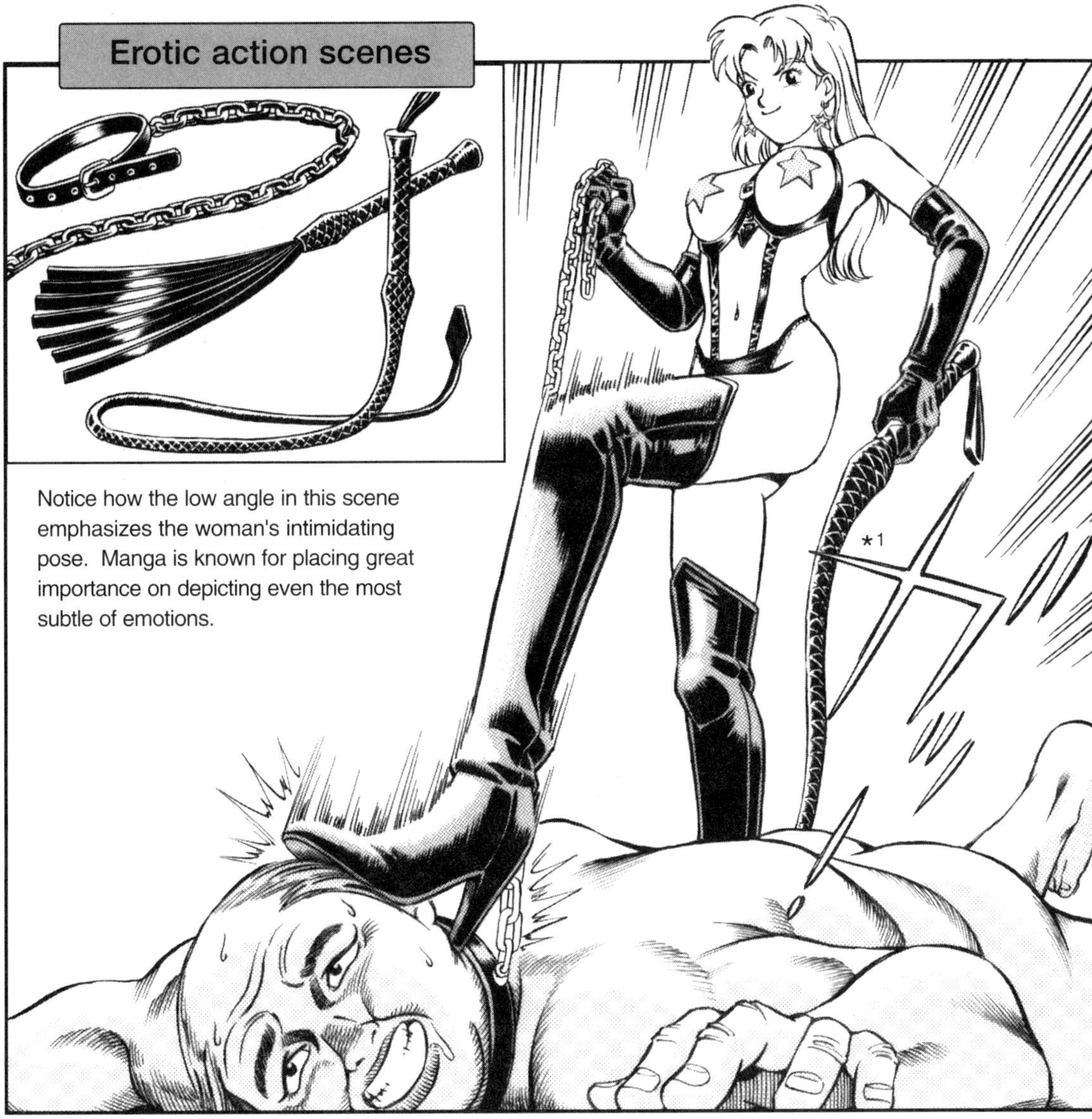

Notice how the low angle in this scene emphasizes the woman's intimidating pose. Manga is known for placing great importance on depicting even the most subtle of emotions.

★1:Thunk!

Sexy fetish wear

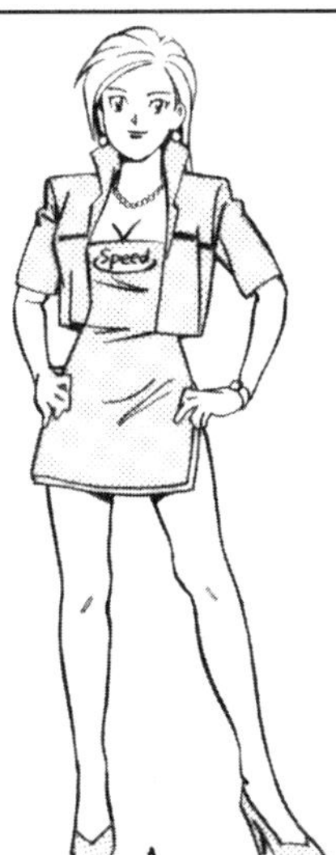

Race queen

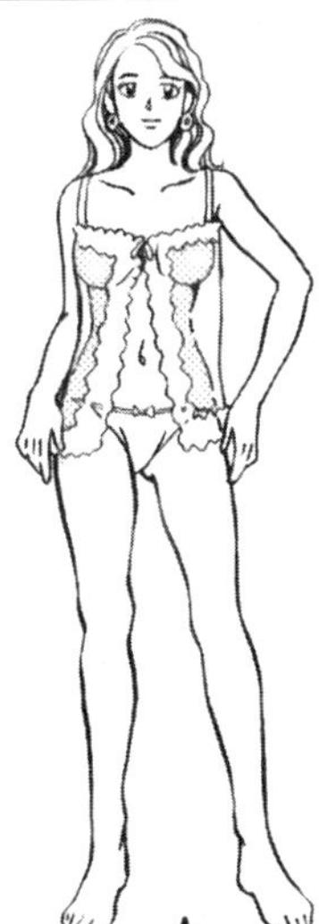

Lingerie

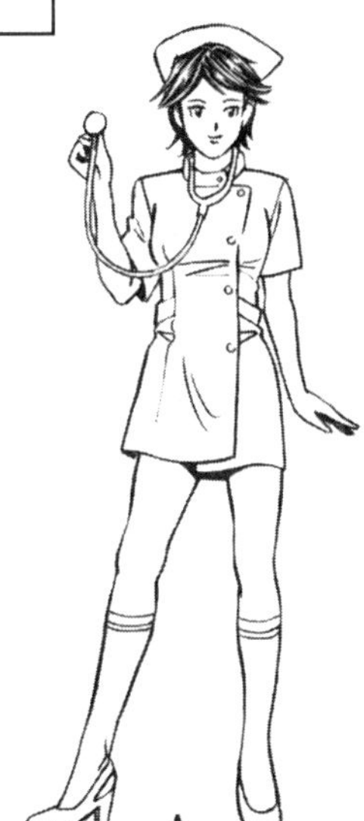

Nurse

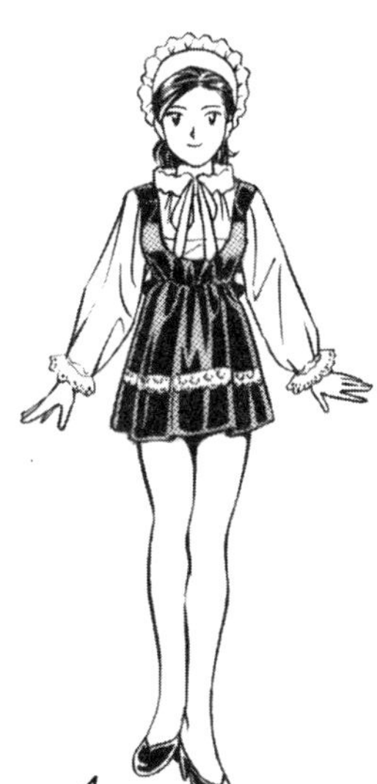

Housemaid

Female action hero

While characters like this may be commonplace in Hollywood movies and martial arts games, they still rarely take center stage in the manga world. They are, however, often cast in supporting roles.

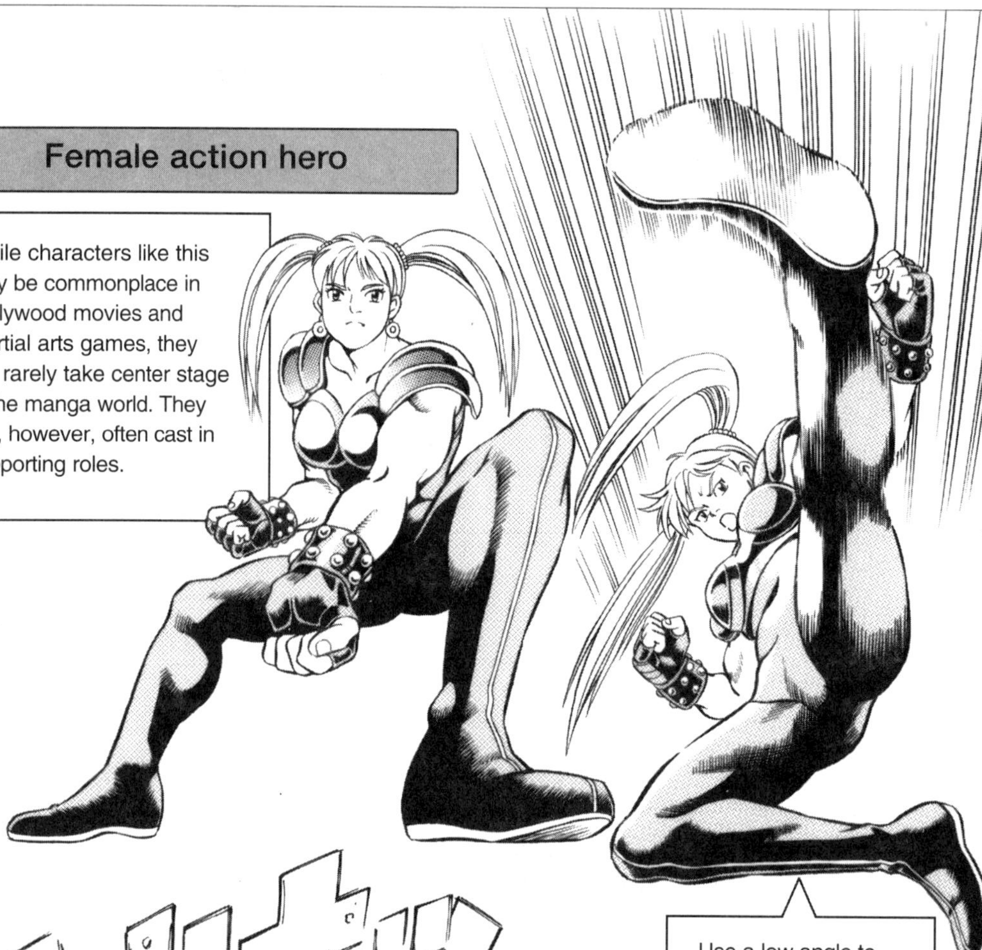

Use a low angle to accentuate the power of her jump kick.

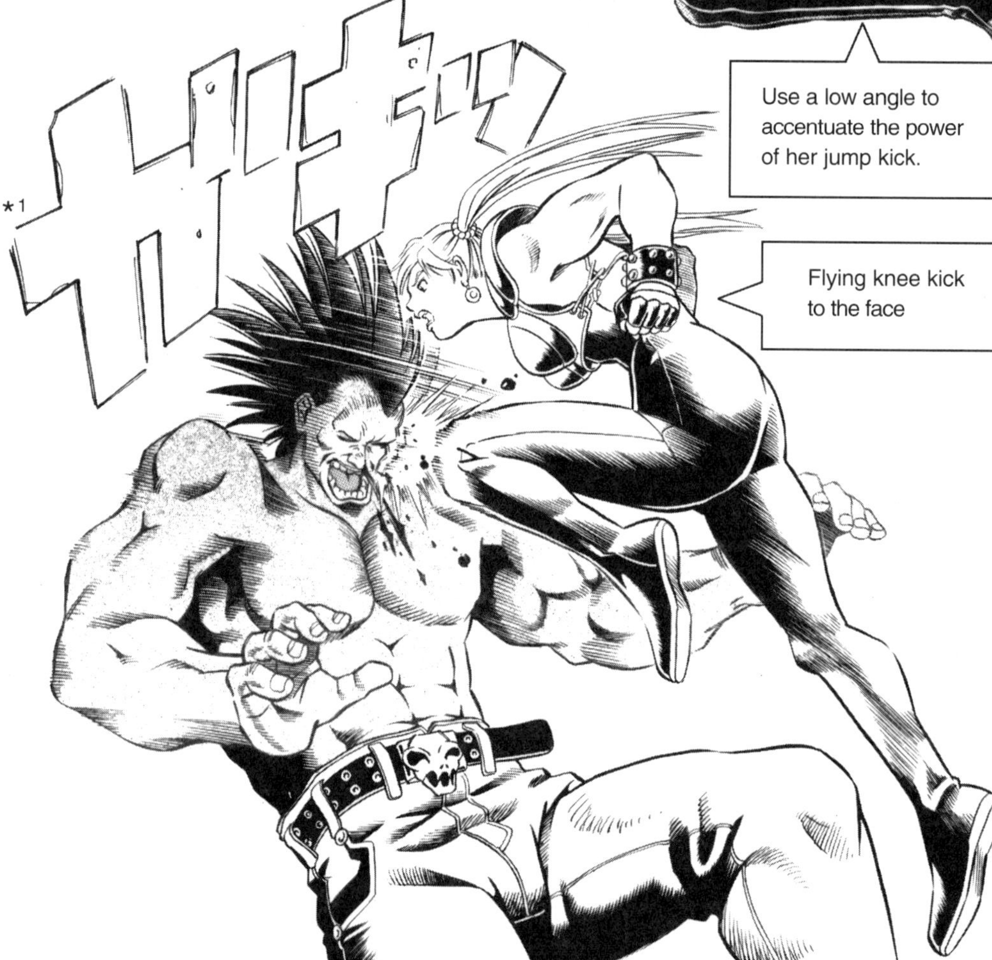

Flying knee kick to the face

★1: Thrakk!

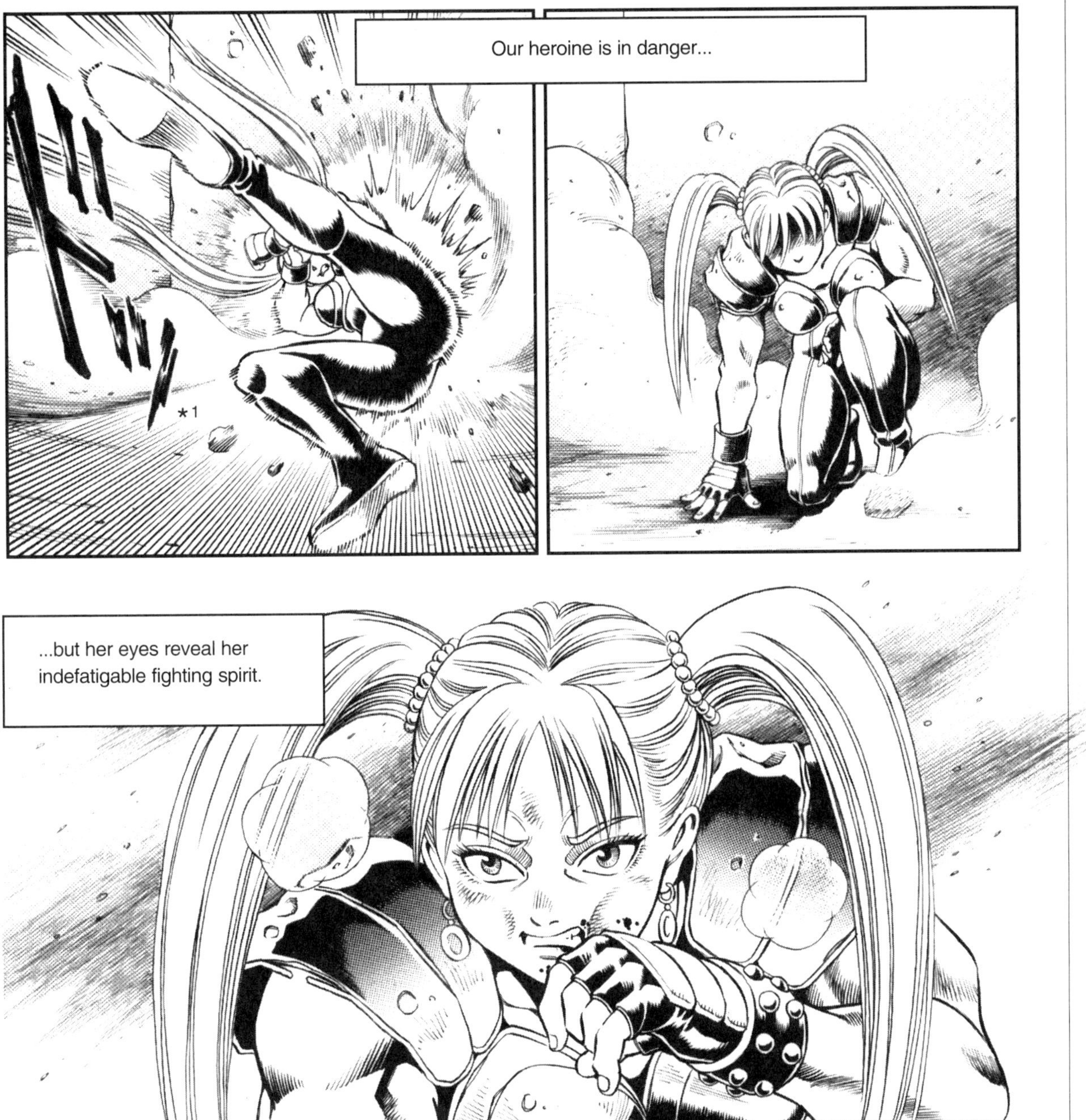

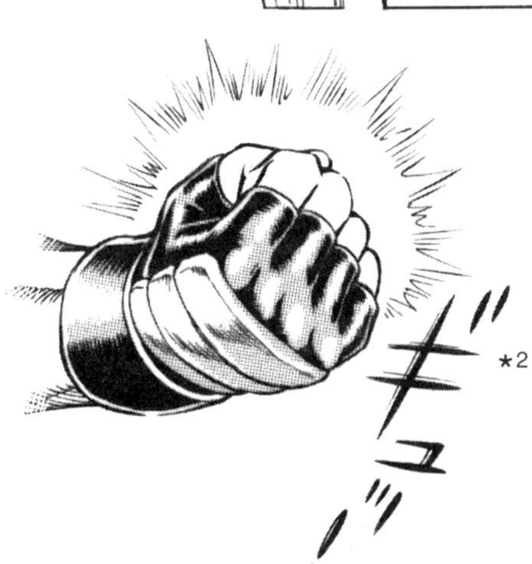

In the preceding pages, we have taken a look at the kinds of characters and action scenes most commonly employed by manga artists. Keep in mind that these are all nothing more than stereotypes; you should not constrain yourself to their stylistic boundaries. After all, there are many other types of manga characters that have not been presented in this book. Furthermore, artists are continually developing new techniques for drawing action scenes and psychological characterization. In the next section, we'll take two original female characters and pit them against each other in a complete, manga style fight sequence.

*1:Fwump! *2:Krick!

How the characters in this book were drawn-Part 3

Kung fu hero

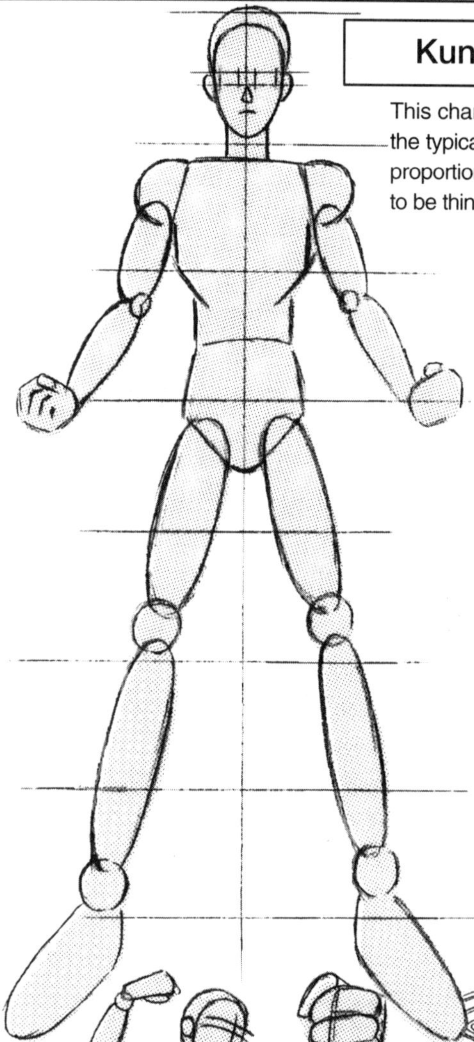

This character, drawn in the typical "eight-head proportion", was designed to be thin and agile.

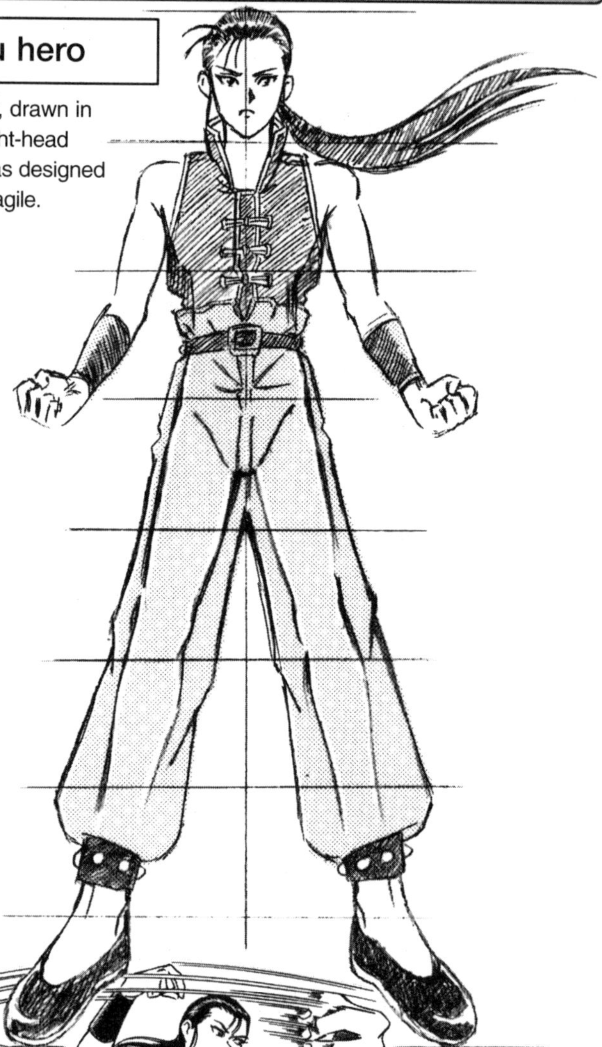

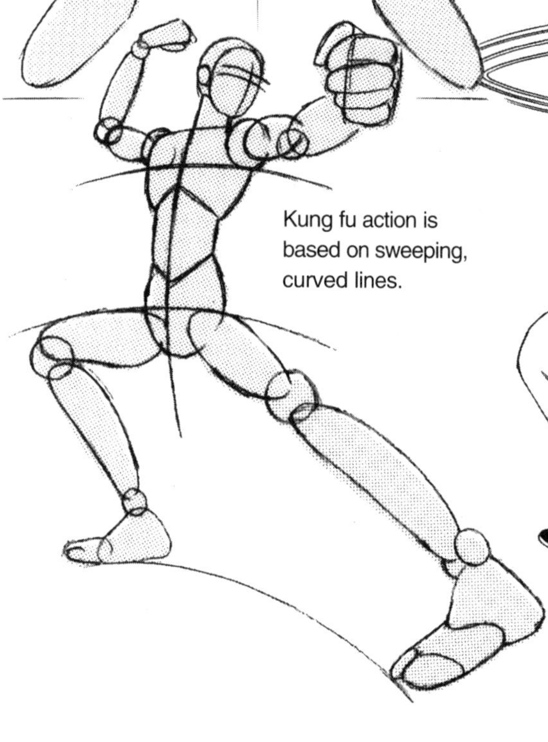

Kung fu action is based on sweeping, curved lines.

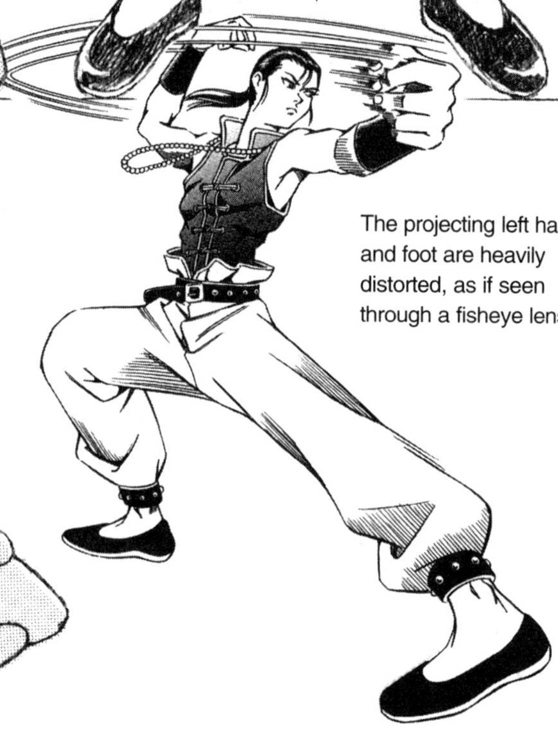

The projecting left hand and foot are heavily distorted, as if seen through a fisheye lens.

Boy hero

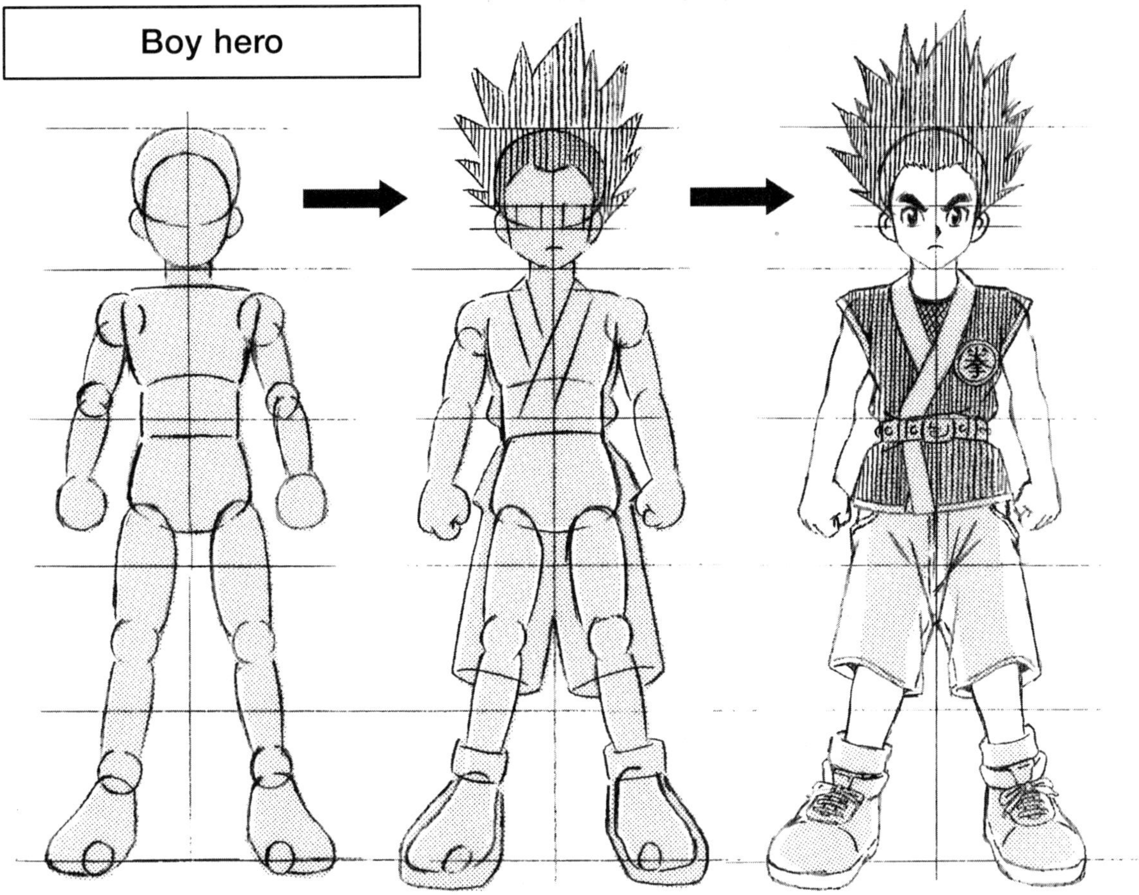

As a general rule, ten-year old kids should be drawn about five-and-a-half heads tall, but since this boy is a manga character, his head is proportionately larger.

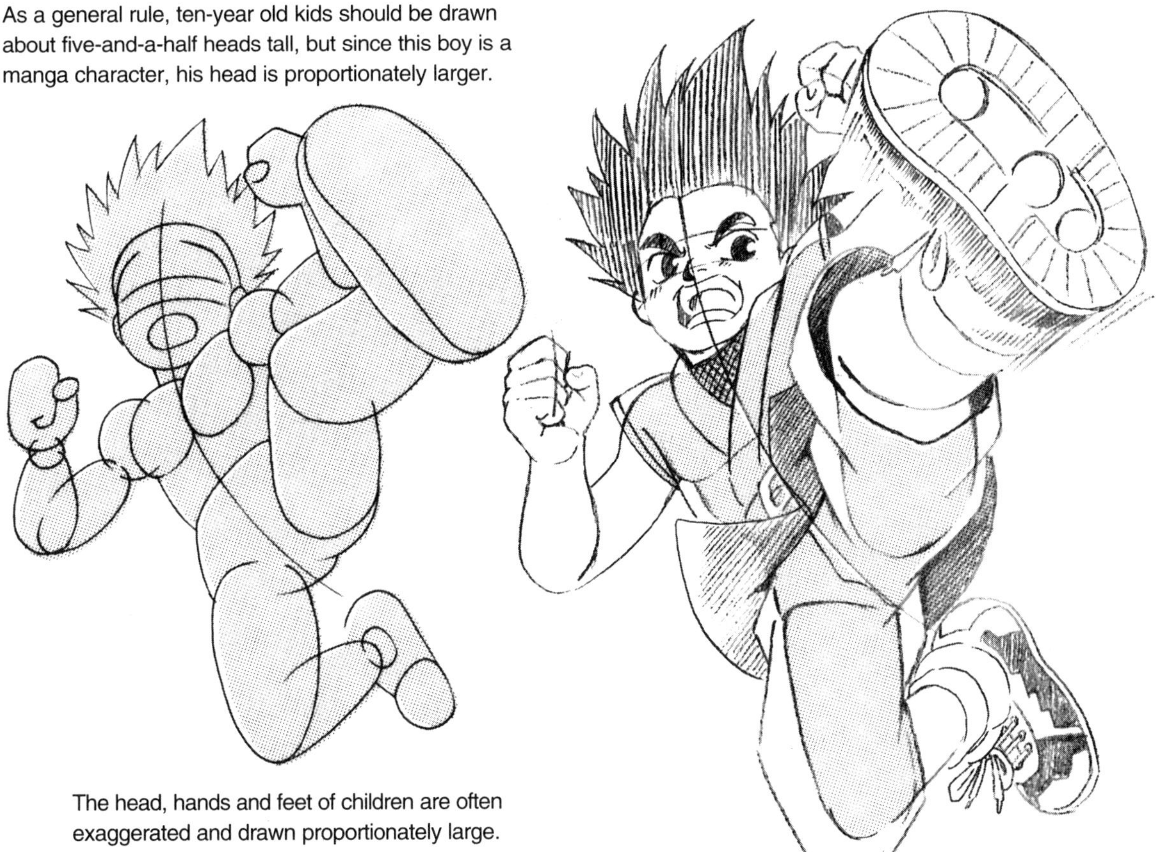

The head, hands and feet of children are often exaggerated and drawn proportionately large.

Drawing a heroine character

1 Think of a department store mannequin when drawing your heroine's figure.

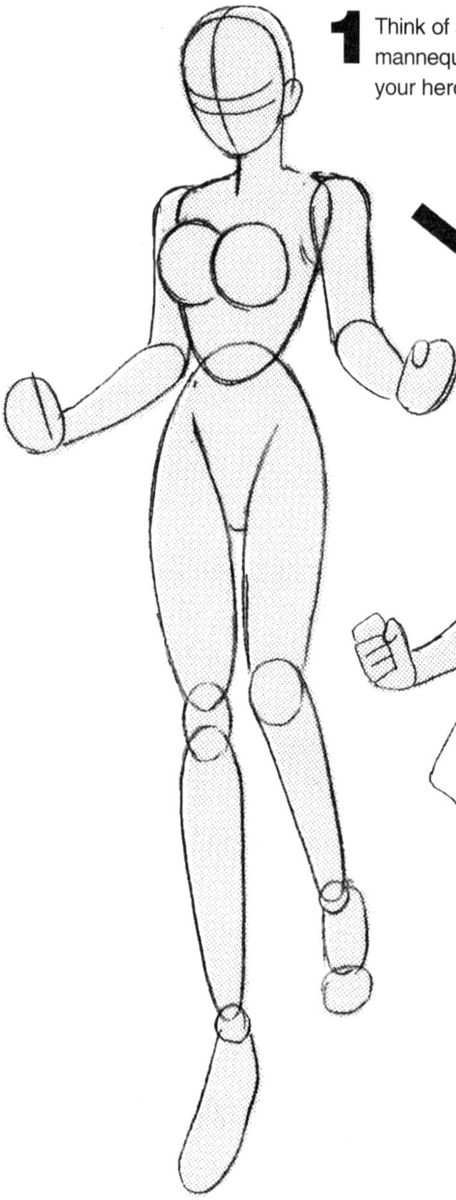

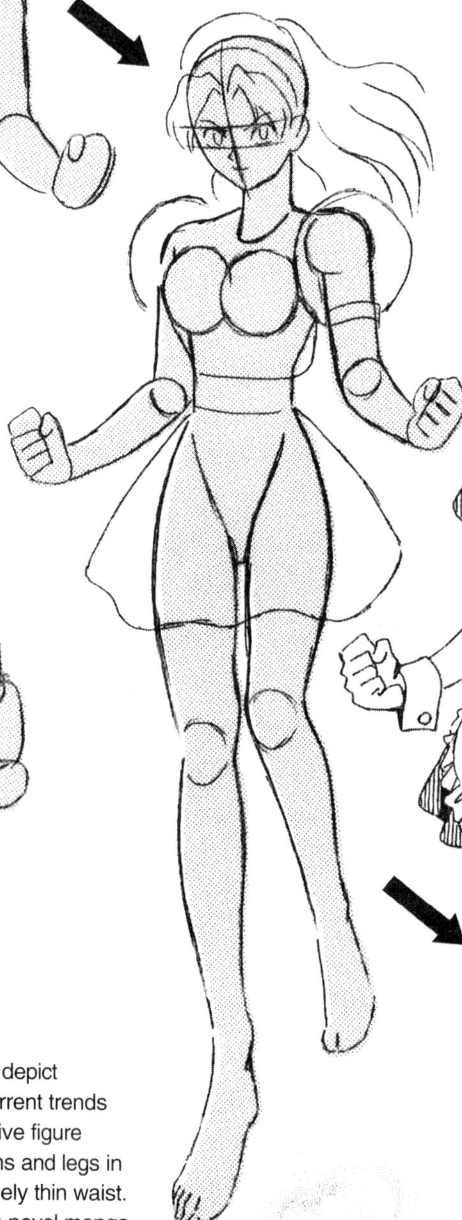

2 Use rounded lines to depict litheness of form. Current trends dictate that an attractive figure should have long arms and legs in addition to an extremely thin waist. However, the graphic novel manga genre tends toward more realistic body proportions.

3 Details are drawn applying sufficient balance to each form. The wrinkles of the apron are shown in this stage.

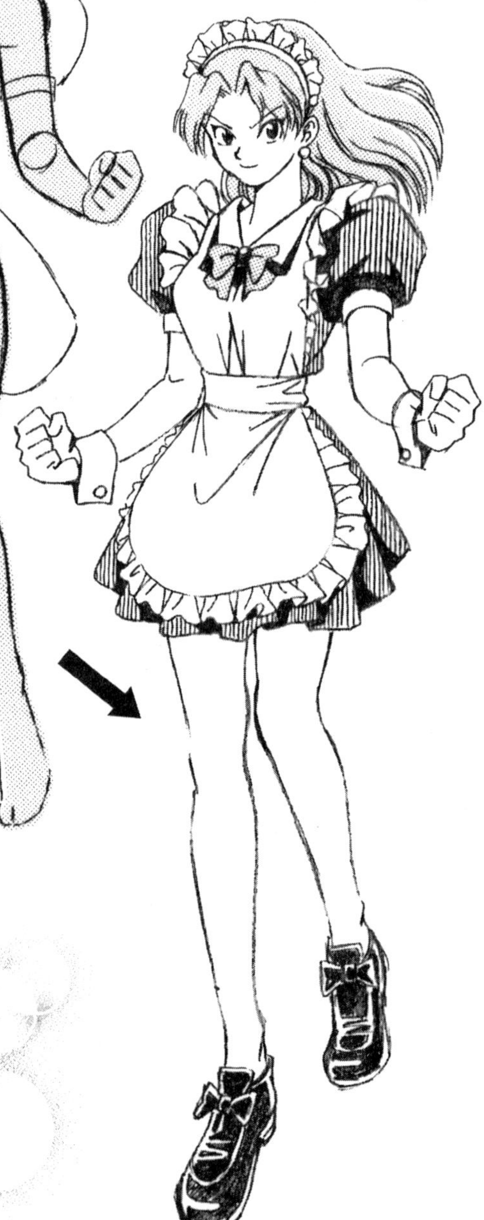

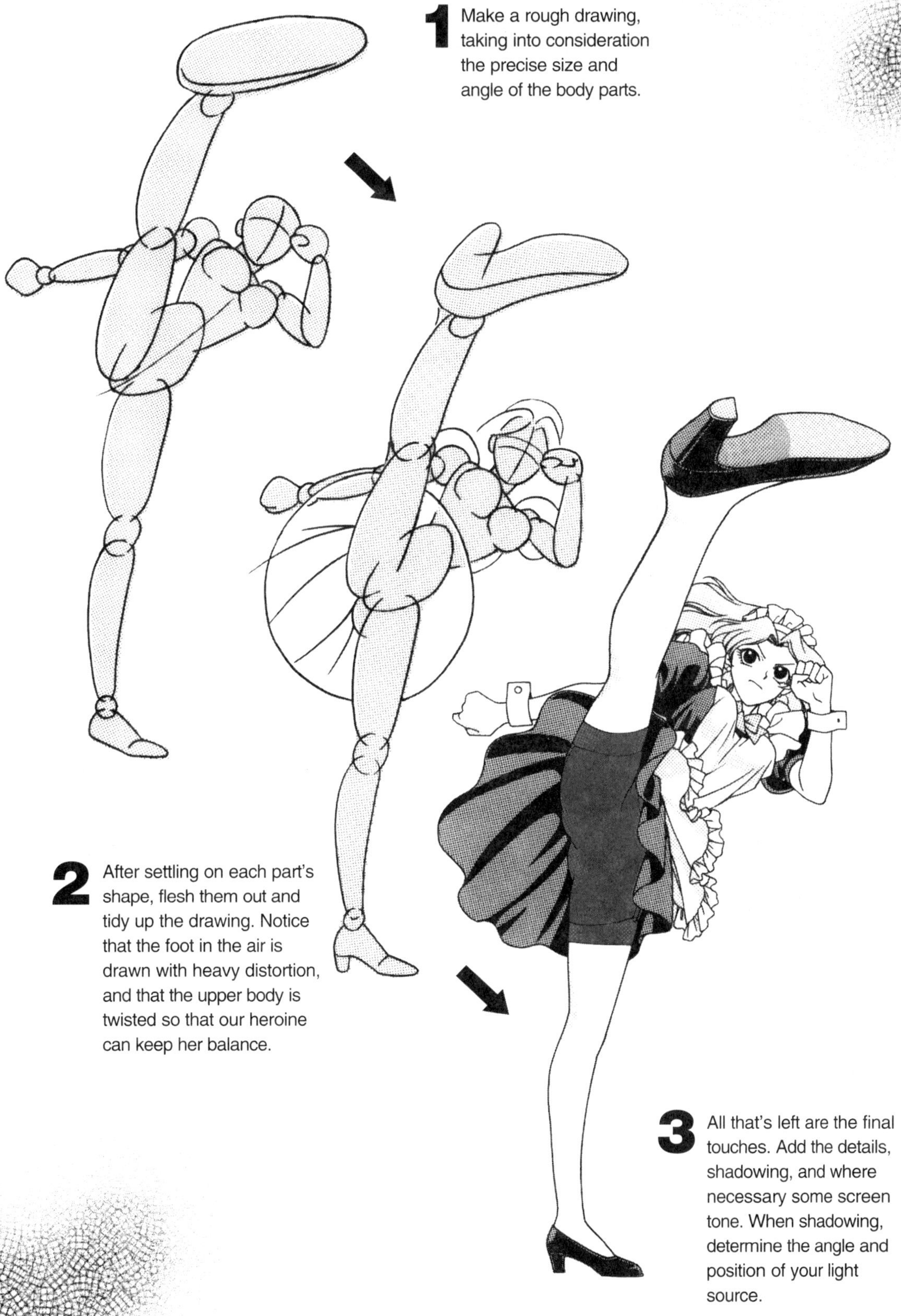

1 Make a rough drawing, taking into consideration the precise size and angle of the body parts.

2 After settling on each part's shape, flesh them out and tidy up the drawing. Notice that the foot in the air is drawn with heavy distortion, and that the upper body is twisted so that our heroine can keep her balance.

3 All that's left are the final touches. Add the details, shadowing, and where necessary some screen tone. When shadowing, determine the angle and position of your light source.

バトルシーンの実践

Let's Draw a Fight Sequence!

Okay! Let's take what we've learned so far and apply it to a real fight sequence that features the two lovely ladies below.

Japanese people are known to have a thing for uniforms and costumes. French maid outfits have proven especially popular in recent years, as housemaid characters have found their way into numerous Japanese anime and manga.

Character design

Miki

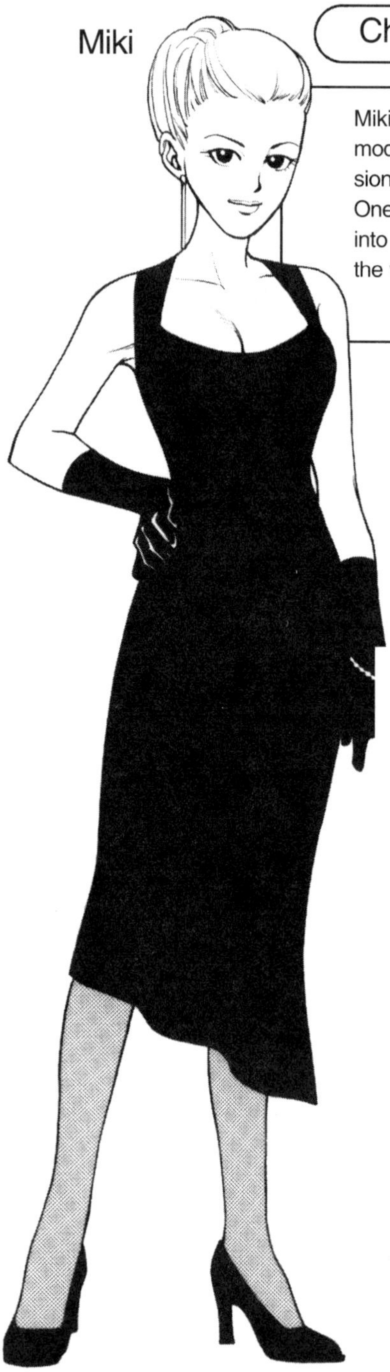

Miki is a fashion magazine model by day and a professional gem thief by night. One evening, she sneaks into a high-class mansion on the way home from a party...

Nanae

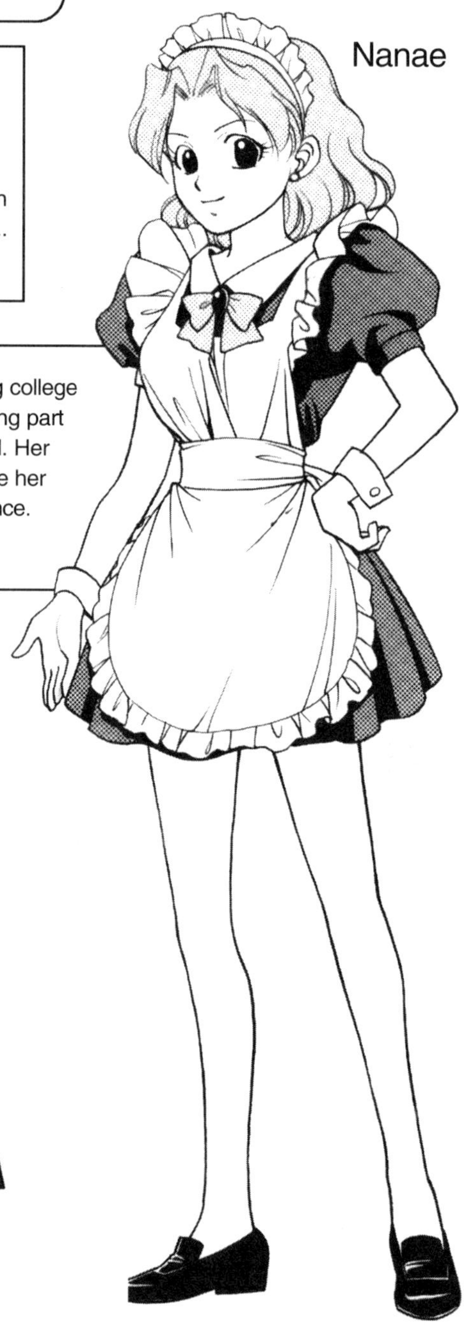

Nanae is a struggling college student who is working part time as a housemaid. Her youthful features belie her strength and confidence.

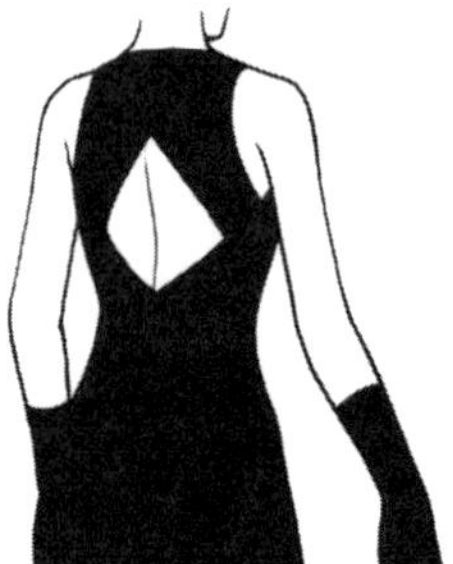

Rear view of Miki

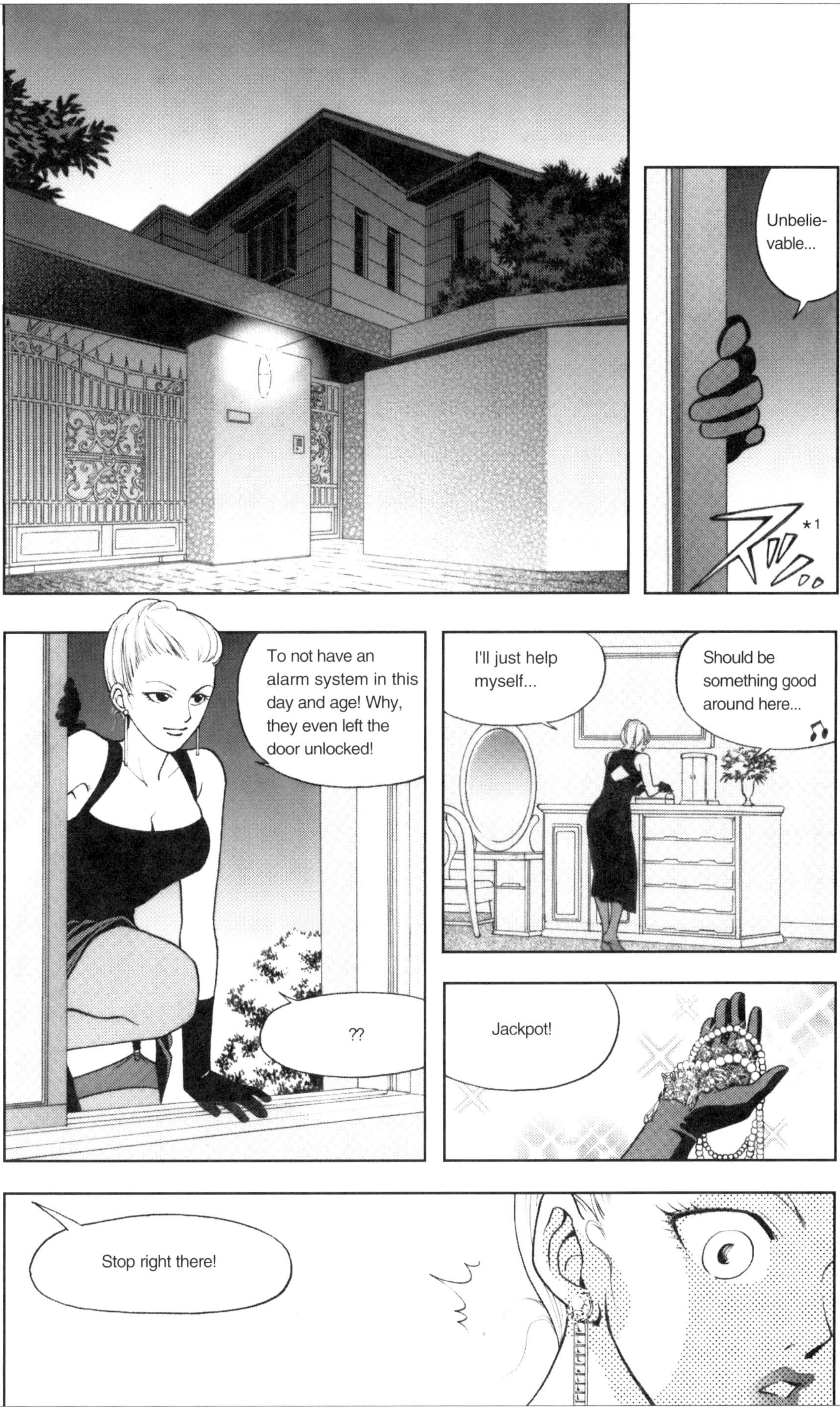
Unbelie-
vable...
★1
To not have an alarm system in this day and age! Why, they even left the door unlocked!
??
I'll just help myself...
Should be something good around here...
Jackpot!
Stop right there!

★1: Fffoosh

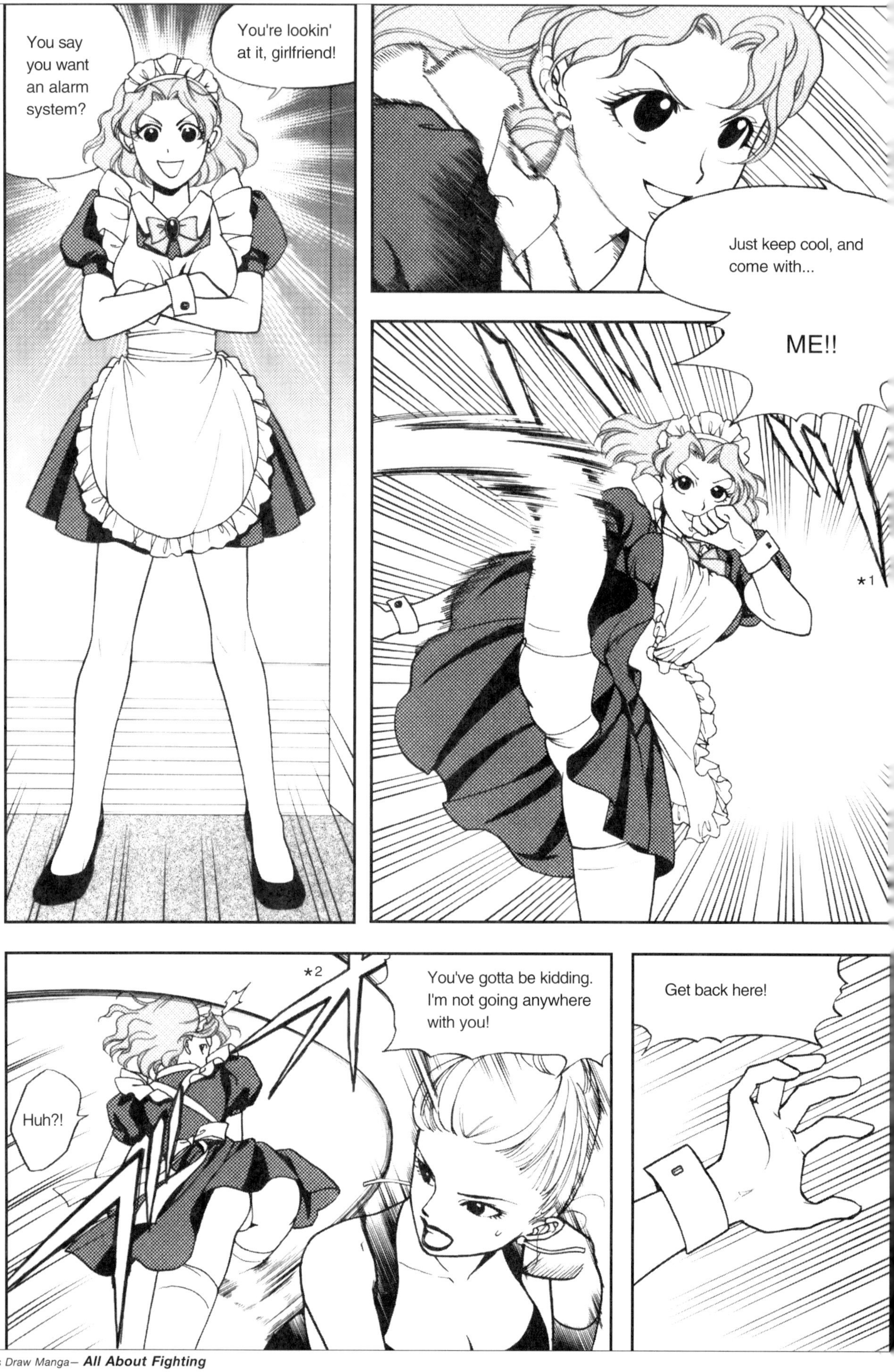

*1:Shlikakaka *2:Fwoosh

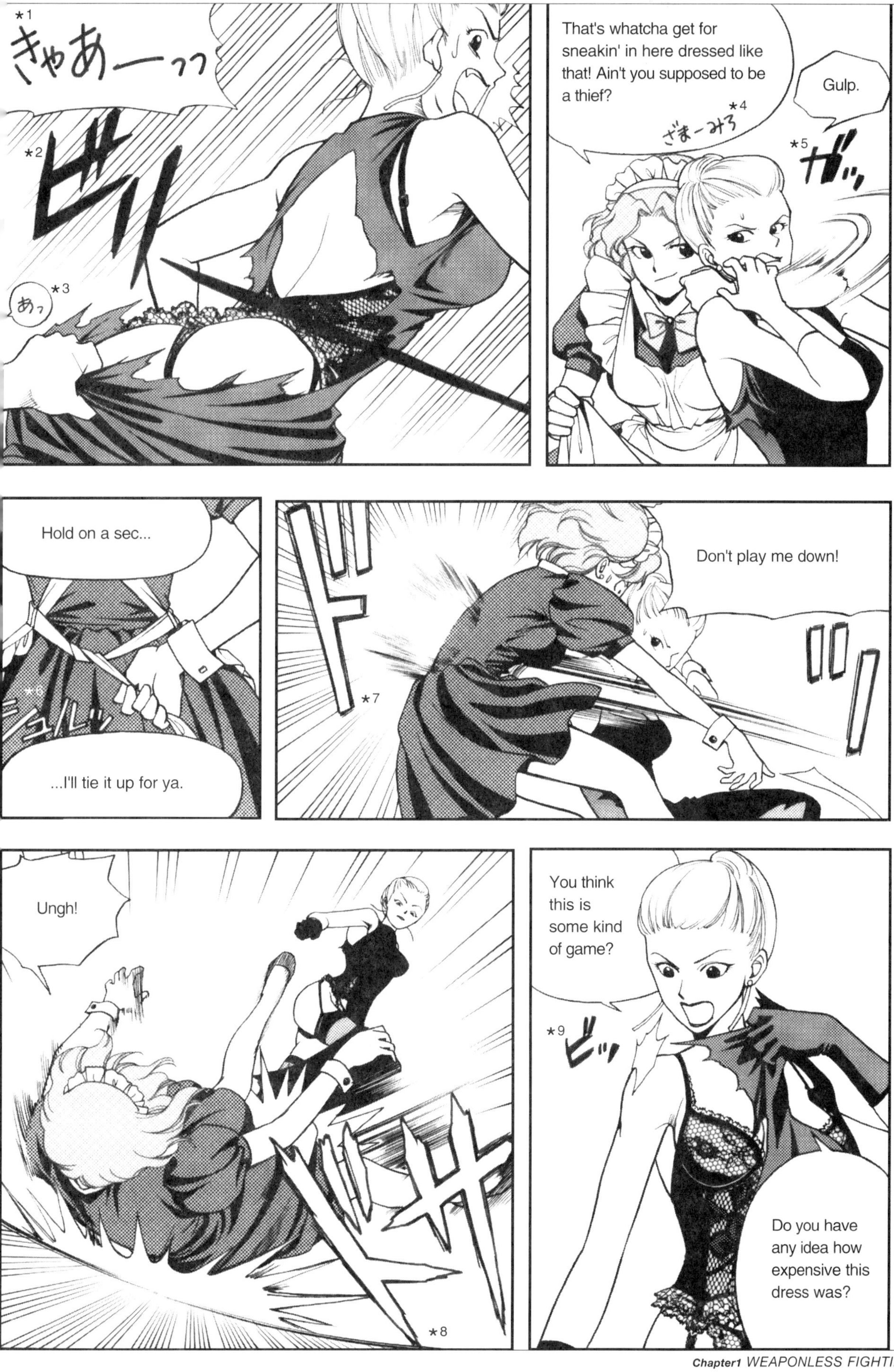

★1:Yaaaaaa!! ★2:Riiip ★3:Oops ★4:Just look at yourself... ★5:Thwip ★6:Slip ★7:Sockk ★8:Thump ★9:Hmph

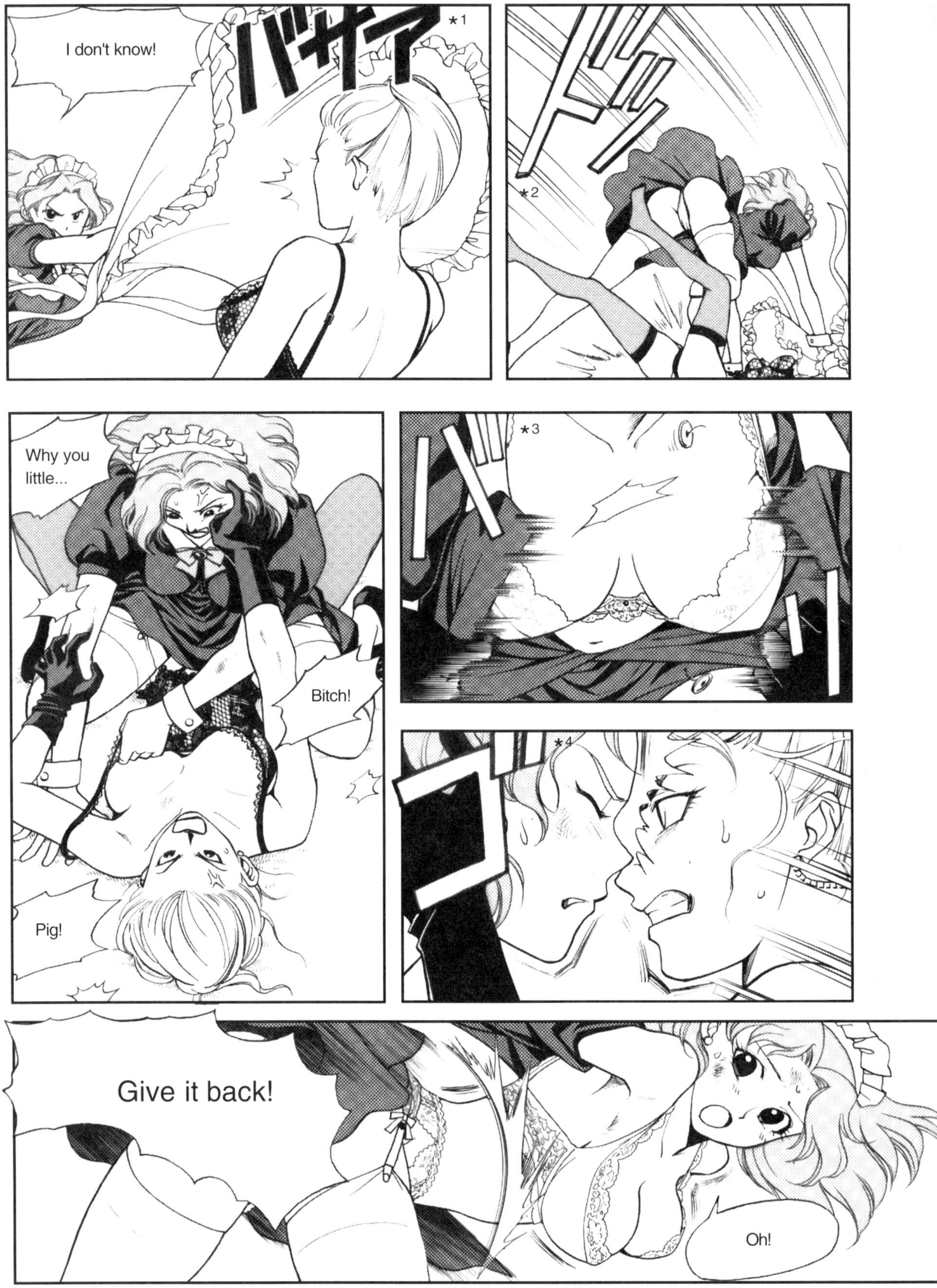

*1:Thwip *2:Thunk! *3:Pop! Pop! Pop! *4:Grrr!

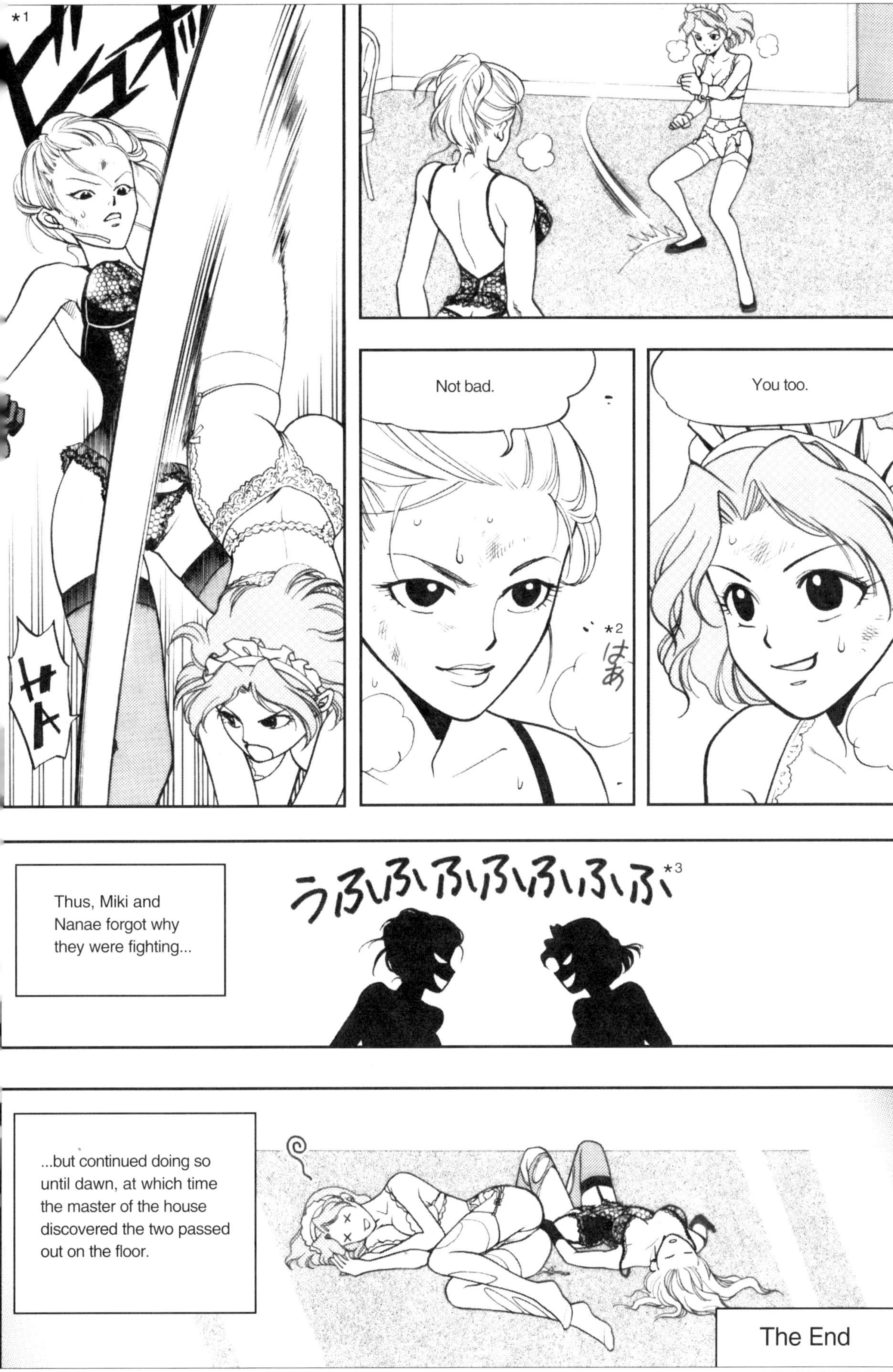

★1:Zishh ★2:Pant ★3:Heh heh heh

状況別アクション
Real-Life Action Scenes

We'll end chapter one with some scenes of violent situations that actually arise in modern-day Japan.

Salaryman fight

The panel to the right shows some businessmen having an after-work drink at a restaurant. Even the polite and mild-mannered Japanese are known to occasionally lose their cool after downing a few glasses. When a heated argument escalates to become a bare-knuckle brawl, the standard line is...

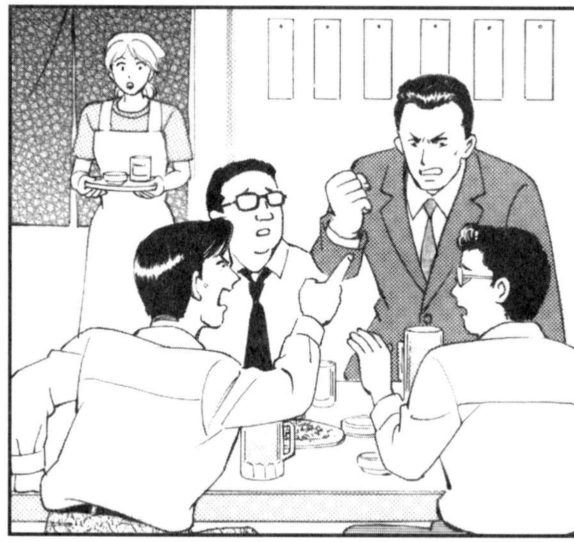

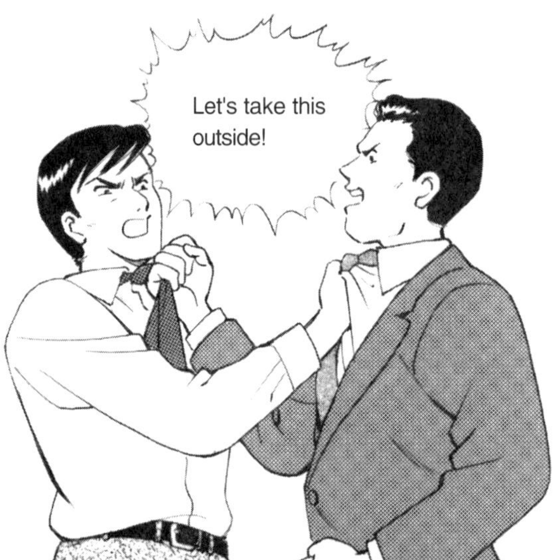

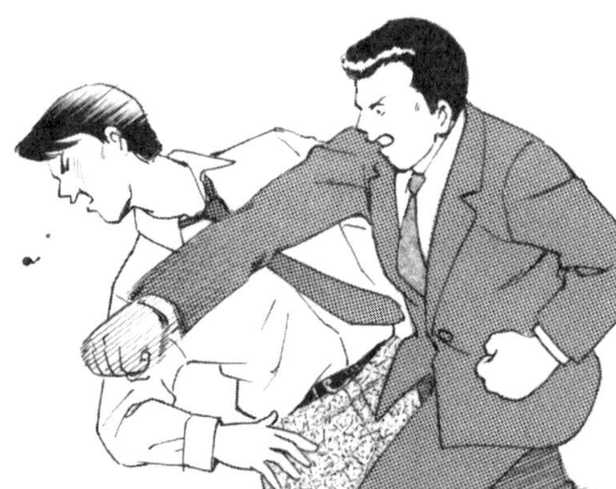

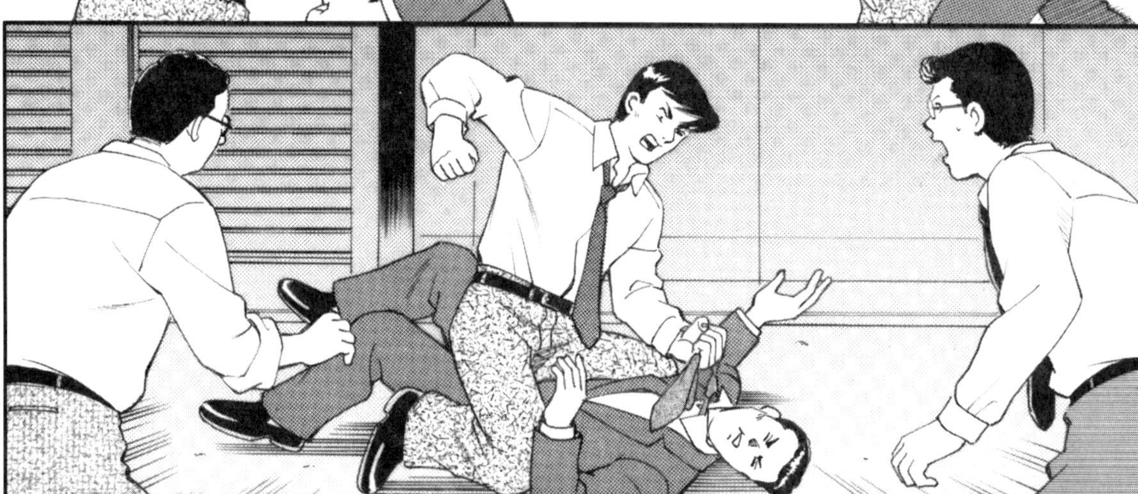

Husband-and-wife fight

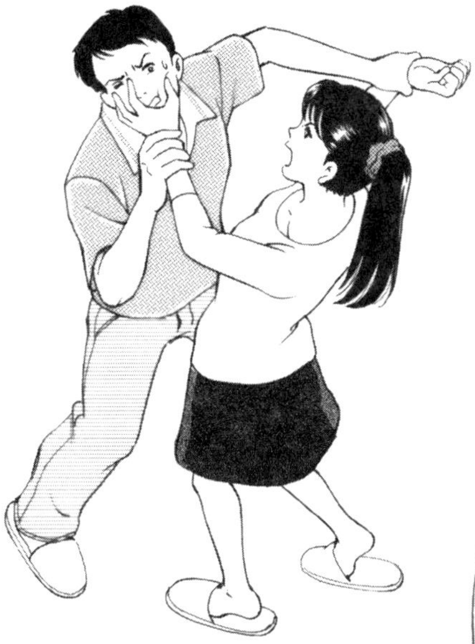

One of the most popular fight scenes used in this situation depicts an angry wife hurling objects at her husband. Of course, the unwritten rule is that she never throws anything of value!

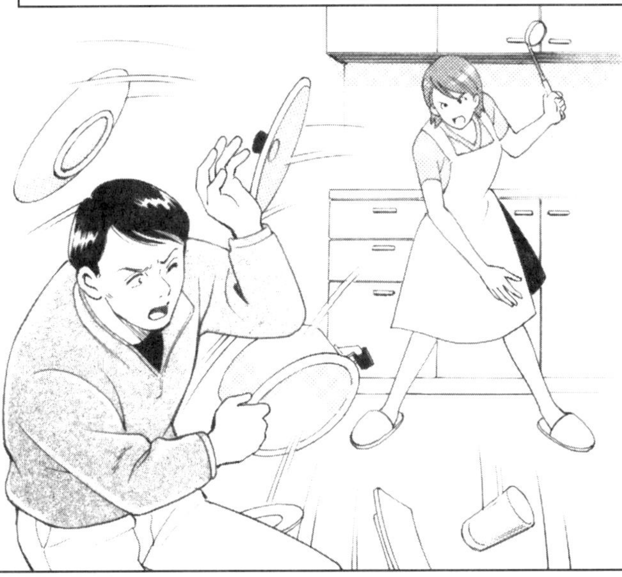

Discount sale scramble

The Japanese are famous for being brand-name fanatics. Eager shoppers will commonly line up in front of a store before it opens so that they can be the first to pounce on a big sale. This amusing drawing shows a group of determined women frantically grasping at sale items.

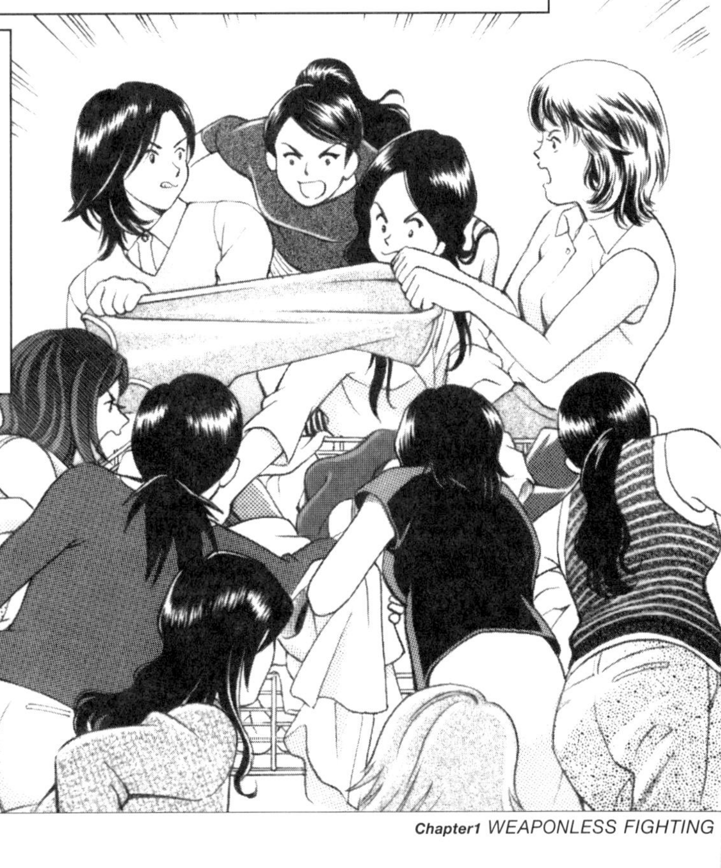

Fighting kids

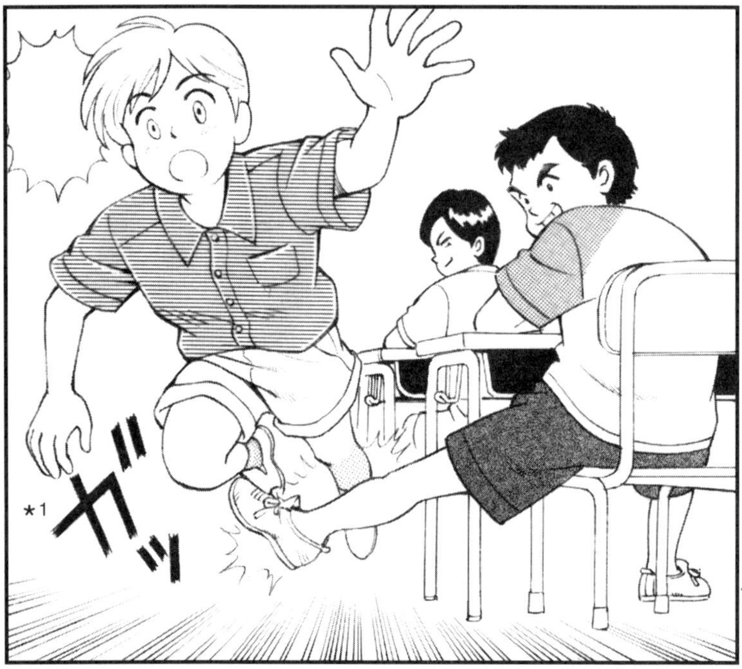

A classic bullying scene is that of a kid getting tripped, typically in a classroom. Such scenes are rarely encountered nowadays, as manga incorporate increasingly malicious images. For better or for worse, manga has become an art form that reflects the realities of our times.

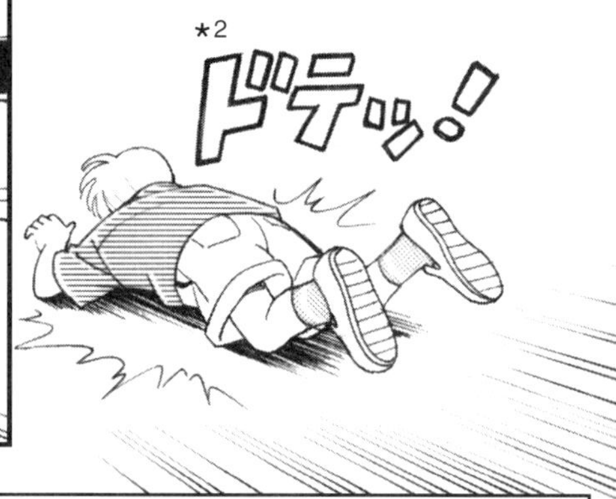

Schoolboy scuffle

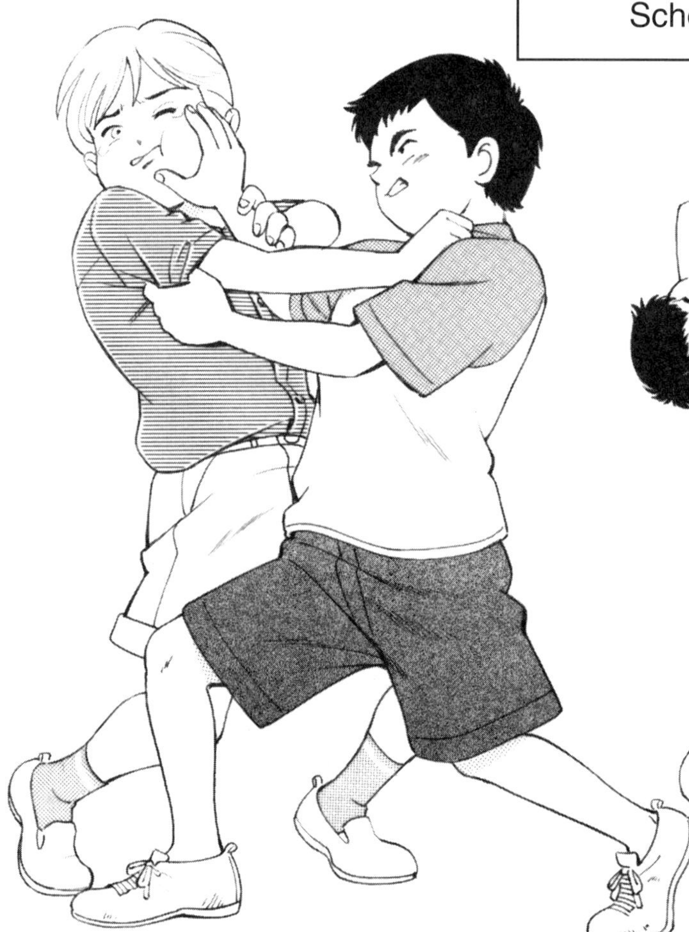

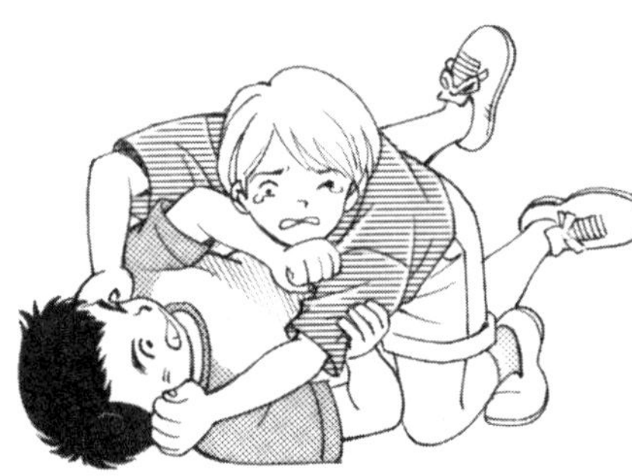

Sobbing boy

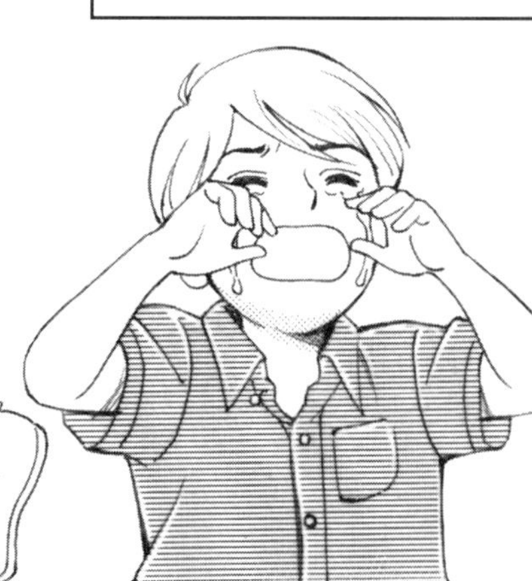

★1:Aaa! ★2:Trip!

CHAPTER 2

「武器で戦う」

ACTION SCENES INVOLVING WEAPONS

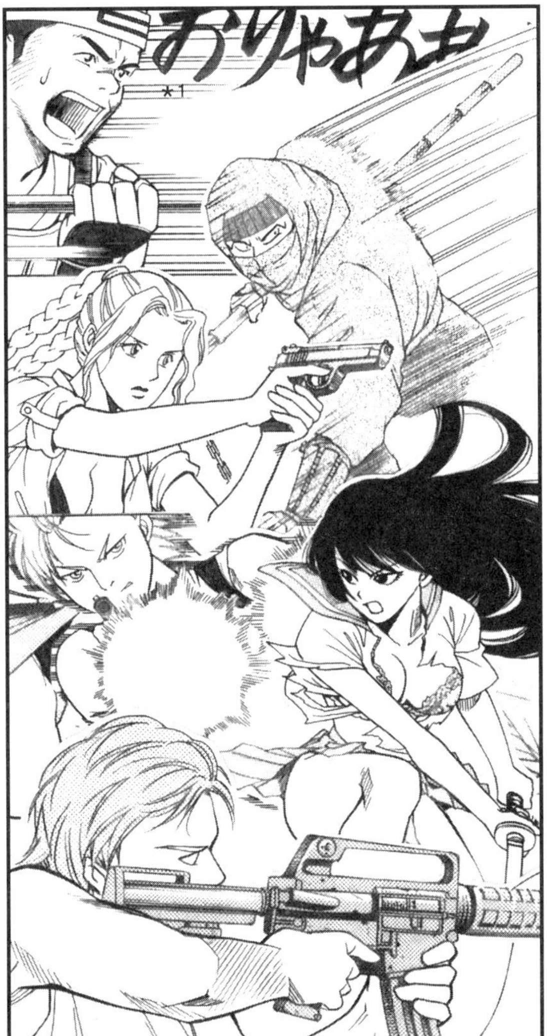

★1: Yehhhh

剣で戦う！
How to Draw a Swordfight!

Although the sword is no longer used in battle these days, it continues to play an essential role in period dramas. In addition, recent years have seen an increasing number of Japanese manga that feature modern-day youth wielding swords. Let's take a closer look at swordfighting scenes in an imaginary world.

Mizuki is a sixteen year-old high school student who just happens to be an expert at Japanese swordfighting. Let's see what happens when she gets pulled into another world.

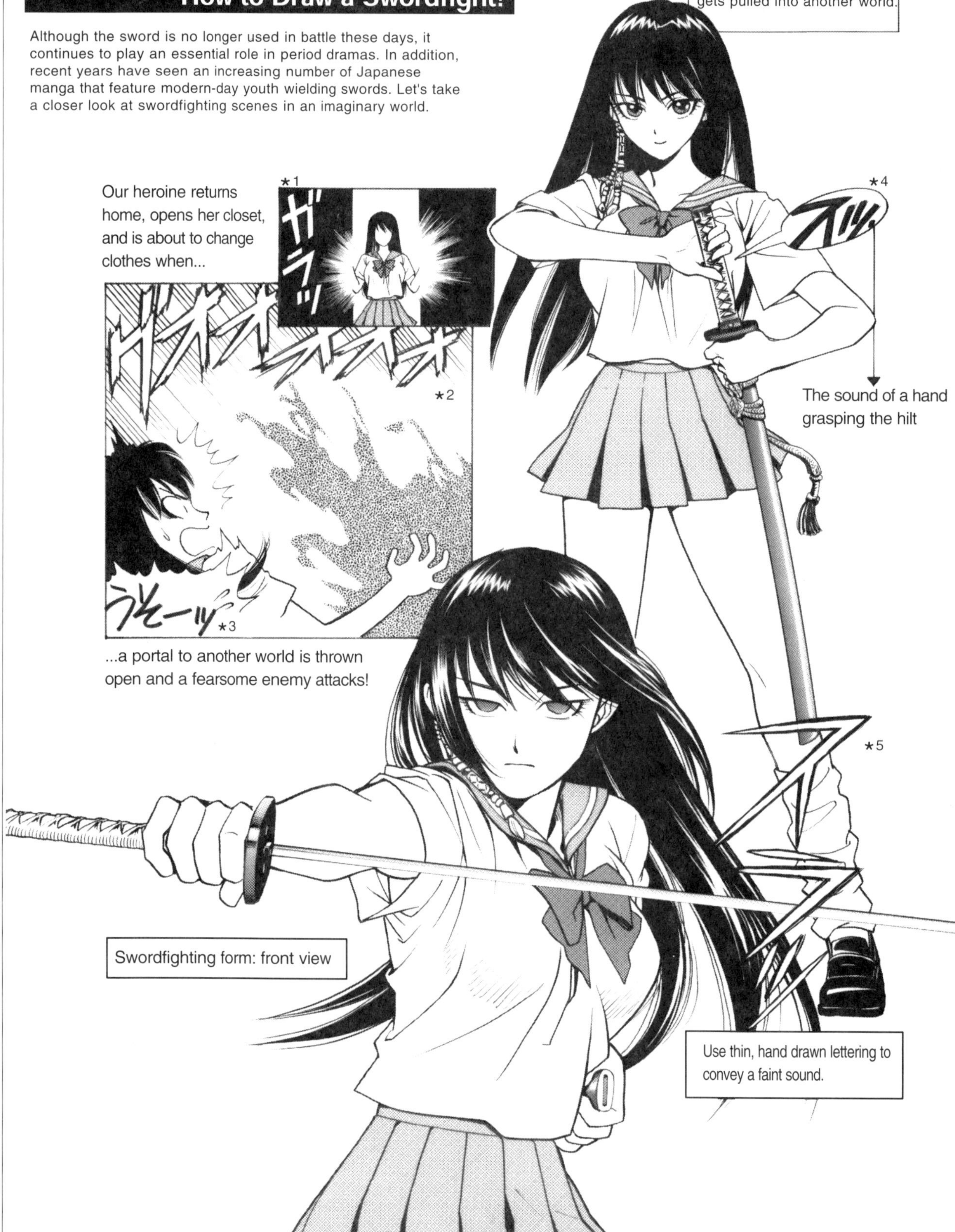

Our heroine returns home, opens her closet, and is about to change clothes when...

...a portal to another world is thrown open and a fearsome enemy attacks!

The sound of a hand grasping the hilt

Swordfighting form: front view

Use thin, hand drawn lettering to convey a faint sound.

★1:Kerthunk ★2:Fawooumph! ★3:What the... ★4:Sfft ★5:Shling!

The Parts of a Japanese Katana (sword)

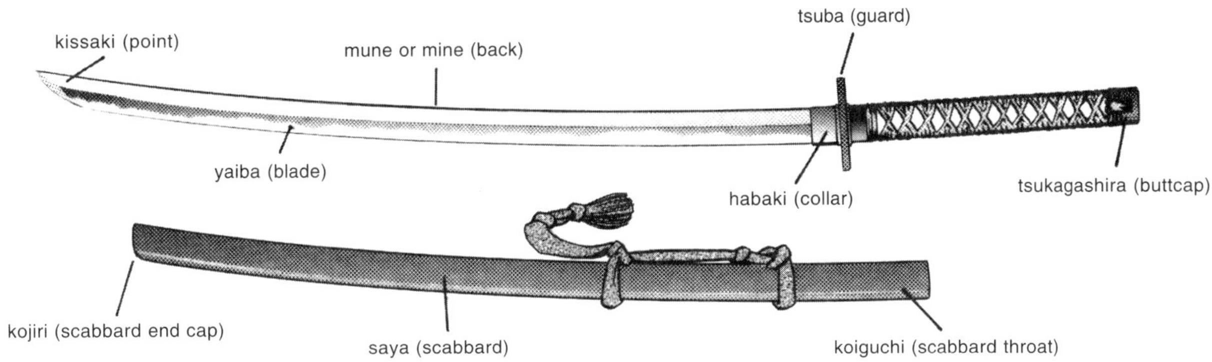

Intruders from the other world
These are Mizuki's relentless assailants. Outlandish attire and features help give them that "otherworldly" look.

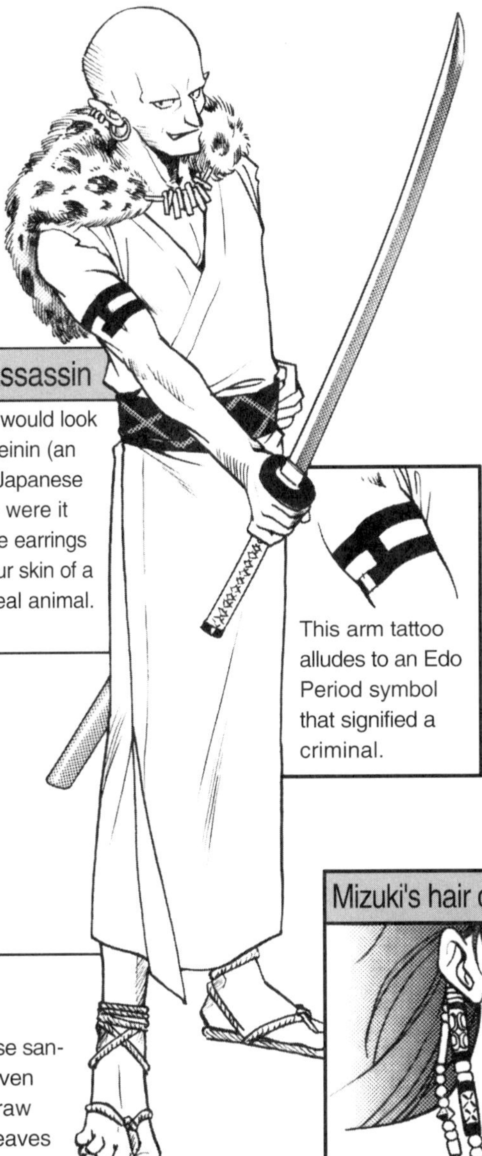

Male assassin

This guy would look like a toseinin (an old-time Japanese gambler) were it not for the earrings and the fur skin of a wild, boreal animal.

This arm tattoo alludes to an Edo Period symbol that signified a criminal.

Waraji
Ancient Japanese sandals woven from straw (dried leaves and stems of the rice plant). Usually worn when making a journey.

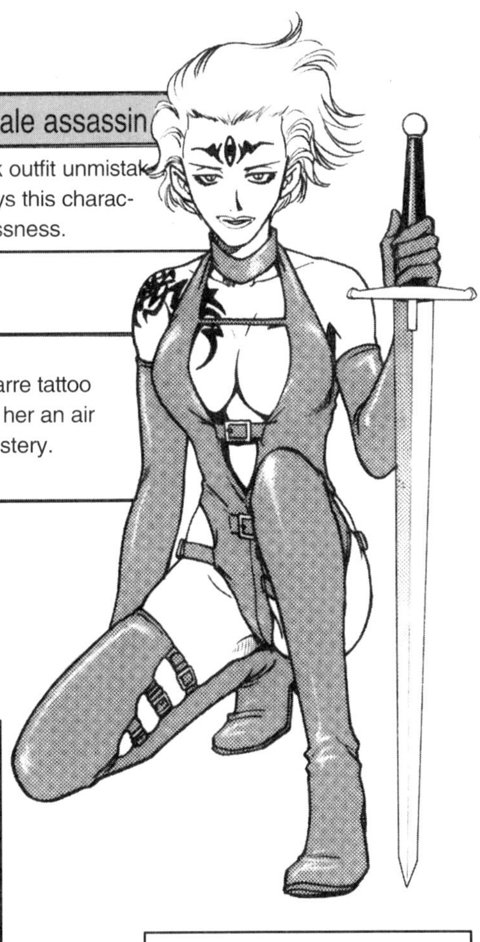

Sexy female assassin

An all-black outfit unmistakably conveys this character's ruthlessness.

A bizarre tattoo lends her an air of mystery.

This assassin's sword is a two-handed medieval type. It is described on a later page.

Mizuki's hair decoration

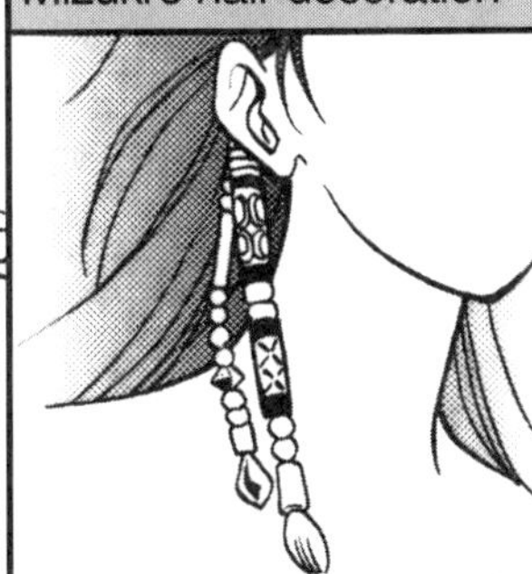

Does it ensheathe a lock of hair, or is it simply hanging off of her ear?

The heroine's background

Our heroine's swordsmanship must be supported by a convincing story.

Long ago, Mizuki's ancestors trained army generals in the art of swordsmanship. The tradition was preserved in her family over the years, and Mizuki became acquainted with the art at an early age.

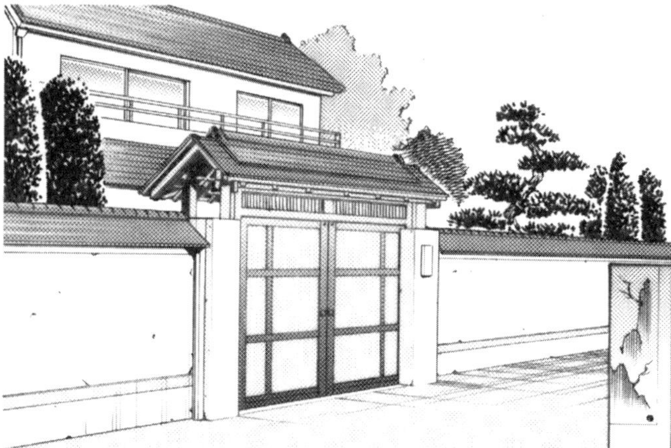

Her family also practiced the exorcism of evil spirits, but never became well known in this regard. Consequently, Mizuki's family failed to make a lasting mark in history.

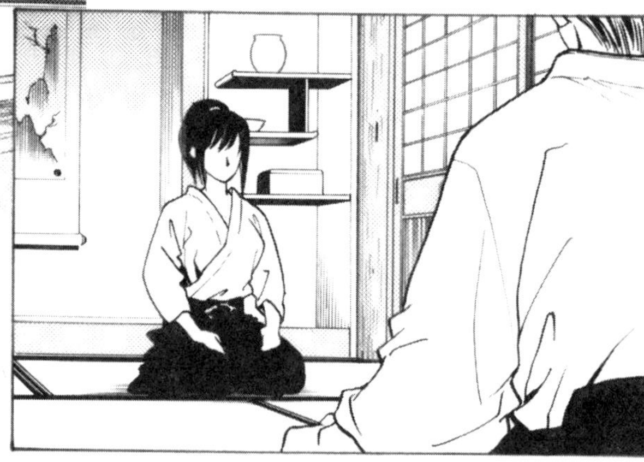

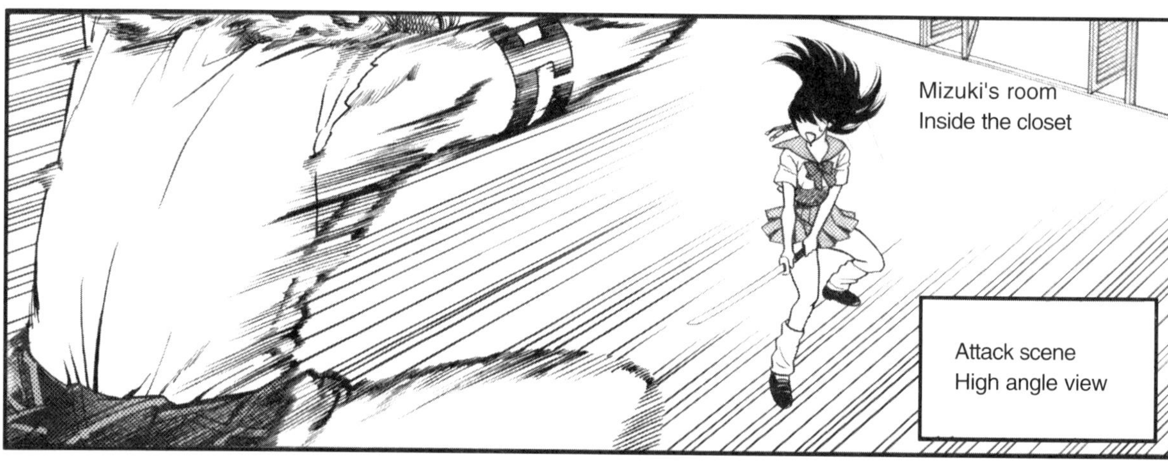

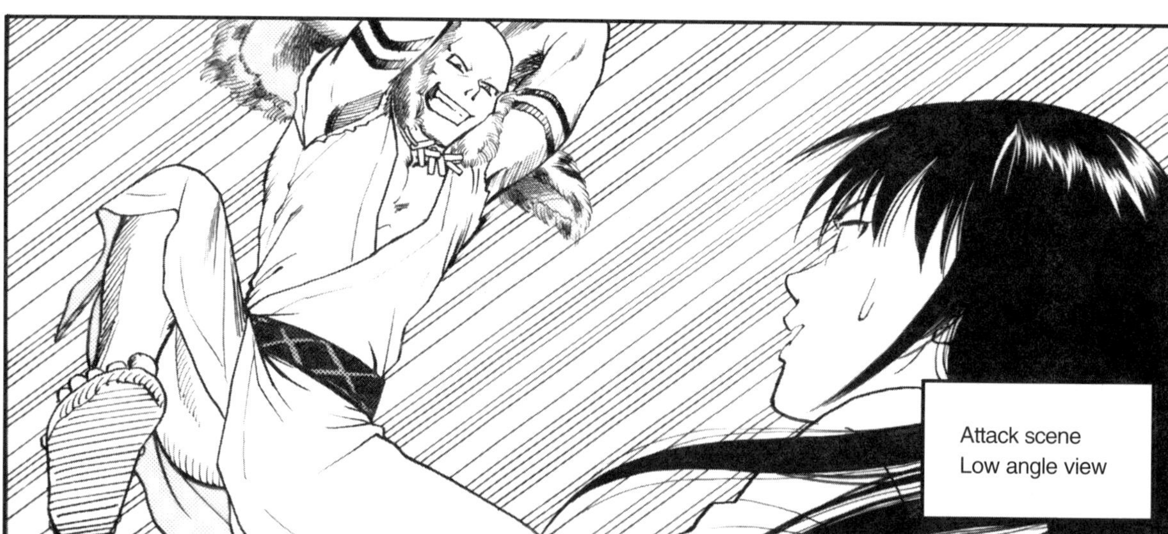

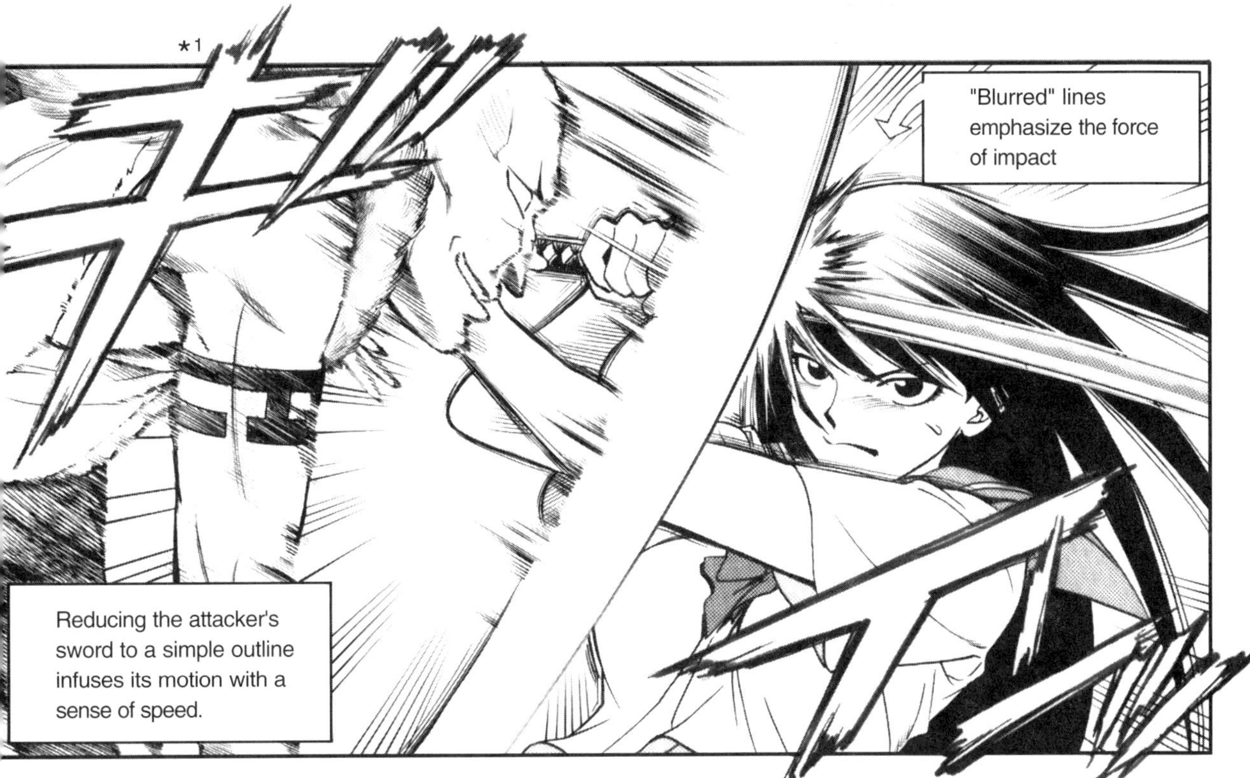

"Blurred" lines emphasize the force of impact

Reducing the attacker's sword to a simple outline infuses its motion with a sense of speed.

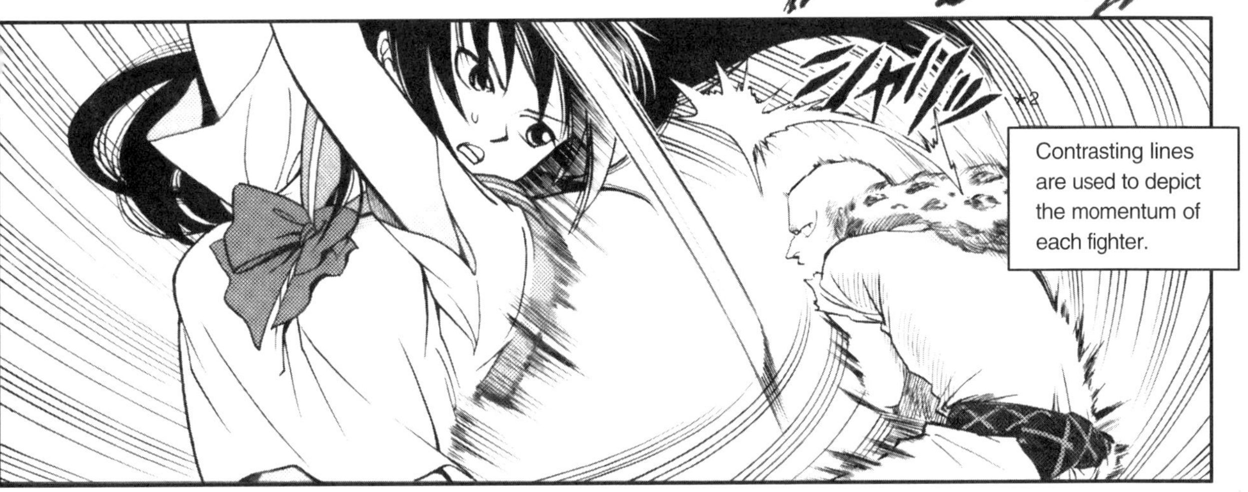

Contrasting lines are used to depict the momentum of each fighter.

Different angles

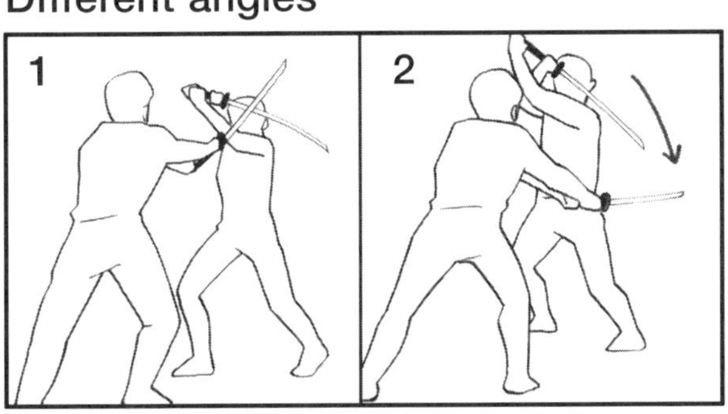

These two panels illustrate the motion of a parry. The panels with Mizuki show only the moment of impact and the repositioned characters after the parry. Everything in between is omitted. This implied movement, together with the liberal use of subjective motion lines, lends manga its characteristic intensity.

Figure 2 from above

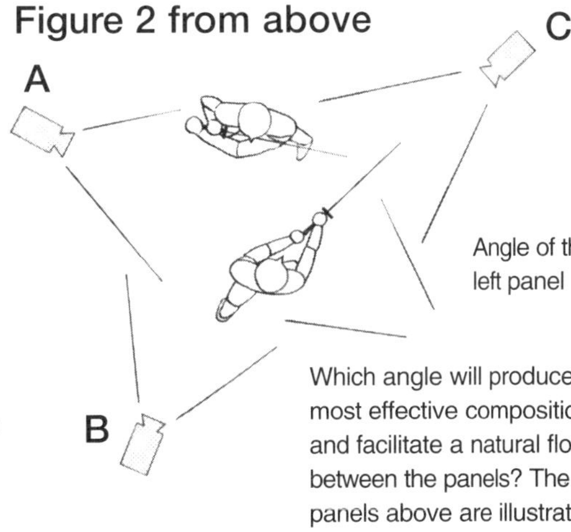

Which angle will produce the most effective composition and facilitate a natural flow between the panels? The panels above are illustrated from angle A.

★1:KaCHING! ★2:Shnikkt

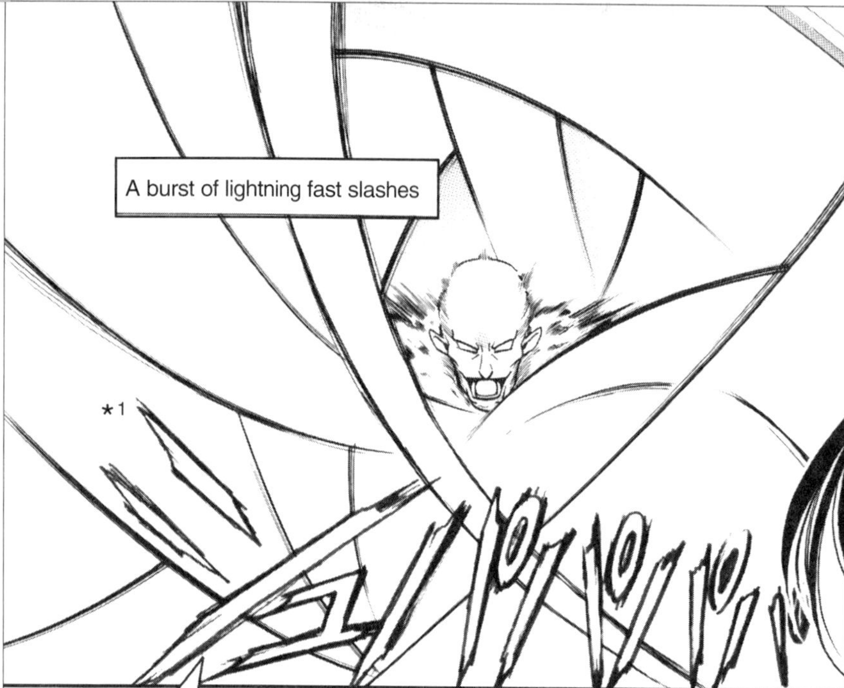

A burst of lightning fast slashes

A consolidation of multiple motions into one panel is a technique occasionally employed by the manga artist. The character is deliberately drawn anchored to one spot.

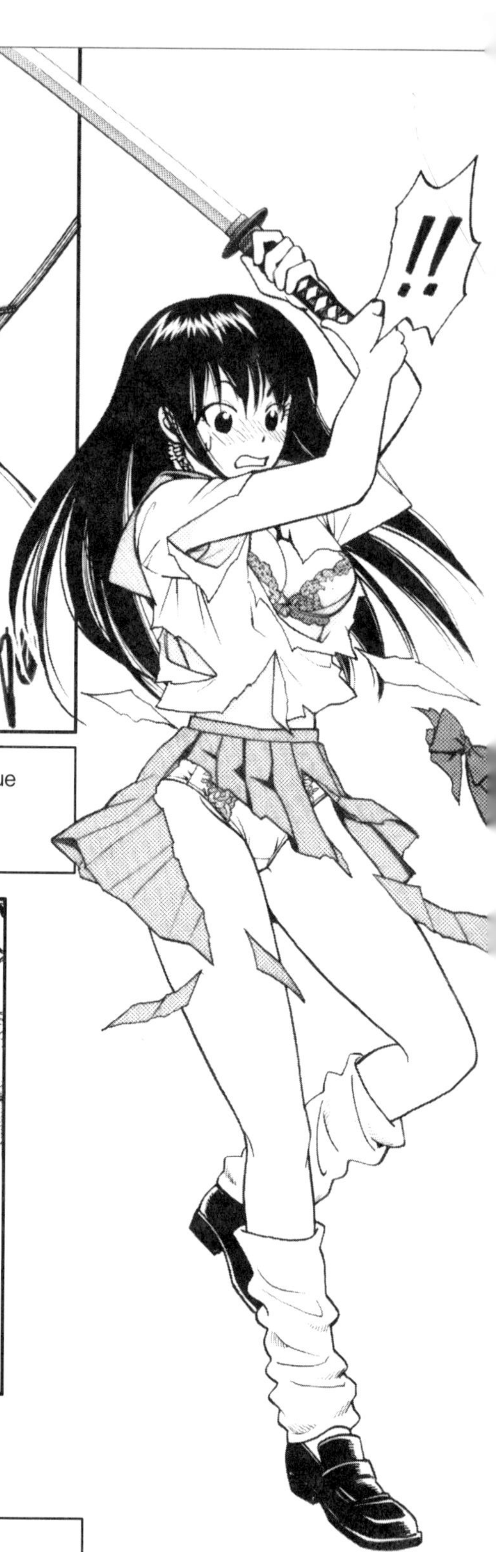

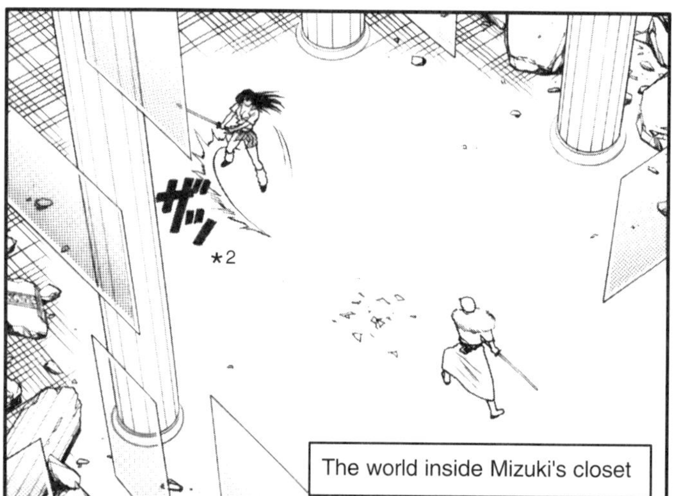

The world inside Mizuki's closet

Our characters wage battle amidst odd-looking ruins and what appear to be floating computer screens. An opening panel like this used to be obligatory for every action scene.

Emotions through the eyes

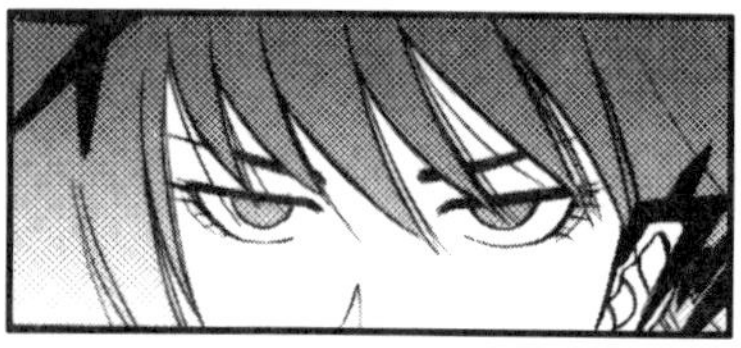

Silent rage
The eyes are narrow and peer out from beneath lowered brows. Think "icy wind" when incorporating sound effects.

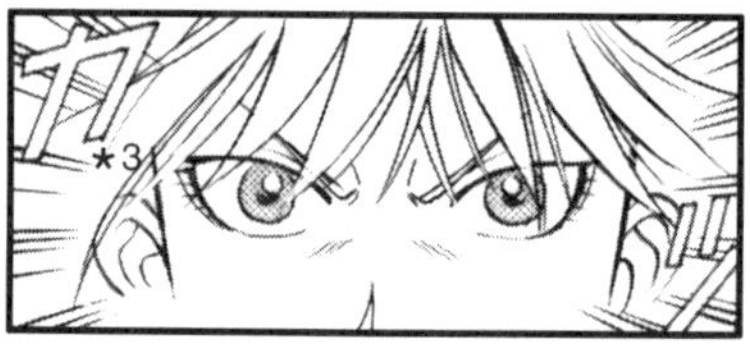

Explosive rage
The eyes are drawn wide open and the hair ruffled. Centrifugal subjective motion lines add to the effect.

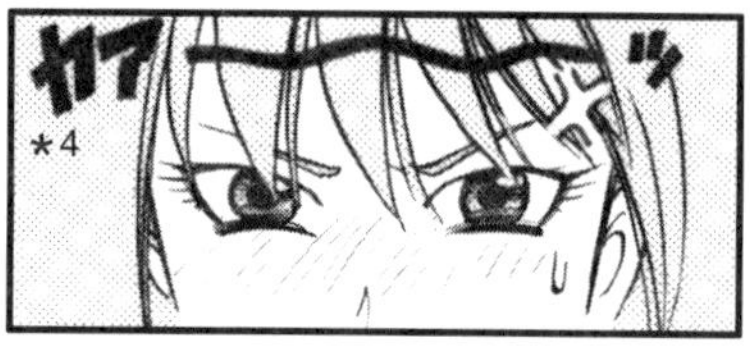

Embarrassed rage
The eyes are slightly narrowed and the cheeks are flushed. Sound effects are drawn across the forehead to depict a character turning purple with rage.

★1:Schflikakakaka! ★2:Flick ★3:Shaa ★4:mmmm

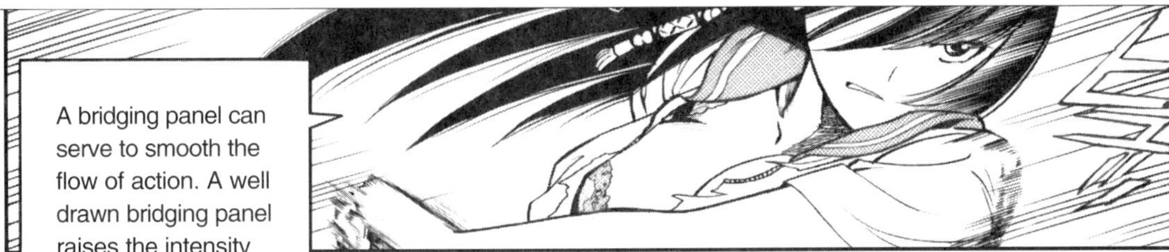

A bridging panel can serve to smooth the flow of action. A well drawn bridging panel raises the intensity level considerably.

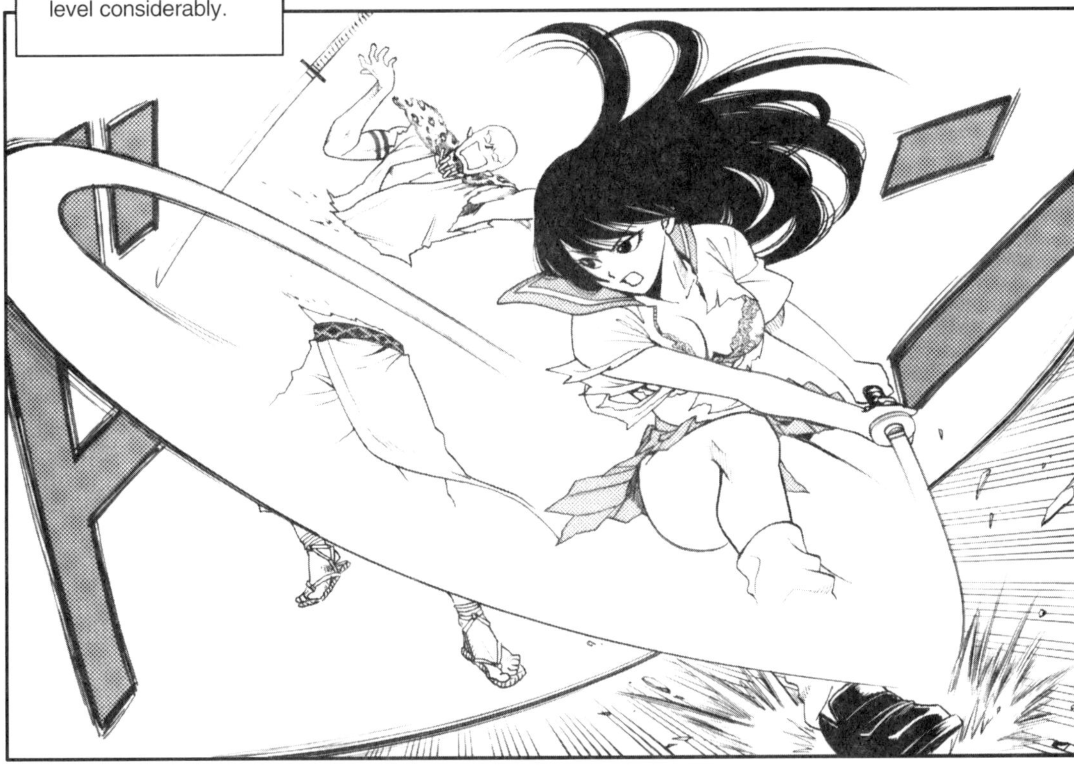

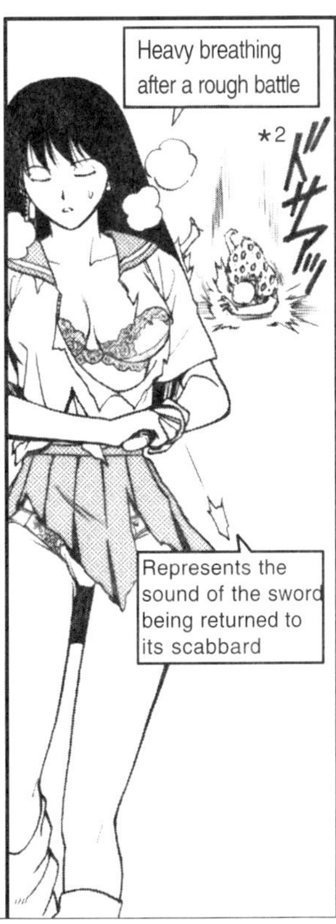

Heavy breathing after a rough battle

Represents the sound of the sword being returned to its scabbard

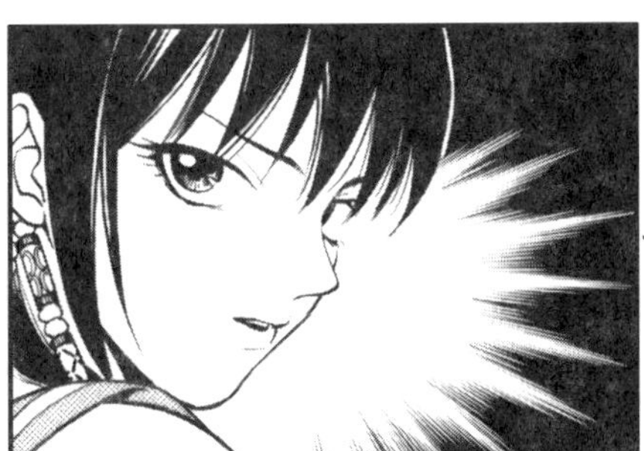

A starburst-like effect is useful for signaling danger, a change in the air, or simply when something is amiss.

Solid

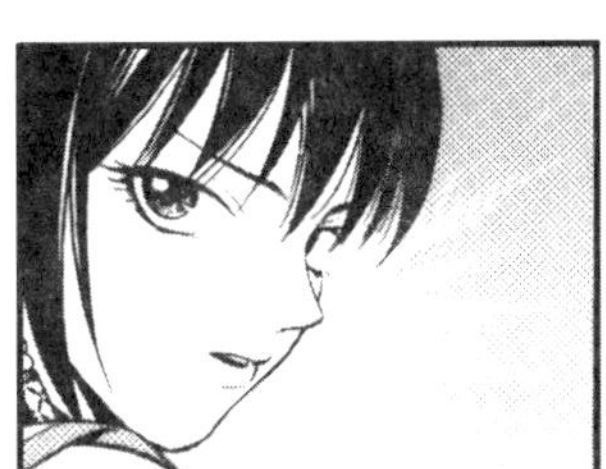

Screen tone

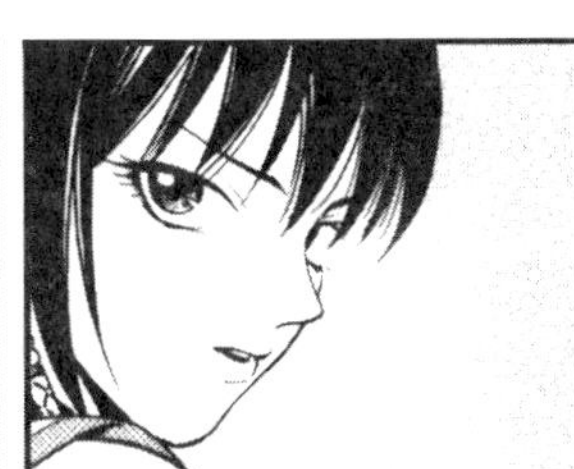

Textured screen tone

★1:Whoosh ★2:Thwump!

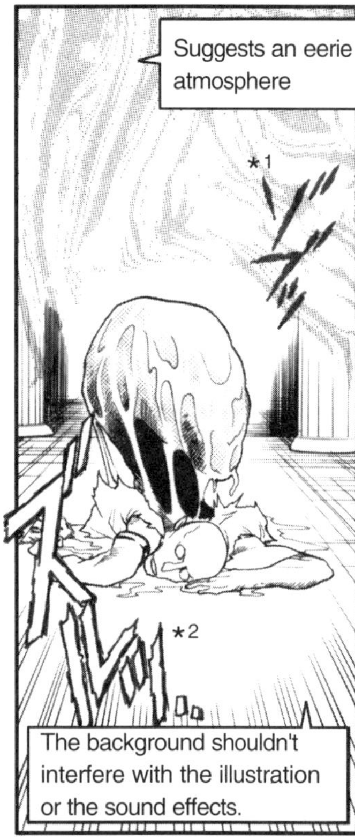

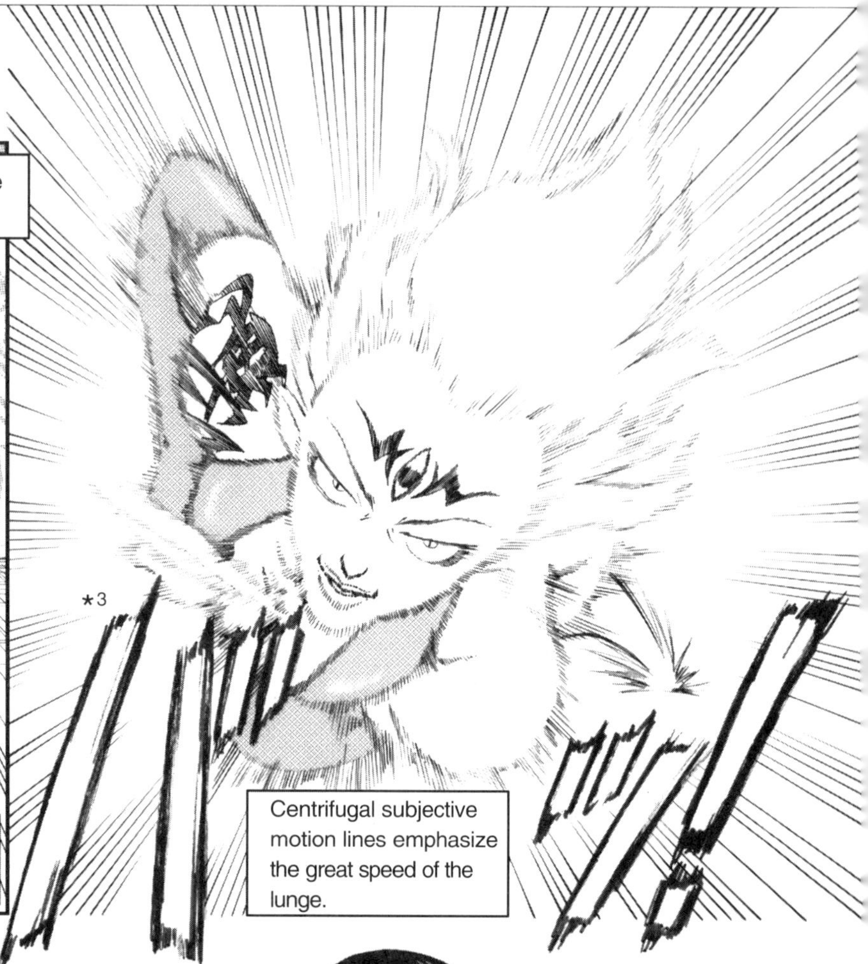

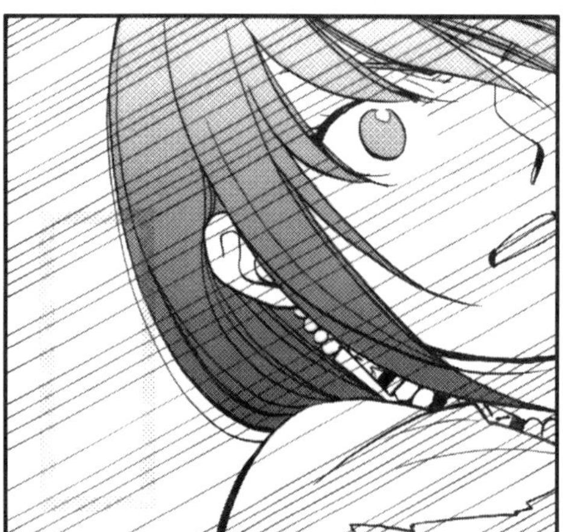

To depict an extremely short time interval, skew the frame area and draw kinetic lines across the character itself. Fill the space at left with a monologue. Something short, like "No!" or "It can't be!" is particularly effective.

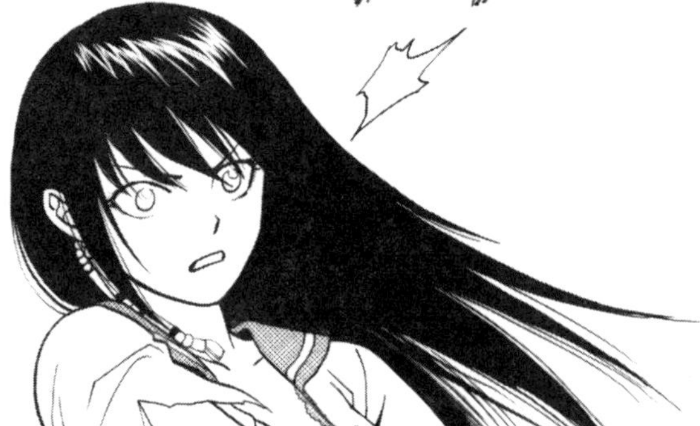

The panel at left is illustrated here solely with a formophor.

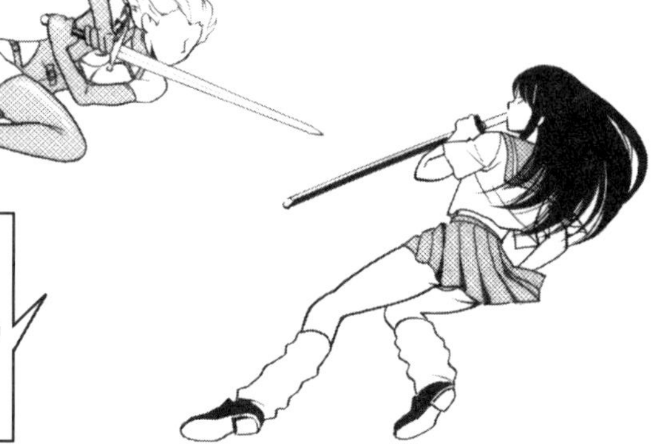

Draw a mid-action panel in freeze-frame for the illusion of slow motion.

★1:Gloop ★2:Splat ★3:Zwooom!

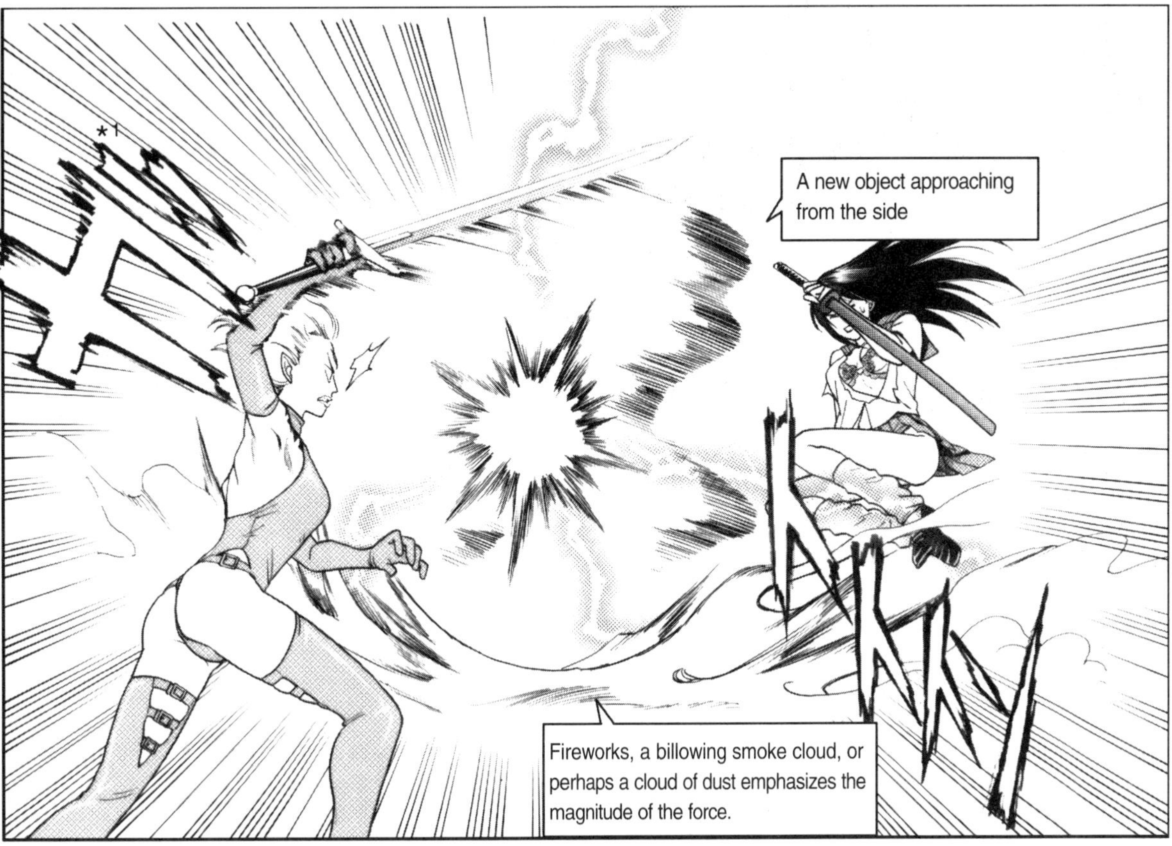

A new object approaching from the side

Fireworks, a billowing smoke cloud, or perhaps a cloud of dust emphasizes the magnitude of the force.

Let's give Mizuki some help.

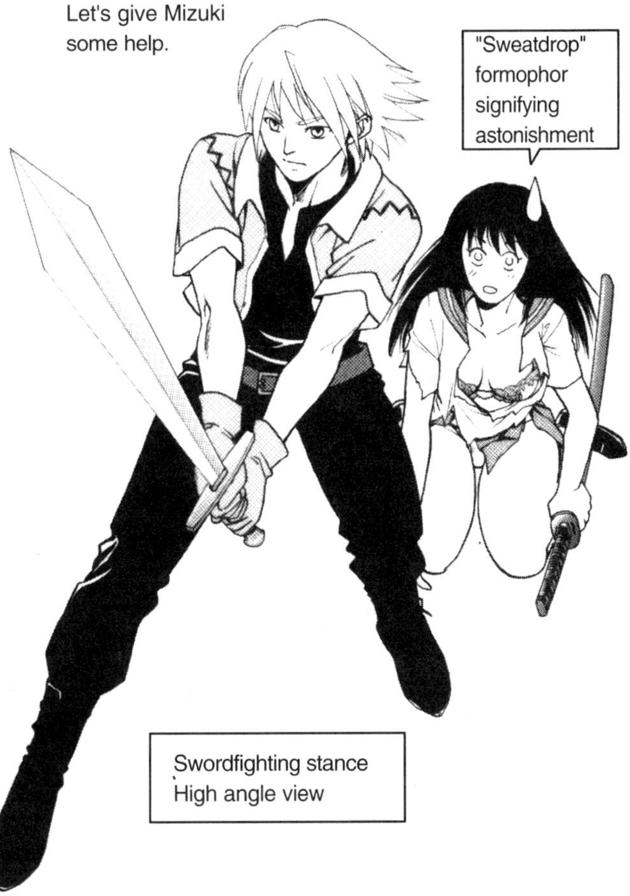

"Sweatdrop" formophor signifying astonishment

Swordfighting stance
High angle view

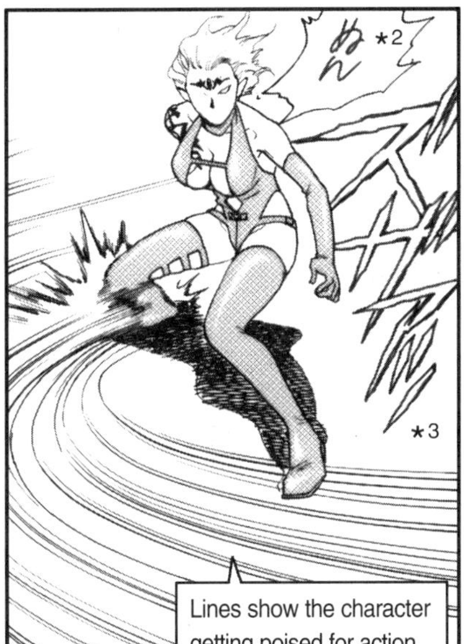

Lines show the character getting poised for action. She is momentarily separated from her opponents before her next attack.

★1:Ka-boom! ★2:Hmph ★3:Swiszsh

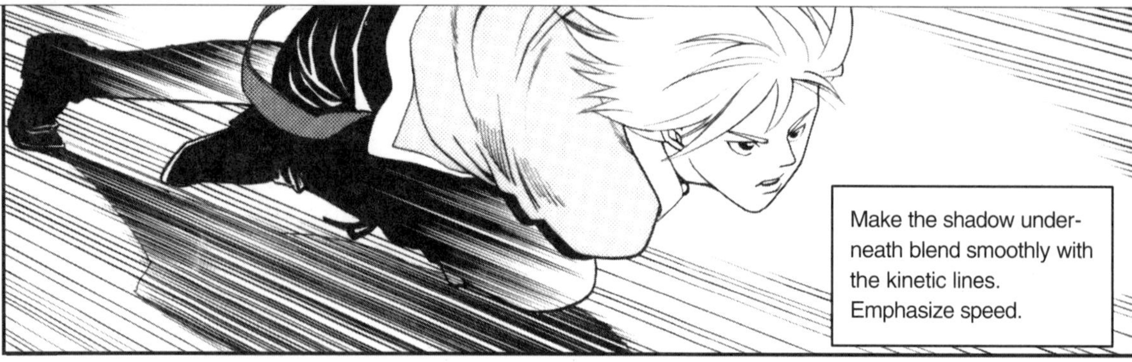

Make the shadow underneath blend smoothly with the kinetic lines. Emphasize speed.

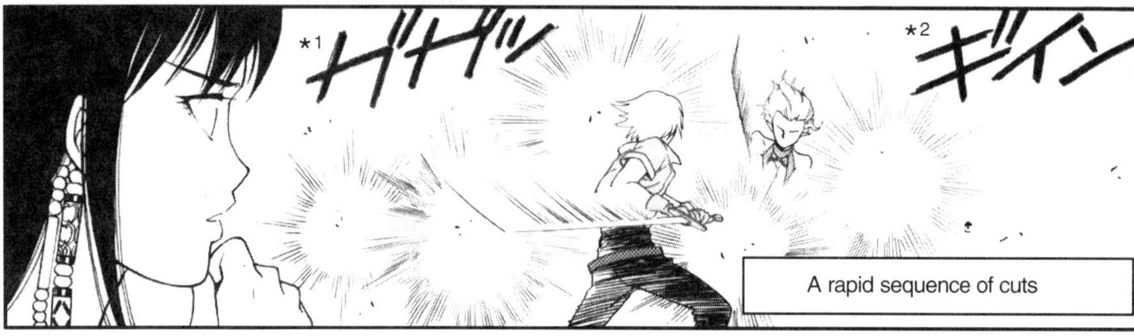

A rapid sequence of cuts

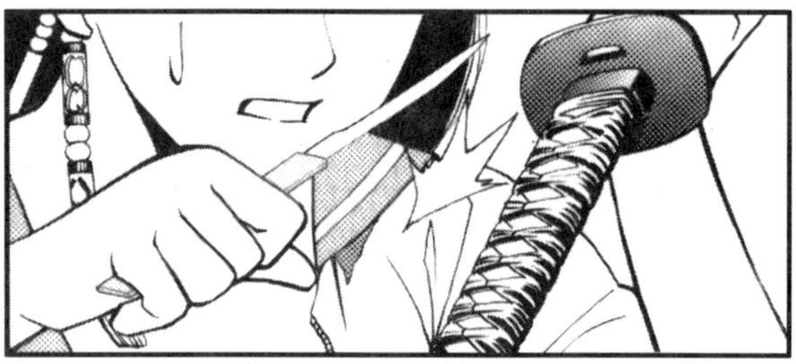

Mizuki pulls out a kozuka knife. Although it is stored inside the sword here, it is normally found hidden in the scabbard.

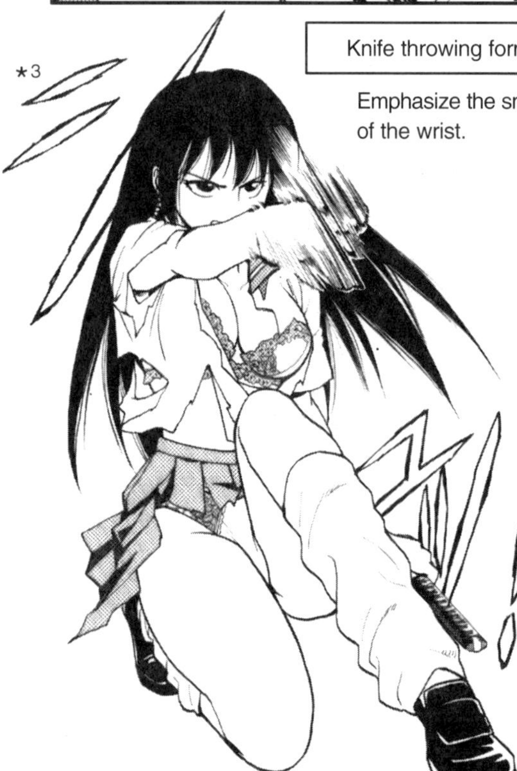

Knife throwing form

Emphasize the snapping of the wrist.

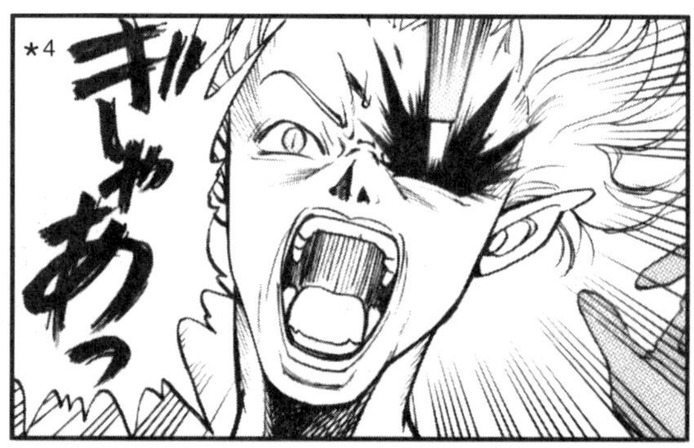

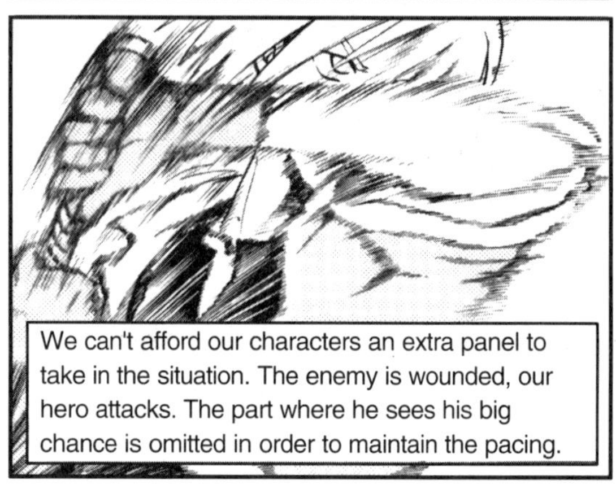

We can't afford our characters an extra panel to take in the situation. The enemy is wounded, our hero attacks. The part where he sees his big chance is omitted in order to maintain the pacing.

★1:Thawhip ★2:Sha-ching! ★3:Fwitt! ★4:Aaaaaargh!!!

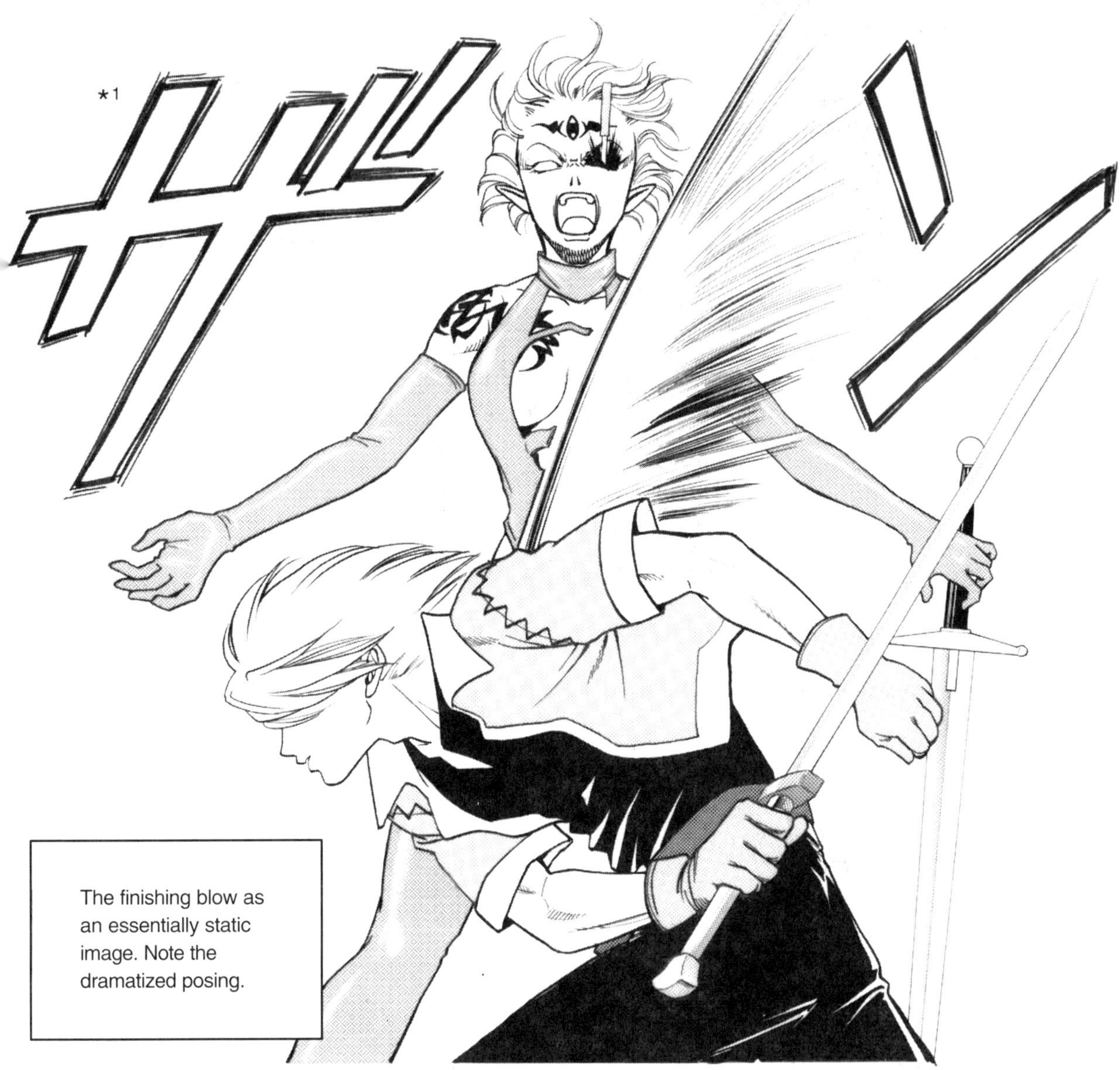

The finishing blow as an essentially static image. Note the dramatized posing.

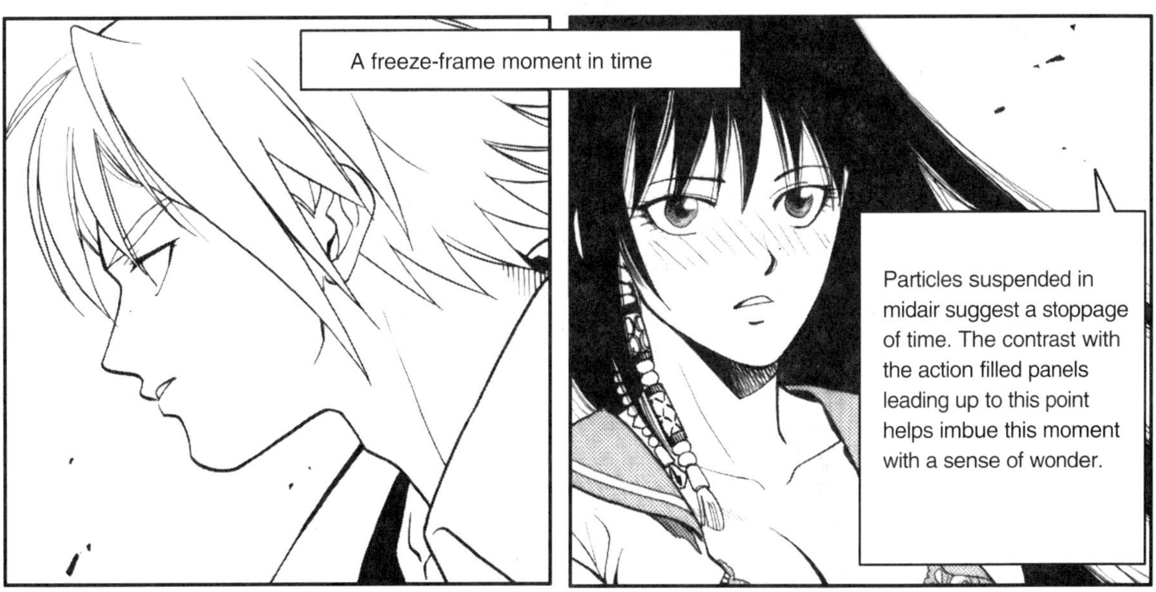

A freeze-frame moment in time

Particles suspended in midair suggest a stoppage of time. The contrast with the action filled panels leading up to this point helps imbue this moment with a sense of wonder.

★1: Shlikt!

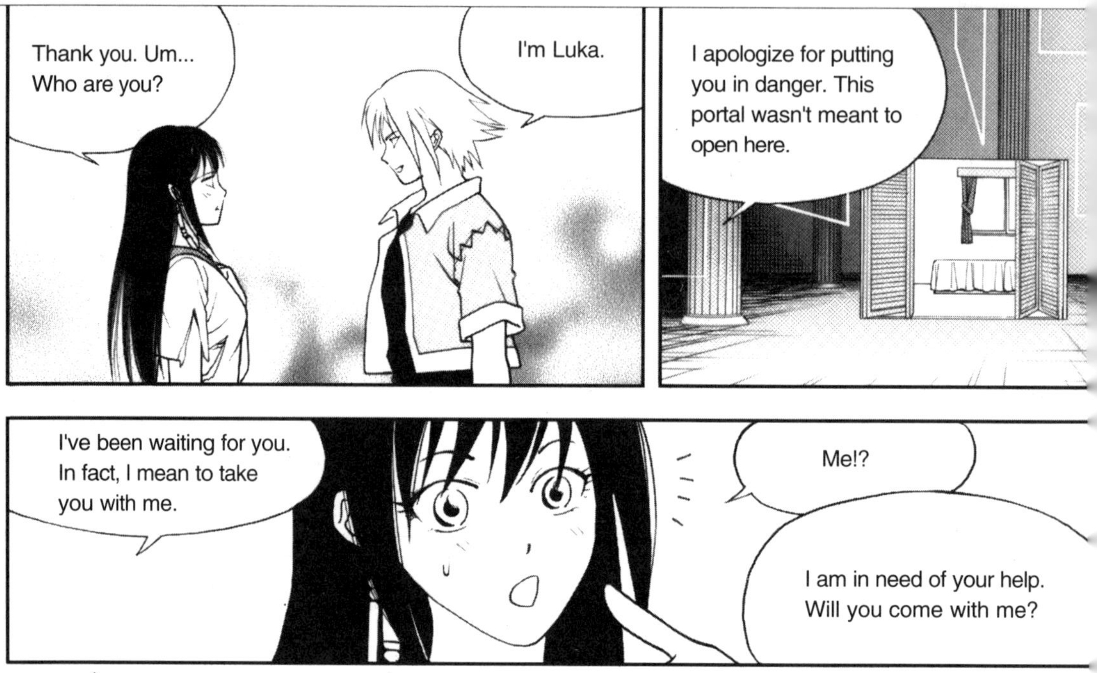

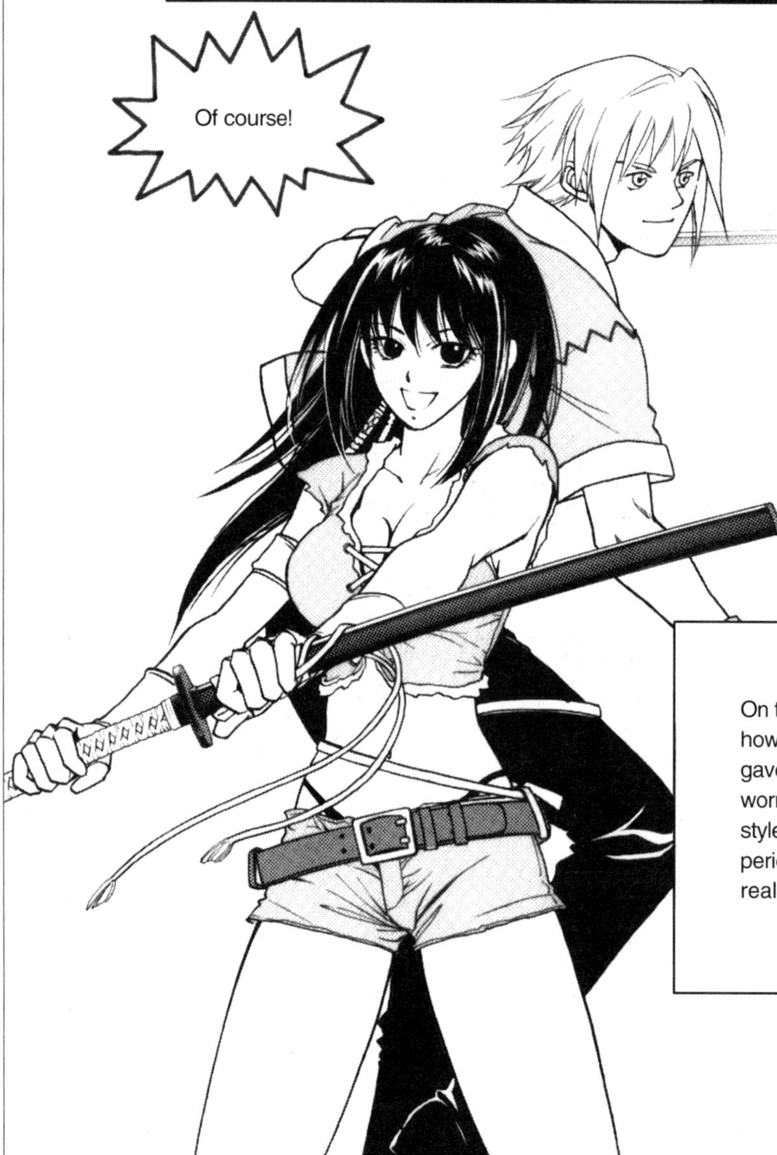

This is how our heroine sets off on her journey into another world. A number of recent manga series have featured characters that leave the everyday world to have adventures in some fantastic realm. In contrast, other manga characters are set inside an imaginary land from the beginning of the story. Although manga can sometimes be difficult to categorize, this genre is generally labeled "fantasy". Such manga often reveal the heavy influence of foreign novels and computer games.

On the preceding pages, we have taken a look at how to draw swordfights. Our imaginary setting gave us the freedom to draw stylistically without worrying too much about real swordfighting styles. Keep in mind however, that illustrating a period samurai manga calls for much more realism.

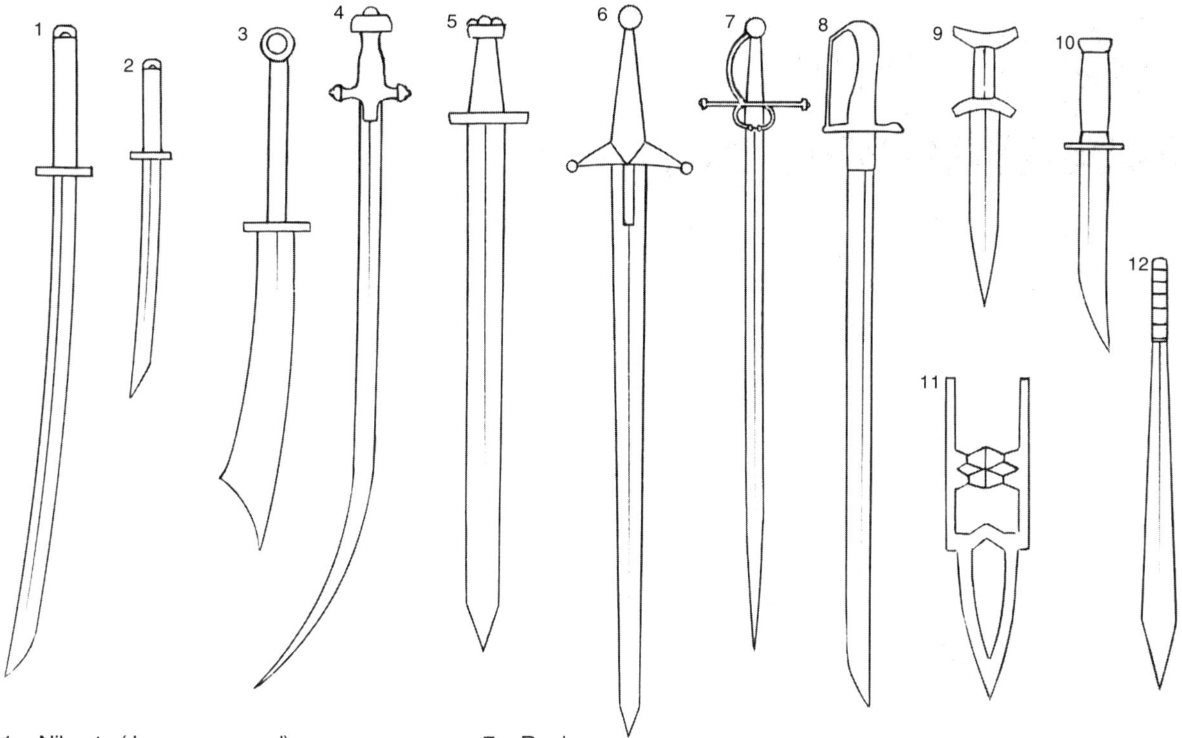

1 Nihonto (Japanese sword)
Two-handed, single-edged. A slightly shorter sword is the wakizashi.

2 Kogatana
Shorter than a wakizashi.

3 Chinese iron sword
Single-edged. A string was typically wound onto the circular section.

4 Talwar
Seventeenth century Indian saber. Curved blade.

5 Scandinavian iron sword
Ninth to tenth centuries. Double-edged.

6 Claymore
Mid-sixteenth century Scottish battle sword. Two-handed.

7 Rapier
Long blade is designed for stabbing. Mid-sixteenth century.

8 Saber
Commonly issued to armies around the world in the eighteenth century.

9 Baselard
Medieval European dagger. Commonly double edged and tapered to a point.

10 Knife
A typical post-World War II blade.

11 Katar
Ancient Indian knife. Can penetrate chain mail armor.

12 East African sword
Double-edged sword wielded by Masai warriors. Lacks a guard.

The blades listed here are but a few of the weapons in existence that can be classified as swords. Cultures around the world have developed swords over many millennia, and they manifest a wide array of forms and functions. To introduce them all would fill an entire volume.

At the least, it would be wise to research how a particular sword is used before incorporating it into a manga scene.

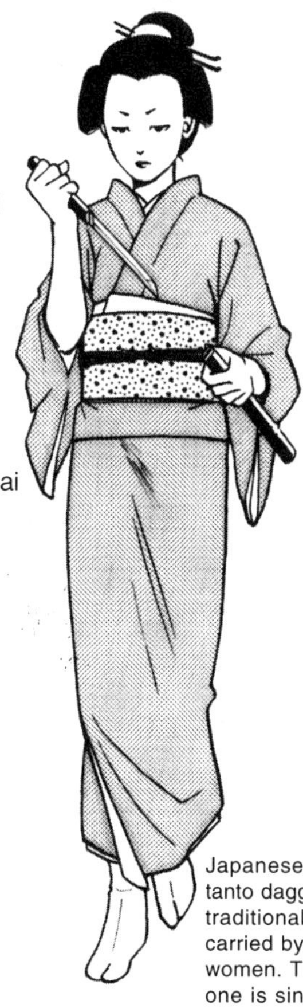

Japanese tanto dagger traditionally carried by women. This one is single edged, but double edged tanto are also common.

銃で戦う!
How to Draw a Gunfight!

Manga are increasingly featuring firearms–no doubt thanks to the influence of Hollywood action flicks. In this chapter, we'll have our characters demonstrate gunfights in various situations.

Handgun poses

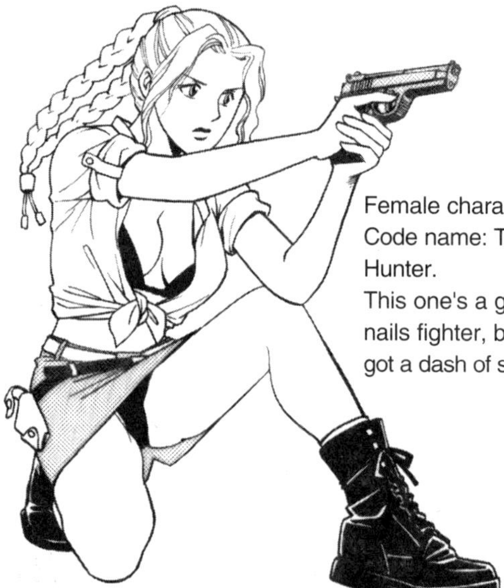

Female character
Code name: Treasure Hunter.
This one's a gritty, hard-as-nails fighter, but she's still got a dash of sex appeal.

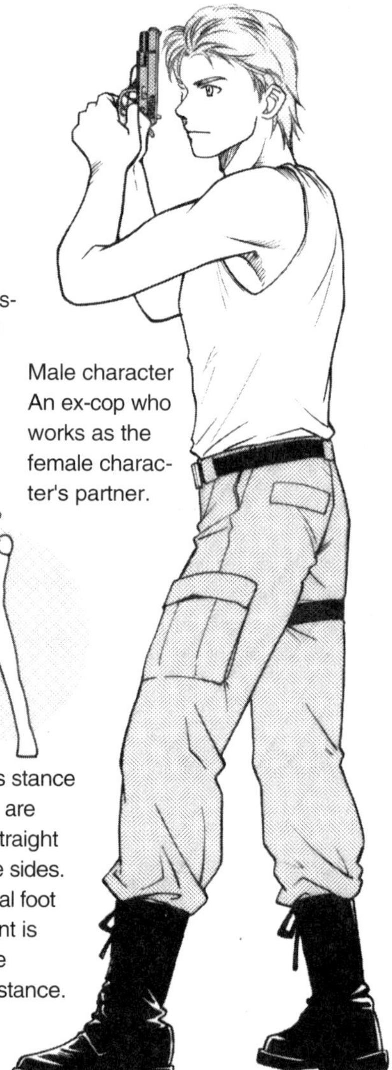

Male character
An ex-cop who works as the female character's partner.

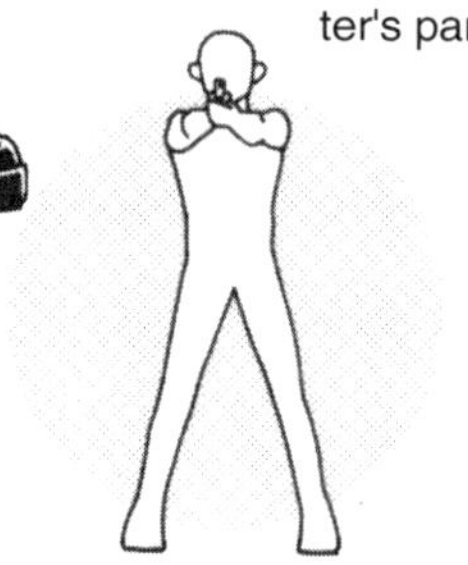

Isosceles stance
The legs are spread straight out to the sides. A diagonal foot placement is called the Weaver stance.

Poster pose
Similar to a Weaver stance

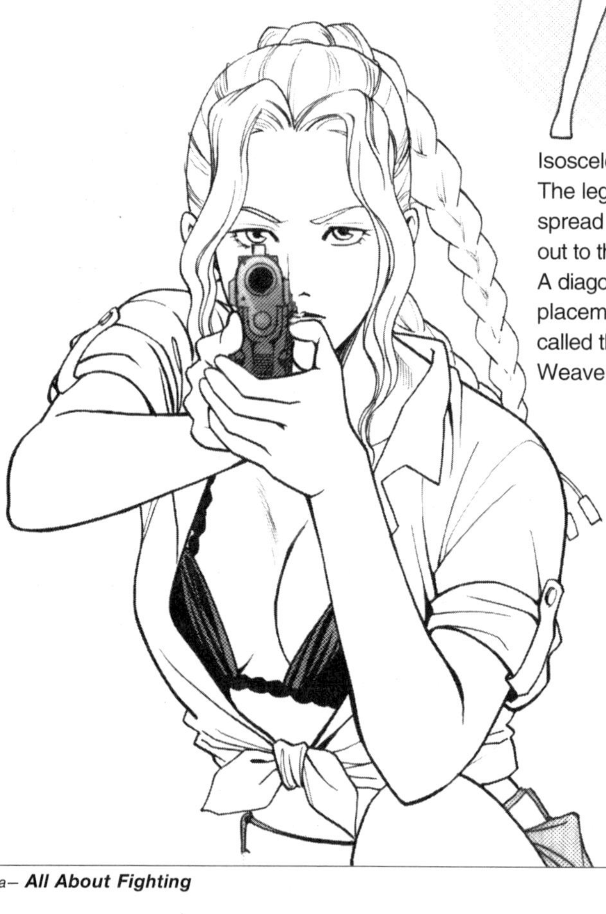

Kneeling position
(front view)

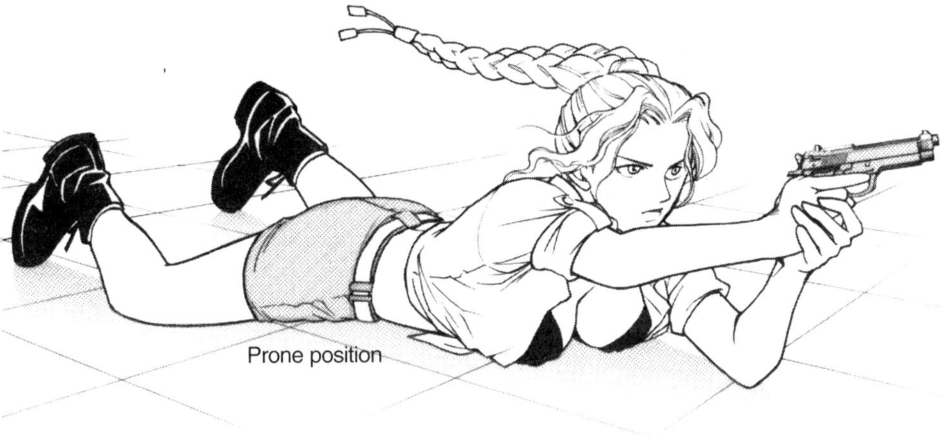

Prone position

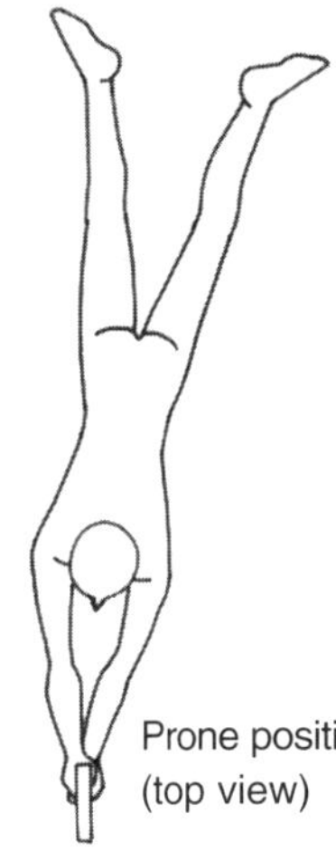

Prone position
(top view)

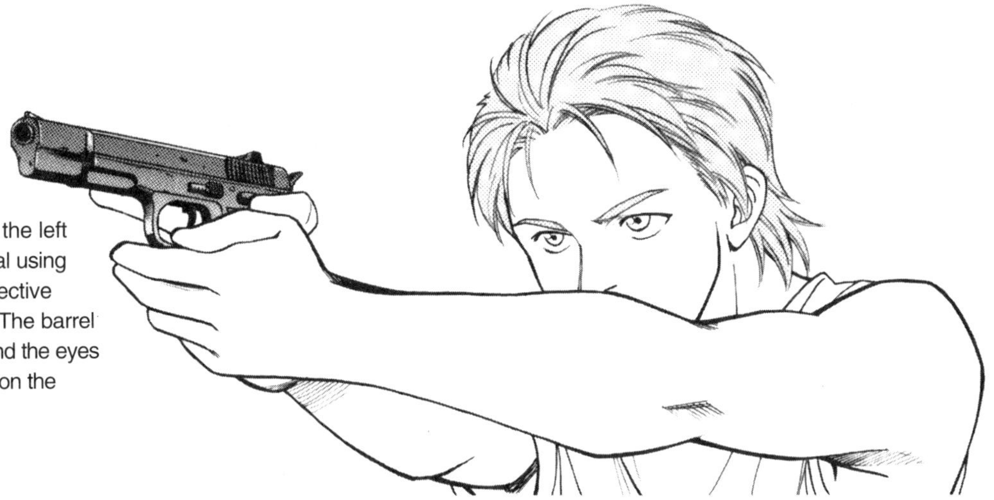

Drawn from the left front diagonal using some perspective techniques. The barrel of the gun and the eyes are focused on the same point.

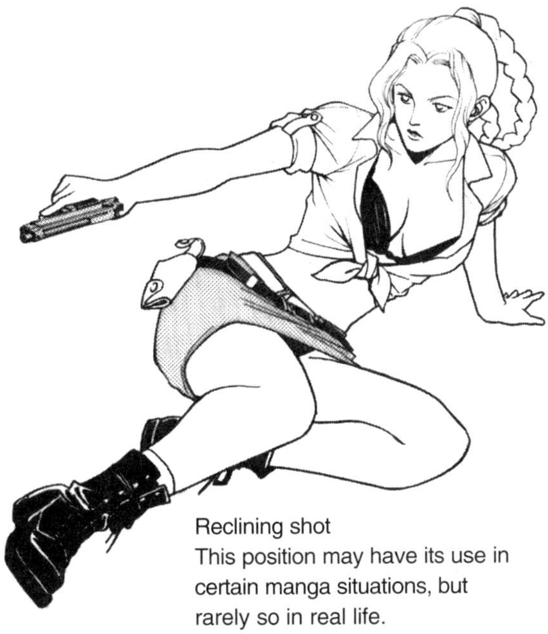

Reclining shot
This position may have its use in certain manga situations, but rarely so in real life.

So far, we've examined some authentic poses (save the drawing at left) that are actually used when firing handguns. Of course, different manga characters will have their own unique poses.

Movies and printed materials are helpful resources when it comes to drawing new poses, but don't forget that videogames these days also feature highly accurate representations of firearm combat (e.g. Biohazard, Tomb Rader, Metal Gear Solid series, etc.).

Drawing handgun action

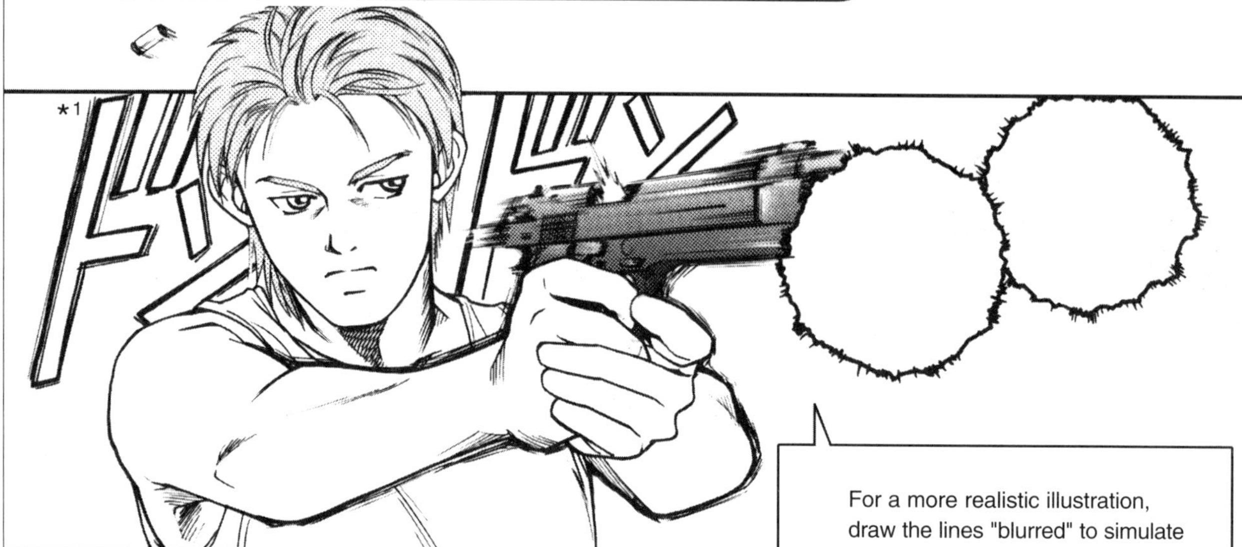

For a more realistic illustration, draw the lines "blurred" to simulate recoil.

Examples of gunfire

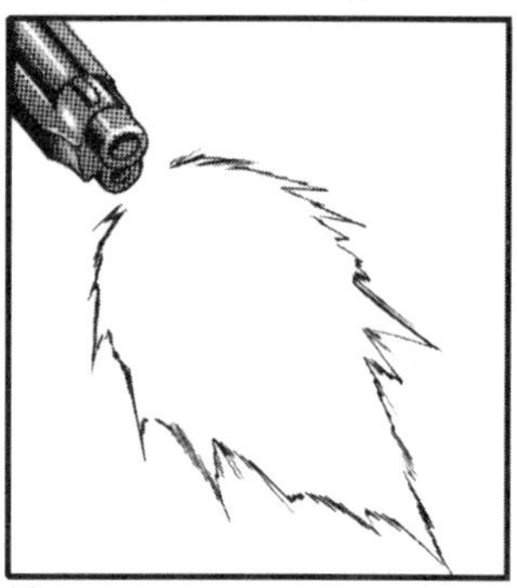

Line

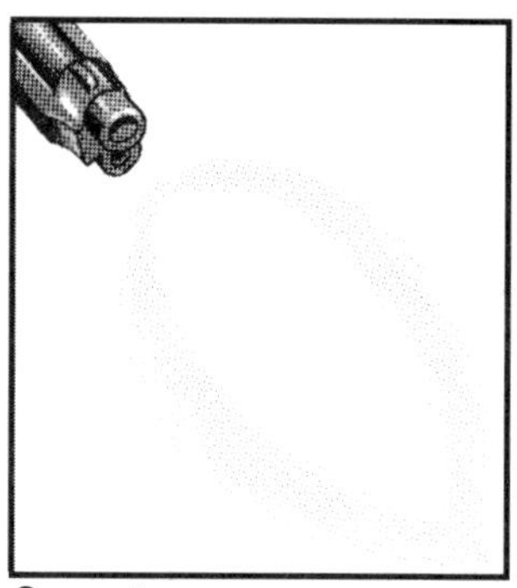

Screen tone

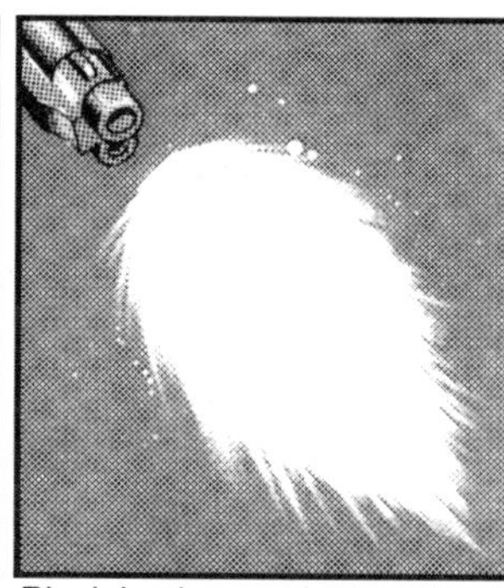

Black background

Illustrators have their own favorite ways of drawing gunfire. Another method is to draw only the smoke curling up from the barrel.

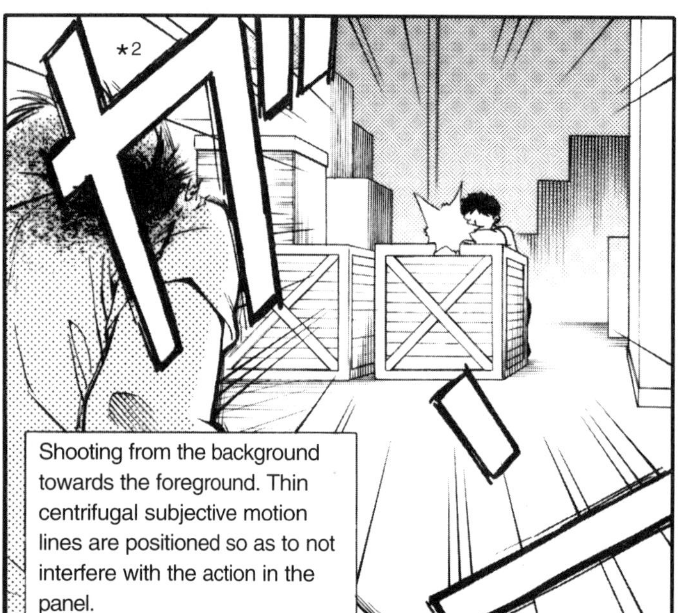

Shooting from the background towards the foreground. Thin centrifugal subjective motion lines are positioned so as to not interfere with the action in the panel.

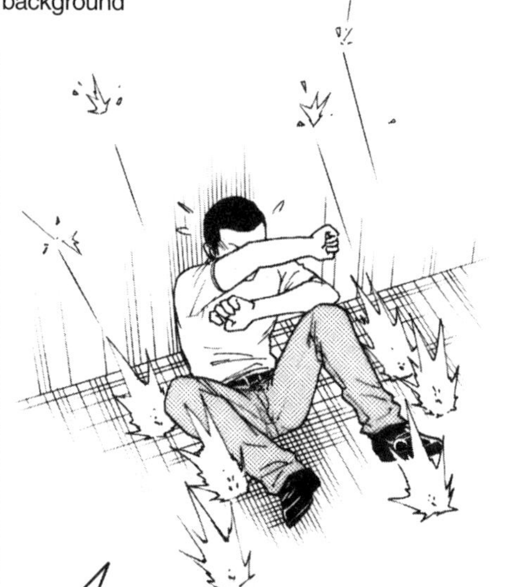

Cowering against a wall amidst a spray of warning shots. Include flying debris and ricocheting bullets for an added sense of realism.

★1:Blam! Blam! ★2:Bang!

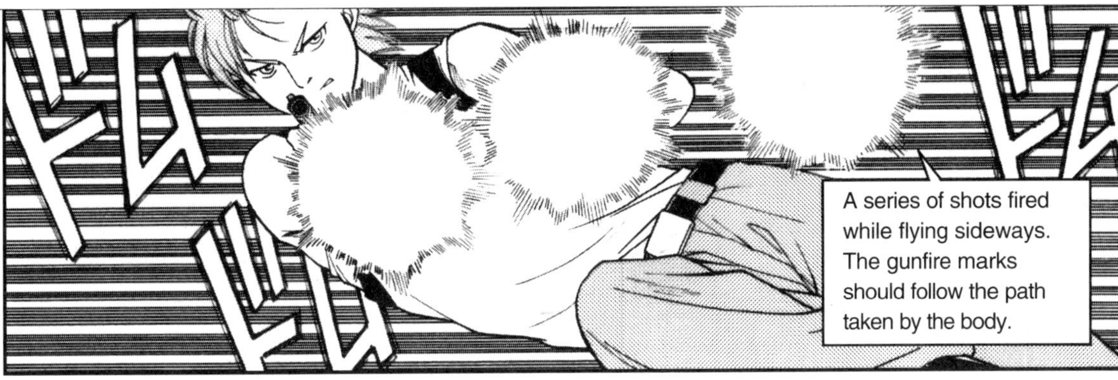

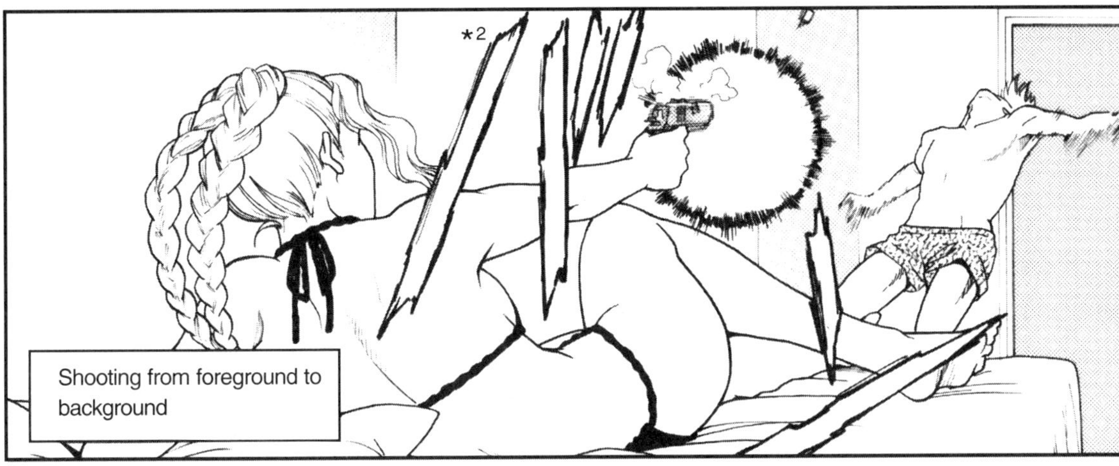

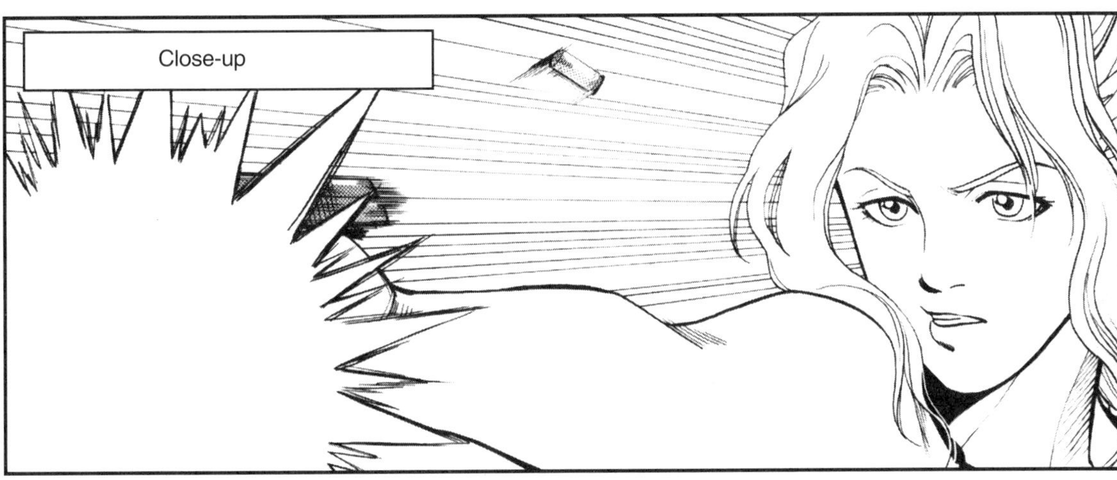

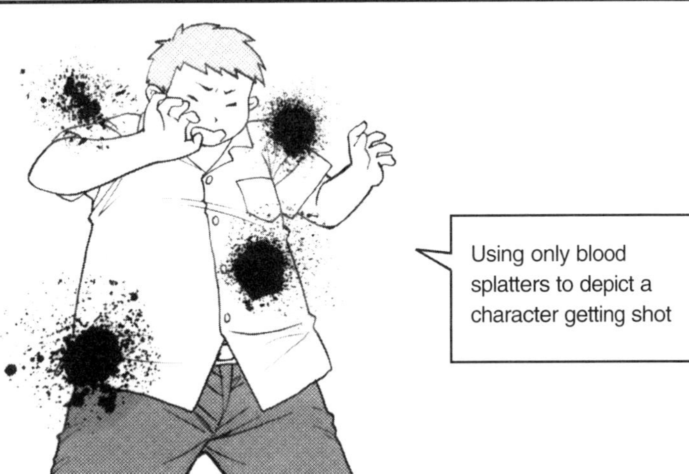

★1:Foomp Foomp Foomp ★2:Bam!

Submachine gun poses

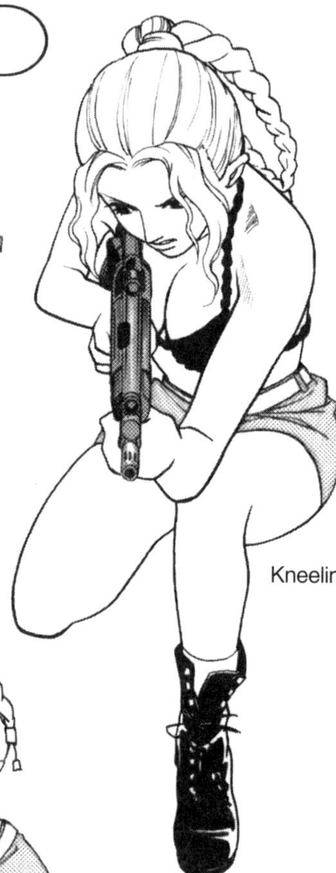

Kneeling position

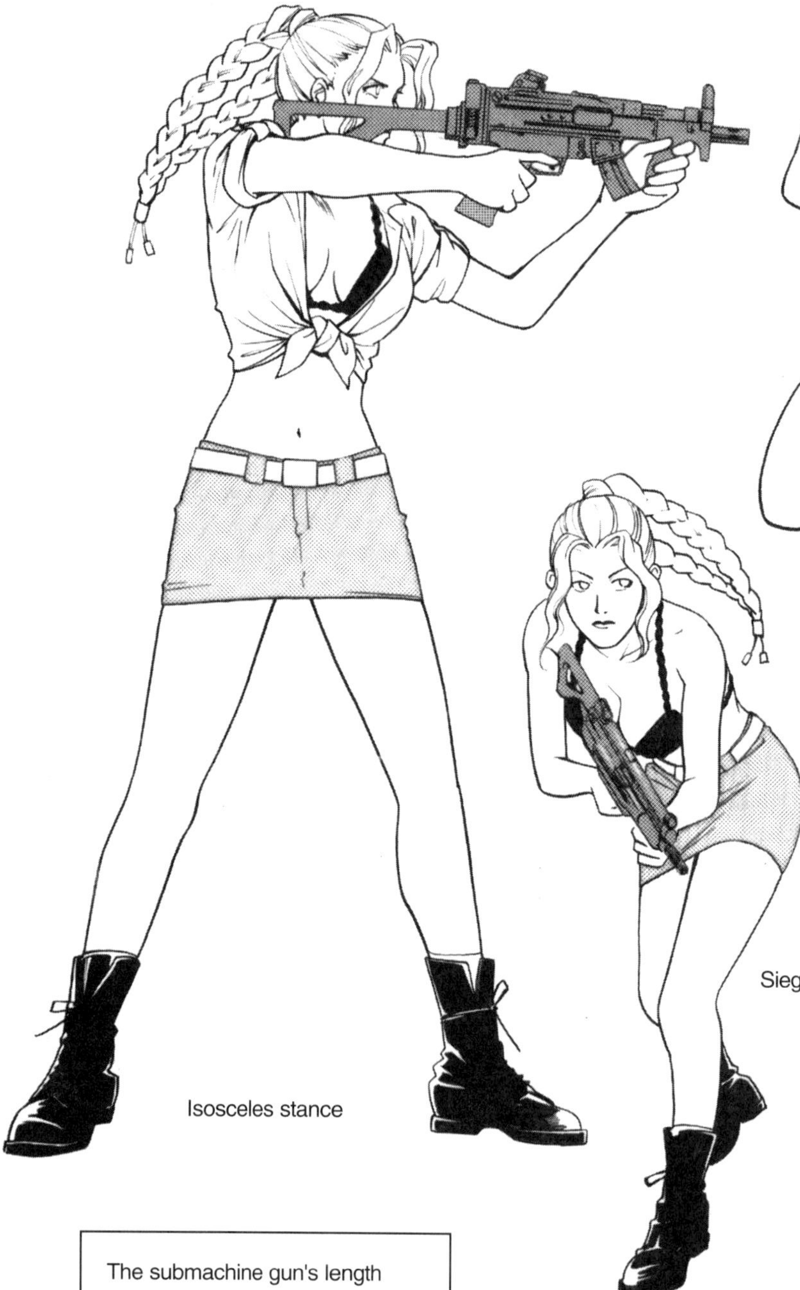

Isosceles stance

Siege stance

The submachine gun's length requires a compact firing stance.

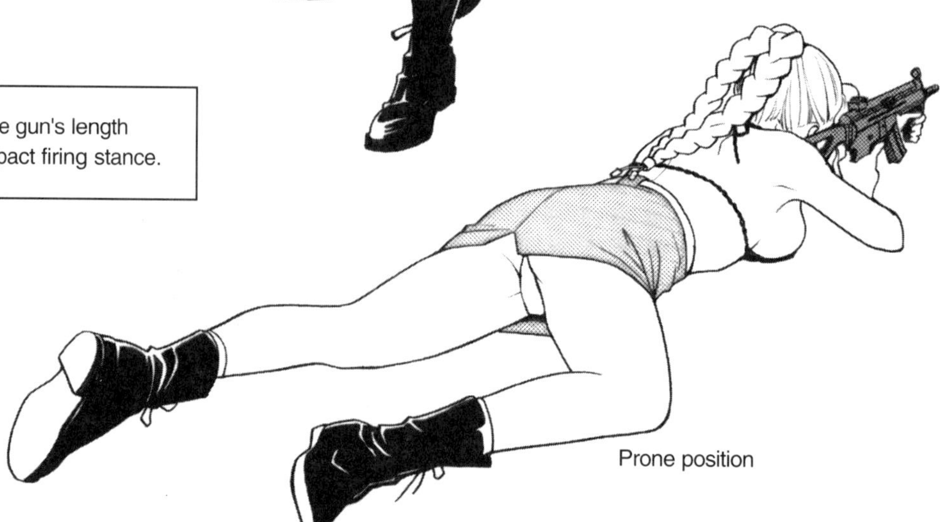

Prone position

A submachine gun gets its name from its ability to use regular handgun ammo. It is also known as a machine pistol and a machine carbine.

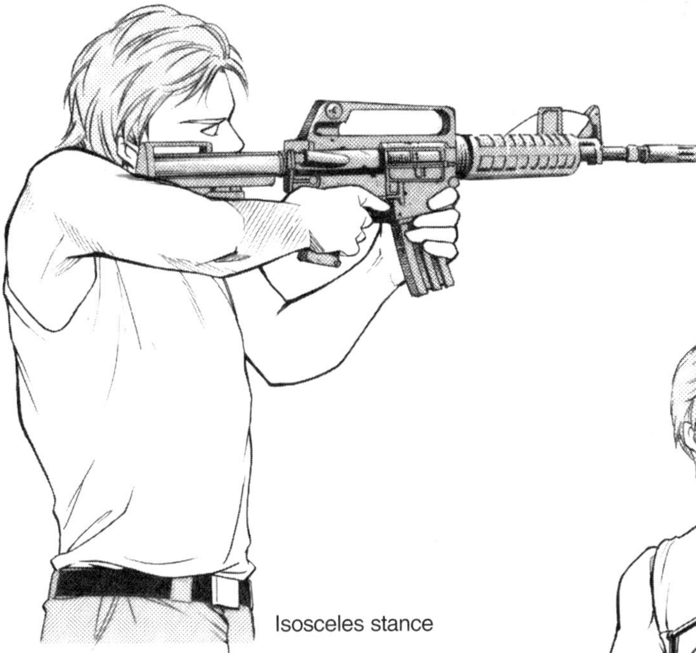

Isosceles stance

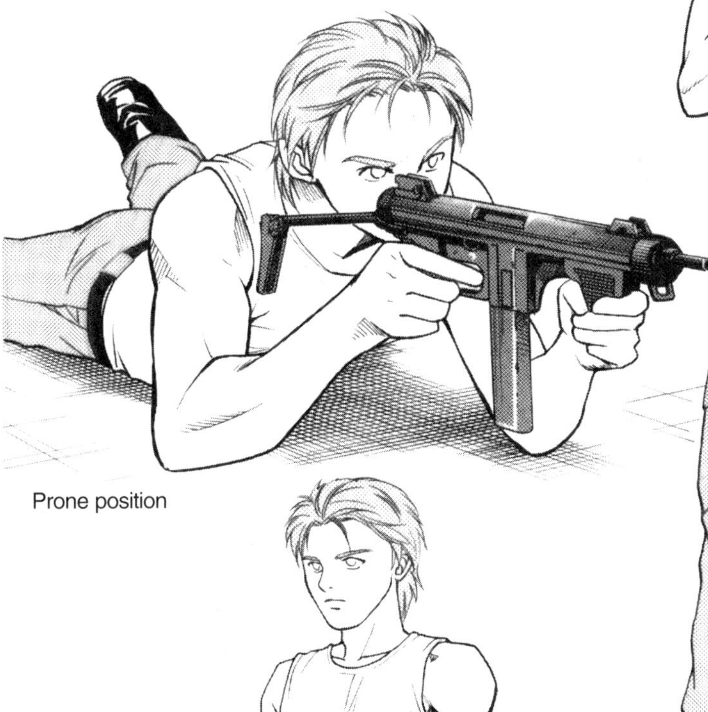

Prone position

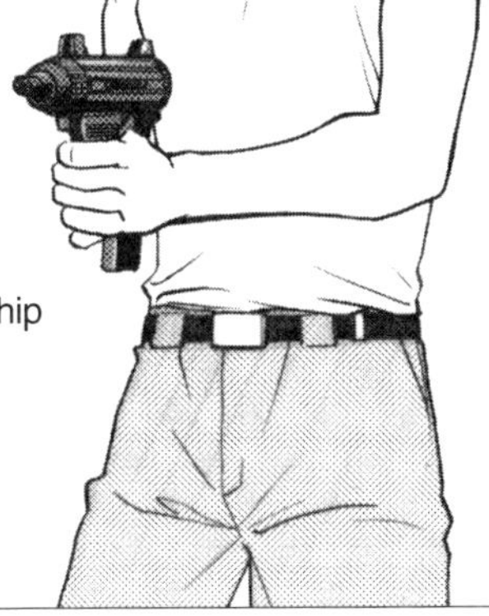

From the hip

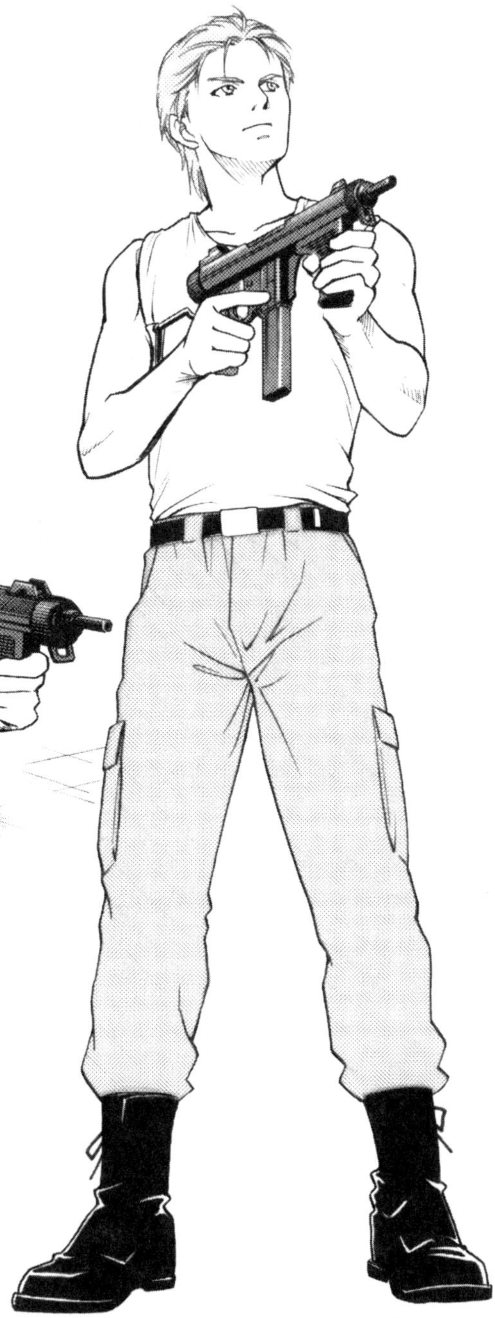

Isosceles stance

Drawing submachine gun action

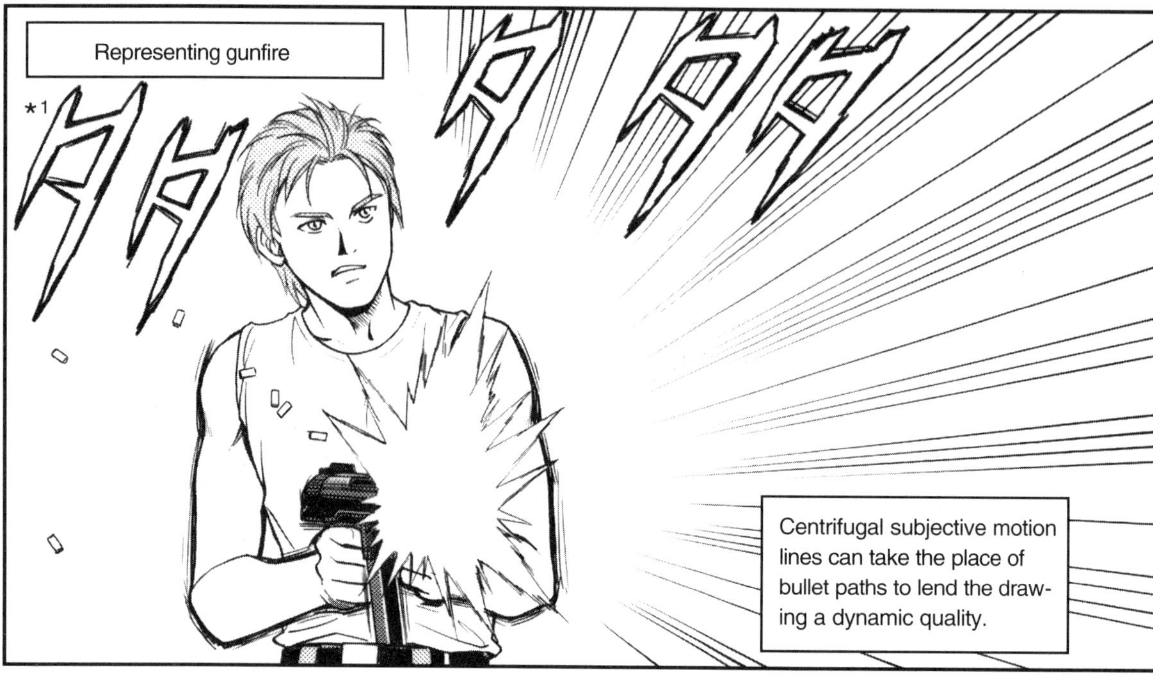

Representing gunfire

Centrifugal subjective motion lines can take the place of bullet paths to lend the drawing a dynamic quality.

The number of bullets released at full automatic is astoundingly fast (6 - 20 shots per second, depending on the firearm). As one might expect, manga action scenes typically include multiple gunshots within one panel.

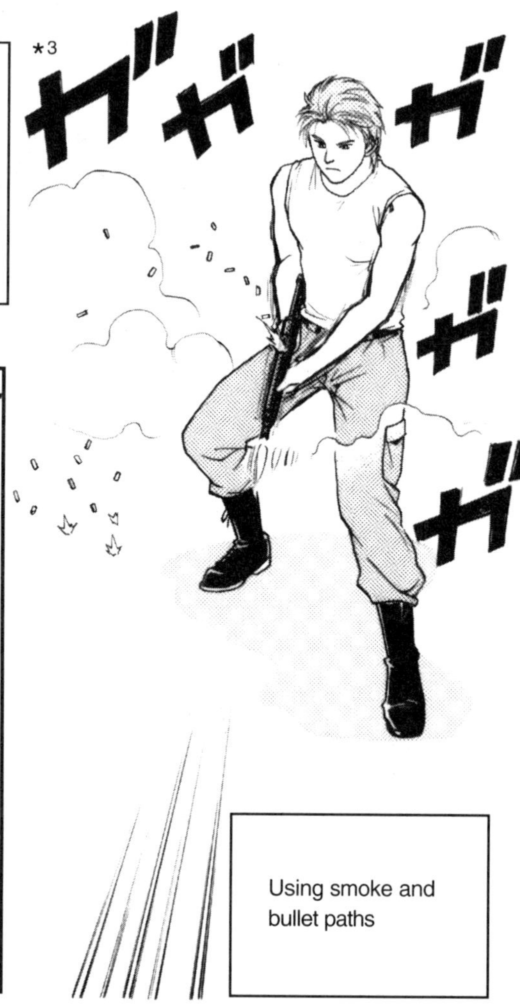

Using smoke and bullet paths

Drawing a character getting shot

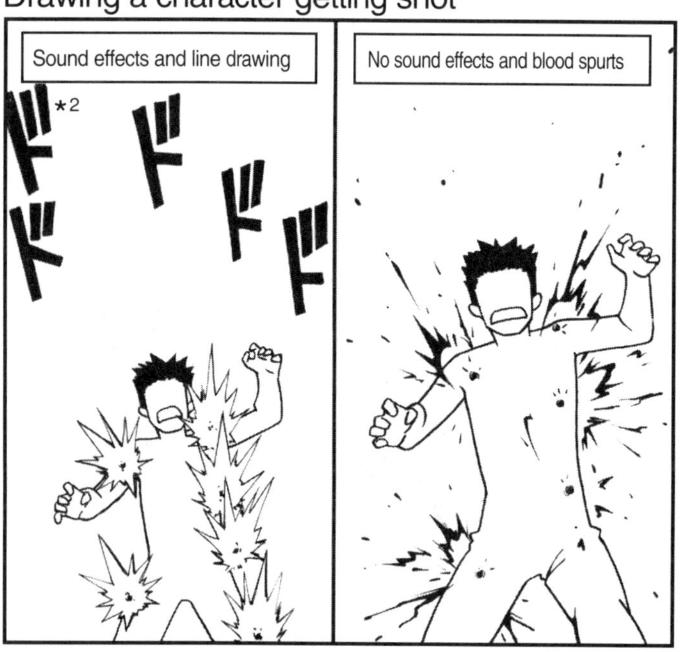

Sound effects and line drawing

No sound effects and blood spurts

*1:Rat-a tat tat tat tat *2:da,da,da,da

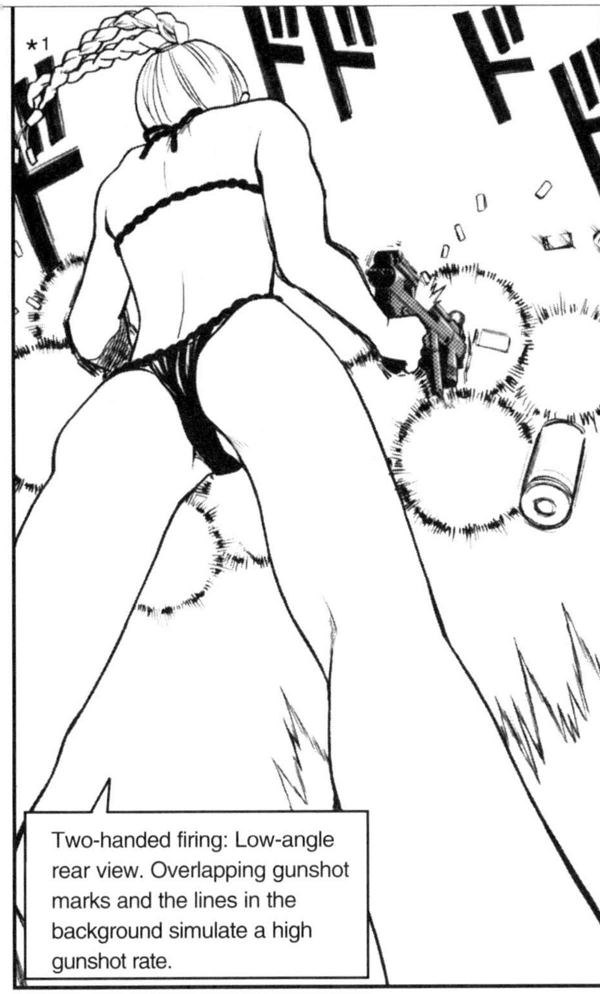

Two-handed firing: Low-angle rear view. Overlapping gunshot marks and the lines in the background simulate a high gunshot rate.

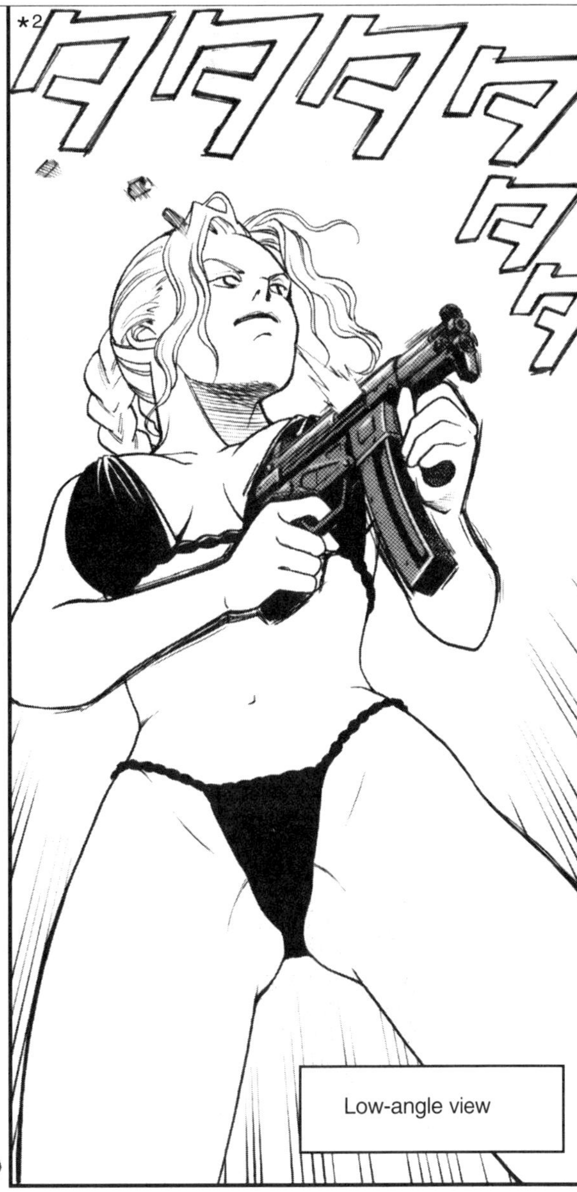

Low-angle view

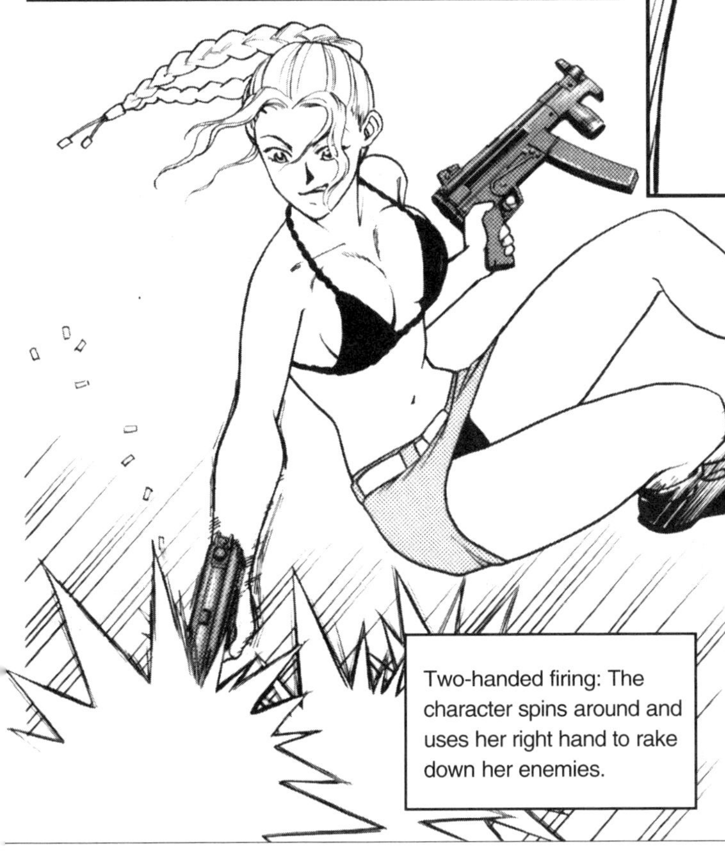

Two-handed firing: The character spins around and uses her right hand to rake down her enemies.

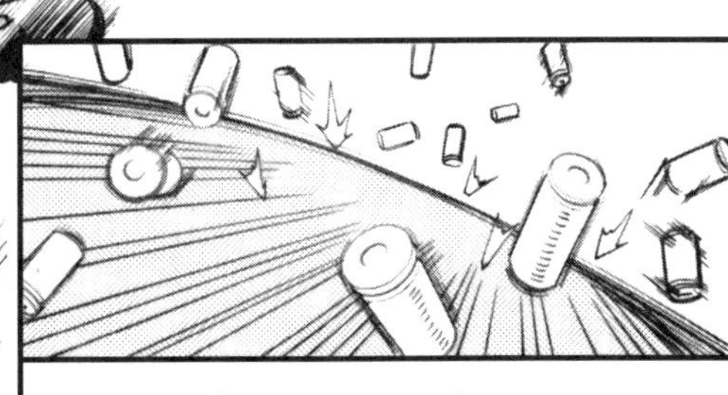

Spent shells may be drawn according to personal preference.

★1:Brrapapapapapa ★2:Rakatakatak

Machine gun and rifle action

Various firing poses

Machine gun

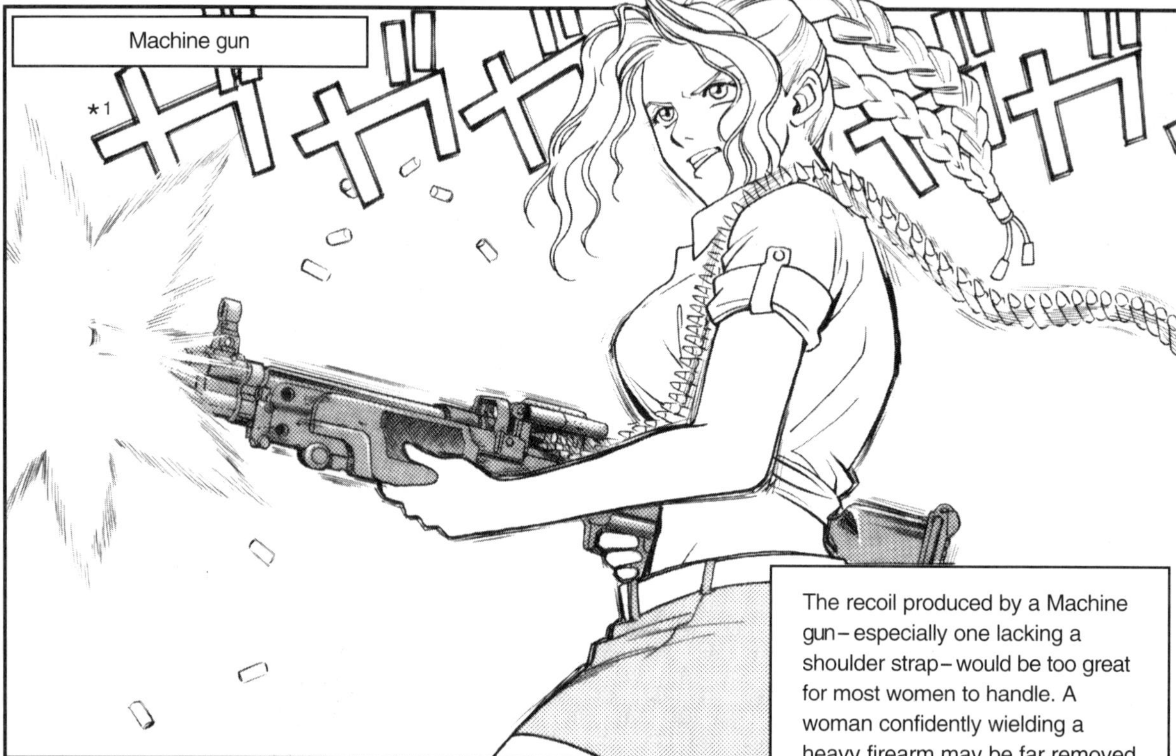

The recoil produced by a Machine gun–especially one lacking a shoulder strap–would be too great for most women to handle. A woman confidently wielding a heavy firearm may be far removed from reality, but perhaps for this very reason, many manga fans are captivated by this kind of character.

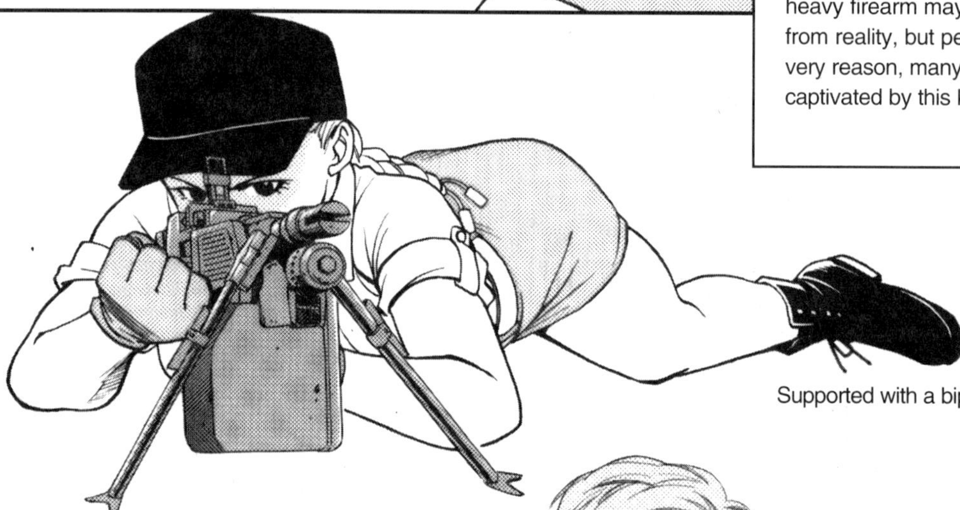

Supported with a bipod

Assault rifle

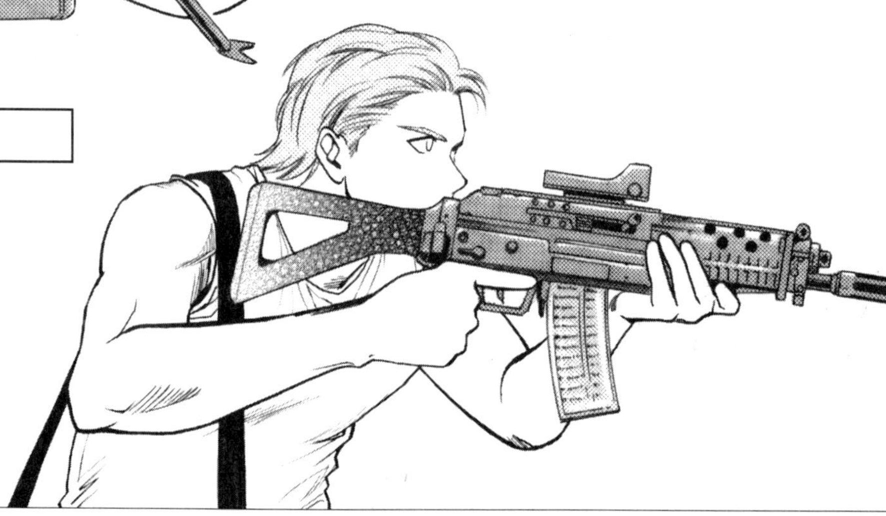

★1:Gakka gak gak gak gak

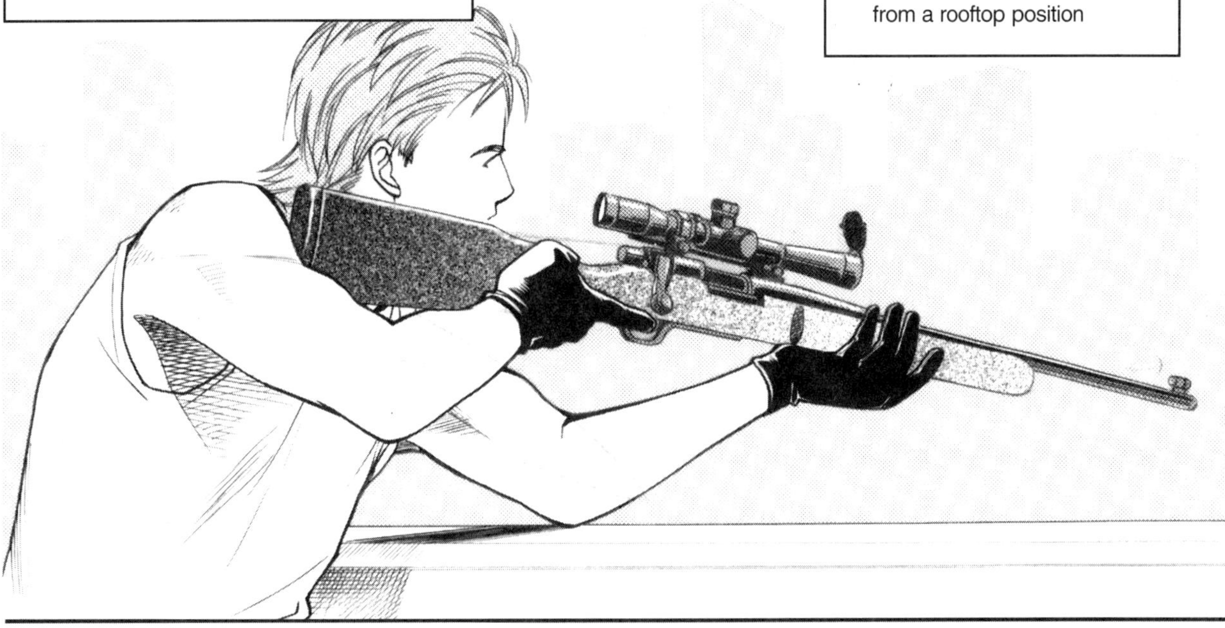

Sniper rifle

Drawing a bead on a target from a rooftop position

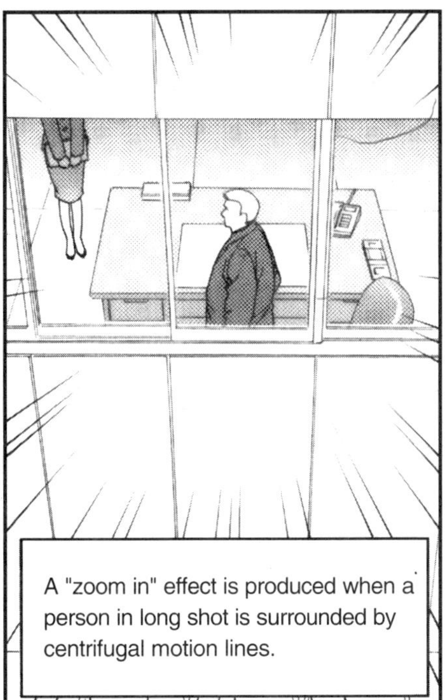

A "zoom in" effect is produced when a person in long shot is surrounded by centrifugal motion lines.

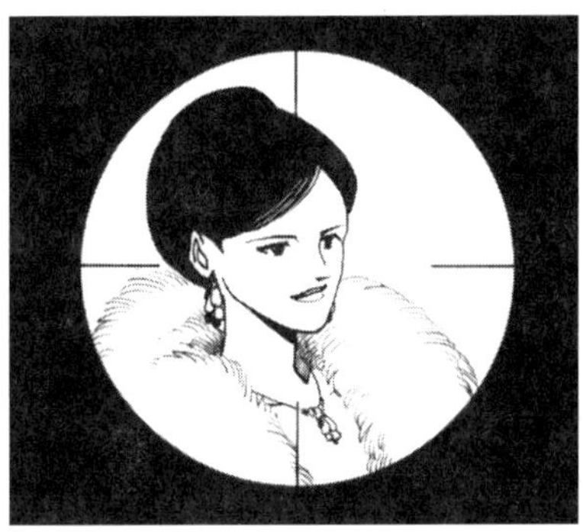

The "scope view" is often seen in movies and television programs. Without ever showing the rifle itself, this view alone can signify a sniper at work.

Types of shoulder weapons
Rifle: a firearm that does not take handgun ammo
Assault rifle: a rifle that can be fired on full automatic
Carbine: a short-barreled rifle
Shotgun: fires shells full of small lead pellets (shot)
The submachine gun is also classified as a shoulder weapon.

The countless gun designs in existence today are the product of their nearly 600-year history. That's why it's essential to conduct some background research before incorporating them into your manga–especially if your storyline includes a lot of gun action. Since the possession of firearms is illegal in Japan, many artists resort to studying model guns. Movies can provide plenty of ideas for action scenes. Some artists go so far as to study foreign military footage to give their manga that extra edge of authenticity. Whatever your method, you have to do your research if you want to draw great looking gun action.

様々な武器で戦う

How to Draw Action Scenes Using Other Weapons!

We'll close chapter two with a look at a few action scenes that incorporate some weapons we haven't seen yet. The characters here are nameless, generic denizens of the manga world.

Bow and arrow

Drawing an arrow from the quiver

★1

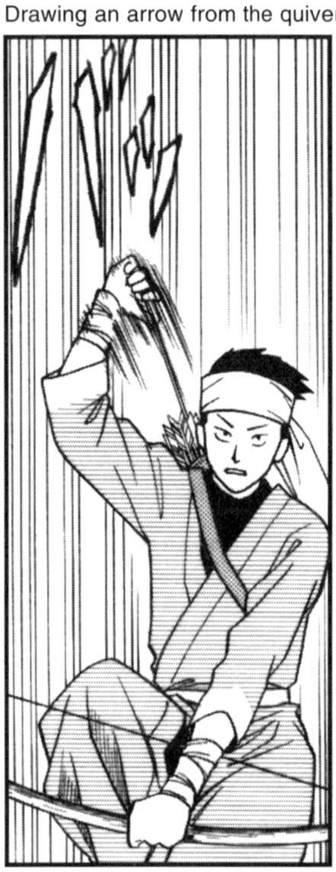

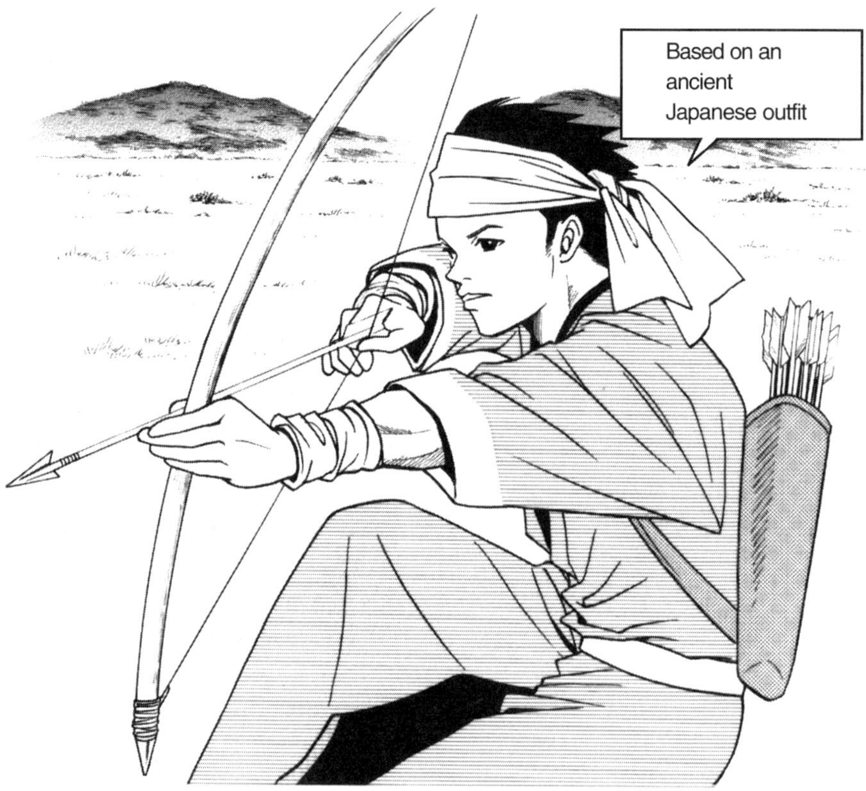

Notching an arrow to the bowstring

Discharging an arrow

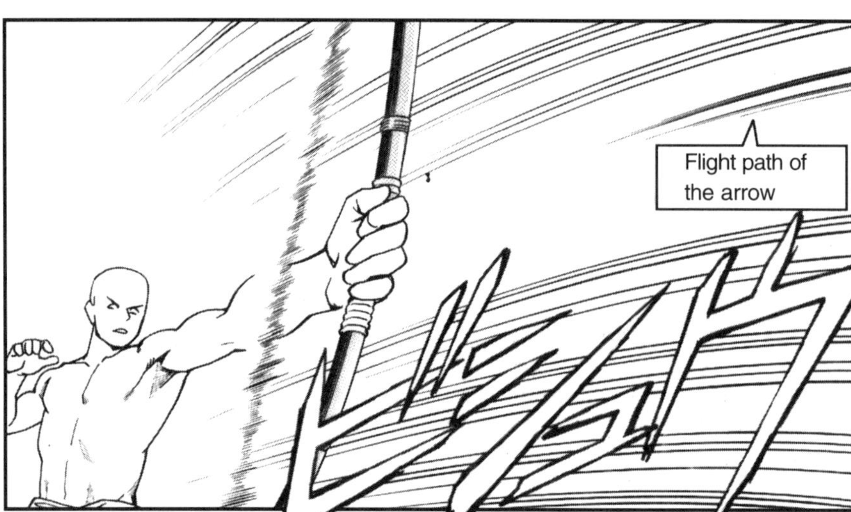

★2

This weapon's simple firing mechanism is comprised of just three parts: bow, bowstring and arrow. Despite its simplicity, its range and accuracy are excellent. The bow itself takes on many different shapes and sizes.

★1:Ffft ★2:Pyoosh

Yari (spear)

The yari is basically a long pole tipped by a thin spearhead. It is a versatile weapon that can be used for slashing, thrusting and throwing. Throughout history, people around the world have used various types of spears in combat.

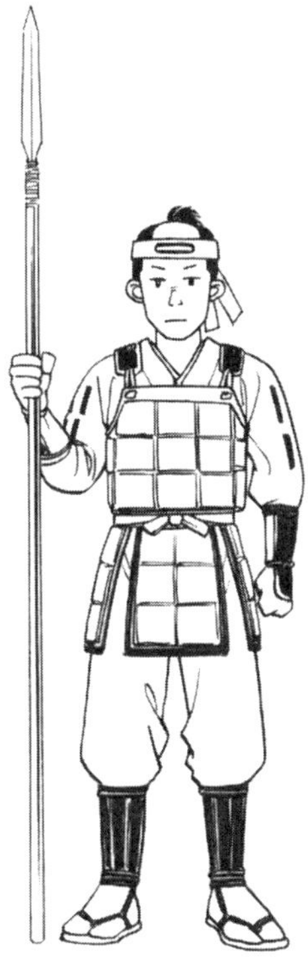

A spear-wielding Japanese foot soldier

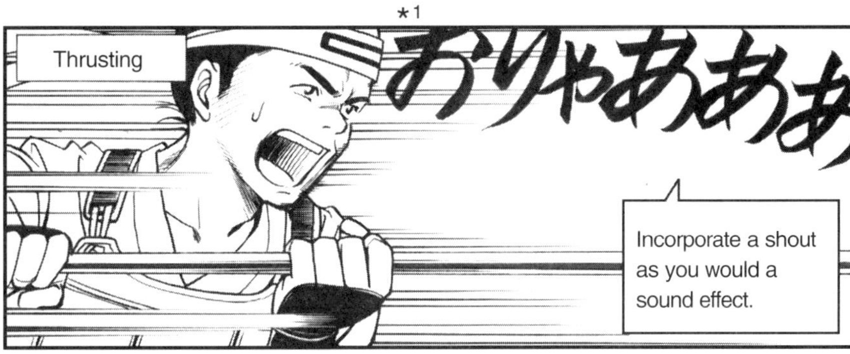

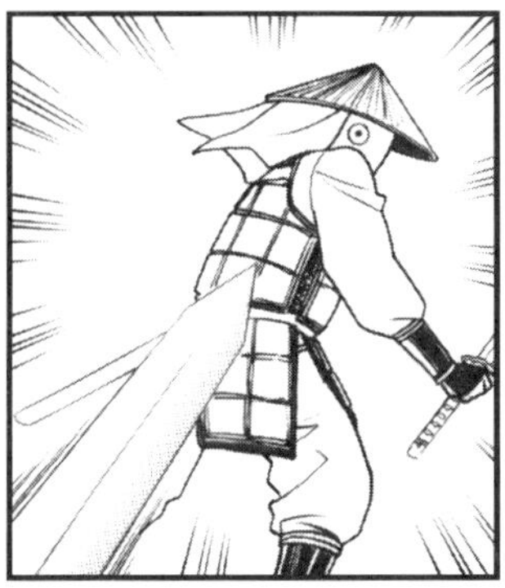

Naginata (glaive)

The naginata is a polearm weapon similar to the yari, except that it is tipped with a blade rather than a spearhead. It was traditionally the weapon of choice for women in samurai families.

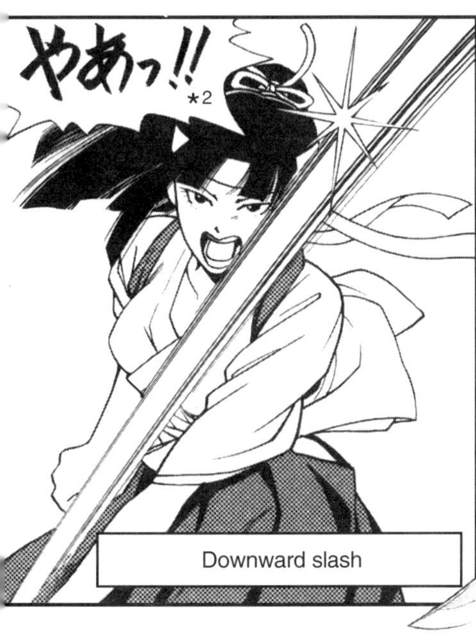

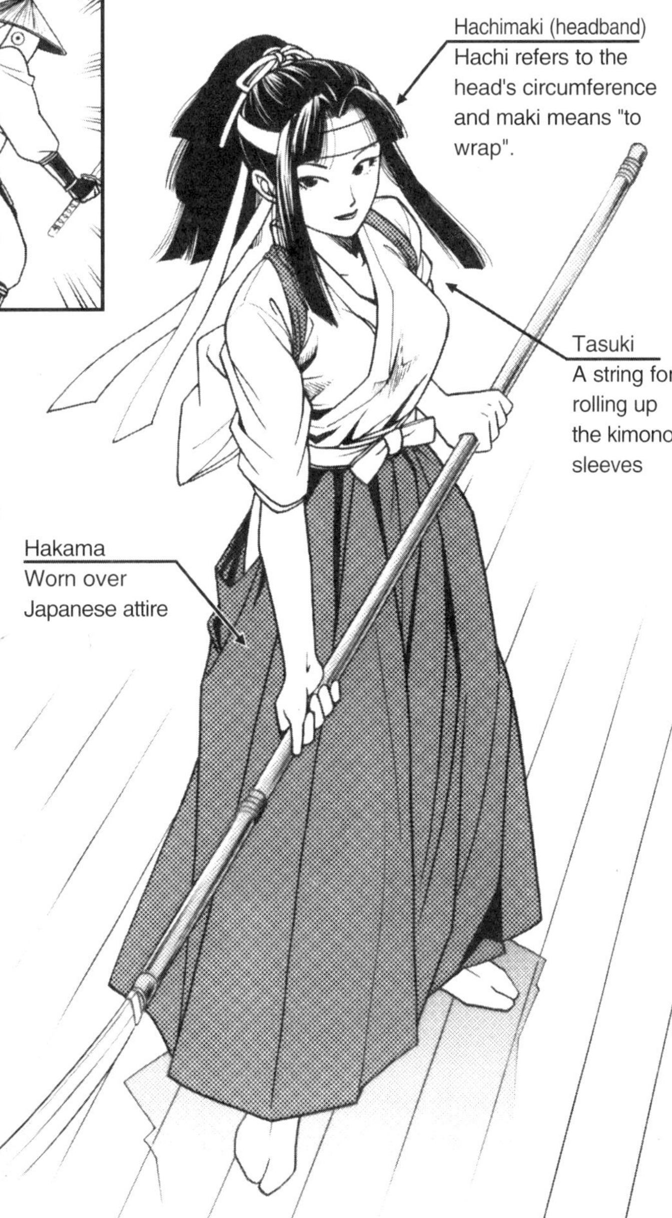

★1:Aryaaaa! ★2:Ya!!

Ninja action

Ninja organizations proliferated during Japan's Sengoku or "warring-states" period. We know that they spied on their enemies and conducted covert intelligence-gathering operations, but the true face of the ninja profession still remains enshrouded in mystery. Interestingly, there were several regional schools of ninjutsu, the most famous being the Iga-ryu and Koga-ryu. The ninja's mythical shadow-dweller image has stirred the imaginations of a great many writers over the years, and today, he frequently appears in the mass media.

The ninja's outfit and gear

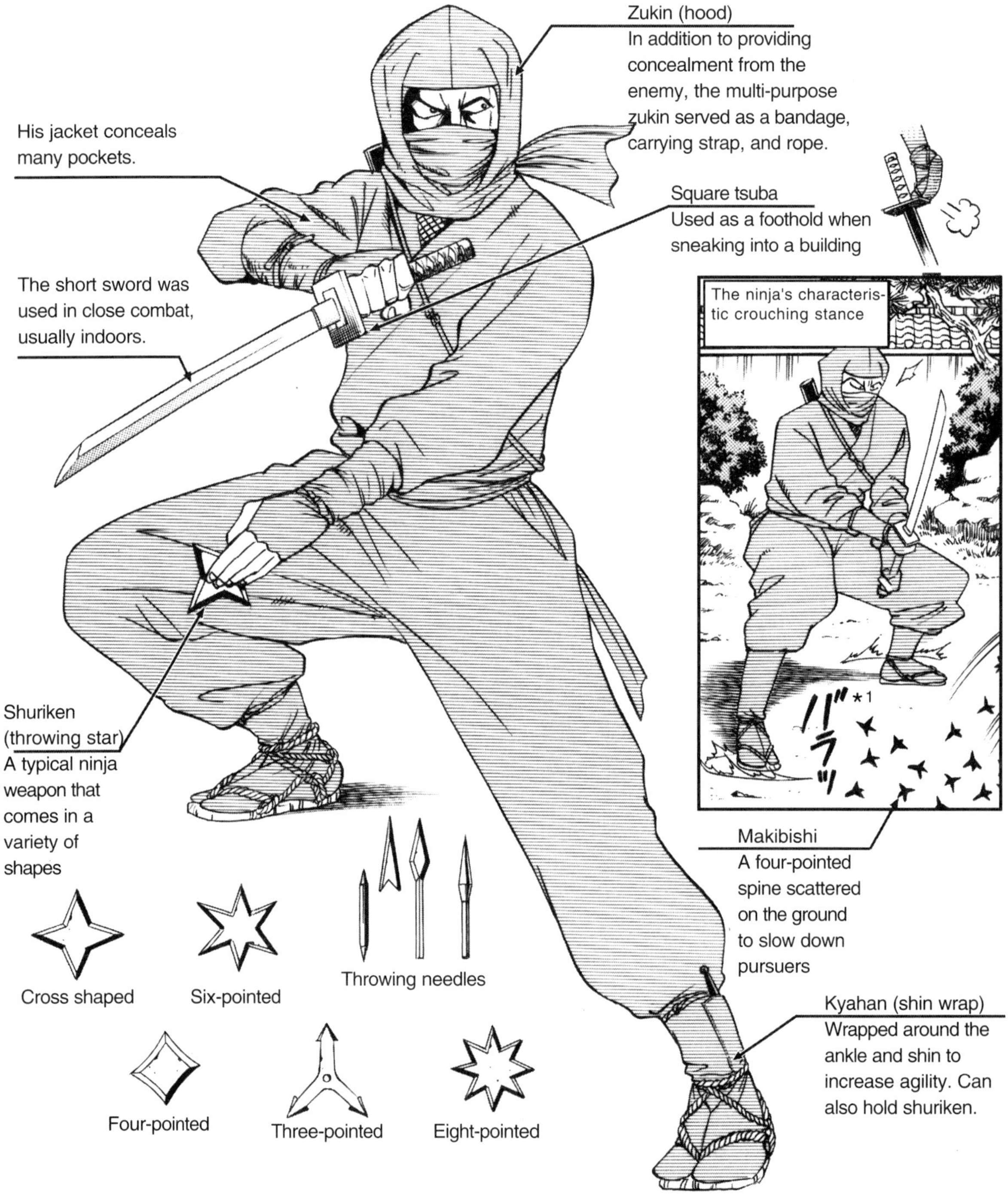

★1:Clakaka

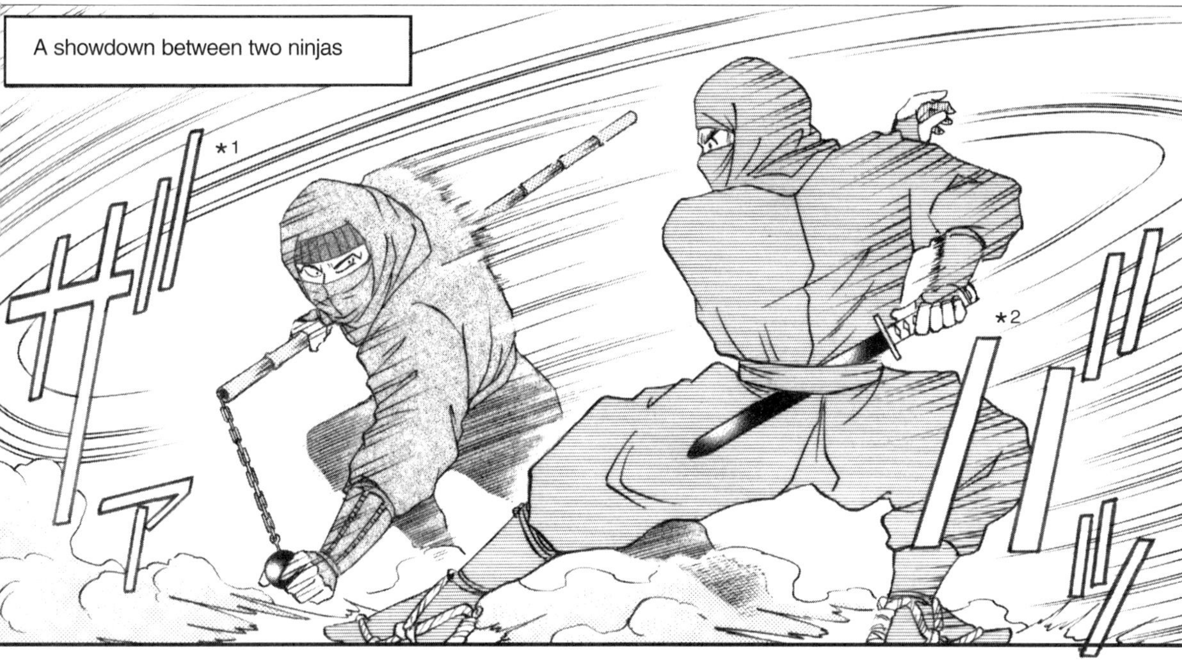

A showdown between two ninjas

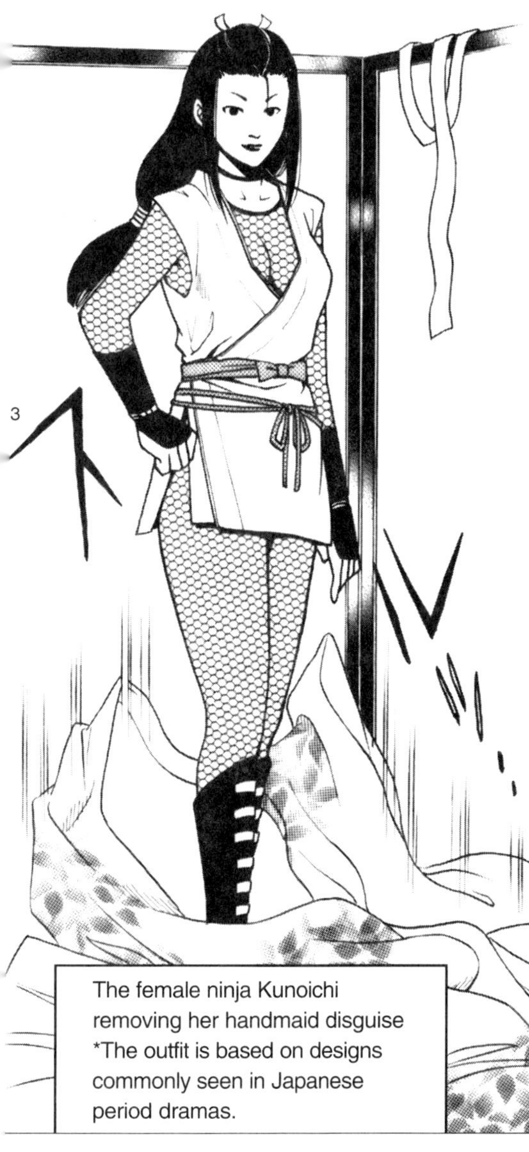

The female ninja Kunoichi removing her handmaid disguise
*The outfit is based on designs commonly seen in Japanese period dramas.

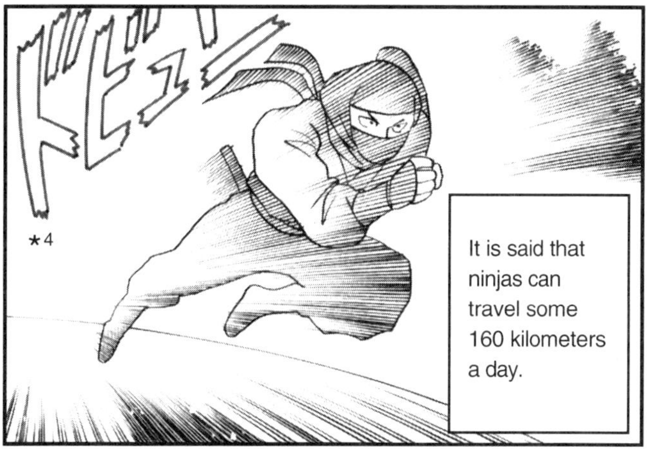

It is said that ninjas can travel some 160 kilometers a day.

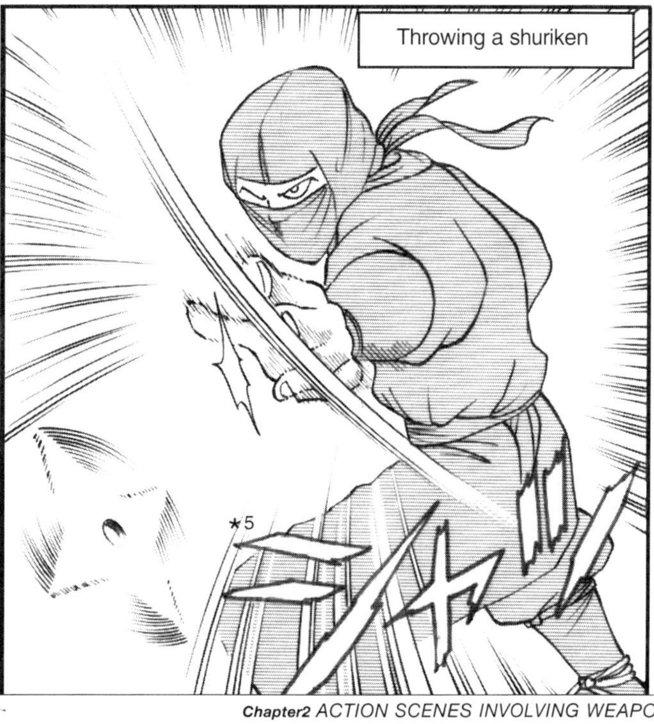

Throwing a shuriken

★1:Skrrsh ★2:Fkkrt ★3:Flutter ★4:Pfoosh ★5:Flifft

SF

SCIENCE FICTION & FANTASY

Thanks to the influence of video games, fantasy manga are enjoying a veritable renaissance in Japan today. The Japanese tend to lump together fantasy and science fiction into one category, but they are actually two distinct genres. The celebrated SF author Arthur C. Clarke defined the genres in this way: "Science Fiction is something that could happen – but usually you wouldn't want it to. Fantasy is something that couldn't happen – though often you only wish it could."

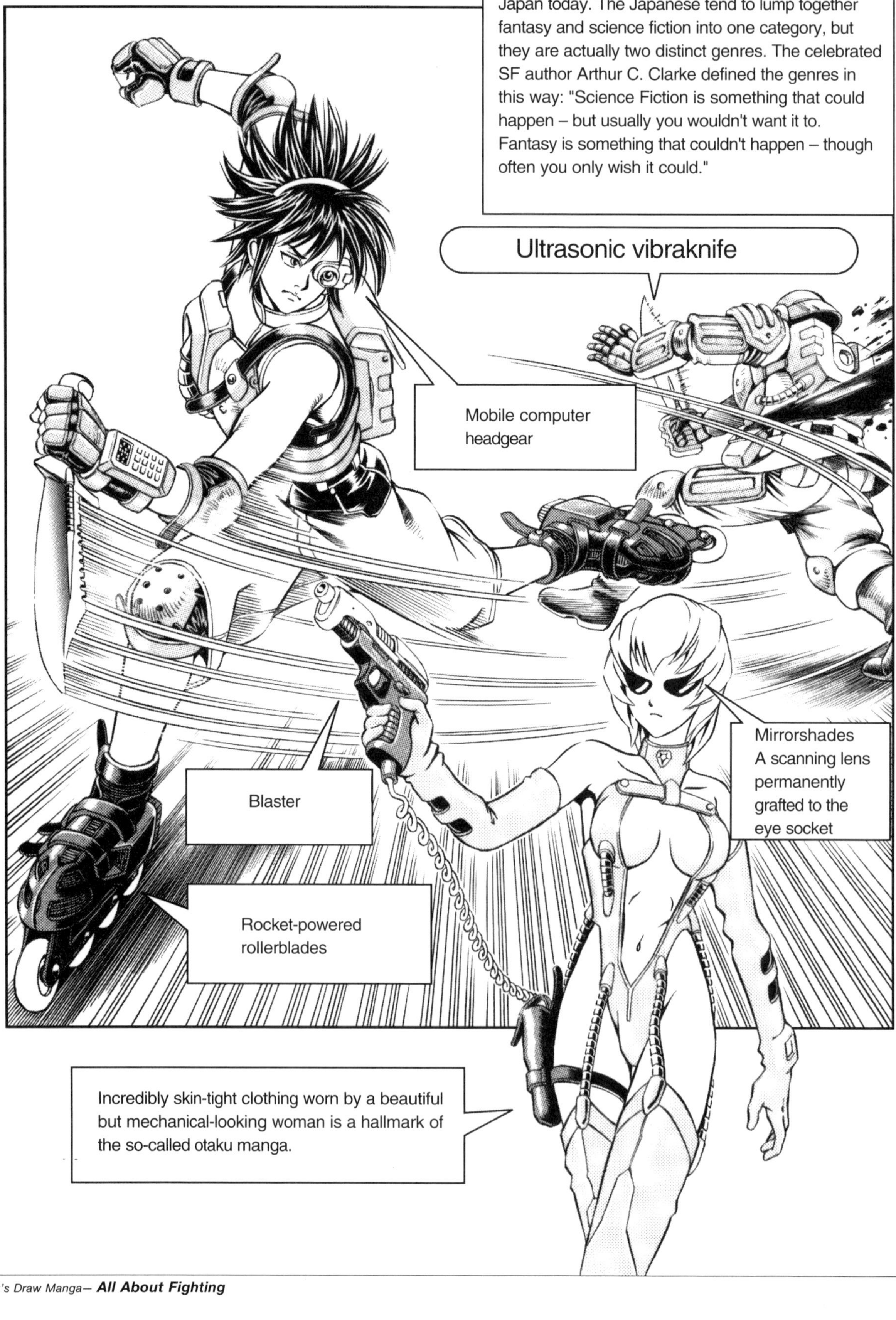

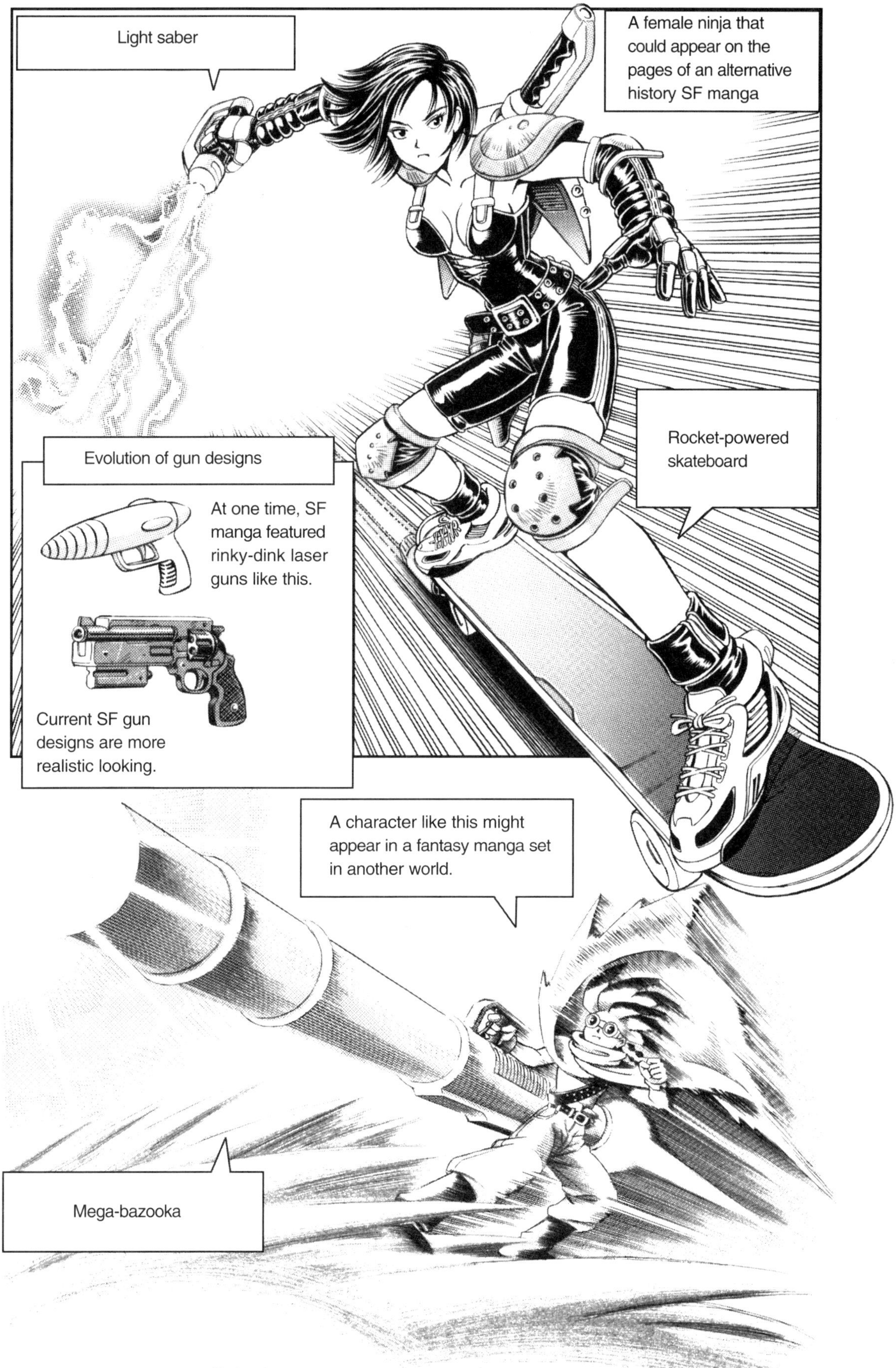
Light saber
A female ninja that could appear on the pages of an alternative history SF manga
Rocket-powered skateboard
Evolution of gun designs
At one time, SF manga featured rinky-dink laser guns like this.
Current SF gun designs are more realistic looking.
A character like this might appear in a fantasy manga set in another world.
Mega-bazooka

Knuckle dusters

A knuckle duster ups the lethality of a punch.

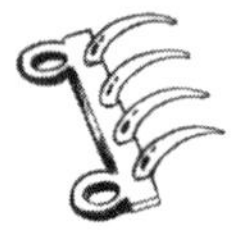

Tiger claw
Origin: India
Japanese ninjas had a similar weapon in their arsenal called a tekokagi.

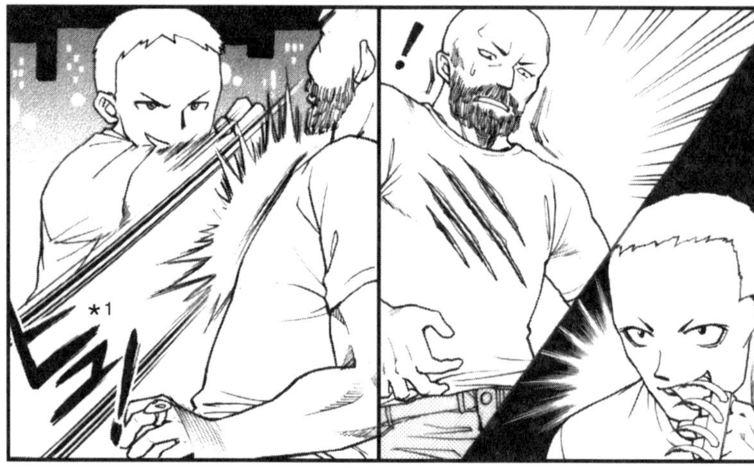

A street-corner brawl between two ruffians

Brass knuckle types

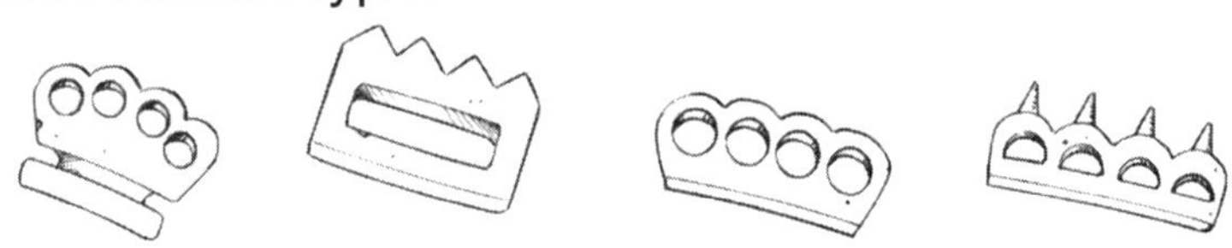

Chakram

A thin, knife-edged ring employed by Arabs in the nineteenth century.

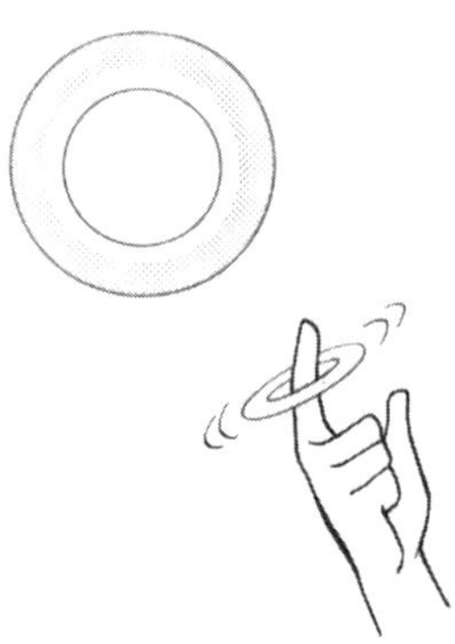

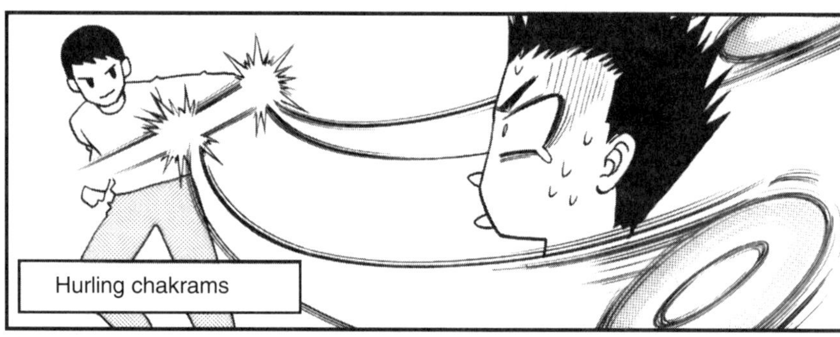

It is unknown whether several chakrams could actually be thrown at once.

Baseball bat

Sports equipment can be used as weapons too!

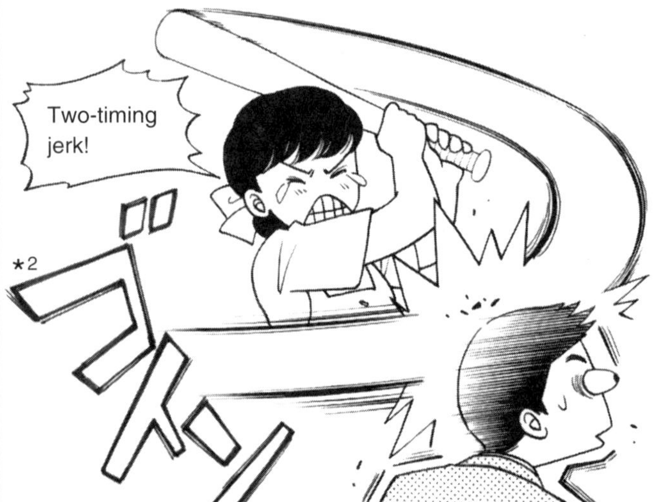

In chapter two, we focused on action scenes that incorporate handheld weapons. If you consider that practically anything around you can be used as a weapon (like the baseball bat), the number of expressive tools at your disposal becomes limited only by your imagination.

★1:Woosh! ★2:Wham!

CHAPTER 3

「特殊な戦闘シーン」

SUPERNATURAL BATTLE SCENES

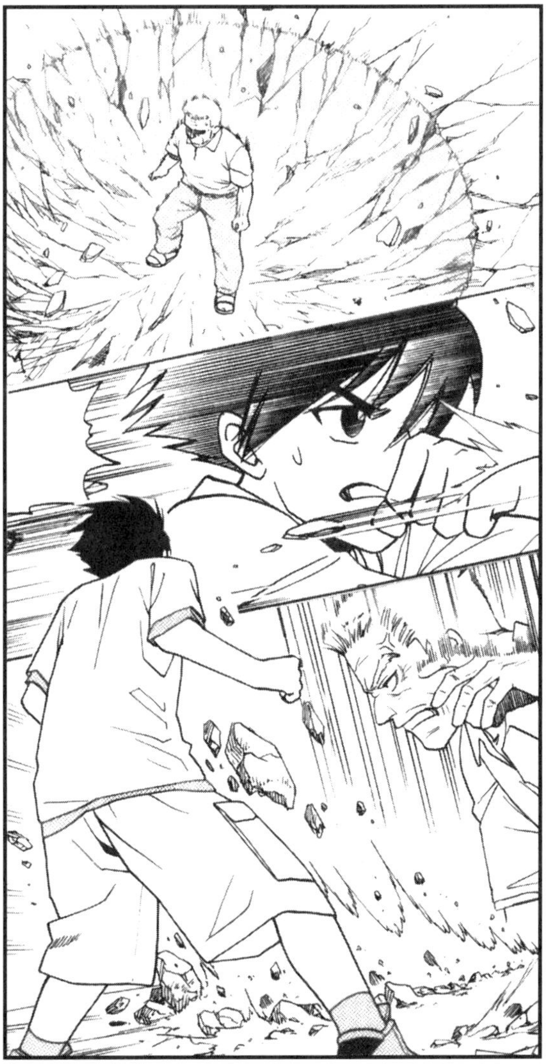

超能力で戦う

How to Draw a Psychokinetic Battle Sequence!

Let's take a look at how to draw a battle between characters wielding supernatural powers. We'll focus on purely psychokinetic characters that can use their mind powers only to affect the physical world. That is to say, they do not control any other psychic powers, such as second sight, clairvoyance, or telepathy.

Character design

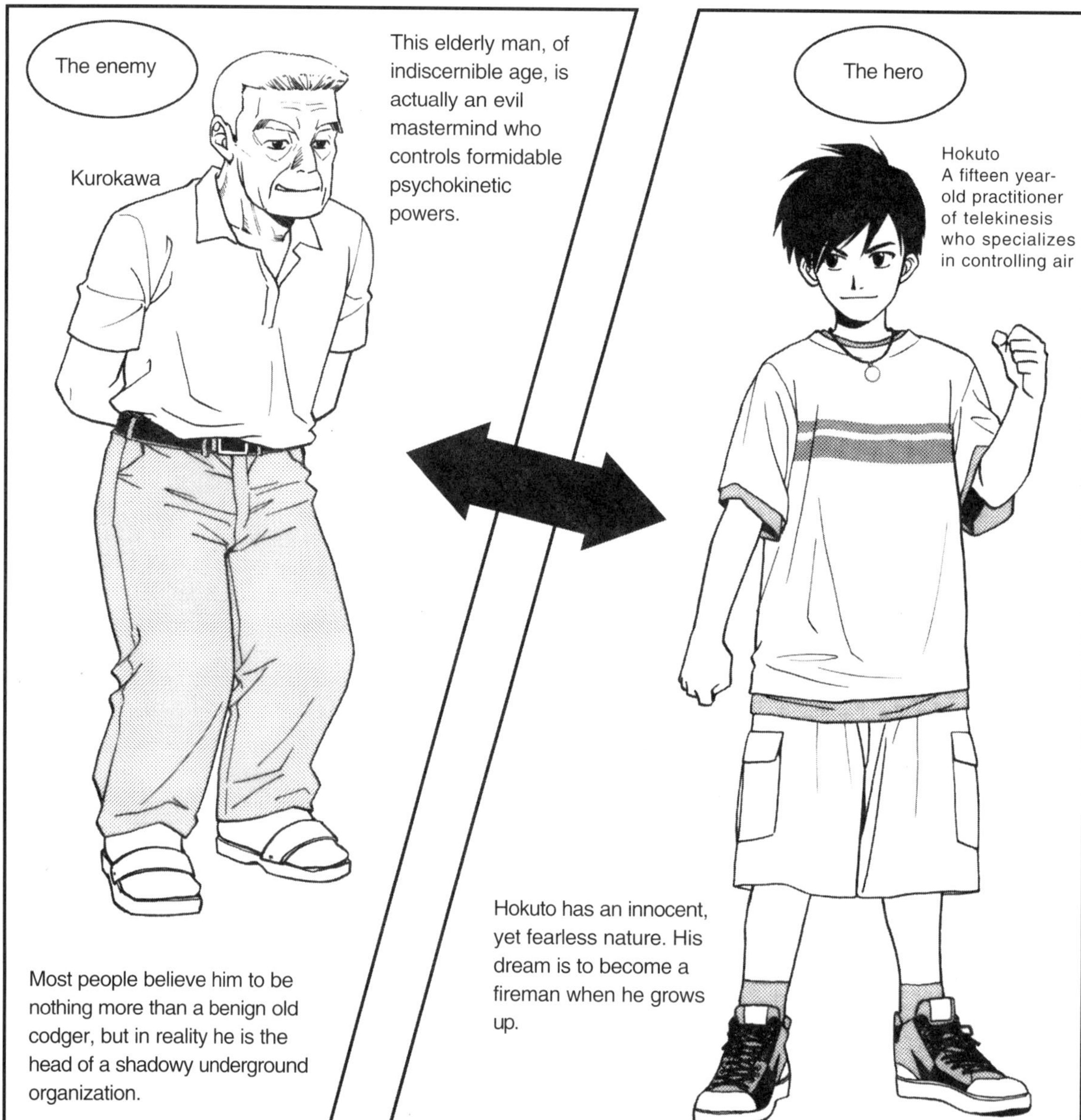

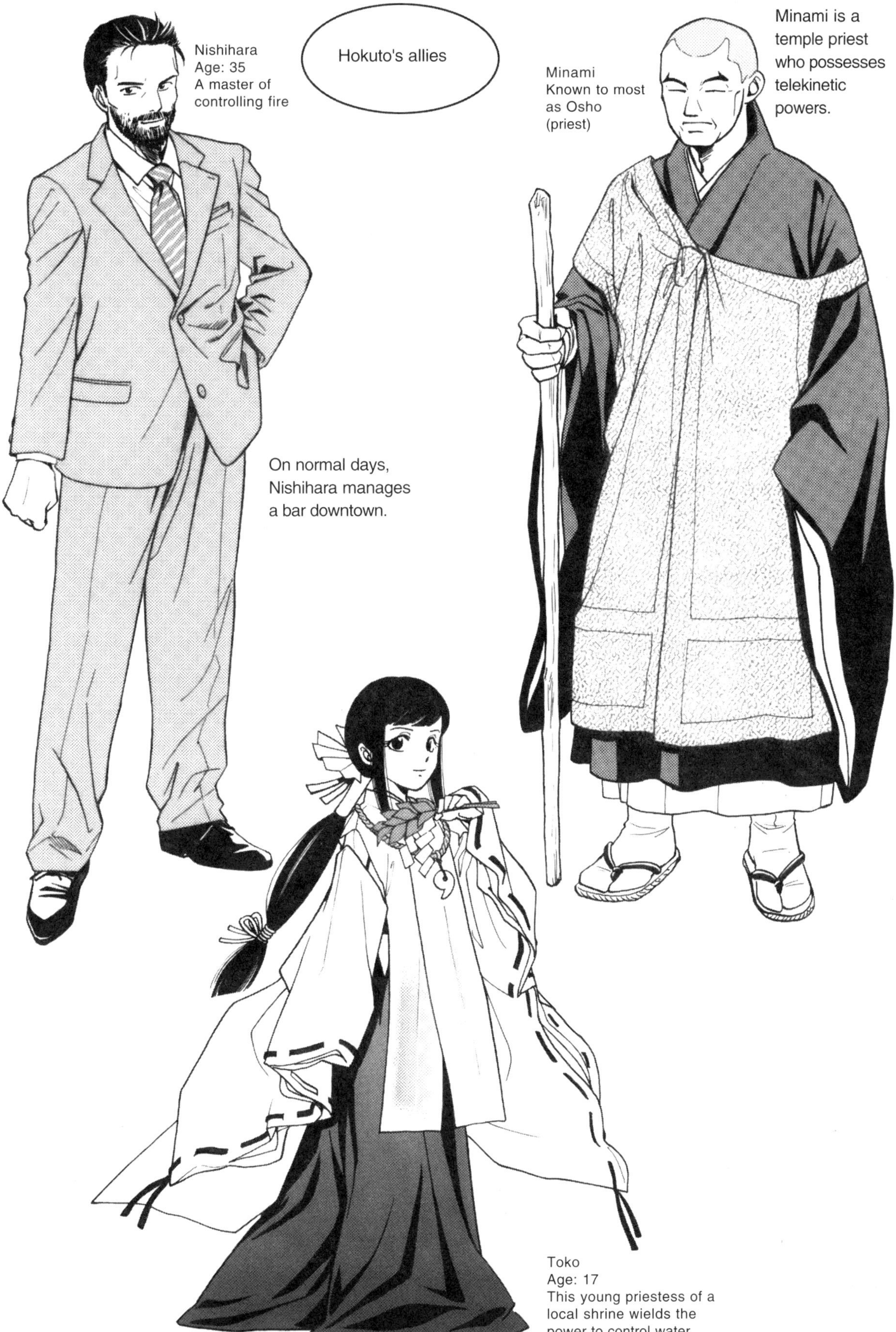
Hokuto's allies
Nishihara
Age: 35
A master of controlling fire
On normal days, Nishihara manages a bar downtown.
Minami
Known to most as Osho (priest)
Minami is a temple priest who possesses telekinetic powers.
Toko
Age: 17
This young priestess of a local shrine wields the power to control water

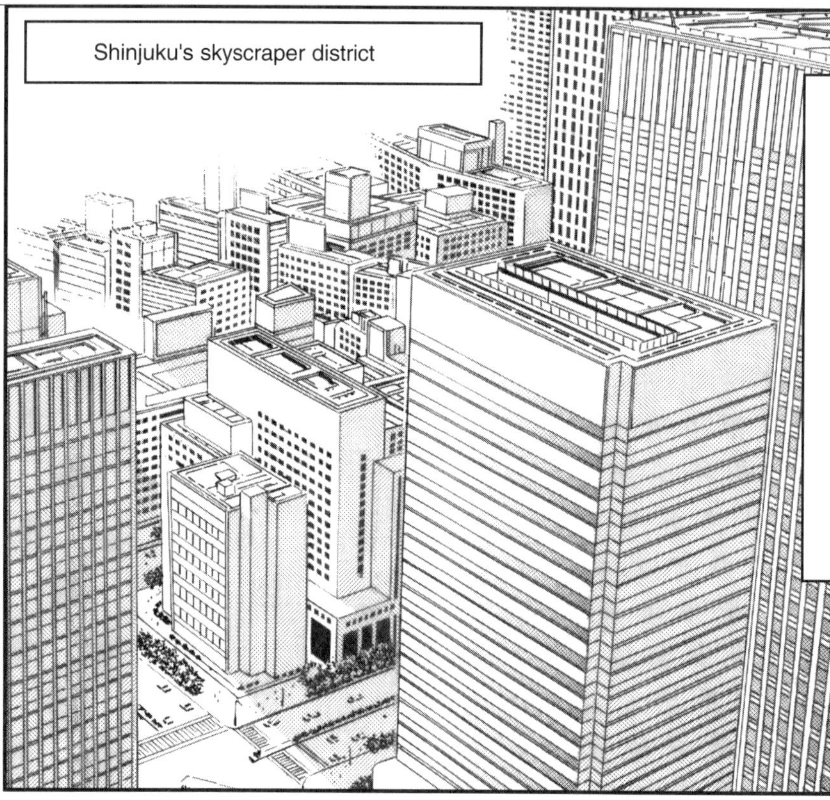

We'll stage our manga's psychokinetic battle in modern day Japan. The story so far: Hokuto and Nishihara have raided the enemy headquarters, but Kurokawa has made a run for it. We join the action on the roof, just as Kurokawa is trying to escape by helicopter.

The skyscrapers in West Shinjuku are the highest in Japan. The nation's largest and most notorious pleasure district, Kabuki-cho, is but a few minutes walk away.

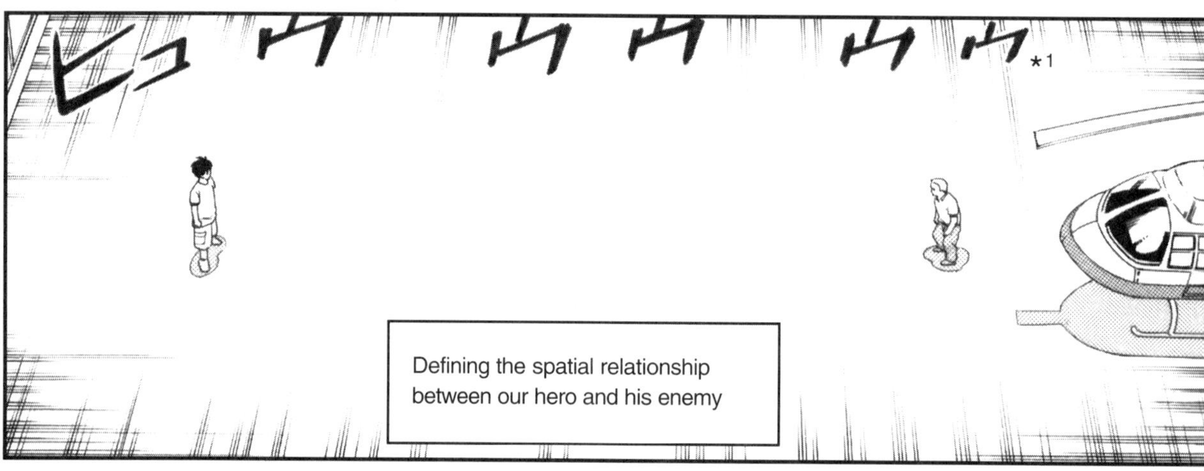

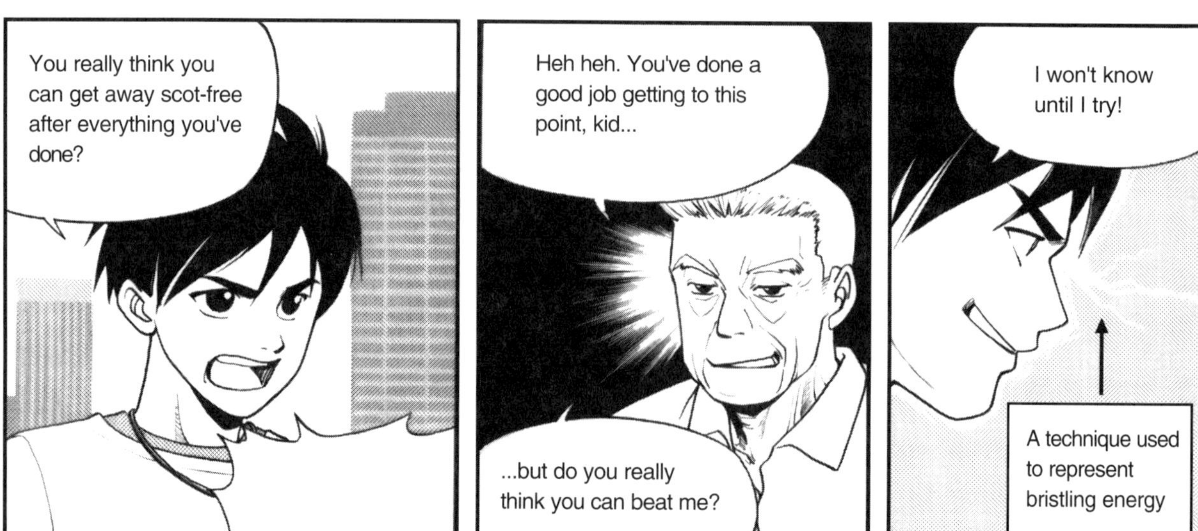

★1:Whoooooshhh

Depicting a tremendous gravitational force

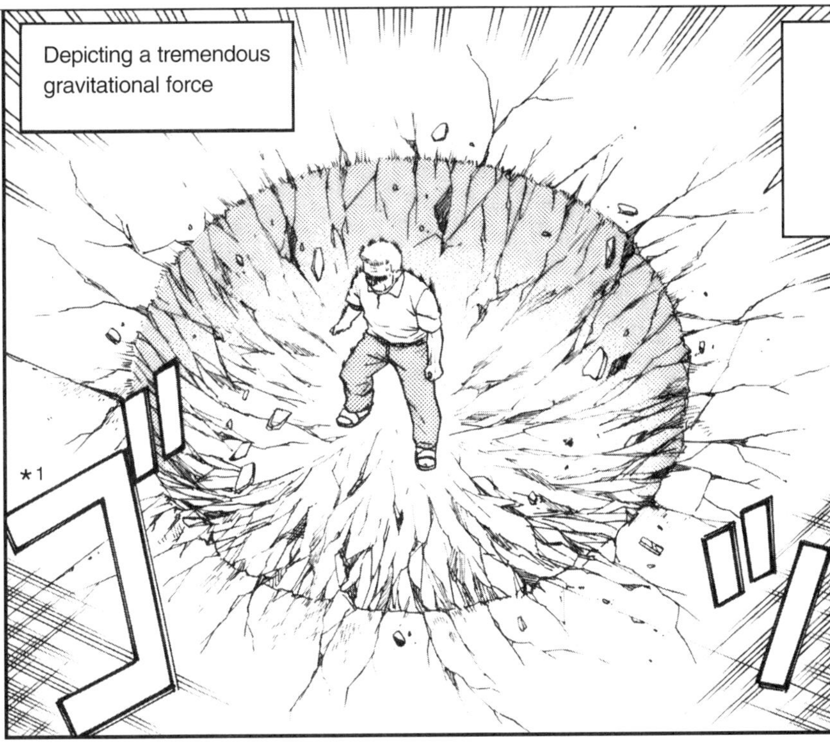

Imagine a giant sphere pressing down from above, smashing a crater in the ground.

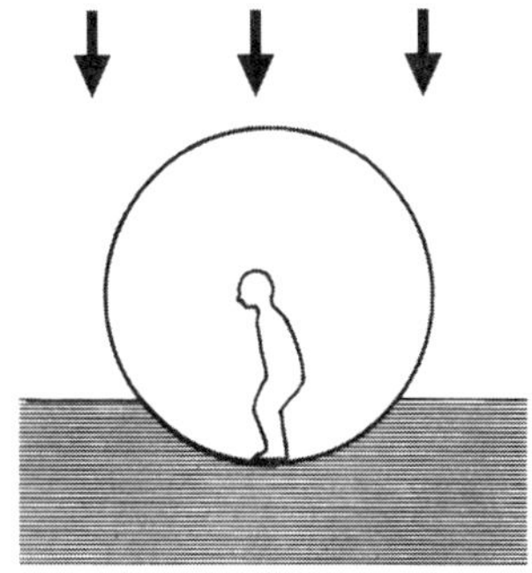

Side view

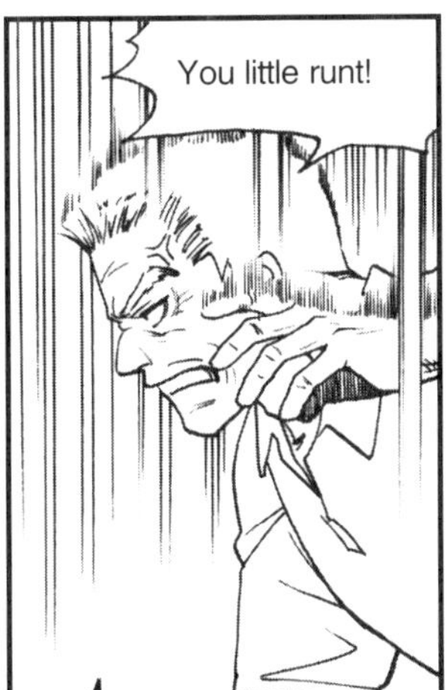

These parallel speed lines (kinetic lines) suggest that the body is moving downward.

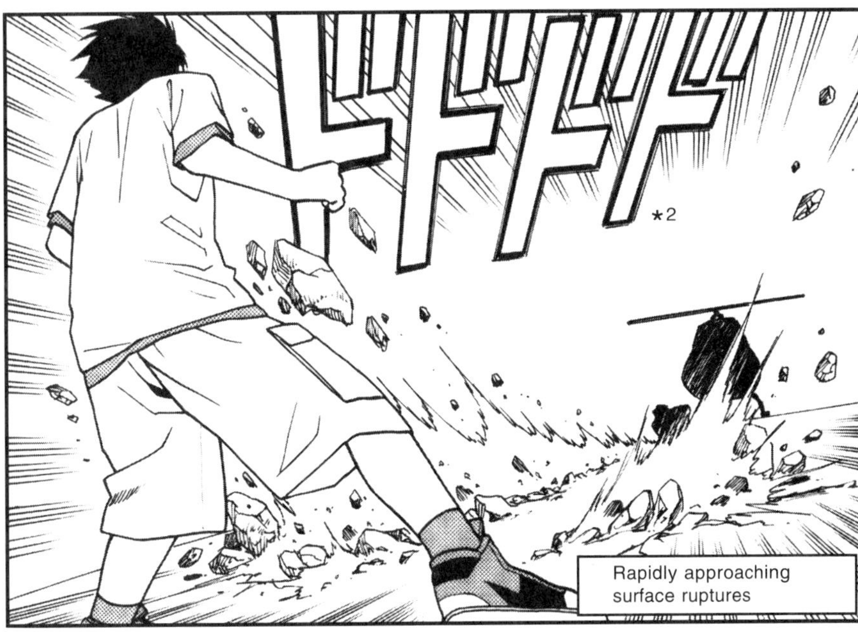

Rapidly approaching surface ruptures

The effect of speed lines

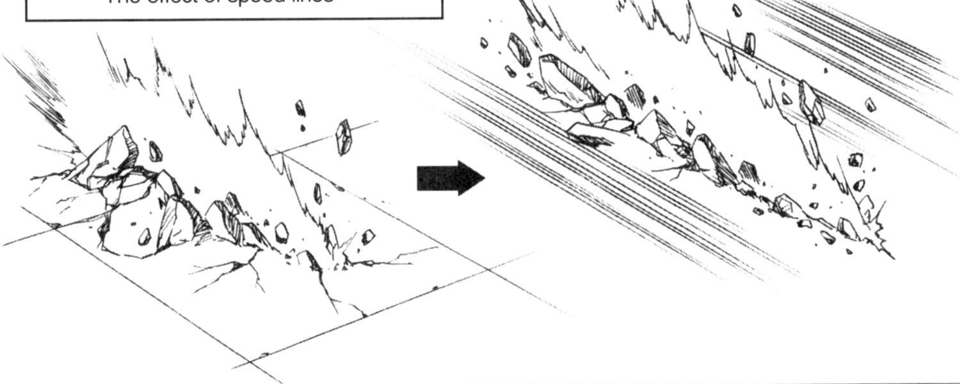

Speed lines give the ruptures a sense of direction and motion.

*1:Boom *2:Grakkkkk

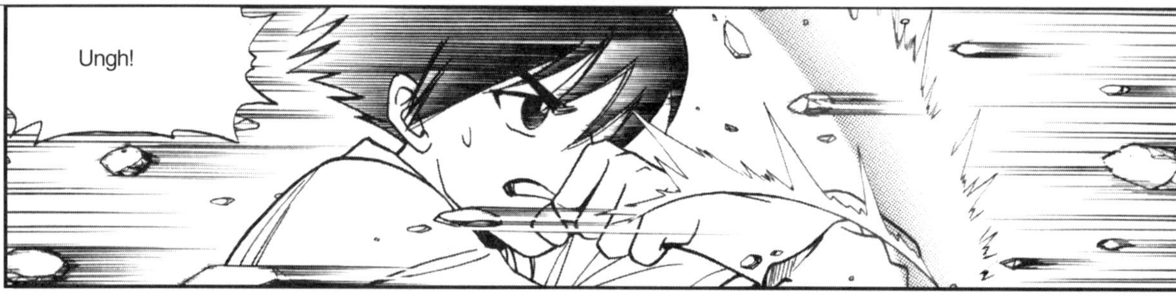

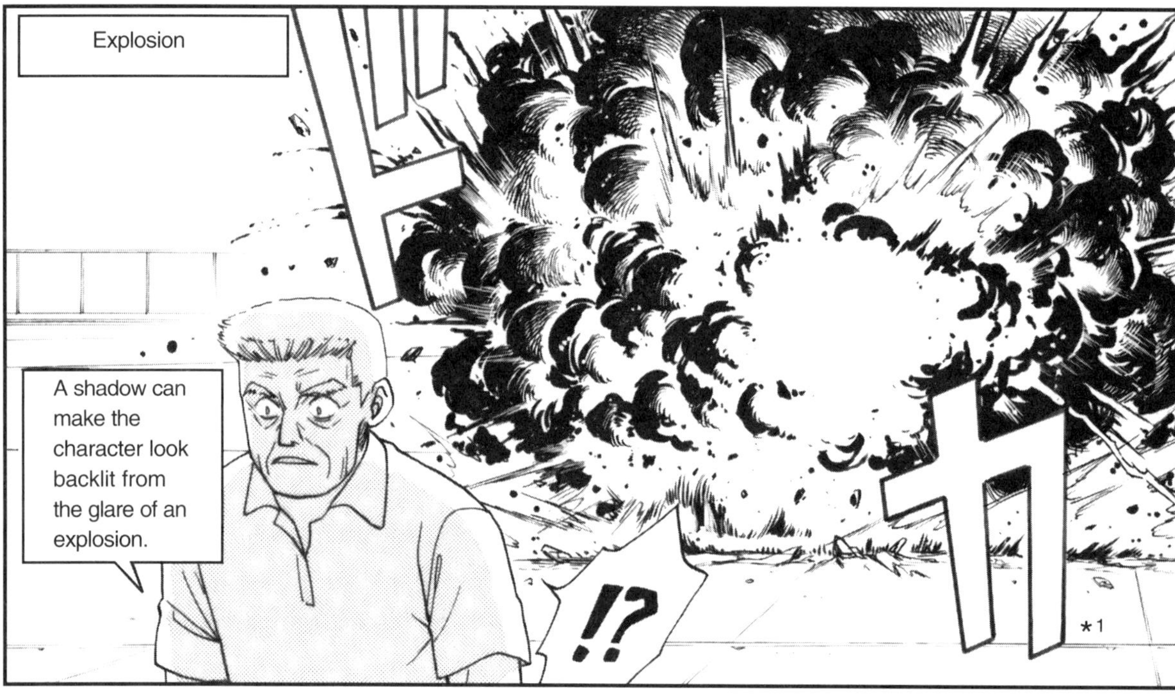

Explosion

Various explosions

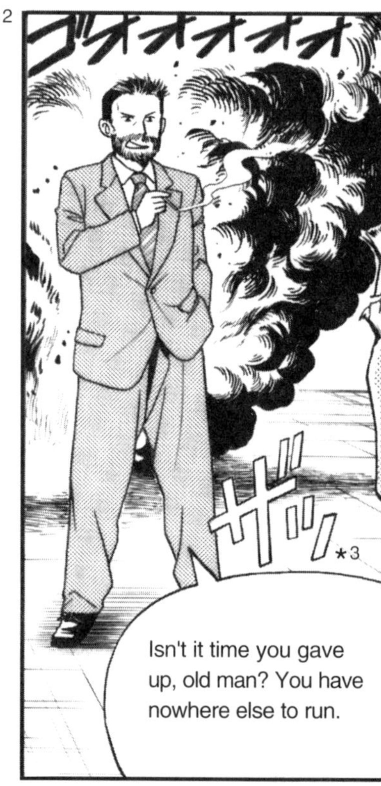

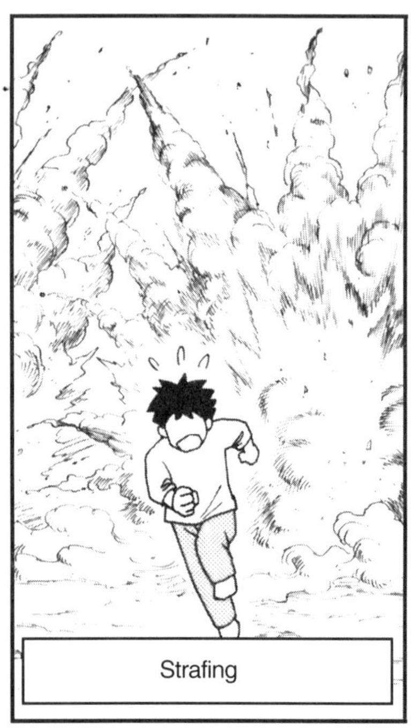
Strafing

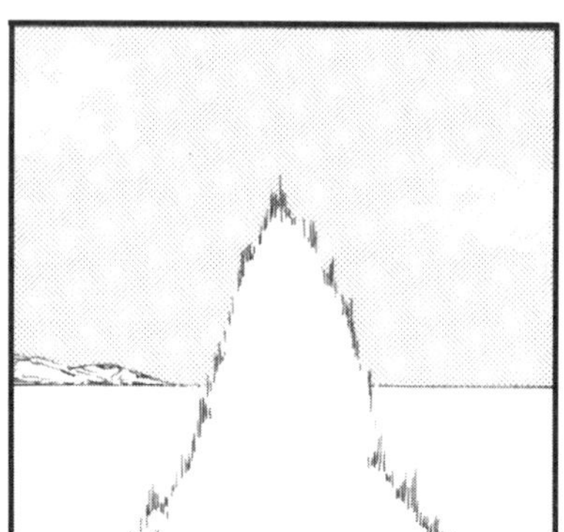
Underwater explosion

★1:Ka-BLAM! ★2:Roaaar ★3:Sssft

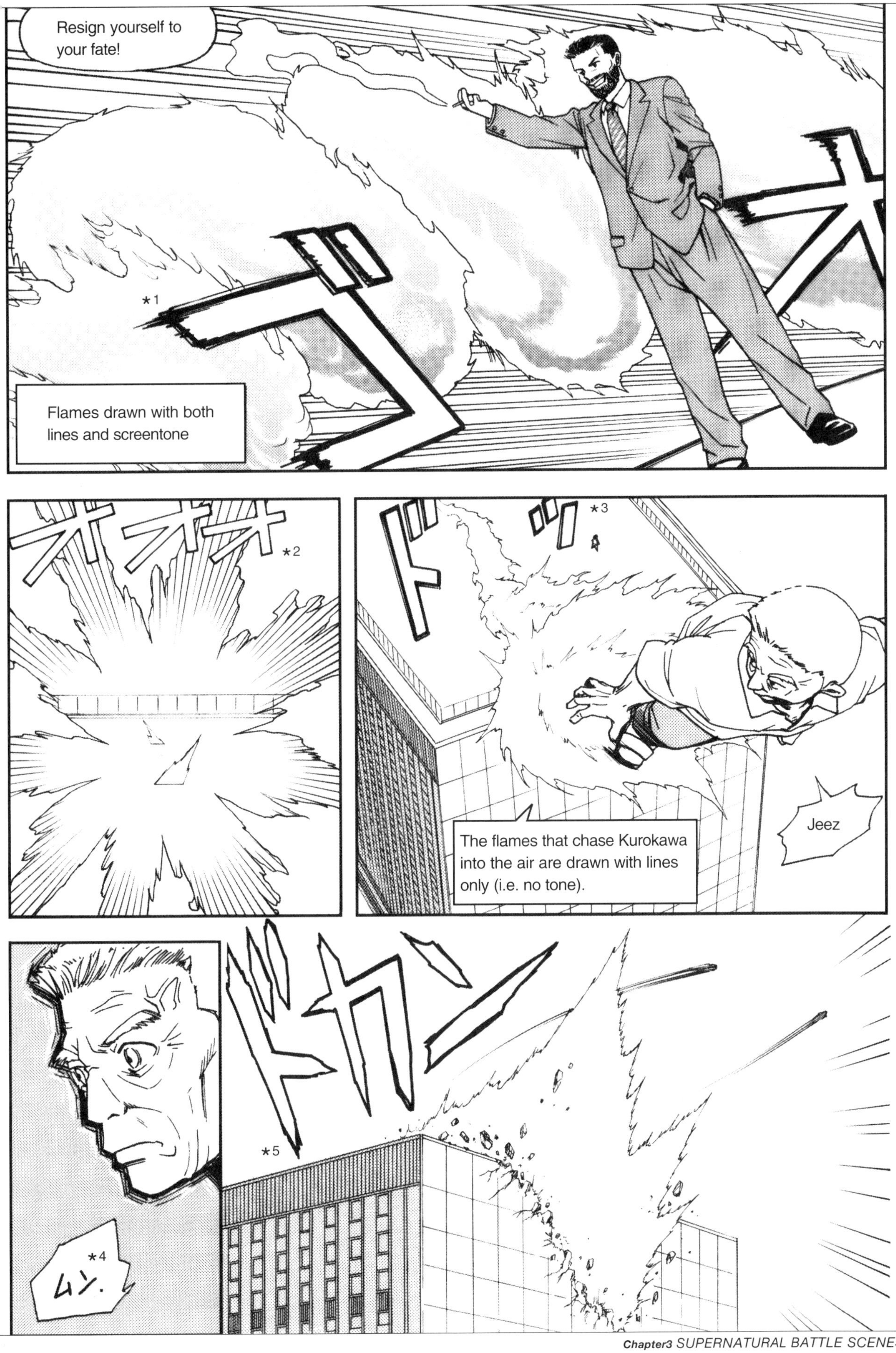

★1:Vrooshh ★2:Kroohh ★3:Brrsh ★4:Hnm! ★5:Ba-BOOM!!

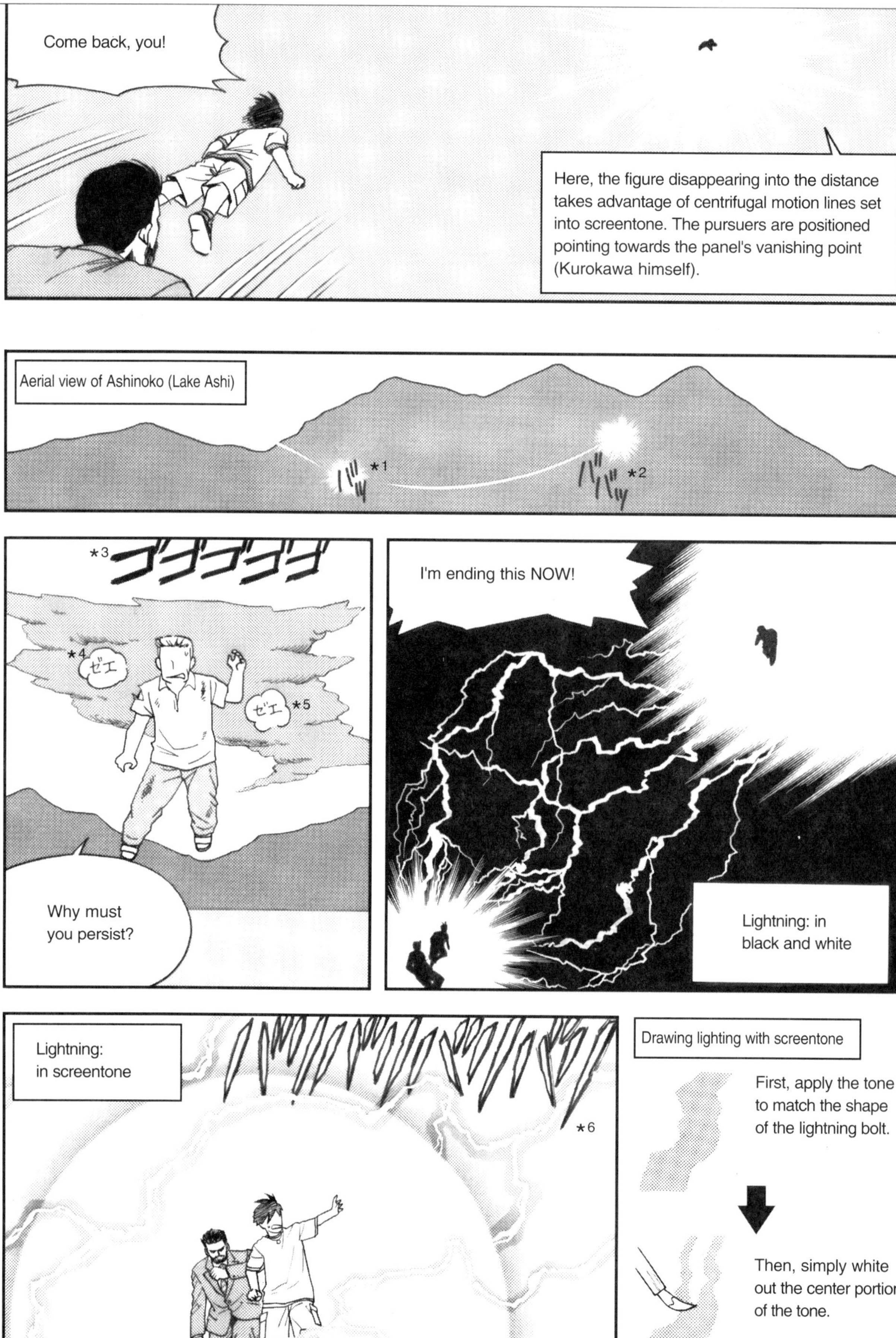

★1:Fzzt ★2:Fzzzt ★3:Rumble ★4:Heave ★5:Heave ★6:Ffrzzaak!!

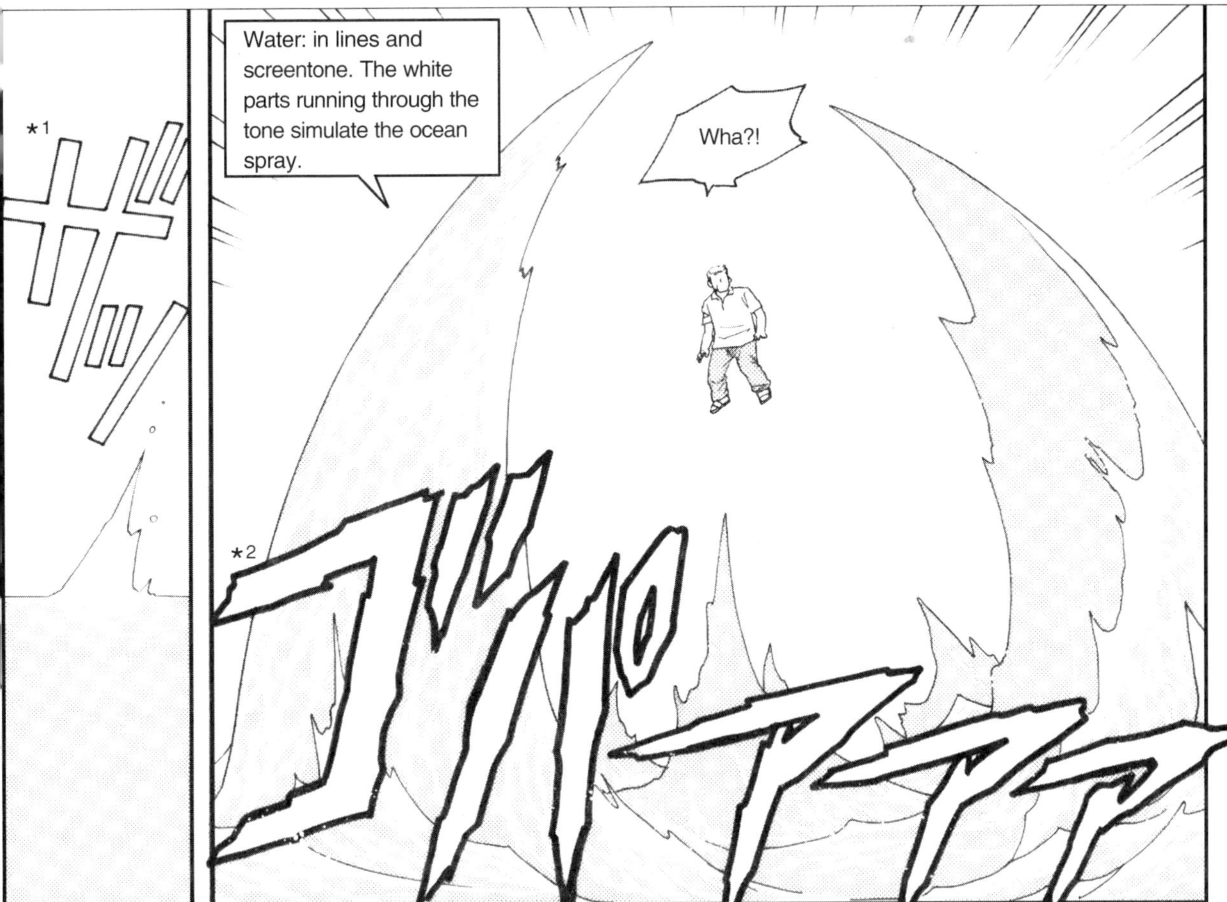

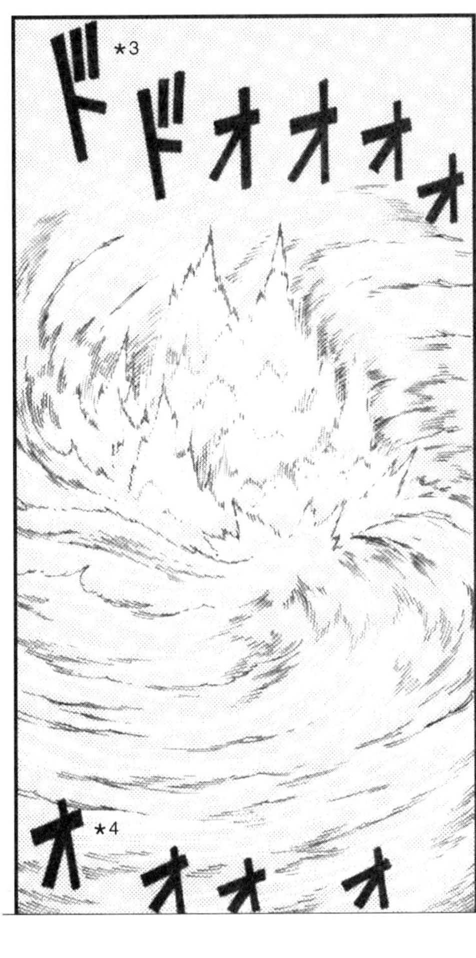

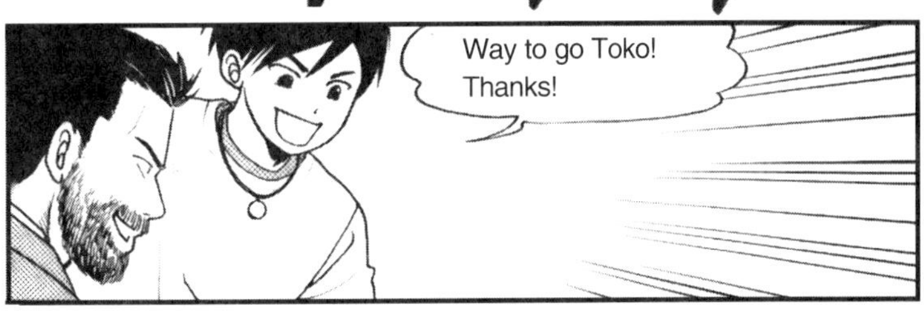

Note: The drawings of fire, water and smoke presented here are just a handful of the innumerable styles in use today. There are as many ways to draw natural phenomena as there are manga artists in the world!

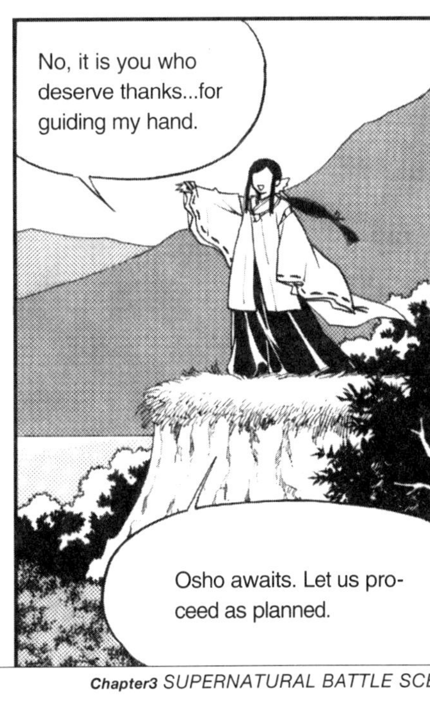

★1:Splish ★2:RROARR ★3:Fwathoom! ★4:Fooom

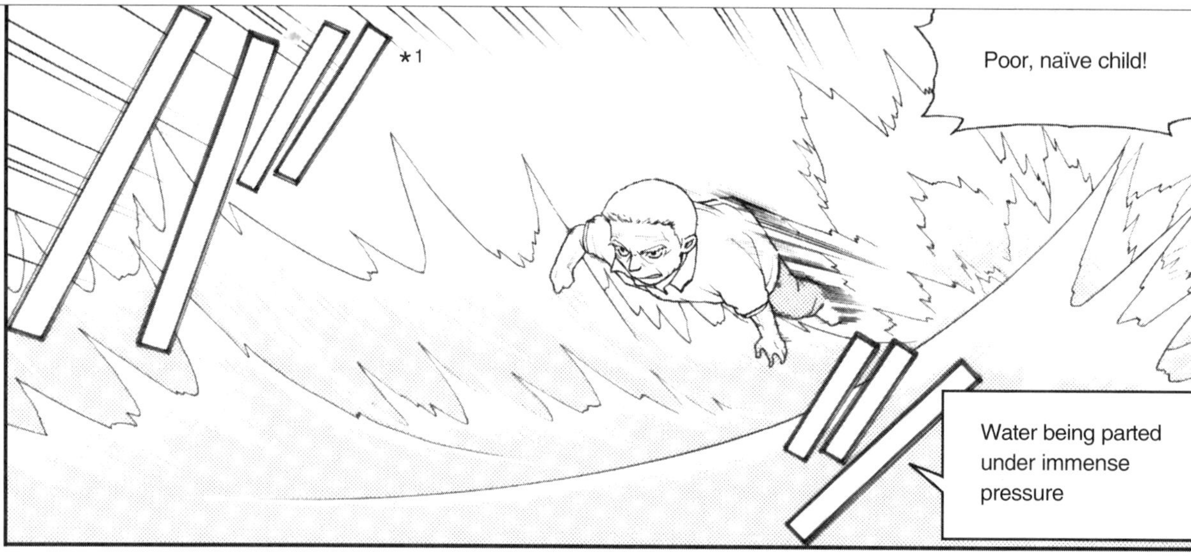

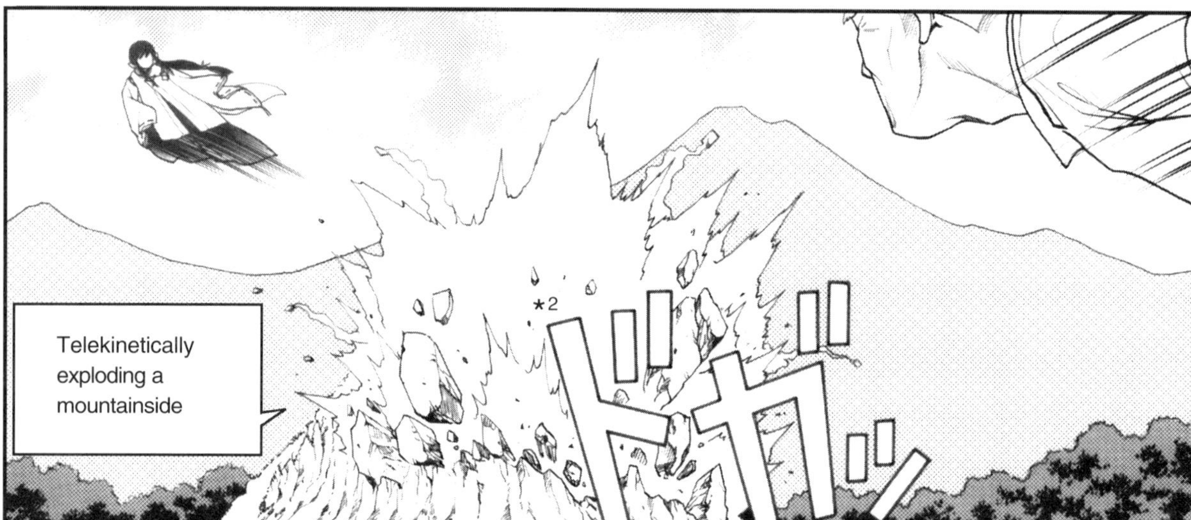

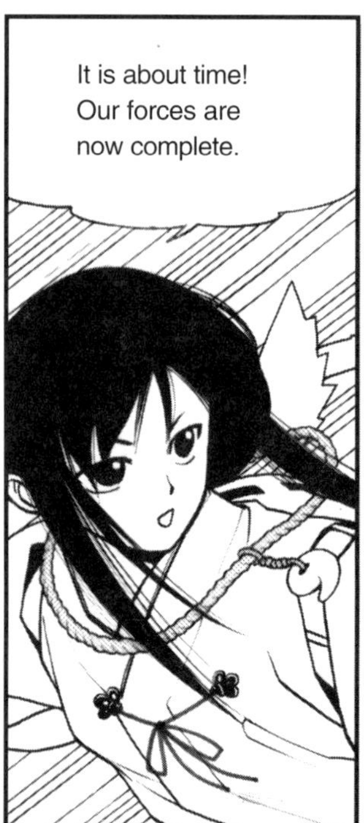

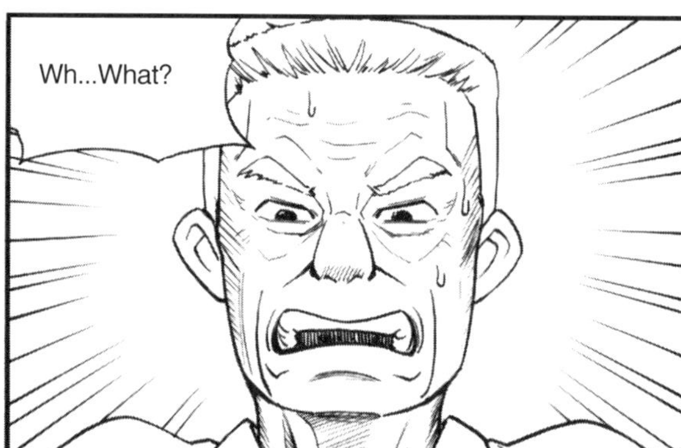

Additional props

Magatama: an ancient Japanese ornament typically made from jade, agate or crystal

Staff: used worldwide as a weapon or as a symbol of authority

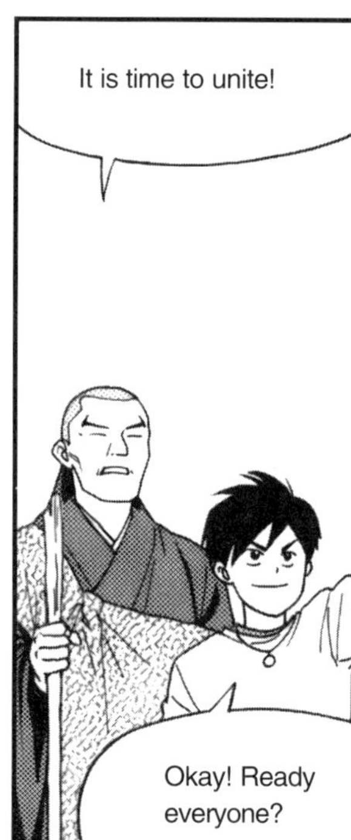

*1:Shkshh *2:Kathoom!

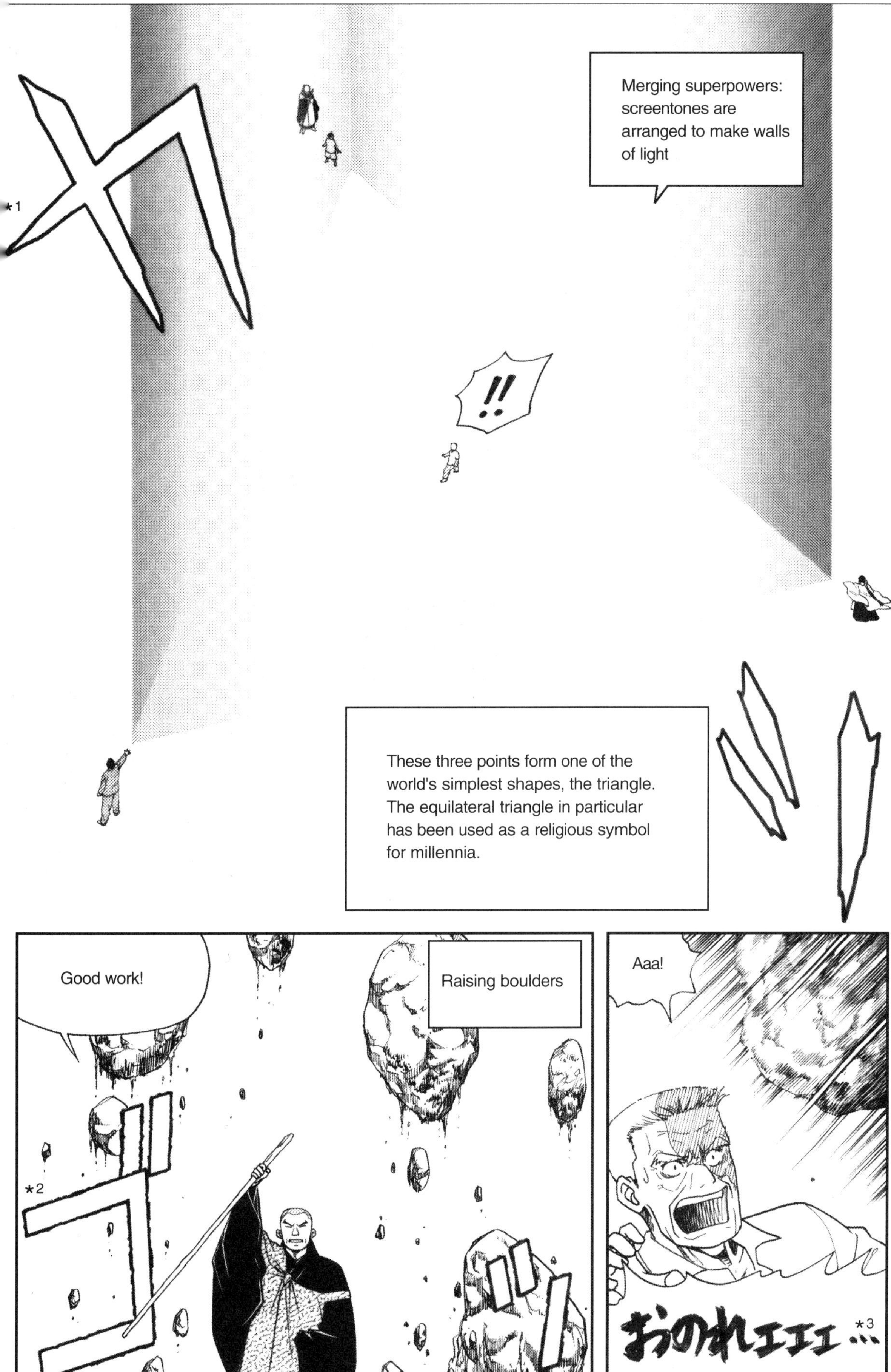

★1:Shing ★2:Krkkk ★3:You'll pay for this!!!

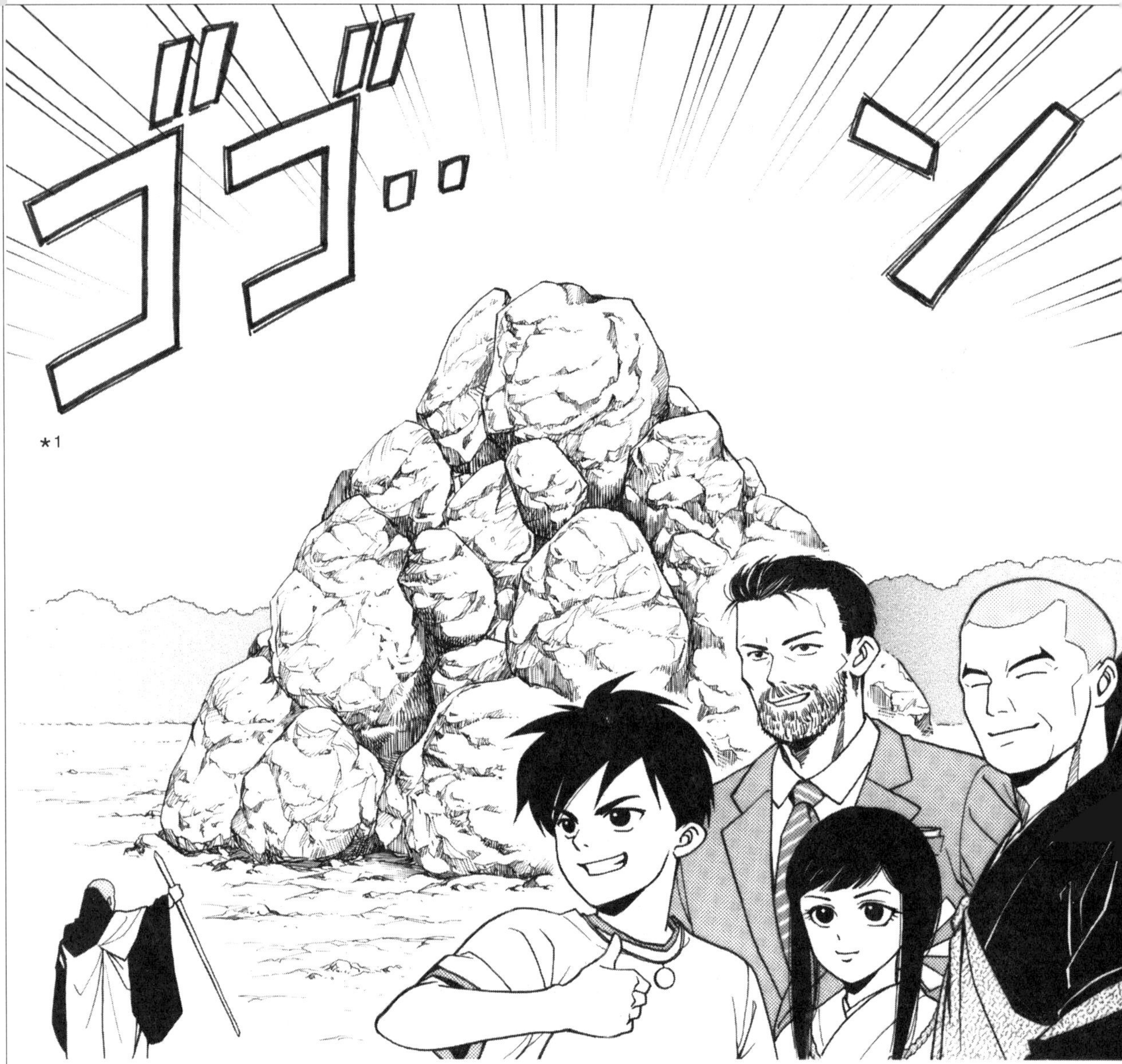

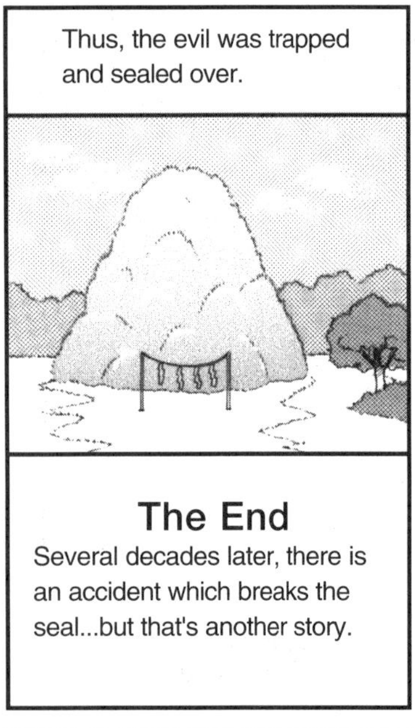

So there we have it, a psychokinetic battle sequence. Typically, a psychokinetic manga character's childhood is marked by sadness and torment. He is a tragic figure that has, on account of his powers, suffered through years of harsh discrimination. Just when he has resigned himself to a bitter fate, he encounters friends and allies who help him foster his unique powers. And that's where the adventure usually begins...
The battle sequence here, for the sake of clarity, was portrayed as a black-and-white struggle of good against evil.

*1:Ker-KLUDD!!

アニマルバトル

Animal Fights!

One particular manga, popular in Japan, features stories of power and revenge punctuated by fearsome battle scenes–all perfectly normal, mind you, were it not for the fact that it revolves completely around the lives of dogs.

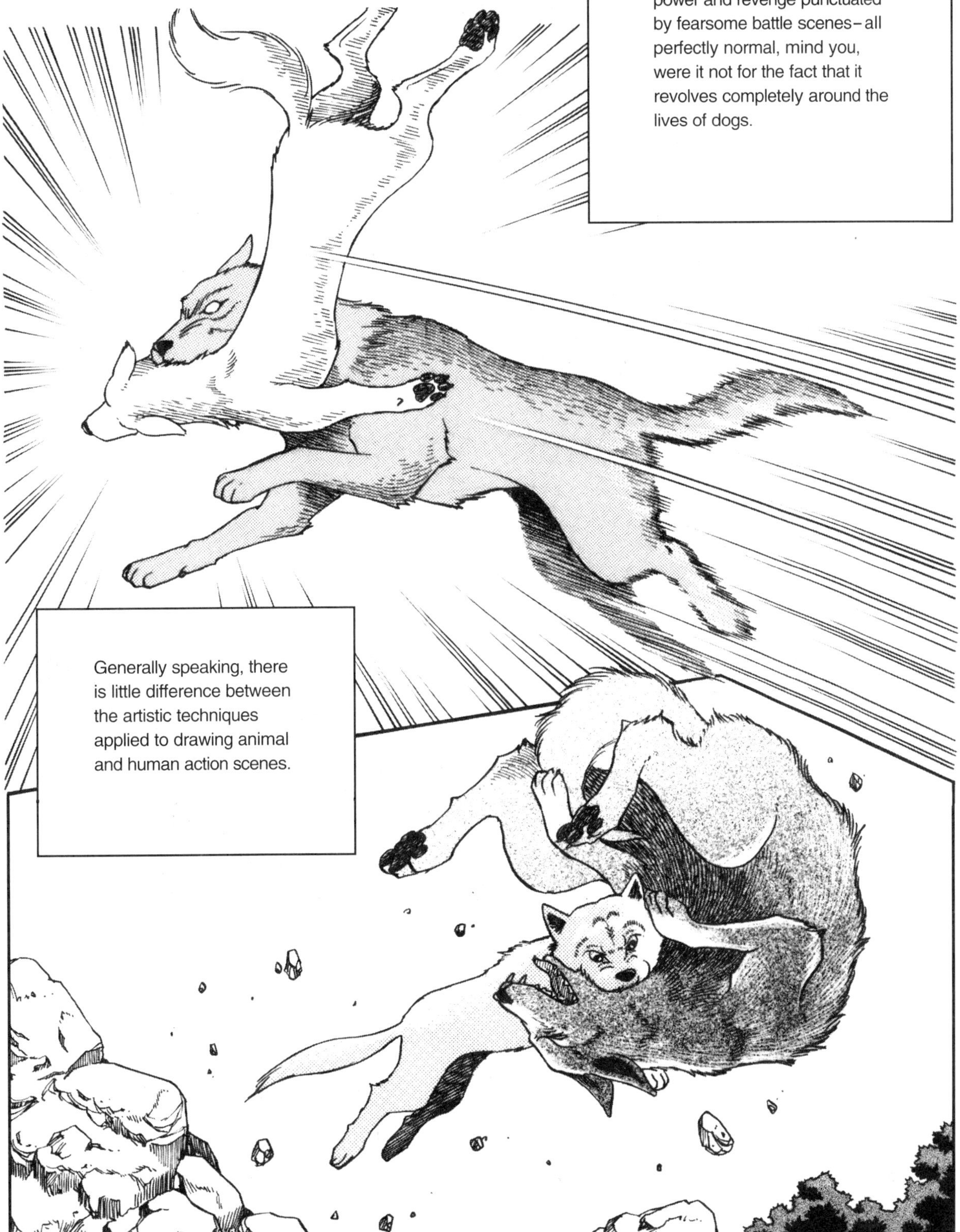

Generally speaking, there is little difference between the artistic techniques applied to drawing animal and human action scenes.

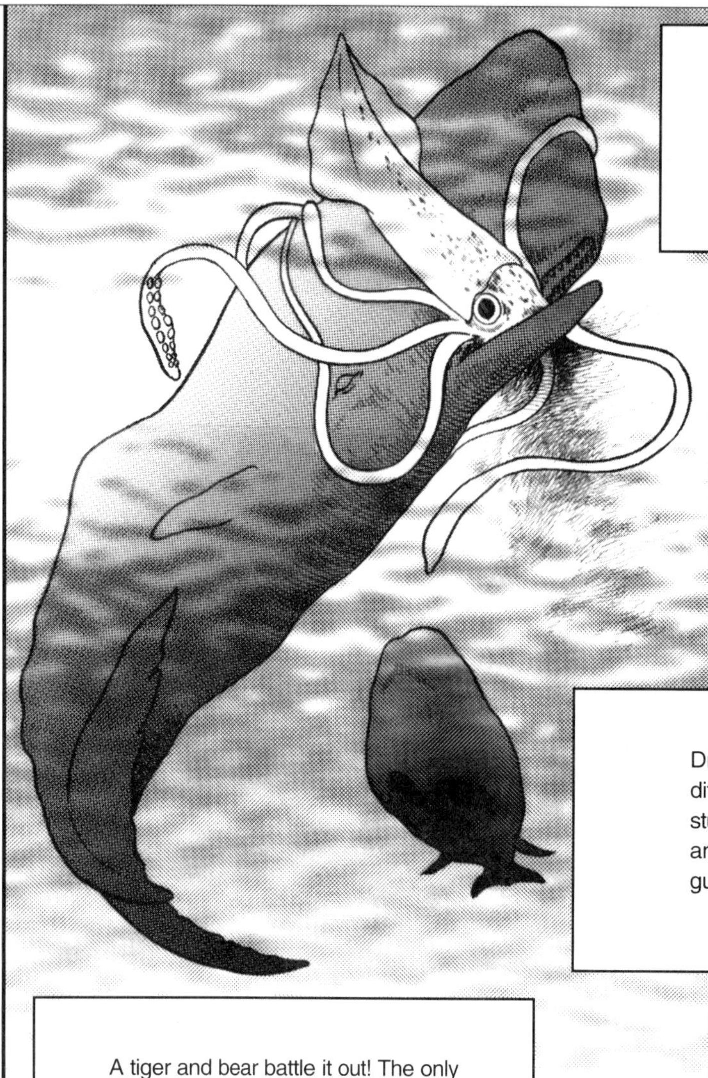

It is rumored that sperm whales and giant squid engage in mortal combat down in the depths of the sea.

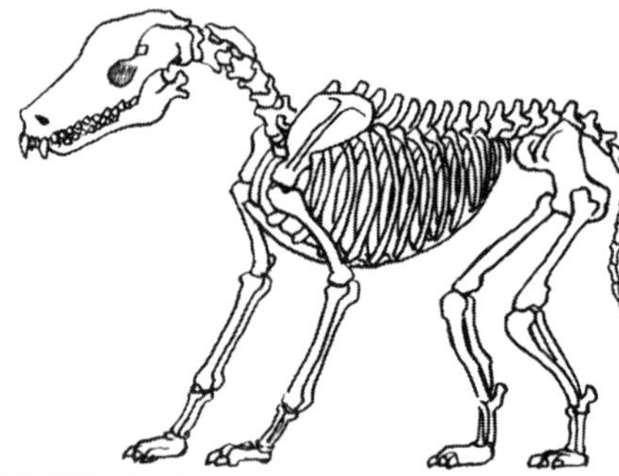

Drawing an animal's form often proves more difficult than drawing a human's. In addition to studying photographs–and, if possible, the animal itself–bone structure is a valuable guide for producing realistic drawings.

A tiger and bear battle it out! The only large, wild animal found in Japan's wilderness is the bear. Perhaps for this reason, it gets more than its fair share of attention in the manga world.

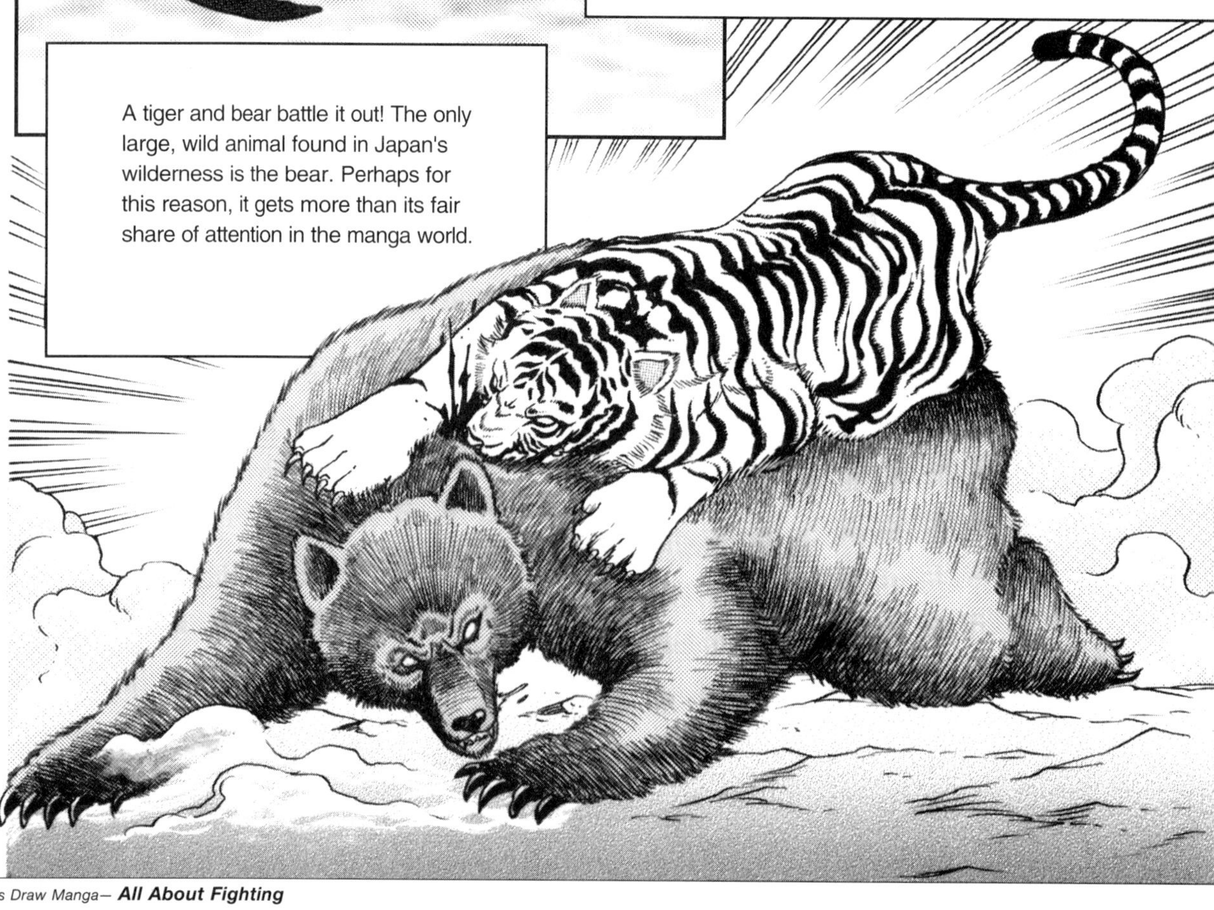

CHAPTER 4

「モンスターバトル」

MONSTER BATTLES

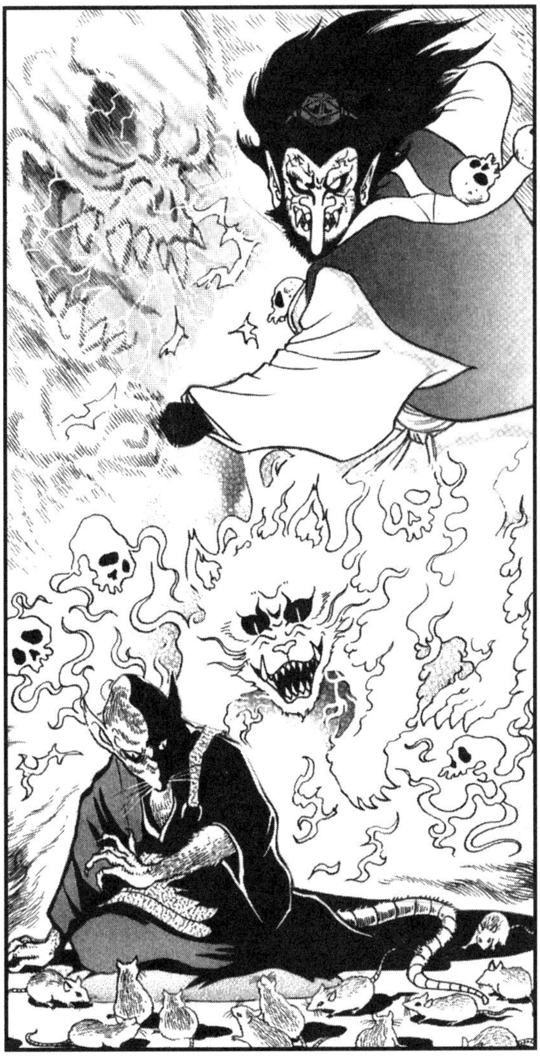

妖怪と戦う
Fighting Youkai!

While these creatures would most likely be generalized as "monsters" in the West, we'll refer to them in this chapter by their Japanese name: youkai. Their remarkable diversity ranges from frightfully shaped demons to creatures that are surprisingly jocular and comical. A particularly large number of youkai are shapeshifters that transform from an animal state.

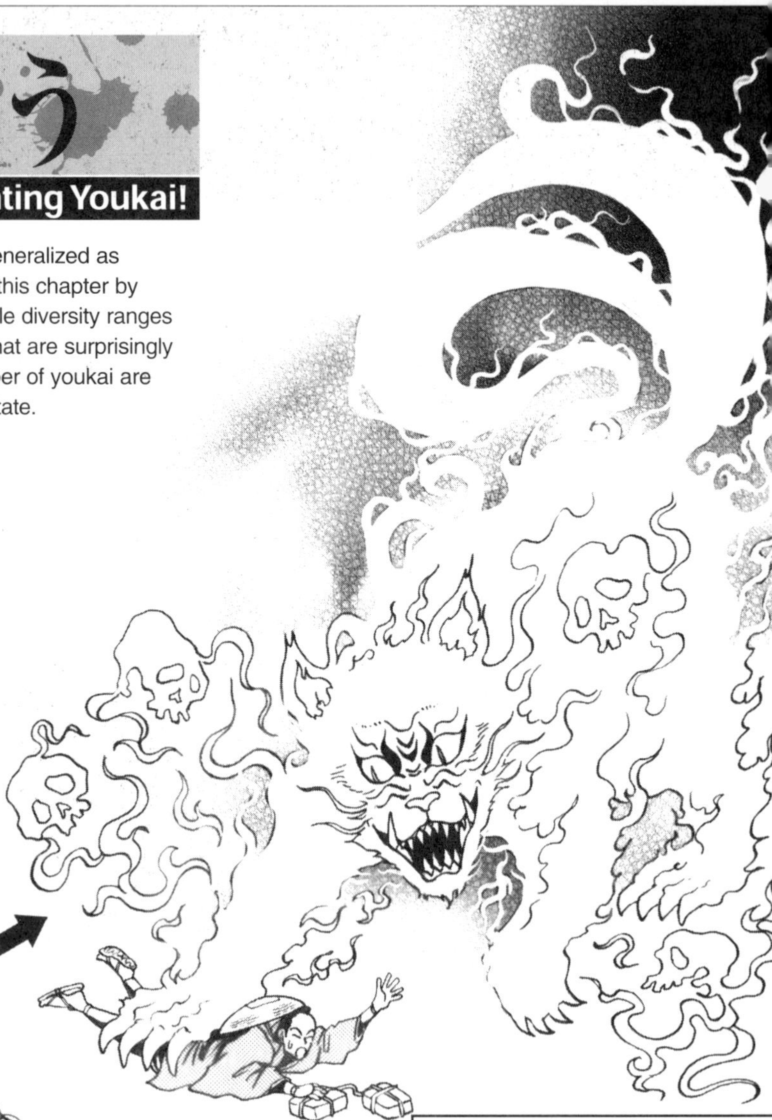

One example of an animal youkai is the nekomata, an old, double-tailed cat that devours humans.

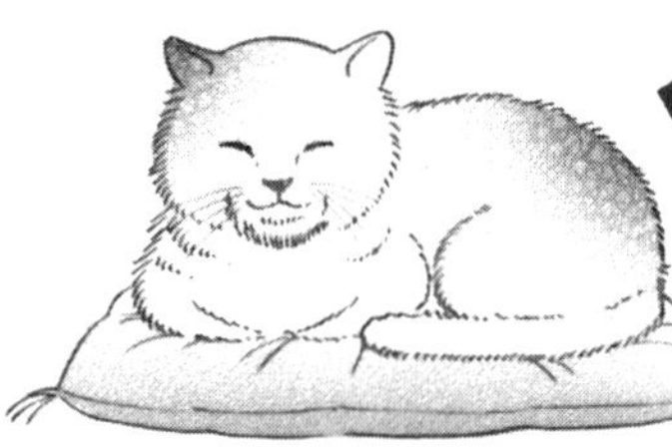

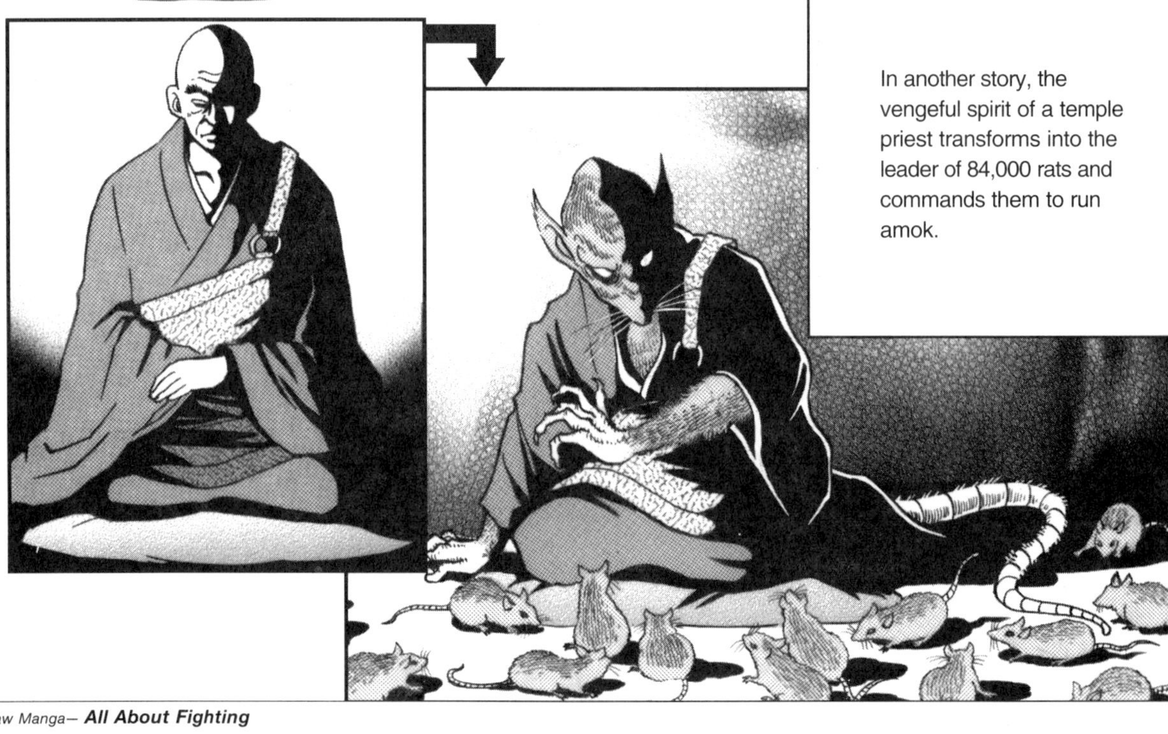

In another story, the vengeful spirit of a temple priest transforms into the leader of 84,000 rats and commands them to run amok.

日本三大妖怪
Japan's Top Three Youkai

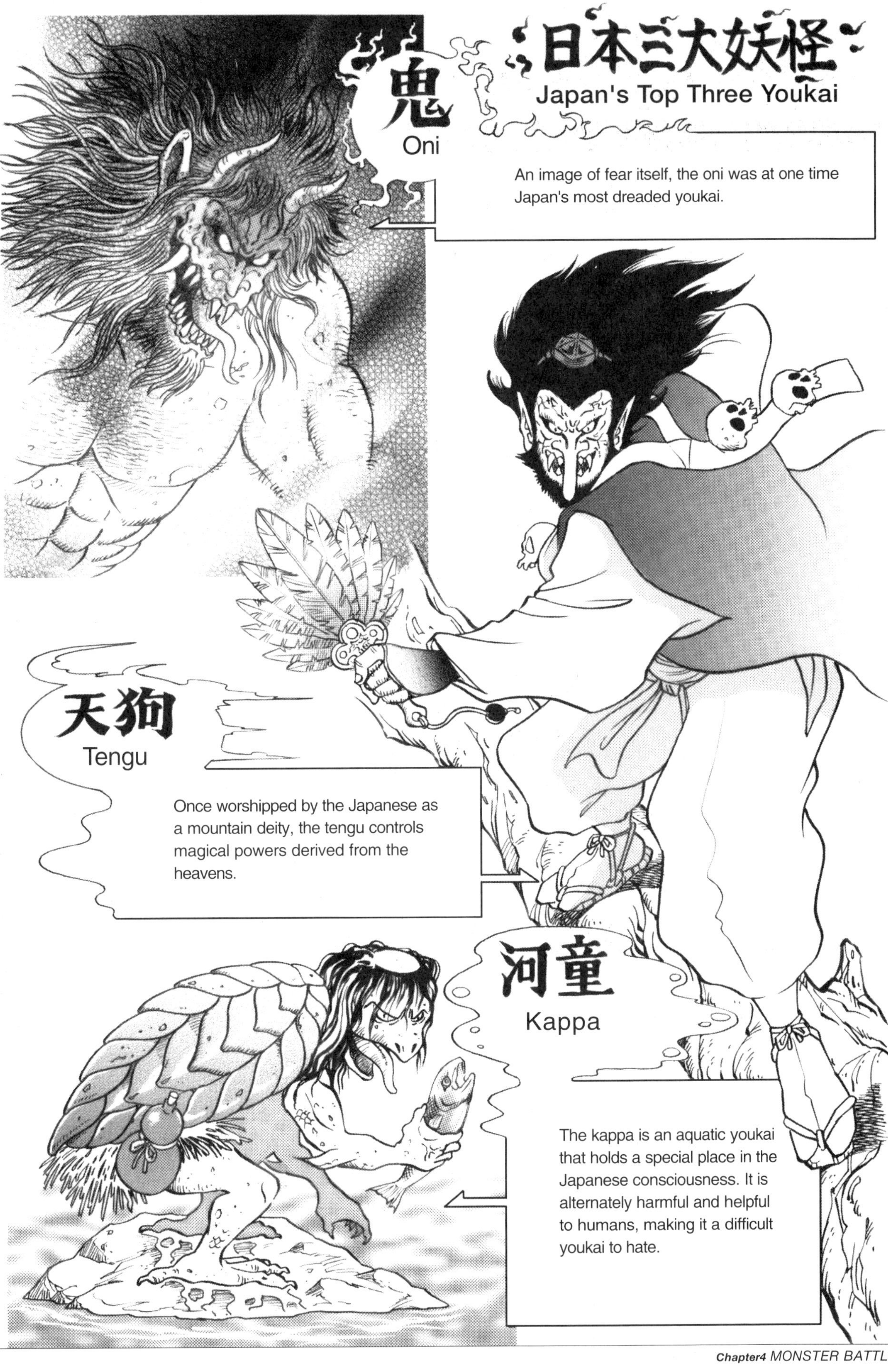

鬼
Oni

An image of fear itself, the oni was at one time Japan's most dreaded youkai.

天狗
Tengu

Once worshipped by the Japanese as a mountain deity, the tengu controls magical powers derived from the heavens.

河童
Kappa

The kappa is an aquatic youkai that holds a special place in the Japanese consciousness. It is alternately harmful and helpful to humans, making it a difficult youkai to hate.

妖怪の嫌うもの…

Youkai Weaknesses

1. Peaches: Most youkai detest this fruit.
2. Salt: The classic substance used to ward off evil. Even today, more than a few Japanese households rely on salt for spiritual protection. Sake (rice wine) is believed to wield comparable powers.
3. Incantations & Buddhist scriptures: Shugenja, or Japanese "ghostbusters", are hired to recite special chants that exterminate youkai.

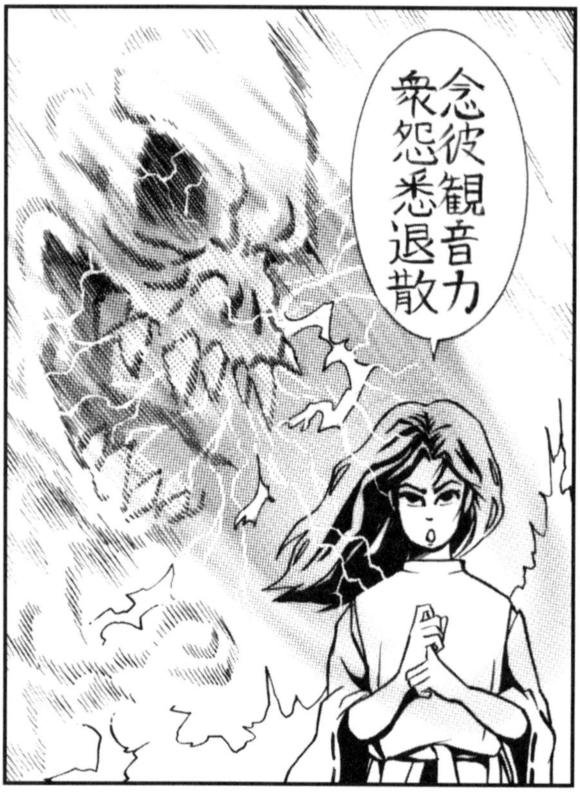

Rather than drive away the youkai themselves, incantations function to eliminate their miasma of evil.

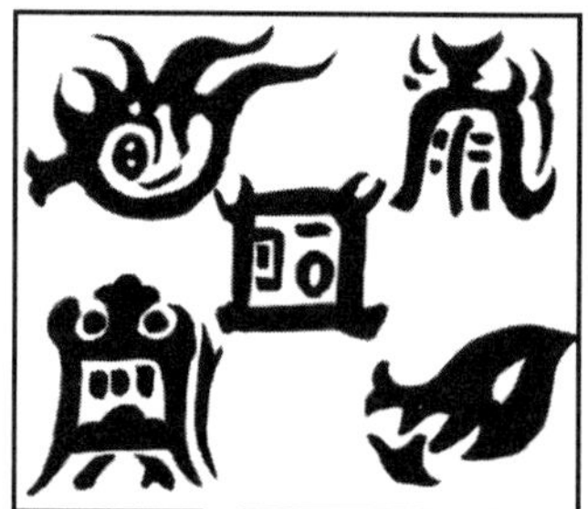

Reifu are mystical symbols that have the power to vanquish youkai.

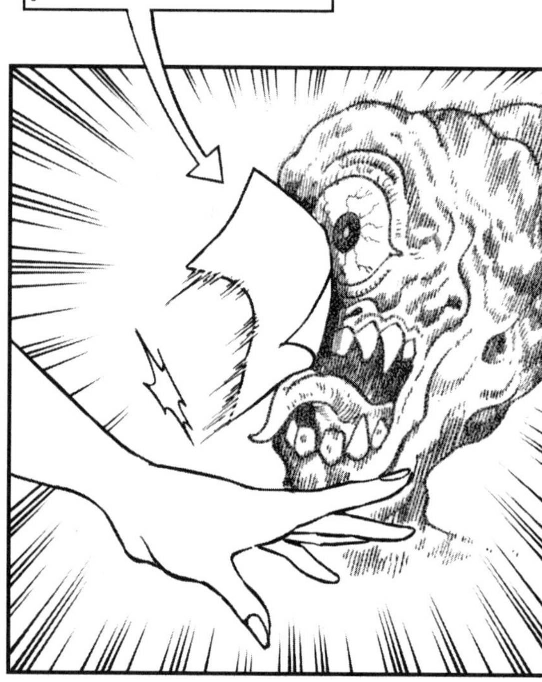

And, just so you know, the kappa's weak point is the plate upon his head.

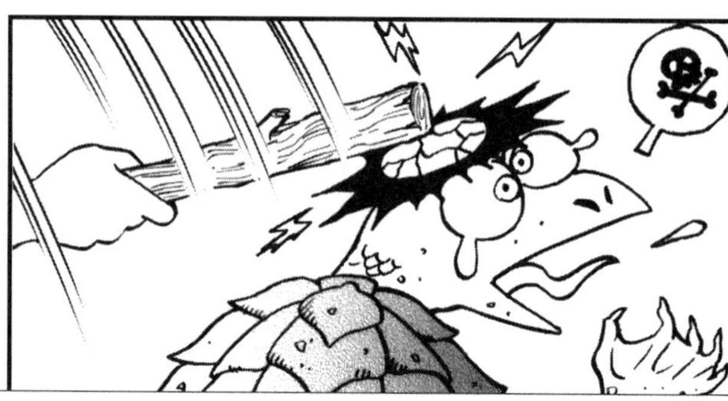

CHAPTER 5

「ロボットバトル」

ROBOT BATTLES

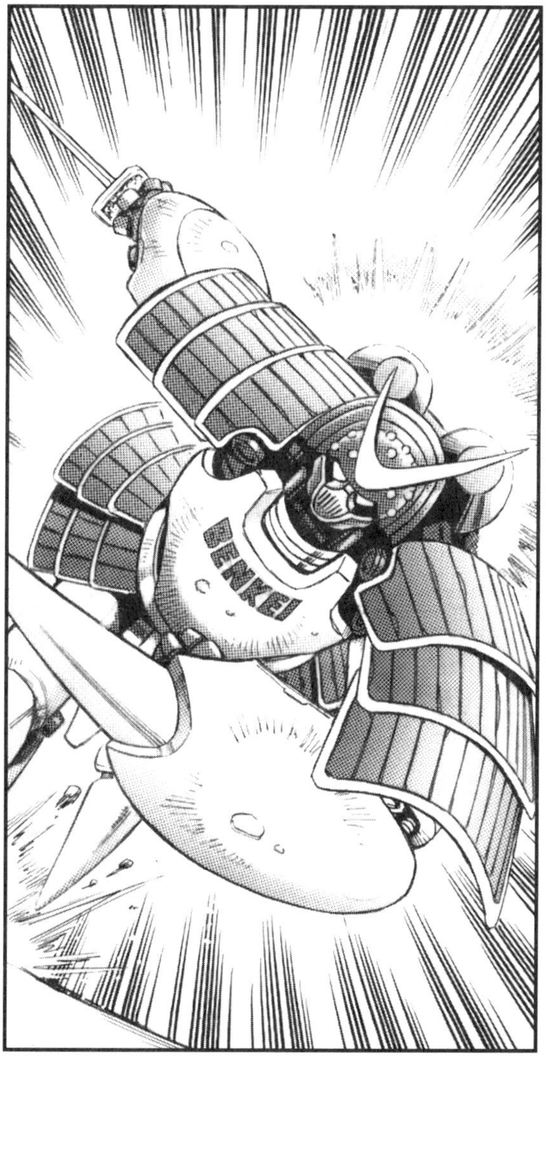

ロボットバトルを描く
How to Draw Robot Battles!

Japan has produced an astonishing number of manga and anime that feature robots. In addition, the genre abounds with highly regarded masterpieces, typically marked by complex and profound storylines. In the final chapter of this book, we'll examine some useful techniques for drawing robots in battle.

The evolution of robot designs

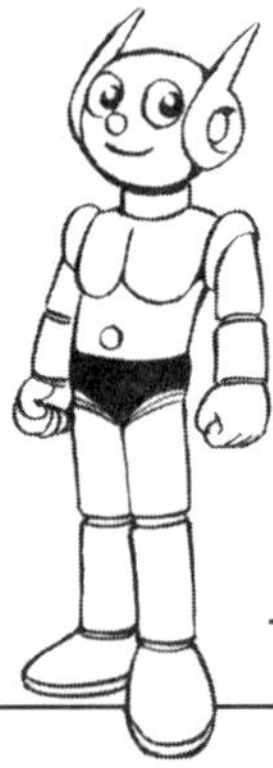

1950 - 1970

A humanoid robot design, popularized at the dawn of the manga age. Commonly portrayed as a friend and companion to man.

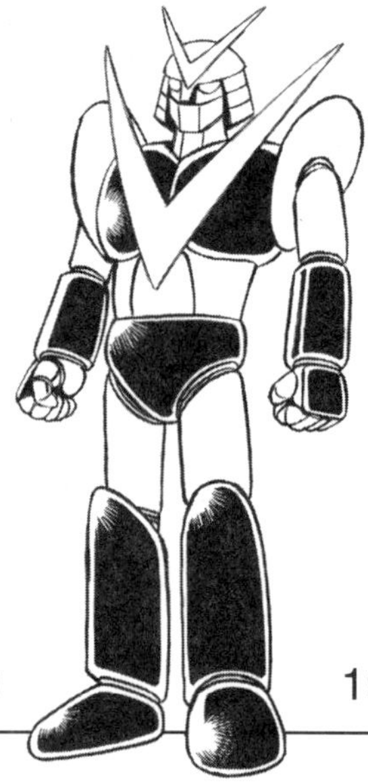

A giant, human-controlled robot. Whether it serves good or evil intents is entirely dependent upon the person manipulating it. Its popularity soared thanks to its ubiquitous presence in anime programs and its numerous tie-ins with toy manufacturers.

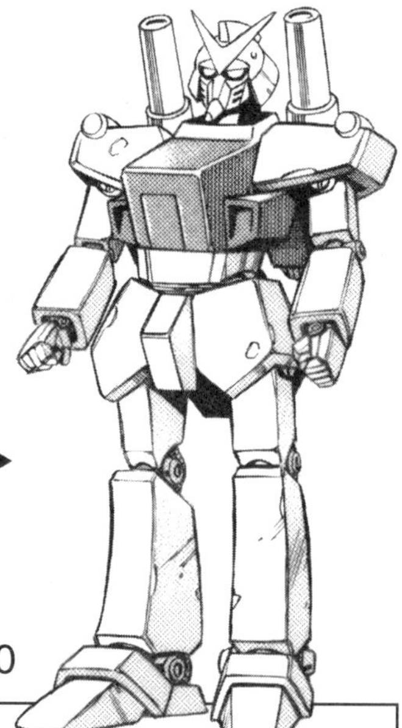

1970 - 1980

A more modern design, characterized by its exposure of joint mechanisms. It is generally portrayed as an advanced piece of military hardware. Storylines focus on the people who pilot these "mechas", and manifest themes deeply rooted in hard-core SF. Has been called the "realistic robot genre".

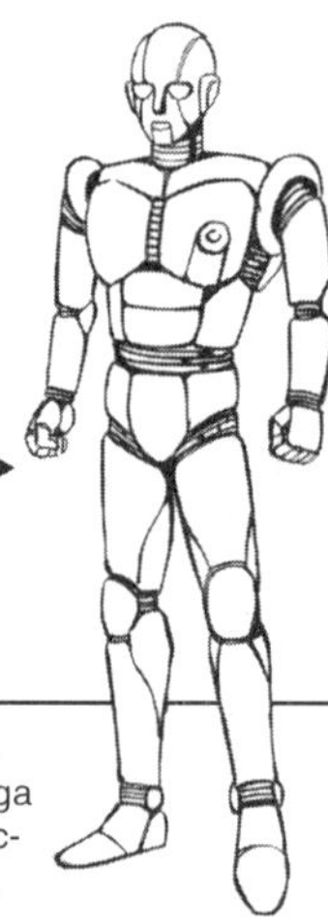

The "android hero", oft-characterized as an avenger of evil. Manga commonly feature human characters that transform into androids. A number also have androids pondering intriguing philosophical questions about the nature of their existence. Themes like this have earned the genre a niche amongst a mature readership.

What will the future hold?

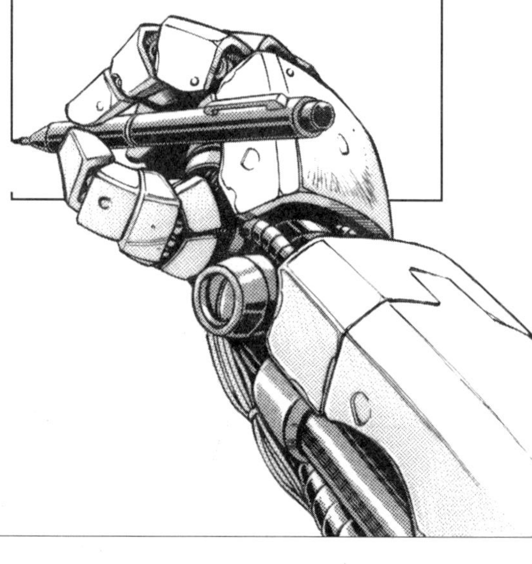

et's Draw Manga - Monsters
y: Plex, Inc.
SBN :1-56970-967-X
RP: $19.95
oftcover w/ Dustjacket,, 7 1/8" x 10 1/8"
pprox: 128 pages in B&W w/partial color
nglish text, Digital Manga Publishing (DMP)
ORTH AMERICAN TERRITORY

Japan is the monster capital of the world without a doubt in anybody's mind. Literally thousands of monsters ranging from gargantuan beasts, human sized villians, and charming cartoon characters have made their appearance in manga, theaters, television, and games, enamoring children across the world for generations due to their original, captivating design. Created by PLEX, Inc., the renowned design office of Bandai, Japan's largest toy manufacturer, this book stands out from the rest of any monster book released in the past, and will surely be the ultimate drawing reference for monster fans of all ages!

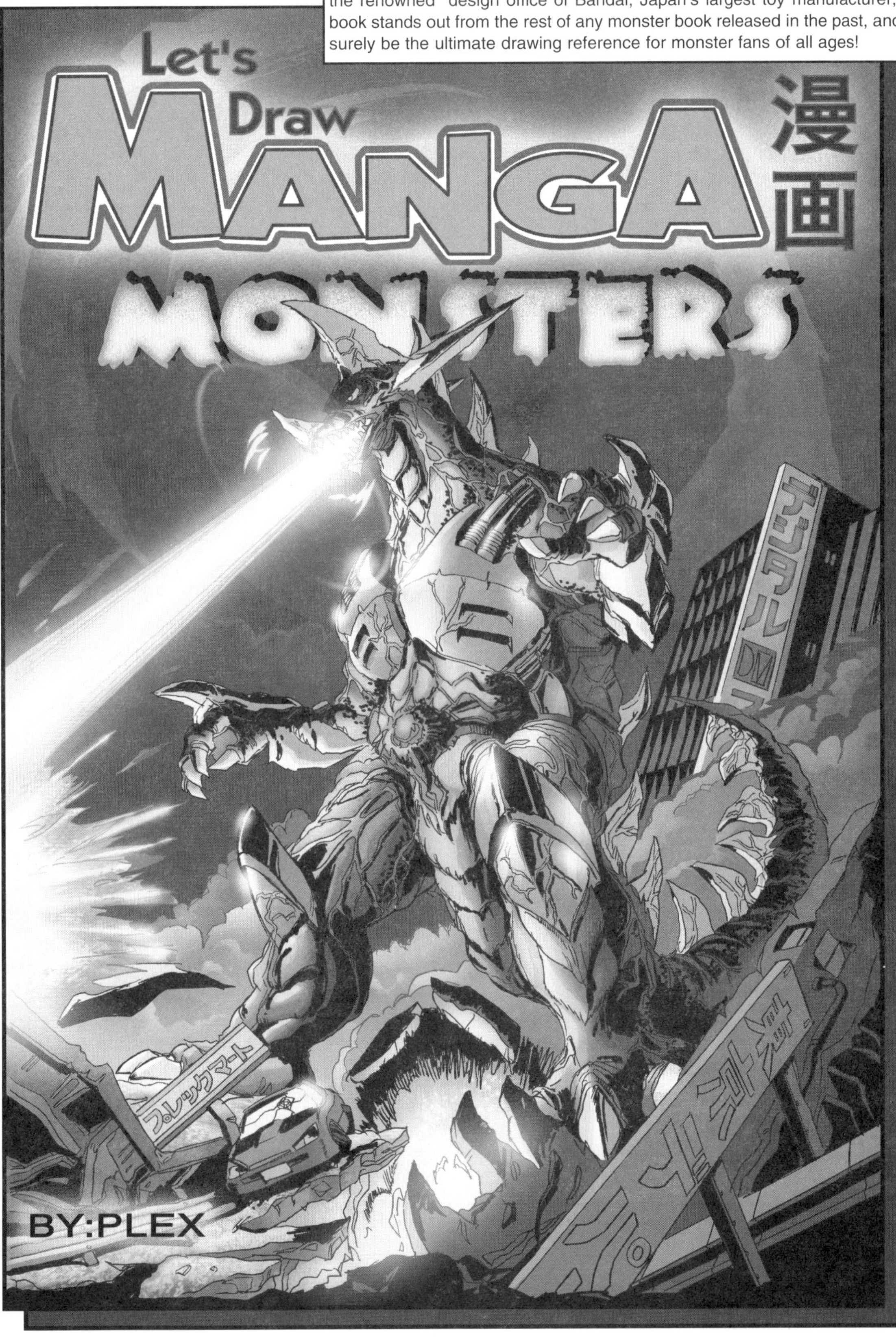

Let's Draw Manga - Tokyo Urban - Hip Hop Culture
By: Big Mouth Factory, Makoto Nakajima
ISBN :1-56970-969-6
SRP: $19.95
Softcover w/ Dustjacket, 7 1/8" x 10 1/8"
Approx: 132 pages in B&W
English text, Digital Manga Publishing (DMP)
NORTH AMERICAN TERRITORY

Learn to draw manga staged in the heart of the trendy Tokyo Urban & Hip Hop scene! With the exploding popularity of manga, there is an increasing interest in Japan amisdst the younger generation like never before. This very unique publication gives us an in depth look of stylizations that make the urban and Hip Hop trend the dominant culture it is amongst youths today. Instructed by Japanese street experts, with a rich variety of characters, both male and female, in their latest fashion, hanging out at the hippest scene in town, this book carries a whole lot of attitude.

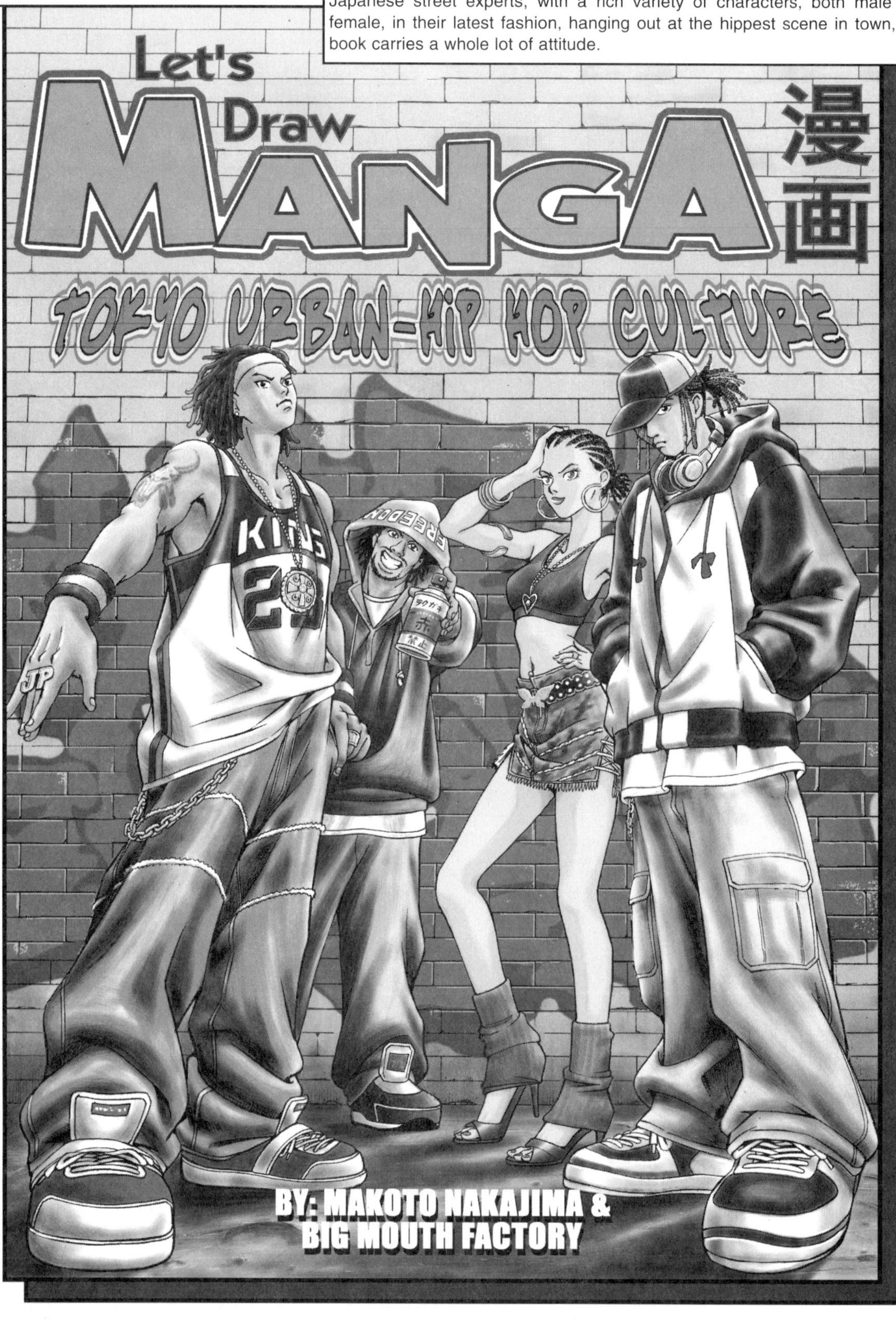